MW00452687

INTERESTING TIMES

INTERESTING TIMES

ARGUMENTS & OBSERVATIONS

Published by:
CURRENT AFFAIRS PRESS
631 St. Charles Ave
New Orleans, LA 70130
currentaffairs.org

Copyright © 2017 by Current Affairs LLC
All Rights Reserved

First U.S. Edition

Distributed on the West Coast by
WATERS & SMITH, LTD
MONSTER CITY, CA

ISBN 978-0-9978447-9-5

No portion of this text may be reprinted
without the express permission of Current Affairs, LLC.
Cover illustrations copyright ©Mike Freiheit
http://mikefreiheit.com

LIBRARY OF CONGRESS CATALOG-IN-PUBLICATION DATA
Robinson, Nathan J. (ed.)
Interesting Times / Nathan J. Robinson
p. cm
Includes bibliographical references
ISBN 978-0-9978447-9-5
1. Cultural analysis 2. Political science 3. Libertarian socialism
4. Social Philosophy 1. Title

To the subscribers,
for making everything possible.

CONTENTS

The Press

Crime & Punishment

Discourse

Money

Horrors

Famous Leftists I Have Loved

Potpourri

Light & Dark

INTERESTING TIMES

ARGUMENTS & OBSERVATIONS

NATHAN J. ROBINSON

CURRENT
AFFAIRS
currentaffairs.org

Introduction

"MAY YOU LIVE IN INTERESTING TIMES" is not, as commonly believed, an ancient Chinese curse. But it's easy to see why people think it is. The livelier the era, generally speaking, the bloodier it is. The 20th century was extremely interesting. It also featured hundreds of millions of violent deaths.

Fortunately, on these terms, our own century is less "interesting" than the last. We don't exactly inhabit an era of universal goodwill and peace, but we have so far managed to avoid a civilization-ending conflict. That may not seem like much to congratulate ourselves about, but it's something. Human history has, generally speaking, consisted in large part of wars and plagues, and the fact that we have avoided destroying the species is actually somewhat impressive given our ever-greater technical capacities for inflicting destruction and chaos on the planet and each other.

But things are still plenty perilous, and often it seems as if something has gone desperately wrong with political and social reality. In the United States, we have managed to elect one of the most shockingly venal and incompetent governments in modern memory. It often seems as if some malevolent force is conspiring to turn our country's people oblivious, heartless, and suspicious.

Hopelessness, however, is one of the most powerful tools that the powerless have for convincing the powerless not to change anything.

The moment one becomes resigned to despair and pessimism, there is no point attempting meaningful political action. This explains why one core right-wing argument is that progress is impossible, because human nature is corrupt and brutal. If you convince people that it's impossible for things to be different than they are, they will be forced to accept the existing arrangement. Gloom is conservative, because gloom counsels surrender to one's circumstances rather than resistance to them.

It's feasible though, to be both unsparingly realistic and continually hopeful. And personally, I think it's the job of political writers to convince people not to give up and become cynical. This is why I don't like to think of myself as a "critic," even though I am—as you will see—very critical. Critics, however correct their judgments may be, offer no helpful vision for the future, no messages of affirmation and reassurance. At a time when risks are so high, but possibilities are so great, anyone who cares about how history will go needs to be willing to say not just that "things are bad" but that "things can be better."

This book collects a small heap of the commentaries I have written for *Current Affairs* over the last two years. In my writing, I try to present a point of view that is biting without being cynical, critical without being miserable. I have attempted to produce work that will make people re-examine their commitments and preconceived notions, without lapsing into nihilism or paralysis.

The essays in this book cover a multitude of different subjects. I have tried to arrange them according to themes. The lines are often blurry, because many topics don't fit neatly into the categories of politics, society, or economics. But in a book this long, it felt necessary to have at least some semblance of organization, so the poor reader did not feel hopelessly deluged with a neverending wall of words.

I hope some common themes emerge over the course of this book. One is, as I say, that of hope without illusion. Another is a sort of "pragmatic utopianism," a mindset that combines a belief in radical transformation with a careful attention to political reality and the means by which one can actually get from A to B. Another theme you'll find is a "moralistic" approach to politics. I'm sure this will border on sanctimony sometimes, even though I don't intend it to. But I believe strongly in having clear values and doing one's best to apply those values consistently.

Consistency itself recurs as a theme. I have tried to make sure that if I say something, I am willing to follow its implications through, even when they may prove politically uncomfortable. I also believe strongly in making sure that one's political arguments can be supported by strong evidence, and in being scrupulously fair to the other side, even when one finds their value system appalling. I am sure I don't always manage to be fair in practice, but I do take it seriously in principle, and I am uncomfortable when my writing drifts into polemic or propaganda.

It's no secret that my work comes from a generally "socialistic" perspective, and that I am on the left. But I take criticisms of socialist ideas seriously and believe they need to be answered carefully and rigorously. This is one reason why my writing can be pedantic and long-winded, spending inordinate amounts of time responding to objections and offering qualifications. I am trying to be thorough and to "show my work," so that if readers buy my arguments, they do so because I have offered exhaustive support for them rather than because I have dazzled them with a zippy polemic. I don't want to preach to an audience of the converted, but to write for people who don't necessarily share my preconceptions, in the hopes of—if not entirely convincing them—at least encouraging them to give leftist ideas a full hearing. I strongly believe that if left values were more widespread, the world would be healthier, friendlier, fairer, and freer, and so I want to make the case for those values as strongly as I can. The concluding essay in this book is called "Socialism as a Set of Principles," and I've ended with it because it sums up the ethical and intellectual starting point from which I address most of the topics in this book.

I am sure I am wrong about a lot of things, especially because this book is so lengthy. (You may call this "self-indulgent." I call it "giving value for money.") If you read everything, and you do not have to, there will almost certainly be at least one point at which you fling the book aside in exasperation at my stupidity. I apologize in advance for the frustration you will inevitably feel at certain points throughout the text. All

I can say in my own defense is that I have tried to produce work that is at least thought-provoking, with all of the words in correct grammatical order. It's not much of a promise, I know. But it does elevate this book above a fair number of others.

The main takeway I'd like to offer is this: the world is extremely difficult to figure out, and nobody can be sure they have the right answers. But that doesn't suggest one should embrace political quietude or mushy centrist politics. The world may be complex, but basic moral values are often very clear and widely shared, and there's no reason to shy away from the exercise of strong judgment, so long as one has a humble appreciation for the limits of one's capacities and a willingness to adjust one's position in response to new facts.

I can't promise you I will answer anything, or solve anything, over the course of these pages. But hopefully I will offer an interesting thought or two, and produce some observations and arguments worthy of serious discussion. If I don't, well, books this bulky can always make for good doorstops or firelighters.

—Nathan J. Robinson
New Orleans, LA
April 2018

Politics &
Ideology

Democracy: Probably a Good Thing

DEMOCRACY, AS I UNDERSTAND IT, broadly refers to participation in political power by the governed. A state is democratic to the extent that the people have a say in its operations, a workplace is democratic to the extent that workers have some control over management decisions. (Almost no workplaces are democratic.) Democracy is also often held to be what is known as "a good thing," on the theory that people probably deserve to be part of the decision-making processes that affect important aspects of their lives. When those decisions are made by unaccountable forces, without popular input, and people are subjected to the will of the state without having any control over it, this is called "authoritarianism." It is commonly considered to be worse than democracy, and has a somewhat dubious track record.

I hope you'll excuse the patronizing civics lecture. I wouldn't have thought it necessary. But, there are, surprisingly enough, a number of people who do not subscribe to the belief that democracy is good. In fact, they believe we may even have too much of it already, and should probably cut back. The populace just has too much of a say in things, and must have its influence curtailed. Benjamin Wittes and Jonathan Rauch of the Brookings Institution have condemned the "cult of democratization" that gives voice to the "ignorance and irrationality" of voters.[1] Writing in the *Los Angeles Times*, James Kirchick concluded that the rise of Jeremy Corbyn in Britain is a "reminder of the perils of too much democracy," and worries that about increasing use of the phrase "the people," "that expression beloved of Third World tyrants and increasingly adopted by leaders in advanced industrial democracies"[2] (also, we should note, beloved of James Madison). Bret Stephens, the *New York Times* conservative affirmative action hire, worried about the problem of "reckless voters" being seduced by dangerous populists.[4] A libertarian philosopher, Jason Brennan, has written an entire book called *Against Democracy*.[5]

Obviously, ever since there has been democracy, there have been those who want to get rid of it. Plato saw in it the seeds of despotism, and as Noam Chomsky has often pointed out, there is a long antidemocratic tradition in American political thought.[6] This runs from the Founders' desire to check popular control to Walter Lippmann's belief that "the public must be put in its place" and the "bewildered herd" ought to be kept "spectators" rather than participants, a sentiment reiterated in the Trilateral Commission's conclusion that democracy needed moderating, because "the effective operation of a democratic political system usually requires some measure of apathy and noninvolvement on the part of some individuals and groups." Wherever there is concentrated power and wealth, those who possess them will naturally wish to ensure a lack of interference from those who do not possess them.

But it's somewhat extraordinary just how open some commentators are in their embrace of elitism and their disdain for the participation of ordinary people in the political process. Brennan's *Against Democracy* advocates "epistocracy," the rule of the knowledgeable, asking why a majority of the stupid "should be allowed to impose its incompetent governance" on a smart minority. *Business Insider*'s Josh Barro, who has proudly embraced elitism,[7] says that "the public should be kept away from policymaking."[8] James Traub, in a *Foreign Policy* article entitled "It's Time for the Elites to Rise Up Against the Ignorant Masses," said that "mindlessly angry" voters of left and right are undermining those who believe in "reality": "Did I say 'ignorant'? Yes, I did. It is necessary to say that people are deluded and that the task of leadership is to un-delude them. Is that 'elitist'? Maybe it is."[9] Daniel Bell comes to the extreme conclusion that "the uncomfortable truth is that the best (perhaps only) way to reduce the political influence of ignorant voters is to deprive them of the vote."[10]

Each of these writers insists that his position is driven by empirical evidence, showing that voters are "objectively" bad at making decisions. Their preferences are incoherent (the classic "lower taxes with more government services" demand) and their knowledge of policy is, on average, negligible. There's a lot of the well-worn Jay Leno-type "X% of voters can't find the U.S. on a map" material.[11] The word "populism" is used as a pejorative, as if anything that appeals to large numbers of people is inherently suspect.

But, and this should hardly need to be said, the fact that you don't like something does not make it "objectively" bad. James Kirchick, for example, bases his case that there is "too much democracy" on the fact that Jeremy Corbyn did well in the British election. But he doesn't actually make an argument for why voters shouldn't be allowed to vote for Jeremy Corbyn. He just says that he doesn't like Corbyn (for a series of bizarre reasons including Corbyn's alleged enthusiasm for Argentine fascism), and therefore Corbyn shouldn't have been one of the available options. The people have made the wrong decision, thus they shouldn't have been allowed to decide at all. (Luke Savage has previously written about how the elite hatred of democracy often occurs when democracy seems to be tending toward left-wing policies like single-payer health care.[12])

This logic, if accepted, doesn't just justify curtailing democracy slightly. It's a call to eliminate it altogether. After all, if people are only given choices when they make the choices you want them to make, this isn't some kind of "partial" democracy. It just leads to fraudulent plebiscites of the kind run by dictators, where you accept the vote if you agree with it and discard it if you don't. Actual democracy means—and again, I can't believe I have to say this—that people have the freedom to make decisions that you think are bad. "This was a bad choice" is only a case for taking away the freedom to choose if we don't believe in the freedom to choose to begin with.

Many of the arguments against democracy depend on carefully fudging important distinctions, or attacking irrelevant positions. "Professional and specialist decision-making is essential, and those who demonize it as elitist or anti-democratic can offer no plausible alternative to it," say Wittes and Rauch. Since nobody actually advocates that there should be no "specialist decision-making" in any part of the government, the point is misleading and irrelevant. Likewise, Lee Drutman says we must give up "on the deeply held belief that American democracy can be solved by giving citizens more opportunities to participate by emailing Congress or voting, and an end to thinking all would be better if more people would just 'get informed on the issues.'"[13] But this isn't a deeply held belief at all; hardly anyone holds it. Who honestly thinks that "emailing Congress" would "solve democracy" or that "all would be better" if people were a little more informed? Nobody. Those who advance these positions are dishonestly caricaturing the democratic position, yet still arguing that "epistocrats" like themselves should be entrusted with unaccountable power. That's one of the contradictions with the pro-"elitist" position: such people argue that they know what people want better than the people know it themselves, but they're unwilling to actually try to fair-mindedly understand what people say they want.

This is a serious problem with the defense of elites: it assumes that there are no rational reasons why people dislike being ruled by a small political class, and that there is no legitimate critique to be made of the policy consensus adopted by that class. Yet one explanation for the rise of populism is precisely that people do not like the world the elites have made: a world in which they live precarious economic existences under a grossly unequal system. To believe that being angry about this is "mindless" is to assume the conclusion one is supposed to prove: being dissatisfied must be irrational, because elites must make good choices, because the choices made by elites are good by definition. Never do they wonder whether, instead of "expertise" and "merit" being the criteria by which people come to inhabit the halls of power, it might be something else (say, social class).

In their paper, Wittes and Rauch offer a telling look at what leaving more things to elites would look like. Wittes and Rauch openly advocate the return of corruption and smoke-filled rooms, saying that "the curtailment of backroom horse-trading and pork-barrel spending stripped legislators of important tools to make deals and build coalitions." They believe that voters should have less of a role in party primaries, since the current system "empower[s] disruptive and extreme outsiders at the expense of more compromise-minded party regulars." (Democratic Party regulars, of course, have long had an extraordinary disproportionate amount of nominating power through the superdelegate system,[14] but apparently Wittes and Rauch think even this is not exclusive enough.) They lament that, even though Donald Trump was manifestly unqualified to be president, the Electoral College could "never seriously conside[r] performing its original failsafe function" to prevent him from taking office, since this would be seen as some kind of impingement on voter sovereignty.

As an example of a government institution that functions without popular oversight, Wittes and Rauch cite the intelligence agencies. They believe that the history of the CIA and NSA, whose policies are made without any substantive input from the public, shows that many parts of government are best left to experts. Of course, they couldn't really have chosen a worse example. The story of these two agencies is a story of everything that goes wrong when parts of the government are released from the constraints of transparency and popular oversight. As Tim Weiner documents in his history of the CIA, *Legacy of Ashes*, the agency's track record is an appalling litany of international crime and financial mismanagement.[15] The agency has squandered billions of dollars on projects of dubious worth, and has engaged repeatedly in illegal subversion of foreign governments, often without authorization from the president or Congress (to whom they have lied). The CIA has given arms to terrorists, tried to assassinate foreign heads of state, collaborated with Nazi war criminals, tortured people at black sites (sometimes to death[16]), and fabricated intelligence. What's more, precisely because oversight is left to "experts" instead of the public, there has been almost no accountability as the CIA has violated law after law (both international and domestic, including spying on American citizens in direct violation of its charter). Likewise with the NSA: Wittes and Rauch cite the NSA's reforms after Edward Snowden's revelations as evidence that it adapts to public opinion. But the Snowden story actually illustrates the core of the problem: because nothing the NSA does is ever subject to public scrutiny, a single individual had to take illegal action in order to bring the agency's behavior to light. Relying on individuals to break the law is not a workable way of ensuring accountability. Wittes and Rauch think the "success" of the intelligence establishment shows that insular, invisible government works. In fact, the intelligence establishment is a case study in the failures and atrocities that result when small groups of people are christened "elites," handed large sums of cash and total legal impunity, and allowed to go forth and do as they please.

But the "anti-democrats" don't just rely on the CIA's record of coups and arms sales in order to make their case: they also have political philosophy on their side, and *Bloomberg*'s Justin Fox notes that "important thinkers from Plato to Machiavelli to the U.S.'s Founding Fathers to John Stuart Mill all proposed limits on democracy."[17] Perhaps, then, this is a good opportunity to note that all appeals to the authority of esteemed historical philosophers are empty. Each of these men had horrific opinions, and the fact that they endorsed some practice should be taken as reason to suspect it rather than endorse it. Machiavelli was writing a manual on how to be a sociopathic tyrant, while Plato thought we should live in a regime of philosopher-kings and that all poets should be systematically expelled from society (actually, that particular idea could possibly stand to be revived). John Stuart Mill spoke eloquently of liberty, but when it came down to it, he believed that some people are "more or less unfit for liberty" even if they "prefer a free government," and are incapable and undeserving of one due to their "indolence, or carelessness, or cowardice."[18] Mill said that in the case of those people, "a civilized government... will require to be in a considerable degree despotic [and impose] a great amount of forcible restraint upon their actions." Mill deemed some "unfit for more than a limited and qualified freedom," giving as an example "the Hindoos, [who] will perjure themselves to screen the man who has robbed them." Probably best not to give much credence to Mill, then, on the subject of when to withhold democracy.

As for the Founding Fathers, well, let's just say that it might not be desirable to adopt their idea of who should be afforded equal participation in power. Even the Declaration of Independence speaks of "merciless Indian savages,"[19] and Thomas Jefferson, that most democratic of framers, felt that certain races of people were biologically incapable of the reasoning necessary for self-governance. In *Notes on the State of Virginia*, Jefferson explained that, in his capable scientific judgment, black people were uglier, smellier, and dumber than whites:

> *Is this difference [between black and white] of no importance? Is it not the foundation of a greater or less share of beauty in the two races? Are not the fine mixtures of red and white, the expressions of every passion by greater or less suffusions of colour in the one, preferable to that eternal monotony, which reigns in the countenances, that immoveable veil of black which covers all the emotions of the other race? Add to these, flowing hair, a more elegant symmetry of form, their own judgment in favour of the whites, declared by their preference of them, as uniformly as is the preference of the Oranootan for the black women over those of his own species... [Blacks] secrete less by the kidnies, and more by the glands of the skin, which gives them a very strong and disagreeable odour. Their existence appears to participate more of sensation than reflection... Comparing them by their faculties of memory, reason, and imagination, it appears to me, that in memory they are equal to the whites; in reason much inferior, as I think one could scarcely be found capable of tracing and comprehending the investigations of Euclid; and that in imagination they are dull, tasteless, and anomalous... Never yet could I find that a black had uttered a thought above the level of plain narration; never see even an elementary trait of painting or sculpture... Their love is ardent, but it kindles the senses only, not the imagination... I advance it therefore as a suspicion only, that*

the blacks, whether originally a distinct race, or made distinct by time and circumstances, are inferior to the whites in the endowments both of body and mind.[20]

I mention this to point out that while there is very much a respectable philosophical tradition on the need for democracy, there is no such respectable tradition justifying autocracy. Whenever ancient political philosophers defended some kind of curtailment on people's rights, they were usually speaking out of their most bigoted instincts, the ones that deemed some civilizations "barbarous" and unfit for self-governance (echoes of which are heard to this day in discussions of whether Arabs are capable of practicing democracy).[21] One serious reason that many great political philosophers have advocated restrictions on democracy is that those philosophers were outright racists, who constructed their theories deliberately to rationalize the exclusion of certain people from participating in government.

Jason Brennan's *Against Democracy* makes the most spirited and comprehensive attempt at a philosophically coherent justification of despotic rule. Brennan's book also offers a useful insight into libertarianism: *Against Democracy* is a good illustration of how supposedly "libertarian" philosophy is often just a defense of oligarchy. Libertarians always insist that they are defending a philosophy of freedom, but what they are in fact defending is the freedom of a few to maintain their status privileges. The rest of us, without money or votes, always tend to remain distinctly unfree.

The actual case Brennan advances can be devastated rather quickly, since it suffers from a central logical flaw that renders the whole core argument worthless. Brennan makes his case against democracy by pointing out all the ways in which people are stupid and fail to govern themselves well. Then, he makes the case for epistocracy by thinking through how smart people might make better decisions. All of this is very persuasive, until we remember that he is comparing "democracy as it actually exists" with "epistocracy as an abstract theory." By comparing real democracy to hypothetical epistocracy (instead of epistocracy as it would actually be implemented), Brennan's book doesn't address a single one of the important questions around restricted suffrage: in practice, wouldn't voting tests probably be used (as they have for their entire history) to disenfranchise the socially powerless? Wouldn't such a system inevitably be abused, and wouldn't "knowledge" just become a stand-in for "things powerful people believe"? (Brennan admits that wealthy white men will probably be considered the most "knowledgable," but does not appear to have a problem with this.) By presenting democracy with all its warts, but giving no thought to how "epistocracies" would work in practice, Brennan avoids confronting the difficult fact that his preferred system of government, if adopted, will almost certainly reinstate Jim Crow.

Thus Brennan's book is ultimately morally disgusting, since it amounts to a manifesto in favor of seizing a right from African Americans that took them centuries of bloodshed to win. (People died for that right, but to the Princeton University Press it's apparently an interesting matter for academic debate.) Brennan believes, in the great Jeffersonian tradition, that most black people are probably too dumb to vote and that we should return to one of the most shameful eras in our politics. He does not have the guts to contemplate what his proposals would look like if implemented, since this would involve having to make difficult arguments. But at least Brennan is honest in revealing the libertarian project as fundamentally opposed to the basic rights of human beings, its grand paeans to liberty being thin cover for taking the vote away from poor people.

Some of today's "anti-democratic" writers profess themselves puzzled that their proposals are controversial. Barro says it seems to "offend modern sensibilities" to question democracy, while Bell says it's "a bit odd that since World World II and especially since the collapse of the Soviet Union, it seems to have become a kind of sacred value that you can't question in Western society." Neither considers why the world's experiences with World War II and the Soviet Union might have turned democracy into a kind of "sacred value" that people were deeply committed to. (Hint: it was because millions of people were brutally slaughtered by undemocratic governments.) And all of these writers seem to treat the elimination or reduction of democracy as a kind of interesting intellectual exercise, rather than an infringement on the fundamental right of human beings to control their own governments.

Only those narrow few who benefit from today's system of elite rule could possibly see such rule as a good thing, or contemplate its further entrenchment. For the rest of us, the old cliché about democracy being the worst form of government except for all the others remains as true as ever. It is certainly preferable to epistocracy and oligarchy, which empower the most arrogant and least self-aware segment of society to make decisions about the lives of those whom they do not understand or care about. However dysfunctional our democracies may get, it will remain true that the people least qualified for power are those who are most convinced that they should have it.

The Clinton Comedy of Errors

It would be very nice never to think about the 2016 election again. It was miserable, and it is over. What is done will never be undone, and there is no sense "re-litigating" yesterday's arguments. We should, to use a popular formulation, look forward not backward. Instead of dwelling on which persons may have made what catastrophic mistakes, opponents of Donald Trump should be spending their time thinking about what to do next and how to do it.

Yet re-examining the forces that led to Trump's defeat of Hillary Clinton is essential for understanding how to prevent a similar result from occurring again. What this does mean, though, is that the most useful examinations of the 2016 race are those conducted with an eye toward drawing lessons. Divvying up responsibility is not a worthwhile exercise for its own sake, and only needs to be done insofar as figuring out causes is a way of preventing future effects.

It's important to be careful, then, in looking back on Hillary Clinton's unsuccessful campaign for the presidency. We can ask whose fault Clinton's loss was, and assign percentages of blameworthiness to James Comey's letter, Bernie Sanders' criticisms, Vladimir Putin's machinations, Bill Clinton's libido, and Hillary's own ineptitude. But that's only useful to the extent that it's useful, and a better question than "Whose fault was this debacle?" might be "What should we gather from this if next time is to be different?" Those two questions overlap (if you know whose fault it is, you can try to make sure they stay in the woods and out of public life). But the point is that for anyone who has progressive political values, the exercise of examining 2016 should be constructive rather than academic.

THIS NEED TO AVOID gratuitously flogging dead horses for one's own satisfaction is important to keep in mind while reading Jonathan Allen and Amie Parnes' *Shattered: Inside Hillary Clinton's Doomed Campaign*. Allen and Parnes had access to numerous Clinton insiders, and their book is full of scrumptious campaign gossip. But while Clinton-haters will be tempted to relish the book's tales of hubris and incompetence, there's no point conducting a needless exercise in schadenfreude. For progressives, the issue is whether the story told in *Shattered* can yield any helpful insights. And it can.

Shattered depicts a calamity of a campaign. While on the surface, Hillary Clinton's team were far more unified and capable than their counterparts in 2008 had been, behind the scenes there was utter discord. The senior staff engaged in constant backstabbing and intrigue, jockeying for access to the candidate and selectively keeping information from one another. Clinton herself never made it exactly clear who had responsibility for what, meaning that staff were in a constant competition to take control. Worse, Clinton was so sealed off from her own campaign that many senior team members had only met her briefly, and interacted with her only when she held conference calls to berate them for their failures. Allen and Parnes call the situation "an unholy mess, fraught with tangled lines of authority, petty jealousies, distorted priorities, and no sense of general purpose," in which "no one was in charge."

Clinton campaign manager Robby Mook comes across very badly indeed, and appears to have been the wrong man for the job. First, he had a Machiavellian streak (the authors call him a "professional political assassin" bent on "neutralizing" competitors), which he seems to have directed less towards defeating Donald Trump than towards squelching his power rivals within the campaign team by selectively depriving them of knowledge.

Second, and worse, he appears to have been an idiot. Mook was a numbers nerd obsessed with data analytics, but had such blind confidence in his statistical calculations that he followed along when they told him to send Hillary to spend the last stretch of the campaign in Arizona[1] rather than Wisconsin.[2] Every single decision he made was based on the elaborate analyses of campaign stats guru Elan Kriegel (a man whose name should live in infamy), from which Mook concluded that it was a "waste of time and energy" to try to persuade undecided voters or to go to rural areas.[3] Mook ignored pleas from state-level organizers for adequate organizing and advertising budgets, and rebuffed everyone who dared to question the algorithm's superior wisdom.[4] They were fools who didn't understand the superiority of cold hard math to fuzzy intuition, and Mook felt they failed to adequately appreciate the superior rationality of his strategy. Thus every time Bill Clinton warned that the campaign was dangerously losing support among the white working class, and "underestimating the significance of Brexit," Mook responded that "the data run counter to your anecdotes." After the election, asked to explain what the hell had happened, Mook blamed the data. (I can't help but be reminded of *The Office*'s Michael Scott obediently following his GPS as it directs him to drive into a lake, because "the machine knows."[5])

Numerous tactical decisions were simply inscrutable. A planned rally in Green Bay, which would have paired Clinton with Barack Obama, was canceled after the Orlando nightclub shooting and never rescheduled.[6] Mook "declined to use pollsters to track voter preferences in the final three weeks of the campaign" even though some advisers warned him that it was an "unwise decision because it robbed him of another data point against which to check the analytics." Bernie Sanders recorded a TV spot promoting Clinton, but the campaign declined to air it, which some insiders thought was a "real head-scratcher" giving the difficulty Clinton was having in swaying former Bernie voters. A campaign staffer confirms that "our failure to reach out to white voters, like literally from the New Hampshire primary on... never changed." Mook was so confident they would win, however, that he had already been considering how to get himself appointed to head the

DNC afterwards. The arrogance was infectious: phone-banking volunteers, who realized there was little enthusiasm for Clinton among the electorate, were puzzled that "campaign staffers were so confident" and "acting like they had this in the bag."

BUT IT WOULD BE A MISTAKE to pin too much blame on Robby Mook as an individual. Allen and Parnes say that Clinton herself was an adherent of the "facts over feelings" dogma, and was so "driven by math... that she couldn't, or wouldn't, see that she was doing nothing to inspire the poor, rural, and working-class white voters." Clinton favored evidence-based decision-making, but often to the point of absurdity. Everything she said or did was focus-grouped, calculated, and reworked by committee in order to be mathematically optimal. A vast speech-writing bureaucracy watered down every public utterance to the point of total vapidity (they even "deliberated over the content of tweets for hours on end," an especially galling revelation when one considers the quality of the resulting tweets).[7] Yet Clinton was somehow puzzled as to why the public found her robotic and inauthentic! Her team even proudly told the *New York Times* of their brand-new plan to make Hillary appear more warm and likable, then they were somehow surprised to discover that the idea of an "authenticity strategy" was considered hilariously oxymoronic.[8]

In commenting on Clinton's selection of Tim Kaine as Vice President, I had written at the time that he was so bland that he seemed to have been selected by algorithm. This turns out to be almost exactly what happened; Clinton didn't know or care much about Kaine, but he was simply the end result of a formulaic process of elimination. Nobody had any notion that he would energize voters; he was merely logically inevitable, having met the maximum number of designated criteria. (Note that if Clinton had picked Bernie Sanders she would have won the election, but this was never even seriously considered.)

Many of Hillary Clinton's supporters have been resentful over the attention paid to the infamous "email scandal," suggesting that Clinton was unfairly damaged in the press over something trivial.[9] But by *Shattered*'s account, Clinton's own poor management of the situation helped drag the story out. Even Barack Obama was exasperated with Clinton. He "couldn't understand what possessed Hillary to set up the private email server" in the first place, and then thought "her handling of the scandal—obfuscate, deny, and evade—amounted to political malpractice."

Clinton did make factually untrue statements to the public about whether she sent or received classified documents on the private email server and her campaign tried to mislead the press into treating the FBI's investigation as less serious than it actually was.[10] (The Clinton campaign falsely insisted that the investigation was a mere "security review" rather than a criminal investigation, and even got the *New York Times* to partially go along.[11]) She spent months refusing to apologize as donors and allies "furiously" pressured her to engage in some public contrition to defuse the issue, and Clinton ally Neera Tanden wrote in an email that "her inability to just do a national interview and communicate genuine feelings of remorse and regret is now, I fear, becoming a character problem." Sometimes Hillary Clinton's public relations instincts were almost unbelievably poor: when a reporter asked her if she had wiped her email server, Clinton replied "What, like with a cloth or something?"[12] This did not exactly scream forthrightness and seriousness.

To her credit, Clinton was at least aware that she was unaware about the psychology of the American voter, at one point admitting "I don't understand what's happening with the country. I can't get my arms around it" and knew she "couldn't grasp the sentiment of the electorate." But throughout the process, she disregarded the advice of those who cautioned her about getting on the wrong side of the prevailing populist tides. She had "ignored warnings from friends not to give the paid speeches" to Goldman Sachs that would ultimately create months of bad press when she pointlessly refused to release the (relatively benign[13]) transcripts. She insisted that one speech should retain a "sappy" reference to the $2400-a-ticket Broadway musical Hamilton, despite several suggestions from speechwriters that it "connected with her liberal donors and cosmopolitan millennial aides but perhaps not the rest of the country."[14] And she spent August hanging out in the Hamptons with wealthy donors and celebrities, attending a swanky fundraiser with Calvin Klein, Jimmy Buffett, Jon Bon Jovi, and Paul McCartney, and joining them for a celebrity sing-along of "Hey Jude." (The *New York Times* ran a story explaining to voters why Hillary had disappeared from the campaign trail entitled "Where Has Hillary Clinton Been? Ask the Ultra-Rich..."[15]) To the parts of the country seething with resentment of coastal elites, this was probably the worst possible way for Clinton to pass the summer months.

BY FAR THE LARGEST PROBLEM with Clinton's campaign, however, and the one that recurs consistently throughout Allen and Parnes' narrative, is the team's total inability to craft a compelling message for the campaign. "There wasn't a real clear sense of why she was in" the race to begin with, and she was consistently "unable to prove to many voters that she was running for the presidency because she had a vision for the country rather than visions of power." Despite Clinton's vow to learn from the mistakes of her loss against Obama, "no one had figured out how to make the campaign about something bigger than Hillary." A speechwriter assigned to draft an address laying out the reasons for Hillary's candidacy found the task nearly impossible; Clinton simply couldn't provide a good reason why she was running. She literally did feel as if it was simply "her turn," and campaign staffers even floated the possibility of using "it's her turn" as a public justification for her candidacy. Just as many people suspected, Clinton didn't run because she had a real idea of how she wanted to change the country (after all, "America Is Already Great"[16]), but simply felt as if she was the most qualified and deserving person for the job. Pressured to come up with a slogan to capture the essence of Clinton's run, the team finally settled on "Breaking Barriers," which the campaign staff all hated and the public instantly forgot.

The one area in which Clinton appears to have truly shined is in debate preparation. Allen and Parnes reveal that she obsessively prepared for her televised encounters with Donald Trump, conducting multiple intensive drills and meticulously memorizing policy details. Staff recalled that "she needed to theorize everything to the ground." Her advisor Philippe Reines went to extraordinary lengths to perfect his Trump impersonation for the rehearsals, even considering dyeing himself orange. Clinton's practice rounds paid off. She was widely seen as having mashed Trump into dust, her carefully-polished and intelligent answers presented a dignified contrast to Trump's sniffing and blustering. (It's amusing to think of how much effort Trump probably put into his own preparation, having given us possibly the most revealing example in U.S. history of what "just going ahead and winging it" in a nationally-televised presidential debate would look like.)

But even Clinton's excessive attention to the debates reveals one of the campaign's core weaknesses. Clinton comes across as subscribing to the "*West Wing* view" of political power,[17] namely that success in politics is produced by having the best argument in favor of your position. On this view, if you win the debates, you are supposed to become president. Thus Kennedy beat Nixon by defeating him in a debate, and Bill Clinton beat George H.W. Bush the same way.[18] It's a perspective that seems to have infected both the Obama administration and the Clinton campaign, each of which appears to have been blindsided by the fact that their right-wing opponents could not be defeated by polite discourse and appeals to reason. As Savage points out, this was the mistake made by Ezra Klein, who wrote that Clinton's three debate performances "left the Trump campaign in ruins,"[19] conflating "the debate" with "the campaign" and contributing to the media consensus that because Hillary had proven Trump to be wrong and unqualified, she was therefore somehow likely to win. In reality, the debates are theater and do not matter. (Or if they do, it is not because of the quality of their arguments but the quality of their persuasive power.)

A similar critique can be made of late-night political comedy; it may be satisfying when John Oliver or Jimmy Kimmel "eviscerates" Donald Trump, but it can also leave us with the false sense that Trump has somehow been "taken down" in some actual meaningful sense, even though it's perfectly possible for someone's power to grow even as they are rhetorically humiliated night after night.[20]

This is the sort of lesson from *Shattered* that goes well beyond Clinton. And in analyzing the book's account, it's important to distinguish between those failings that are unique to Clinton and her 2016 political team and those that represent wider tendencies in the Democratic Party. The Clinton-specific traits are less relevant, since she is gone from the political world (unless, God forbid, she actually does run for Mayor of New York or Chelsea Clinton takes a break from occupying a string of vague sinecures to pursue a congressional seat).[21] But some things are deep-rooted and will come back again and again until Democrats wake up and fix them.

The defects that are Clinton-specific (or, at least, not fundamental to contemporary Democratic politics) are managerial incompetence and Nixonian levels of cronyism and paranoia. Clinton was obsessed with loyalty, "prizing [it] most among human traits" (above, e.g., virtue). She had downloaded and rooted through the emails of all her 2008 campaign staff to determine who had screwed her, and tried to sniff out "acts of betrayal." She even assigned "loyalty scores" to various members of Congress, "from one for the most loyal to seven for those who had committed the most egregious acts of treachery." She and Bill had worked to unseat those who made the list of traitors. Even among trusted staff, secrets were kept closely guarded. When Hillary Clinton became sick with pneumonia, important campaign officials were kept in the dark, causing them to send mixed messages to the press and look as if they were hiding something. After the 2008 campaign, Clinton had wondered what had created the campaign's destructive atmosphere of suspicion and mutual hostility, and she decided to reset in 2016 with a whole new group of people. This time it happened again, yet she still found herself perplexed as to what or who the common denominator could be. (Another theme of *Shattered* is that the Clintons never, ever blame themselves for anything that goes wrong.)

On the incompetence front, as other reviewers have noted, much of Shattered reads like a discarded story outline from *Veep*. In one of the book's more amusing moments, a Clinton staffer mishears a request to book a major TV interview with "Bianna." The staffer hears "Brianna" instead, and books the interview with the tough-minded Brianna Keilar of CNN, rather than the desired Bianna Golodryga of *Yahoo! News*, who is married to a Clinton advisor and thus expected to be a soft touch. (The resulting encounter did not go well.) Actually, while this anecdote has been widely commented on,[22] it's a little unfair to read too much into it. All politics is *Veep*-like to one extent or another, and misunderstandings and bunglings are the Washington way. The true case for incompetence comes from Clinton's inability to manage a campaign team or plot an electoral strategy.

THESE PARTICULAR ASPECTS of the Clinton campaign can theoretically be corrected for in the future, without changing the party much. Barack Obama demonstrated that Wall Street-friendly Democratic centrism can be politically deft and free of Nixonism. It can even be somewhat inspiring, despite ultimately being vacuous. But some of the tendencies displayed in *Shattered* are inevitable, and bound to recur without serious structural reforms to the Democratic Party.

First, the Clinton campaign's inability to forge a coherent vision for the country was no accident. Goodness knows they tried; dozens of smart people sat around in rooms for months trying to figure out why Hillary Clinton was running and what she wanted to do. But it was an unanswerable question, because the answer is that she didn't really want to do anything and wasn't really running for any good reason. She couldn't give them an answer, so obviously they couldn't give her one. And that's honestly not because Hillary Clinton is a uniquely egotistical and myopic person. Instead, she's simply one of many adherents to a kind of "managerial" liberalism, which sees its aspirations for governance less in terms of some clear vision for how the world ought to be, and more as an enterprise in which small groups of smart, qualified, decent-but-pragmatic people should be appointed to preside over the status quo, perhaps tweaking here and there as they see fit. This philosophy means politics is not a fight to enact serious and principled moral commitments, but is little more than a résumé-measuring contest. The

Democratic Party doesn't stand for anything in particular, other than the fact that it isn't vulgar, irrational, racist, and unqualified like Donald Trump.

Politics thereby becomes hollow, drained of its core, with a lot of expertise but without an underlying set of values. The Clinton campaign puzzled over the fact that they had "laid out a million detailed policies" without the public being able to remember a single one of them. But that shouldn't have been surprising; if you're not motivated by a coherent set of principles, then your ideas won't be coherent either. One reason Republicans are highly effective at messaging is that their worldview holds together and is intelligible. Freedom is good, markets are freedom, therefore markets are good and government is bad. Once you know what you stand for and why, it's easy to deliver a clear message, and even Herman Cain, with his colossally stupid "9-9-9" tax plan, produced a more memorable policy proposal than anything to come from the squabbling of Clinton's Authenticity Committee.[23] (And it would be a mistake to think that Republicans are unfairly advantaged by the fact that dumb, oversimplified policies are the easily communicated ones. The Civil Rights movement paired demands for complex legislation with elementary appeals to morality, and Martin Luther King's speeches are things of both great intellectual subtlety and astonishing clarity and cogency. Heck, the original Martin Luther also managed to get his theses across, even though there were 95 of them.[24])

At no point in *Shattered* does anyone in the Clinton campaign display a sign of caring about anything beyond the narrow goal of getting elected. The decision of whether to promise criminal justice reform is not taken based on whether it's morally reprehensible for a country to keep multiple millions of its own people in cages, but on a calculus of whether it would make African American millennials marginally more likely to turn up to the polls. Clinton did not emphasize issues of gender and race in the campaign because she cared about them the most (after all, in 2008, she had been equally happy to cast her appeal explicitly toward white people instead).[25] Rather, Robby Mook's algorithm had concluded that each dollar spent on encouraging black and Hispanic Democrats to vote was more probable to yield a return than a dollar spent trying to persuade an undecided working-class white voter.

This is what can happen when you stay in politics too long. You get in because you want to do some good. Then, for the sake of expediency, you make a moral compromise here and there. Yet if you don't have a sense of what you're ultimately firmly committed to, sooner or later you'll just be doing whatever it takes in order to reach higher office. You begin by rationalizing that the ends justify the means. But if you're not careful, things will soon become all means and no ends. Politics will become about itself rather than about whatever it is you started off trying to do. Of course, political ideas must be pragmatic and grounded. But Clintonian politics takes this to its amoral extreme, never taking a stand for reasons of conviction rather than because it polls well. This is what gives you things like Clinton's infamously mealy-mouthed public statement on the Dakota Access Pipeline, which pleased neither side.[26] Ezra Klein euphemistically refers to this as Hillary Clinton's desire to listen to and incorporate all people's perspectives,[27] but it's actually just a cowardly refusal to stand for anything.[28]

There's something else missing from the world depicted in *Shattered*: democracy. For the Clinton campaign, people are voters. They are there to elect you, and they mostly exist as boxes on a spreadsheet. Outside the campaign cycle, they are nonentities. Inside the campaign cycle, you only talk to them if you have to. Mook wasn't trying to engage people in a larger political project; he was trying to coax as many as possible into dragging themselves to the polls and filling in a bubble for Hillary. There was no sense of trying to get people to join in; on-the-ground organizing was only done to the degree absolutely necessary, with television advertising frequently preferred. But if the Democratic Party is actually going to take back power, it can't simply consist of a small team of elite campaign operatives and an electorate whose only function is to vote every two to four years. Ordinary people have to be encouraged to participate in the political life of their communities, and the fact that they haven't is one reason that Democratic representation in state governments has been plummeting.[29]

Perhaps the things the Democrats need at the moment can be summed up as follows:

1. Vision
2. Authenticity
3. Strategy

In other words: What do you care about? Are you the sort of person that people should trust to do something abut it? And do you have a plan for how to do it? Clinton's answers to these three questions, respectively, were "Nothing," "No," and "Yes." She had a plan, but it wasn't really a plan for anything, because neither she nor anybody on her team actually had an underlying animating vision of what they are trying to help the world to become. Democrats would do well to think about the Vision-Authenticity-Strategy formulation, because unless they can convince the public that they possess these things, it's hard to see how the Republican dominance of government can be reversed.[30]

Now, LET ME JUST DEAL BRIEFLY with what I'm sure will be the principal objection to the various above critiques and suggestions: Hillary Clinton's loss was not the fault of Clinton herself or her campaign team or the Democratic Party. Instead, she was subject to external sabotage from James Comey[31] and the Russians.[32] Democrats should not be looking inward and examining themselves but outward at the unfair interventions that turned a popular vote victory into an Electoral College loss. This appears to have been Clinton's own perspective on the reasons for her defeat; in conversations after the election, according to Allen and Parnes, she "kept pointing her finger at Comey and Russia."

But ultimately, there's a simple response to this objection: Very well. You're completely correct. Also it doesn't matter.

First, let's be clear on what we mean by identifying something that "caused" the result. Because the election was extremely close, and well under 100,000 people would have had to change their minds for the result to be different, hundreds and hundreds of factors can be identified as "but for" causes of the result, i.e. *but for* the existence of Factor

X, Clinton would have won. So, say we narrow our 500 "but for" causes down to 4: the Clinton campaign's incompetence, the Russian leaking of embarrassing internal documents, obstinate voters who refused to come out for Clinton, and James Comey's letter. If we assume for the moment that we think each of these had an equal effect, we can see how it's the case that in the absence of any one of them, the result would have changed:

Threshold to tip election

CLINTON	RUSSIANS	VOTERS	COMEY

That means that the decision of which factor to pick out for blame is subjective. Since both Comey's letter and Clinton's incompetence are equal causes, in that without one of them the result would have tipped in the other direction, the person who blames Comey and the person who blames Clinton are equally correct. Again, the actual chart would have about 5 million causes rather than 4. But the point is that we have to decide which to focus our attention on.

Thus the statement "The Clinton campaign lost because it lacked vision, authenticity, and strategy" is consistent with the statement "If it wasn't for James Comey's letter, Hillary Clinton would have won the election." But personally, I believe it's far more important to focus on the causes that you can change in the future. You don't know what the FBI director will do, and you can't affect whether he does it or not. What you can do is affect what your side does. So the Democrats cannot determine whether James Comey will choose to give a damning last-minute statement implying their candidate is a criminal. But they can determine whether or not to run a candidate who is under FBI investigation in the first place.[33]

Note that even if you think Comey was the major cause of Clinton's loss, it still might be advisable to turn your attention elsewhere:

If you fix the other things, then even a highly impactful Comey letter won't tip the election. And correspondingly, even if you prove that Clinton's own actions were 99% responsible for her loss, a Clinton supporter would be technically correct in identifying Comey as causing the outcome:

CLINTON

In any scenario, it's probably best to figure out what your party itself can do to address the situation. After all, if we're really adding up causes, Donald Trump himself is probably the primary one, yet it would be a waste of time to sit around blaming Donald Trump, if it's also true that you ran a horrible campaign that alienated people.

You can also think certain things acted as precipitating causes without necessarily being at fault. For example, you might think that WikiLeaks was a direct cause of the result, but not think them at fault because it's their job to post the material they receive. The same goes for the *New York Times* covering the email story; it might have contributed to the outcome, but you might think this isn't their fault because they're journalists and that's what they do. Likewise James Comey; you might believe he was doing his job as he saw fit. And Bernie Sanders: Clinton may have lost both because she gave speeches to Goldman Sachs and because Bernie Sanders repeatedly criticized her for it, but you might think that one of those things is more justified than the other.

"Which things can you change to improve outcomes?" is one question. But then there's the question of which things you *should* change. In 1992, for example, Bill Clinton realized that Democrats could win more elections if they adopted the Republican platform of slashing welfare and locking up young black men. This did change outcomes. But it was also heinous. And personally, I think you're changing something about the party, you should change "Democrats enriching themselves from Wall Street speeches" rather than "people pointing out that Democrats are enriching themselves from Wall Street speeches."[34]

Shattered is both tragic and comic. It's tragic because Donald Trump becomes president at the end. But it's comic in that it depicts a bunch of egotistical and hyper-confident people arrogantly pursuing an obviously foolish strategy, dismissing every critic as irrational and un-pragmatic, only to completely fall on their faces. There was, Allen and Parnes tell us, "nothing like the aimlessness and dysfunction of Hillary Clinton's second campaign for the presidency—except maybe those of her first bid for the White House." And however horrible it may be to have Donald Trump as commander in chief (it is incredibly, deeply horrible and threatens all of human civilization), reading *Shattered* one cannot help but get a tiny amount of satisfaction from the fact that Mook and Clinton's cynical and contemptuous attitude toward the American public didn't actually produce the result that they were certain it would. One wishes they had won, but one is also a tiny bit glad that they lost.

Vision, authenticity, strategy. You need to have clear sense of what you want to do and why you want to do it. You need to show people that you mean it and believe in it. And you need to have an idea of how to get from here to there. The Clinton campaign had no vision, was inauthentic, and botched its strategy. But that's not a problem unique to Hillary Clinton, and singling her out for too much criticism is unfair and, yes, sexist (especially because Bill is much worse). This is a party-wide failure, and it will require more than just banishing the Clintons from politics. If the Democrats are to have a future, they must offer something better, more honest, and more inspiring. With Republicans dominating the government, we cannot afford to end up shattered again.

The Racism Versus Economics Debate, Again

I WOULD HAVE THOUGHT we could have moved on by now. Both before and after the 2016 election, there were months of acrimonious debate over the question of whether Trump voters were motivated by racial hatred or anxiety over their economic prospects. And I thought the general conclusion would have been that the premise was wrong to begin with, that you couldn't talk about "Trump voters" as a single unit, because the category includes a broad spectrum of people with a varying set of motivations. Some of them liked Trump's rhetoric on jobs and globalization, some liked his rhetoric on immigration and Islam, and some liked all of it. Both of the appeals obviously contributed to his victory. (Those of us on the left, however, frequently suggested that Democrats should focus on winning over the economically-motivated Trump voters, rather than the wealthy bigots, because the ones anxious about jobs are the ones whose support Democrats have a greater chance of peeling off.)

The "racism or economics" debate is a pretty easy one to resolve, then. Trump's campaign was based on bigotry, but also fueled by a backlash to the unfairness of the contemporary globalized economy. And many workers fell for his promises to bring jobs back, just as racists got excited over his stigmatization of Mexican immigrants. A question that appears contentious and intractable actually has a fairly obvious answer.

But well after the election was over, British journalist Mehdi Hasan attempted to reignite the debate once more, with an essay in *The Intercept* arguing that racism was the primary cause of Trump's victory and that Democrats who say Trump voters were hurting economically are "trafficking in alternative facts."[1] Hasan's conclusions are blunt and unqualified: "The race was about race," he says. "It's not the economy. It's the racism, stupid." Hasan singles out Bernie Sanders and Elizabeth Warren for criticism, saying that by claiming Trump voters were economically motivated, Sanders and Warren are ignoring the "stubborn facts" and "coddling... those who happily embraced an openly xenophobic candidate."

Hasan repeats arguments that have been made over and over for two years, from *Salon*[2] to *Vox*[3] to *The Atlantic*.[4] Many liberal pundits have consistently dismissed the idea that Trump voters acted out of defensible economic motives, instead suggesting that they were just as deplorable as Hillary Clinton made them out to be. (In fact, these commentators go further than Clinton, who was trying to draw a distinction between those who were deplorable and those who should be respected and listened to.) The position is somewhat surprising coming from Hasan, though, who has often seemed sympathetic to the Sanders left, and it's doubly surprising for appearing in *The Intercept*, which has been consistently critical of *Vox*-ian liberalism.

If Mehdi Hasan thinks this is true, then, it is worth dealing with the evidence. His argument for the proposition that the election was "about race" is as follows: There are a series of statistical correlations between racism and Trump support. Donald Trump did better than Mitt Romney or John McCain among voters with high racial resentment. The best way to predict whether any given person is a Trump supporter is to ask them whether they think Barack Obama is a Muslim. If they say yes, they're almost certainly a Trump supporter. ("This is economic anxiety? Really?" comments Hasan incredulously.) Those who hold negative racial stereotypes about African Americans are far more likely to be Trump supporters. ("Sorry, but how can any of these prejudices be blamed on free trade or low wages?") On the other hand, having a low income did not predict support for Trump, and Trump supporters actually tend to have higher incomes than Clinton supporters. And while there may be "economic anxiety" among Trump voters, it tends to be the product of racial resentment rather than its cause; in 2016, people who were racist tended to be economically anxious, while people who were economically anxious did not thereby become racist.

These are the entirety of the facts that Hasan presents to support his conclusion that the election was "about" race and that Bernie Sanders is factually wrong to say things like "millions of Americans registered a protest vote on Tuesday, expressing their fierce opposition to an economic and political system that puts wealthy and corporate interests over their own."[5]

I have long been critical of those in the political press who loudly insist on their superior allegiance to Fact and Truth.[6] By contrast with Hasan, who quotes John Adams saying that facts are "stubborn things," I tend to believe facts are fundamentally slippery things. Statements that are literally factually true can often be highly misleading, and sometimes you do actually need the addition (not substitution) of some "alternative facts" in order to understand what is really going on. For example: I can cite GDP growth as proof that Americans are doing well economically. But it's not until I understand the distribution of the economic benefits across society that I will know how the majority of Americans are actually doing. Or I can cite the fact that lifespans are increasing as evidence that American healthcare is "making us live longer." But it might be that richer people are living longer while poorer people are actually living less long, making the word "us" erroneous. If a fact is true, but is incomplete, then it might actually leave us more ignorant than we were before.

This is precisely the situation with Hasan's statistics. They are carefully selected to support his argument, with the statistics that don't support it simply ignored. He, like many others who have written "it's about racism" pieces, depends heavily on evidence that racism "predicts" support for Trump while income doesn't, meaning that racists are more likely to be Trump supporters while poor people aren't more likely to be Trump supporters.

But if we think about this statistic for a moment, we can see why it's a dubious way of proving that Trump support was "about" race. First, the statement "Most racists are Trump supporters" should never be confused with the statement "Most Trump supporters are racists." Of course most racists are Trump supporters; racists tend to be on the political right, because the political left defines itself heavily by its commitment to advancing the social position of racial minorities. It would be shocking if racism *didn't* predict support for Trump, because it would mean that racists had decided to ignore David Duke's endorsement of Trump[7] and vote for a candidate who embraced the language of "intersectional" social justice feminism.[8] Nor is it surprising that Trump did better with racists than his more centrist predecessors. The more racist your campaign rhetoric is, the more the racists like you.

The income statistic is similarly unsurprising. Of course Trump's supporters tend to be higher income. Republicans are the party of low taxes on the rich, and Trump wants to lower taxes on the rich. Democrats are the party of social programs for the poor. So poor people were always going to disproportionately be for Clinton, and rich people were going to disproportionately be for Trump. Furthermore, since Democrats are disproportionately the party of racial minorities, and racial minorities tend to be less wealthy than white people (due in part to several hundred years of black enslavement), the racially diverse Democratic base will ensure that poverty doesn't predict Trump support.

Note how neither of these facts speak to the actual question. If we want to understand the relative role of race and economics in creating votes for Donald Trump, it doesn't really help us to know that racists tend to be Trump voters. Imagine we have 100 voters, 10 of whom are high-income racists and 90 of whom are low-income non-racists concerned about the economy. Well, we know our 10 rich racists will probably vote for Donald Trump. And we know that being a low-income non-racist doesn't really predict support for Donald Trump, so let's say those votes split equally, or even break slightly in favor of Clinton. We count the votes, and the result is: 54 Trump, 46 Clinton. Trump gets 10 rich racists, plus 44 poor non-racists. Clinton gets 46 poor non-racists.

We can see, then, what can be concealed by statistics showing that "wealthy racists tend to support Trump" and "poor and economically anxious people tend to support Clinton." Those two statistics are consistent with a situation in which the vast majority of Trump's support occurs for economic reasons rather than racial ones. Yes, it's true, the presence of racists in Trump's coalition put Trump "over the top." But it's also true to say that the Democrats losing half of all economically anxious people put Trump over the top, and if you focused on the racism, you'd be focusing on the minor part of Trump's overall support.

In laying out this hypothetical, I am not attempting to show that this is actually what happened. The two statistics ("racists support Trump" and "poor people support Clinton") are also consistent with a situation in which 100% of Trump's supporters are racist. Instead, I am demonstrating that the two premises in and of themselves can't lead us to the conclusion that countless pundits have drawn over[9] and over[10] from them, which is that Trump's support was about racism.

Hasan calls the idea that Trump "appealed to the economic anxieties of Americans" a fiction and concludes that "instead, attitudes about race, religion, and immigration trump (pun intended) economics." But what he has proved is that racial attitudes trump economics as predictors of a particular individual person's support for Donald Trump, not that racial attitudes trump economics as the main issue Trump voters cared about or the main reason for his success. If we take the question "Was the election about race or about economics?" to mean "What was the relative role of race issues and economic issues in determining the outcome of the election?" then Hasan's evidence does not actually address the question.

To get closer to a real answer, we might do better to look at what the most important issues were to Trump voters. What attracted them to Trump? Do they care more about economics or about race? We can begin to get an answer from a Pew poll conducted in July of 2016, which ranked issues by their importance to voters, broken down by the candidate they were supporting.[11] Among voters generally, the economy was considered a "very important" issue to 84%, with immigration only the sixth-most important issue. Among Trump supporters, though, economic issues were considered very important to 90%, compared to 80% of Clinton supporters. For Trump supporters, immigration was the third-most important issue, with 79% considering it very important. Thus nearly every Trump supporter was "very" concerned about economic issues, and economic issues won out by at least 10% over immigration.

We still don't know very much from this. But we do know that a good chunk of Trump supporters cared about economics without caring as much about immigration (and we must assume that all Trump voters who cared about immigration were racists in order to accept Hasan's conclusion). Of course, "being worried about the economy" can mean a lot of things; a rich man can be worried about his tax rate increasing, and we don't know anything about racial attitudes from this survey. But it should caution us against coming to simple conclusions like "the election was about race."

Even if we stick to demonstrations of the factors that predict Trump support, we find Hasan burying crucial evidence. He quotes a Gallup report that, in his words, "found that Trump supporters, far from being the 'left behind' or the losers of globalization, 'earn relatively high household incomes and are no less likely to be unemployed or exposed to competition through trade or immigration.'" But let's look at the original context of that quote:

> *[Trump's] supporters are less educated and more likely to work in blue collar occupations, but they earn relatively high household incomes and are no less likely to be unemployed or exposed to competition through trade or immigration. On the other hand, living in racially isolated communities with worse health outcomes, lower social mobility, less social capital, greater reliance on social security income and less reliance on capital income, predicts higher levels of Trump support.*[12]

Hasan's presentation of the Gallup analysis therefore borders on intellectual dishonesty. If you quote the bit about high average incomes and no lower likelihood of unemployment (facts which, as I explained before, we would expect given the general composition of the Republican base compared to the Democratic one), but you don't quote the part about bad health outcomes, blue collar jobs, and low social mobility, then you're selecting only those facts that confirm your worldview and refusing to deal with the ones that contradict it.

This is the trouble with these types of pieces generally. They accuse others of ignoring "the facts," but they don't really care about facts themselves. Otherwise, why wouldn't you mention the fact that the economy was "very important" to 90% of Trump supporters? Why wouldn't Hasan even deal with that statistic, even if he had a good argument for why it should be disregarded? It's the duty of a responsible political analyst to address the evidence that undermines their position.

Hasan is likewise unfair in his characterization of the Sanders/Warren position on Trump voters. He says that "for Sanders, Warren and others on the left, the economy is what matters most and class is everything." But Sanders repeatedly accused Trump of running a "campaign of bigotry" and whipping up nativist sentiments. Sanders says that "millions" of Trump voters voted out of economic concerns. But he does not deny that large numbers of Trump's voters may be racist. (He has explicitly acknowledged that "some are."[13])

In fact, I don't know a single leftist who denies that Trump ran a racist campaign that energized racist voters. The leftist position is, rather, that there are many ("millions of") Trump voters who were drawn to his anti-Establishment stance because of their economic hardships, that Democrats should have had a better message to target those particular Trump voters, and that suggesting Trump voters as a unit are racist is both politically unwise and unsupported by evidence. Hasan is extremely derisive toward this position, with his repeated suggestion that it's factually ignorant, even stupid. But he doesn't offer any actual proof for why it's wrong. Instead, he willfully mischaracterizes it.

Actually, the left-wing stance here should be extremely uncontroversial. It doesn't even have to presume that the majority, or even a very large percentage, of Trump voters were "economically anxious" rather than racist. Consider the 100-voter scenario from earlier. Say we have 48 rich racists and 52 poor anxious people. Trump snags all the racists by default, but then manages to lure 4 anxious poor people through his message on trade. Trump wins. In that situation, it's still worth pointing out that Democrats needed a better economic message, and that economics were an important determinant of the outcome. A lot of the misguided attempts to decide what the election was "about" result from failures to think about marginal differences. If most Trump voters were racist, and a minority were economically anxious, and the election was decided by a small number of votes in Rust Belt states (which it was), then politically you might reasonably decide that it's not worth focusing on the racists (who will never vote for you) and instead you should craft a rhetorical appeal to the economically anxious Rust Belt voters who can mean the difference between winning and losing.[14])

I should add here that the necessity of fairness applies no matter which side of this you think is correct. If I say "90% of Trump voters thought the economy was the most important issue, therefore the race was about economics," and I do not mention or deal with the disproportionate amount of racial prejudice among Trump voters, I am also cherry-picking the facts that support my preferred conclusion. Anyone who tells you the one issue that the election was "about," and cites factors that "predict" support, without telling you the full range of relevant information, is arguing either ignorantly or dishonestly. They are not putting all of the facts on the table; rather, they are just giving the evidence that supports their own position. This is partisanship and bias, which nobody should engage in. Having a well-defined set of political commitments does not justify misrepresentations of the truth.

The truth about race and economics in the election is easy to grasp. They both mattered, and we can focus on whichever we choose. (Personally, I think that means focusing whatever is most useful or instructive, and that the question "Do Trump supporters tend to be racist?" is less consequential than "Are there enough non-racist, economically anxious Trump voters to where economic anxiety played a significant role in his margin of victory thereby meaning Democrats need to address the issue more?") And if Mehdi Hasan were as committed to Facts and Truth as he professes himself to be, he would be happy to concede this rather than perpetuating a pernicious misrepresentation.

Why You Don't Listen When They Tell You That You'll Fail

CLICHÉS ARE OFTEN CLICHÉS BECAUSE THEY'RE TRUE, and there's a lot of truth to that old one: first they ignore you, then they laugh at you, then they attack you, then you win. Since being elected to head the party in 2015, British Labour leader Jeremy Corbyn had largely been written off as a pitiful and incompetent joke. But after two years as leader, he secured the largest increase in Labour's vote share since 1945, and destroyed the Conservatives' hold on government overnight.[1] Some jokes do not stay funny for long.

Tory prime minister Theresa May called for March 2017's "snap election" because she believed there was no way she could lose. With a substantial Conservative majority already, and the Labour Party having been universally declared moribund, it seemed like the perfect moment for May to consolidate her gains in advance of the upcoming Brexit negotiations. May was so extraordinarily certain that the Conservatives were poised for victory that she didn't even bother to take part in the televised debates against the other parties.[2] But the campaign quickly became a lesson in hubris. Conservatives began with a more than 20-point polling lead over Labour,[3] but in the month or so before the vote, everything began to unravel. Labour released a well-received policy manifesto while Theresa May struggled to defend her party's disastrous proposal for what was branded a "dementia tax."[4] And despite multiple horrific terrorist attacks, May was unable to even seize on the issue of national security. As part of the right's ongoing effort to slash the size of government, May had overseen massive reductions in the numbers of police officers.[5] ("Austerity means terror" is an effective message to neutralize the Conservative notion that you can simultaneously fire a bunch of public sector workers and keep the country stable and secure.) May performed badly on television,[6] while Corbyn plunged himself into campaigning, drawing huge crowds and becoming steadily more confident and effective. The poll gap shrunk daily; one week before the election, one poll even put Labour ahead of the Conservatives.[7]

Election night was a bloodbath for the Conservatives. They won the most seats, of course; there was no way they wouldn't. But instead of increasing their majority, they lost it entirely, falling short of the number of MPs necessary in order to actually form a government. In order to continue in power, they were forced to strike a deal with Northern Ireland's far-right—and deeply homophobic—Democratic Unionist Party.[8] (It's ironic that a Conservative Party that spent the campaign trying to tie Jeremy Corbyn to Irish paramilitaries could only govern by joining with a party that has... ties to Irish paramilitaries.) Headlines the next day ranged from the comparatively mild ("MAY-HEM" in *The Daily Star* and "THERESA DISMAY: HER GAMBLE IS DISASTER" in *The Sun*) to the outright malicious ("BLOODY IDIOT" in *The New European*). The consensus verdict, even among members of May's party, was that the election was a catastrophic blunder, possibly the miscalculation of the century.

PART OF THE STORY OF THE BRITISH ELECTION is about the implosion of the Conservative Party, and the stunning levels of arrogance, ineptitude, and obliviousness demonstrated by Theresa May. But more significant was the extraordinary degree to which Corbyn's Labour Party shattered expectations after being told repeatedly that it was destined for decimation. Corbyn attracted a wave of support from young people (who actually showed up to the polls for once, giving credence to the theory that the reason they don't vote is not because they're lazy but because they're uninspired by the usual choices on offer). He ran a positive campaign focused on the party manifesto, which actually contained concrete promises as well as plans for how to pay for them.[9] And he laid out a clear and compassionate vision for Britain in plain-spoken and relatable terms. It turns out that if you offer people something real, and you are sincere and straightforward in your convictions, they will take a chance on your ideas.

But these were not the aspects of the election dwelled on by the *New York Times* and the *Washington Post*, whose coverage downplayed the importance of Corbyn in the event. To them, the election wasn't Labour's gain, it was a Conservative loss, and this wasn't a tide of support for left-wing ideas, but a "confused" Britain uncertain of itself. The *Times* didn't really know how Corbyn himself fit into the story, describing him as a "far-left urbanite" eccentrically obsessed with Nicaragua and jam.[10] (And possibly a terrorist sympathizer.) Because, for the American press, it is simply a matter of dogma that a left-wing program cannot attract mass electoral support, the British election had to be viewed mostly as a referendum on Brexit, or the product of some other mysterious force such as a national identity crisis. It could not possibly be that people actually liked what Corbyn's Labour stood for.

But what happened in the election was a victory for Corbyn, and for left-wing ideas more broadly. The party's turnaround began precisely at the moment when it released its policy manifesto; i.e. when the general public finally got a sense of what the Labour Party actually intended to do in power. The party managed almost-unprecedented gains; there has been nothing like it since Tony Blair's famous rise in 1997. Labour even managed to gain a parliamentary seat in Canterbury that had been held by Conservatives for 176 years.[11] As a result of Labour's success, the UK Parliament has more women, more LGBTQ people, and more racial diversity than ever before in its history.[12] The increase in vote share was just downright impressive.

Already on election night, certain media commentators were rushing to say that the Labour Party did so well in spite of Corbyn rather than because of him,[13] and that a different Labour leader would have won outright rather than simply diminishing the Conservatives' margin. Note, first, that this argument still silently concedes that all of the prophecies for Labour's doom under Corbyn were false. But it also requires us to believe that a different Labour leader could have gone beyond an already historic set of gains. And given who Corbyn's opponents have been in the previous leadership elections (a fungible pack of stuffed shirts whose names people barely remember), it is hard to imagine any of them doing better. Would tens of thousands of people have showed up to an Andy Burnham rally? Would Owen Smith or Yvette Cooper have enthused a generation of young voters and campaigners? Since all of them were politically indistinguishable from Ed Miliband and Gordon Brown, who had already hemorrhaged Labour votes during their time in the leadership, we know full well that the answer to both of these questions is "Hell no they wouldn't have."

Corbyn's steady ascent is an encouraging testament to the power of persistence. Before his surprise selection as leader in 2015, Corbyn spent over thirty years in parliament as a marginal figure. Members of his own party thought of him as a political irrelevance, to the extent that they thought about him at all. "You really don't have to worry about Jeremy Corbyn suddenly taking over," Tony Blair told an interviewer in 1996,[14] which would certainly hold true for a while. Back in the 1980s, when the BBC ran a story about the "scruffy" Labour back-benchers who were flouting parliamentary dress codes (Corbyn, a chief offender, wore a jumper hand-knitted for him by his mum),[15] he was misidentified by the presenter as "Robin" Corbyn. Yet, mocked and ignored, he continued to diligently and patiently engage in activism, organizing against war and nuclear weapons, and for economic equality and environmental justice.

It was possibly fortunate that by the time he was elected leader, Corbyn had gone through those decades of learning how to focus on one's agenda and ignore what people are saying (or not saying). The media campaign against Corbyn was, from his first day at the head of the party, savage. During the early months, he was attacked for everything from riding "a Chairman Mao-style bicycle" (a.k.a. "a bicycle")[16] to being "disloyal" for standing silently during the national anthem rather than belting it out with patriotic gusto.[17] His clothes were rubbish, he had a bizarre and possibly unhealthy obsession with manhole covers,[18] and his policies were "from the 1970s"[19] (always treated as an automatic slur, as though everything from the 70's must be the equivalent of floral ties and brown linoleum rather than, say, *Ziggy Stardust*). Oh, and what was more, he hated Jews and couldn't decide which was his true BFF: Hamas or the IRA.

In fact, there is actual empirical research on the media coverage of Corbyn, showing just how negative it has been. A report from scholars at the London School of Economics revealed the media had been "systematically vilifying the leader of the biggest opposition party, assassinating his character, ridiculing his personality and delegitimising his ideas and politics."[20] A quantitative analysis from Loughborough University showed that the Labour Party was receiving an incredibly disproportionate amount of negative versus positive media coverage when compared with other parties.[21]

By the end of the election campaign, after Corbyn had used television interviews and public appearances to convince the public he might not actually be Islington's answer to Fidel Castro, the tabloid papers had become desperate. They began throwing everything they could at him. "APOLOGISTS FOR TERROR," said *The Daily Mail* of Labour's leaders. *The Sun* bleated about "JEZZA'S JIHADI COMRADES" and implied that its readership should vote Tory in memory of the London bridge stabbing attack victims. One front page had a bulleted list of indictments against Corbyn, including "TERRORISTS' FRIEND," "NUCLEAR SURRENDER," and "MARXIST EXTREMIST."

This wasn't limited to the trashiest outlets in the British press. The BBC was unduly nasty too, with Jeremy Paxman interrupting and hectoring Corbyn and *Question Time* staging an attempt to bully Corbyn into agreeing that he would nuke another country if he needed to.[22] Over here, even moderately sympathetic *New York Times* columnists were calling Corbyn an anti-American Marxist and comparing him with Marine Le Pen.[23] An overtly biased article in the news section carried the headline "For Britain's Labour Party, a Mild Defeat May Be Worst of All,"[24] and argued that the better Corbyn did, the worse off Labour would be, because "less ideological" centrists would continue to lose their influence in the party. (It did not occur to the *Times* that centrism is itself an ideology.)

But throughout Corbyn's leadership, one of the most unexpectedly shameful media players has been the traditionally left-leaning *Guardian,* whose news department pushed misleading attack headlines ("Jeremy Corbyn accused of incompetence by MPs over antisemitic abuse"[25]), and whose opinion pages published a long series of vicious denunciations by columnists and contributors. Jonathan Freedland wrote article after article insisting that Corbyn was "handing Britain to the Tories."[26] Polly Toynbee asked readers: "Was ever there a more crassly inept politician than Jeremy Corbyn, whose every impulse is to make the wrong call on everything? ... Politics has rarely looked grimmer."[27] London mayor Sadiq Khan used the *Guardian* to endorse Corbyn's opponent in the second leadership contest, saying that Corbyn "has already proved that he is unable to organise an effective team, and has failed to win the trust and respect of the British people."[28] Even the paper's leftiest columnist, Owen Jones, quickly lost faith in Corbyn. Jones declared Corbyn's leadership a failure and said that he would find it "hard to vote for [Corbyn] again."[29] (Jones has now apologized for the premature obituary.) The *Guardian* editors allowed a man named Nick Cohen to publish what must have been one of the most vicious and most vulgar (and now, most wrong) columns ever printed in a newspaper op-ed page. Addressing Corbyn supporters, he said:

> *Far from building a new consensus for previously unthinkable leftist ideas, Corbyn's victory has allowed the right to run riot. I won't insult your intelligence by asking whether you also believe the bullshit you were fed about a "genuinely radical" Labour party attracting people who did not vote to turn out for him... In my respectful opinion, your only honourable response will be to stop being a fucking fool by changing your fucking mind.*[30]

In spite of all of this, the moment Labour's poll numbers started to climb, the *Guardian* suddenly reversed itself. The change was almost overnight and almost verged on the ridiculous. Instantly gone were the floods of stories implying Corbyn was an anti-Semite.[31] Instead, *Guardian* readers began to hear that Corbyn's attentive attitude toward his vegetable garden is reason to think he'd make a good Prime Minister.[32] (It isn't.) Columnist Suzanne Moore had spent eighteen straight months trying to undermine Corbyn ("No one thinks Corbyn can win… What vainglorious egotism, this willingness to kill a party for the thing he loves"; "a party without a point led by a rebel without a cause"; "weak and immoral" with "serial and tragic incompetence"; his politics feel like a "slow motion punch to the face"; plus a column arguing that Corbyn hates joy).[33] But immediately after the election, Moore began lambasting the *Sun* and *Express* newspapers for having tried to undermine Corbyn![34] If you wanted to know whether these people are truly shameless, well, they are.

Of course, all of the commentators who spent so long heaping abuse on Corbyn will continue to pump out blog posts and columns. The mainstream media (or "capitalist hyena press" as it's sometimes colorfully—and rightly—called) never change, and pundits effectively have life tenure no matter how many times they are wrong. Fortunately, one thing the election revealed is that most of their efforts are in vain. When voters are angry enough, and someone appeals to them with a powerful enough program, no amount of propaganda can be totally effective. Of course, it's true that—vile as the Murdoch noise machine might be—there's a special danger from liberal public intellectuals like Cohen, Moore, and Freedland, who portray themselves as pragmatic friends of the progressive cause while actually undermining it. But ultimately, none of it matters too much. Thankfully, pundits are shouting into the abyss, and nobody is listening.

There are a few lessons we can learn from the British election. First, political reality can change very, very quickly, and nobody should declare that they know the limits of what is or is not possible. Predictions are a fool's game, and instead of becoming resigned to the reality one lives in, one must strategize to build the reality one wishes to see. Pessimism is suicidal, but it's also a lie: nobody knows what we are capable of if we don't give up. Jeremy Corbyn, like Bernie Sanders, had to go through 40 years of political obscurity before his moment came. Now, he could be Prime Minister. Patience, courage, and hope should always be maintained.

The idea that a left-wing agenda makes you "unelectable" has been definitively disproven. It doesn't. The anti-Tory vote didn't go to the Liberal Democrats. It went to Labour. Corbyn's Labour. 1970s, neo-Marxist, stodgy, pie-in-the-sky, can't-win-anything Labour. The idea that you have to run to the center in order to get enough votes is simply false. What you have to do is be good at politics, which means giving people something they actually want to vote for.

But this is key: Corbyn didn't do well purely because he put forth left-wing policies. He did well because he campaigned well, and because he convinced people that those left-wing policies would actually be good. He also made them actually seem *possible,* which is crucial. People need to be able to visualize what another kind of politics would actually look like in practice; Margaret Thatcher's "there is no alternative" has been phenomenally effective at cramping people's imaginations and making even moderate steps toward social democracy seem fantastically unattainable. Corbyn gave them confidence that something different was could be done. This means getting past people's disillusionment and pursuing the nearly-impossible task, in an age of mass cynicism, of getting the disaffected to think that their vote might actually count, that going to the polls is not a waste of time.

The manifesto was essential. It received widespread praise, and rightly so. That's because it presented both a set of broad values *and* a number of specific plans for how these values would translate into governance. It was overflowing with ideas and ambitions, from introducing a "right to own," making employees the buyer of first refusal when the company they work for is up for sale" to "moving towards a 20:1 gap between the highest and lowest paid." Importantly, the manifesto was "costed," meaning Labour also presented a plan for how sufficient revenue would be raised to cover its various proposals. That forestalled the right's usual criticism of the left, which is that they make big promises but have no idea how they're going to pay for them. (The Conservative manifesto, by contrast, was a fiscal disaster and didn't add up.[35]) As I read the Labour plan, I sincerely wished that some benevolent multi-millionaire would have spent their fortune putting a physical copy of it in the hands of every man, woman, and child in the United Kingdom. (Regrettably, there is no such thing as a benevolent multi-millionaire, and people were far more interested in watching *Britain's Got Talent* than the BBC's televised leadership election[36]—though, to be fair, that night's *BGT* guest performers were the cast of *Bat Out of Hell: The Musical* doing a medley of Meat Loaf songs, so the ratings disparity is somewhat understandable.)

The importance of the manifesto showed that you have to be pragmatic as well as principled. It's essential not to allow centrists to be correct when they say that people on the left don't actually know how to achieve their goals; there need to be specific plans in place. But the election also showed that character is just as important as policy. People like Corbyn because he genuinely isn't like other politicians. He is unpolished, unshaven, and *human*. One problem that has plagued both American Democrats and the British Labour Party has been that so many of its candidates seem robotic and impossible to relate to. Corbyn, for whatever his eccentricities, is a person that people genuinely like. Convincing people to buy into you as a person is just as important as presenting the right ideas, and it's important to have an authentic and honest character.

The British election also provides increasing support for the—quite obvious already—idea that Bernie would have won. (Or at least, stood a very good chance.) It's *not* impossible to build national support as a left-wing candidate, if the circumstances are right, you're a likable person, you're straight with people, and you campaign well. Of course, political conditions in the two countries are very different. But it's notable that many centrist Labour figures were saying the same things about Corbyn that centrist Democrats have long said about Sanders. After this election, they're not going to be saying those things anymore.

In fact, the role of centrists is worth dwelling on briefly. For nearly two years, those who opposed Corbyn's ascent to the leadership relentlessly attempted to have him thrown out of his position. Even after he had been elected by a commanding majority, they insisted on holding another election and running a challenger against him. (Corbyn only increased his percentage of the vote.[37]) Despite clear evidence that the membership of the Labour Party wanted Corbyn to lead it, Labour MPs issued a no-confidence vote, refused to work with him, smeared him publicly, and generally refused to acknowledge his legitimacy or attempt to work constructively with him on building the party.[38] It's sad and infuriating to think what could have happened if such people had accepted Corbyn right away and turned against the Tories, rather than insisting on perpetuating a doomed internal struggle within Labour.

It's funny: here in the U.S., I remember how fanatically centrist Democrats insisted that left-wing voters needed to suck it up and accept that Hillary Clinton was the party's nominee, and that uniting behind her was the only way Trump could be beaten. You had to vote for the "lesser evil" rather than holding out for purity. (I happened to agree with that.) But I have a feeling this logic only applies one way: if the nominee is a centrist, then we all have to vote lesser-evil, work for the greater good, and silence our internal differences. But if the candidate is a leftist, they can be eaten alive. If Bernie Sanders had been the Democratic nominee, I wonder if centrist Democrats would have been insisting on "lesser-evilism," or if they would actually have preferred "more" evil. I somewhat suspect that many of them would have actually jumped ship and encouraged Michael Bloomberg to run, even if this meant handing the election to Trump. (Maybe that's why Bernie wouldn't actually have won.)

I can't help but be infuriated by someone like, for example, J.K. Rowling. Rowling has ten million Twitter followers. Many of them are, obviously, young people, who adore her. She insists that she is pro-equality and anti-Tory, and broadly supports Labour values. Yet she spent month after month publicly trashing Jeremy Corbyn,[39] saying that the Labour

Party was dead and that he had killed it. Even when it became clear that this was false, she didn't reverse course and encourage people to vote for him. The turnout of young people was crucial in this election, yet Rowling decided not to use her platform even to encourage her young fans to register to vote. Labour came just a few parliamentary seats from being able to form a coalition government. According to the *Independent,* because of a number of close races, Corbyn "was just 2,227 votes away from the chance to be Prime Minister."[40] Imagine if those, like J.K. Rowling, who put so much effort into trying to get the public to fear and despise Corbyn, had lifted a finger to try to get him elected. At this moment, Labour would be implementing its agenda, and the Age of Austerity would be over. The narrow Tory victory is the fault of everybody who stubbornly refused to help Corbyn, from British Labour figures like Owen Smith and Sadiq Khan who pissed on him to American Democrats like Obama campaign manager Jim Messina who actually worked to re-elect Theresa May,[41] and Howard Dean who championed the Liberal Democrats.[42]

The name Tony Blair should live in particular infamy. Blair used every ounce of whatever public influence he had left ("Even if you hate me," he pleaded) to keep Corbyn down. Writing in the *Guardian* (where else?), he mocked those who disagreed with him:

> *When people like me come forward and say elect Jeremy Corbyn as leader and it will be an electoral disaster, his enthusiastic new supporters roll their eyes... Anyone listening? Nope. In fact, the opposite. It actually makes them more likely to support him. It is like a driver coming to a roadblock on a road they've never travelled before and three grizzled veterans say: "Don't go any further, we have been up and down this road many times and we're warning you there are falling rocks, mudslides, dangerous hairpin bends and then a sheer drop." And the driver says: "Screw you, stop patronising me. I know what I'm doing."*[43]

As it turned turned out, "Screw you, stop patronizing me, I know what I'm doing" was precisely the correct thing to say to Tony Blair.

Allocating blame to the responsible parties is actually important, because in order for Labour to win next time, we need to know why it didn't manage to win the first time. And it's frustrating that Labour came so close to actually unseating the Conservatives. But the predominating feeling should still be one of elation rather than bitterness. This was an incredible event in global politics, one that showed that the supposedly impossible may actually be perfectly possible after all.

Jeremy Corbyn's massive political upset is inspiring not just because it demonstrates the viability of left-wing ideas. It's also encouraging on a human level: this is why you don't listen to people who tell you that you'll fail. It's why, in both politics and life, when Tony Blair's "grizzled truck drivers" tell you not to go down that road because there are falling rocks, the courageous among us respond "Well, I guess I'd better watch out for rocks, then." This is not just a story about the repudiation of status quo politics. It's a story about not giving in, and about doing your damndest to prove the haters wrong. You will be ignored. You will be laughed at. You will be attacked. But sooner or later, you'll win.

The Difference Between Liberalism and Leftism

IT IS REASONABLE TO WONDER whether the divide between liberalism and leftism actually matters very much. Why does there actually *need* to be so much animosity between the Clinton and Sanders factions of the Democratic Party? (Or the Blair and Corbyn factions in the UK's Labour Party.) Why on earth did the race for DNC chair between Keith Ellison and Tom Perez grow so vicious, given their substantially similar progressive credentials?[1] With Donald Trump poised to ravage the planet, either through boiling it slowly over time[2] or blowing it up instantaneously with his vast nuclear arsenal,[3] it would seem time for liberals and leftists to emphasize their similarities rather than their differences. Squabbling over minutiae is a fine way to ensure political irrelevance, and if everyone agrees that right-wing policies are poisonous and immoral, then surely the differences *among* progressive and leftish people can be worked out later.

It's also true that, according to one view, the differences between liberals and leftists are not even differences of substance, but differences of political strategy. The claim of people like Clinton and Blair is that, while they share the core progressive principles of compassion and equality, they are simply more hard-nosed and pragmatic.[4] They are more cynical about the limits of political possibility, and believe that change happens slowly. From this perspective, the core difference between Clinton and

Sanders is *not* their ultimate end goals (they both want a world of progressive values), but how to get there.

If that's the case, and the core of the divide is over "compromise" versus "purity," or "a view that major progress happens slowly" versus "a demand that it happens immediately," then the disagreements here should be friendly ones. Unity should be pretty easy, because we're literally trying to help one another pursue the same objective. I want the same things you do, but I simply think that I have a more effective way of getting them.

But while this is often the kind of language with which moderate liberals distinguish themselves from more "radical" progressive factions, I don't actually think it *does* accurately describe the nature of the liberal/left divide. And while conservatives would lump all these varying political tendencies together as a generic political tendency called "the left," there are some internal conflicts that are both fundamental and irresolvable. It is not simply a disagreement over tactics among people who share ideals. The two sets of ideals are different, and come from two entirely different worldviews.

The core divergence in these worldviews is in their beliefs about the nature of contemporary political and economic institutions. The difference here is not "how quickly these institutions should change," but whether changes to them should be fundamental structural changes or not. The leftist sees capitalism as a horror, and believes that so long as money and profit rule the earth, human beings will be made miserable and will destroy themselves. The liberal does not actually believe this. Rather, the liberal believes that while there are problems with capitalism, it can be salvaged if given a few tweaks here and there. Nancy Pelosi said of the present Democratic party: "We're capitalist."[5] But when Bernie Sanders is asked if he is a capitalist, he answers flatly: "No."[6] Sanders is a socialist, and socialism is not capitalism, and there is no possibility of healing the ideological rift between the two. Liberals believe that the economic and political system is a machine that has broken down and needs fixing. Leftists believe that the machine is not "broken." Rather, it is working perfectly well; the problem is that it is a *death machine* designed to chew up human lives. You don't fix the death machine, you smash it to bits.

I was recently reminded of the nature of the difference while glancing through Timothy Snyder's (very) short bestselling book *On Tyranny*.[7] Snyder is a historian of fascism, who believes that the rise of Donald Trump has parallels with 20th century authoritarian movements, and he offers twenty "lessons" for how ordinary people should act under tyrannical regimes. (Trump actually goes undiscussed in the book, but it is quite clear throughout what Snyder is referring to when he talks about contemporary tyranny.) Some of Snyder's lessons reminded me strongly of why, despite our mutual antipathy for Trump,[8] there is such a serious contrast between his beliefs (as a liberal) and my own (as a leftist).

One Snyder lesson was particularly striking: Number 19—"Be a Patriot." Snyder's exhortation to patriotism runs as follows:

> *What is patriotism? Let us begin with what patriotism is not. It is not patriotic to dodge the draft and to mock war heroes and their families... It is not patriotic to compare one's search for sexual partners in New York with the military service in Vietnam that one has dodged.* [Snyder's use of this oddly specific act is a good representation of just how clear it is that the book is about Trump despite treating the president as a Voldemort-esque unmentionable.] *It is not patriotic to avoid paying taxes... It is not patriotic to admire foreign dictators... It is not patriotic to cite Russian propaganda at rallies. It is not patriotic to share an adviser with Russian oligarchs. It is not patriotic to solicit foreign policy advice from someone who owns shares in a Russian energy company...* [Snyder's list of things that are not patriotic goes on further.] *[P]atriotism involves serving your own country. [A patriot] wants the nation to live up to its ideals... A patriot has universal values.*

Snyder's patriotism passage stuck out to me, because I realized I totally rejected a core part of his message: the idea that "patriotism" is a good thing to begin with. Patriotism has always seemed to me to be a profoundly irrational notion; I believe one should love and serve humanity, not one's particular arbitrary geopolitical segment of humanity. Snyder's problem with Trump is that Trump is *not enough* of a patriot. But I see *all* rhetoric of patriotism as profoundly conservative and antithetical to everything I believe. In fact, I find Snyder's whole case to be based on deeply conservative principles. Rhetoric against "draft dodgers"? The idea that one shouldn't listen to the advice of someone with shares in a foreign company? What the hell kind of liberalism is this?

But that's why I say the divide has something to do with one's view of political and economic institutions as either fundamentally good or not. The liberal sees the conservative patriot wearing a flag pin and says: "A flag pin isn't what makes you a patriot." The leftist says: "Patriotism is an incoherent and chauvinistic notion." The liberal says, "We're the *real* ones who love America," while the leftist says, "What is America?" or "I don't see what it would mean to love or hate a flawed conceptual entity." The liberal says, "I'm standing up for what the Founding Fathers *actually* believed" while the leftist says, "The Founding Fathers endorsed the ownership of human beings. Some owned human beings themselves, and beat or raped these human beings. I will not measure the worth of something by what the Founding Fathers thought about it." Certainly, the word "liberal" is an unfortunately overbroad and imprecise term, but it's fair to say that some strains of liberalism actually have more values in common with conservatism than with leftism, in that they affirm key conservative premises that leftists abhor (e.g. all of that "America is the greatest country in the history of the world" poppycock).

I don't think this difference is merely rhetorical. Sometimes it is; the ACLU often sees as politically and legally advantageous to frame everything it does as a defense of the great and noble values embodied in the Constitution, instead of pointing out that many of the Constitution's values are not particularly great or noble. But there is also a strong sense in which the liberal *affirms* the nation's core ideological underpinnings, while the leftist rejects them. (Some other divides: the liberal view of the Vietnam War is that it was well-intentioned but doomed and badly handled. The leftist view is that it was evil in both intention and execution.

Likewise with Iraq: was George W. Bush a well-meaning bungler or a predatory war criminal?[9])

Snyder's suggestions for resisting tyranny are in conflict with leftism in other ways. Most of them are *individualistic*: they focus on people as isolated units. Thus they include:

> ♦ *Believe in truth.*
> ♦ *Be calm when the unthinkable arrives.*
> ♦ *Contribute to good causes.*
> ♦ *Listen for dangerous words.*
> ♦ *Practice "corporeal" politics.* [Sarcastic quotation marks my own.]
> ♦ *Make eye contact and small talk.*
> ♦ *Establish a private life.*

Amusingly, most of these seem like woefully ineffective weapons against fascism. At best they are useless. ("Make small talk"?!) At worst, like prescriptions for "revolutionary self care" (e.g. learning to play an instrument as revolutionary act), they provide convenient rationalizations for people's inaction, allowing them to feel as if they are being politically active by doing the same thing they were probably going to do anyway.[10] Read the news! Hug your friends! The idea that these things constitute meaningful resistance to Trump could be held only by somebody who wasn't actually thinking about what serious political change looks like.

Leftists, on the other hand, are constantly talking about "building a mass movement" and "taking power." They don't just want to change our lifestyles, or get people to donate a bit more here and there to a good cause. The leftist believes in upending everything, which "corporeal" politics very much do not. ("Put your body in unfamiliar places," Snyder says. One can only contemplate what the reaction would have been if Snyder had handed copies of his "lessons for resisting tyranny" to the residents of Warsaw in 1943.)

That *could* be classified as simply another tactical difference: the leftist tells Snyder that his plans won't work, but we *do* all want the same things. But I think it goes somewhat beyond that. I hate the word "neo-liberalism" and have mostly banned it from *Current Affairs* (to the extent that it's even meaningful, as Noam Chomsky has pointed out, "it's not new and it's not liberal"), but I do think something has happened over the past few decades where moderate members of traditionally left parties have become incredibly reluctant to challenge the status quo in any serious way. As Luke Savage has written about the "*West Wing* view" of politics, today's Democratic Party is dominated by political aspirations that mostly consist of having good *character* rather than effecting serious structural change.[11] As Snyder's book shows, this ideology doesn't really espouse a clear set of political ends, and is focused intensely on individual action rather than collective action. Snyder, for example, does not discuss the need to build an effective labor movement, which is a core part of any serious attempt to regain progressive political power, and a necessity if the Trumps of the world are to be stopped. But he does believe we should make eye contact and read the *New York Times* more.

So I don't think it's the case that liberalism is just a slower-moving form of leftism. There are real ideological differences. Barack Obama wished to pretend that underneath it all, Americans really just believed the same things.[12] But they don't. Their interests and convictions collide. And the only way you can make it so that they do "believe the same things" is to operate in such a realm of gray abstraction that you sap progressivism of any and all elements that seriously challenge the status quo. If you make it so that the difference between a Trump economic policy and a Clinton economic policy is the difference between trying to appoint the CEO of Carls Jr. as Labor Secretary[13] and trying to appoint the CEO of Starbucks as Labor Secretary,[14] then yes, there won't be much of a serious ideological divide among American political elites. But people on the left can never sign on to such an approach, because it ditches their core commitment to restructuring the economy from the ground up.

Does this mean that anti-Trump forces are doomed to political infighting on everything? No, I don't think so. Because even if you ultimately cannot reconcile your values with someone else's, you can still forge temporary alliances for the purposes of achieving common political goals.

Pelosi and Sanders share the goal of ridding the world of Trump, and it is possible to collaborate based on what we *do* have in common. That's why Bernie Sanders endorsed Hillary Clinton and told his followers to vote for her. The fact that, at the end of the day, the liberal/left conflict is real and intractable does not preclude a liberal/left coalition in undermining the Trump agenda. It just means that this coalition is ultimately destined to be temporary.

None of what I have said will be news to leftists, most of whom know full well that their disagreements with Democrats go well beyond the merely tactical. But I think it's worth spelling out clearly, because it's reasonable to wonder just how deep the division really goes, versus how much of it is unnecessary warring over issues of strategy. And while I am a firm believer that the enemy of my enemy is my temporarily politically useful coalition partner, the answer is that the divide goes very deep indeed.

How To Be a Socialist Without Being an Apologist For Atrocities

IT'S INCREDIBLY EASY to be both in favor of socialism and against the crimes committed by 20th century communist regimes. All it takes is a consistent, principled opposition to authoritarianism. I don't like it when bosses mistreat and abuse their workers. And I don't like it when governments mistreat and abuse their people. A system in which people must work for low wages, struggling to afford housing, healthcare, and education, is abhorrent and should be gotten rid of. A system in which people must either work or be sent to forced re-education camps is even more abhorrent. We can dream of a world that has neither gulags nor indentured servitude, and I am such a romantic idealist that I believe such a world might even be possible...

Bret Stephens, in the *New York Times,* has attempted to convince readers that the choice is binary.[1] The millennials who criticize contemporary capitalism (i.e. the majority of them, who identify more strongly as socialists) have forgotten the history of the 20th century, he says. They know that Nazis and Apartheid South Africa were bad, but they don't have the same horror at Stalinism and the Khmer Rouge. "Why is Marxism still taken seriously on college campuses and in the progressive press?" Stephens asks. "Do the same people who rightly demand the removal of Confederate statues ever feel even a shiver of inner revulsion at hipsters in Lenin or Mao T-shirts?"

Leftists, Stephens says, engage in excuse-making. They justify atrocities committed by revolutionaries that they would condemn if those same acts were committed by capitalists:

> *They will insist that there is an essential difference between Nazism and Communism—between race-hatred and class-hatred; Buchenwald and the gulag—that morally favors the latter. They will attempt to dissociate Communist theory from practice in an effort to acquit the former. They will balance acknowledgment of the repression and mass murder of Communism with references to its "real advances and achievements." They will say that true communism has never been tried. They will write about Stalinist playwright Lillian Hellman in tones of sympathy and understanding they never extend to film director Elia Kazan.*

The ultimate consequence of this is extremely dangerous, he says. Because leftists fail to reckon with the truth about communism, they will end up justifying anything done in the name of The People. They "cheered along" Venezuela's socialist government as it collapsed into "dictatorship and humanitarian ruin" and people like Bernie Sanders condemn Wall Street without recognizing that "efforts to criminalize capitalism and financial services also have predictable results." The "line running from 'progressive social commitments' to catastrophic economic results is short and straight."

Alright. First of all, I am not sure how many millennial hipsters Bret Stephens spends time around, but I tend to see very few of them in Mao Zedong t-shirts (and if they *were* in Mao Zedong T-shirts, those shirts would almost certainly be dumb ironic jokes making Mao look ridiculous, e.g. "hipster Mao" or "LMAO," rather than the honest advocacy of collectivized farming systems). I have only ever encountered one authentic millennial Maoist, and let's just say I don't think there's any danger he'll be leading the next Great Proletarian Cultural Revolution.

There are two main parts to Stephens' argument: first, that leftists have a double standard, rationalizing communism and failing to appreciate just how bad it was, and second, that if leftists honestly faced the realities of that history, they would see that their criticisms of capitalism can only lead us toward terror and misery. The first point has some merit. The second is a steaming pile of manure.

Much of what Stephens categorizes as rationalization is nothing of the kind. There *is* an actual difference between racial hatred and class hatred, and it's an important one: race is an immutable characteristic, while class isn't. If I am a rich landlord, I can stop being a rich landlord any day of the week by simply giving all of my property away. It's much more fair to hate someone for something they do than for some aspect of themselves they cannot change, and hatred of the rich stems from the fact that rich people, through their actions, make the world more unjust. Whenever people who have a lot of money make this silly argument that prejudice against the wealthy is the same as prejudice against Jews, they imply that rich people can't help but be selfish. But it's good to remind them that they could cease to be victims of "prejudice" any time they like.

Stephens also suggests that saying communism remains a sound theory or has "never been tried" amounts to an apology for dictatorships. I think here he misunderstands what the actual argument is, at least in its more sensible version. When anyone points me to the Soviet Union or Castro's Cuba and says "Well, there's your socialism," my answer isn't "well, they didn't try hard enough." It's that these regimes bear absolutely no relationship to the principle for which I am fighting. They weren't egalitarian in any sense; they were dictatorships. Thus to say "Well, look what a disaster an egalitarian society is" is to mistake the nature of the Soviet Union. The history of these states shows what is wrong with *authoritarian* societies, in which people are *not* equal, and shows the fallacy of thinking you can achieve egalitarian ends through authoritarian means. This is precisely what George Orwell was trying to demonstrate, though almost everybody seems to have missed his point.[2] Orwell was a committed socialist, but he knew that socialism was about giving workers ownership over the means of production, which they don't have if they're being told what to produce at gunpoint. *Animal Farm* is not about the dangers of socialism, it's about the dangers of using revolutions to justify totalitarianism.

The history of the Soviet Union doesn't really tell us much about "communism," if communism is a stateless society where people share everything equally: it was a society dominated by the state, in which power was distributed according to a strict hierarchy. (Likewise, Kim Jong Un's "Democratic People's Republic of Korea" doesn't tell us much about democracy or republics.) When Emma Goldman and Alexander Berkman visited the Soviet Union, they were horrified by the scale of the repression. "Liberty is a luxury not to be permitted at the present stage of development," Lenin told them.[3] Goldman concluded that "it would be fantastic to consider it in any sense Communistic." (Her pamphlet "There Is No Communism In Russia" argues that if the Soviet Union was to be called communist, the word must have no meaning.[4]) Bertrand Russell visited Lenin and was alarmed by his indifference to human freedom. Russell left disillusioned, "not as to Communism in itself, but as to the wisdom of holding a creed so firmly that for its sake men are willing to inflict widespread misery."[5] Lenin himself acknowledged that he was implementing a form of "state capitalism."[6]

The primary lesson here is not about "egalitarianism" or "socialism" or even "communism" since Castro, Mao, Stalin, and Lenin did not actually attempt to implement any of those ideas. Instead, the lesson is about what happens when you have a political ideology that contains a built-in justification for any amount of horrific violence. The bad part of Marxism is not the part that says workers should cease to be exploited, but the part about the "dictatorship of the proletariat." The dominant "communist" tendencies of the 20th century aimed to liberate people, but they offered no actual ethical limits on what you could do in the name of "liberation." That doesn't mean liberation is bad, it means ethics are indispensable and that the Marxist disdain for "moralizing" is scary and ominous.

It actually is important, then, to do precisely what Stephens condemns: to distinguish "advances and achievements" from "indefensible atrocities." If your society manages to have impressively low infant mortality and impressively high literacy,[7] but tortures political prisoners, we might want to adopt your literacy program while declining to recreate your secret police. Because I am capable of holding two ideas in my head at the same time, and do not think in caveman-like grunts of "This good" and "This bad," I can draw distinctions between the positive and negative aspects of a political program. I like the bit about allowing workers to reap greater benefits from their labor. I don't like the bit about putting dissidents in front of firing squads. And it seems to me as if an intelligent person ought to be capable of disaggregating those things and seeing that you can be in favor of readjusting the balance of wealth without being in favor of show trials and purges. Conservatives see a necessary connection between these things, but (ironically enough) this is because they don't actually know much about the history of socialism, and the long tradition of libertarian socialists who have been critical of totalitarian thinking from the very beginning. The critiques that Bakunin made of Marx exactly predicted the nature of the Soviet Union, decades before it came about:

> [Marxists] insist that only dictatorship (of course their own) can create freedom for the people. We reply that all dictatorship has no objective other than self-perpetuation, and that slavery is all it can generate and instill in the people who suffer it. Freedom can be created only by freedom, by a total rebellion of the people, and by a voluntary organization of the people from the bottom up.[8]

Bakunin said that strong states, of the kind advocated by Marxists, would inevitably produce "military and bureaucratic centralization" and that the only difference between this kind of government and a monarchy is that a monarchy oppresses and robs the people in the name of the King, while the proletarian dictatorship does it in the name of "the people." But, he said, "the people will feel no better if the stick with which they are being beaten is labeled 'the people's stick.'" (Bakunin himself was often loathsome, an anti-Semite with violent tendencies,[9] but again, this is the magic of thoughtful reasoning: I am able to accept the sensible parts of his ideology and discard the insane ones.)

The most objectionable part of Stephens' case is his suggestion that criticism of Wall Street is a step down the road to the Gulag, and that "progressive social commitments" necessarily lead to "economic catastrophe." Gulags only become possible if you have an ideology, like Leninism, that justifies Gulags. If you are a leftist like Bertrand Russell, who visited Lenin and was disturbed by his lack of interest in liberty, then the conclusion is not that you should stop trying to make the economy more fair, it's that you shouldn't ever be willing to make millions of people miserable in the name of pursuing an ideal. Ideals are still good, but there need to be strict limits on what acts those ideals can justify. Just as "liberté, égalité, fraternité" did not become invalid aspirations when Robespierre started cutting off heads, and the U.S. invasion of Vietnam didn't discredit the idea of representative democracy, communist atrocities are a warning against committing atrocities in pursuit of fairness, not against fairness.

Stephens is right in one respect, however: there are still some on the left who don't think that way. In recent interviews and op-eds, Tariq Ali has praised Lenin for his love of "democracy," without mentioning the Red Terror, the Cheka, and the stifling bureaucratic misery Goldman and Berkman discovered when they first set foot in Lenin's Soviet Union.[10] Terry Eagleton's *Why Marx Was Right* dismisses worries that Marxism will inevitably be used to justify horrible crimes, essentially by saying that revolutions are never easy and power is an inevitable feature of human life.[11] (Examine Chapters 8 and 9 and see if you feel reassured that Eagleton's Marxism contains any ideological backstop to limit the amount of corpses it would be willing to pile up.) It is is concerning how little time has been spent analyzing what should be a central question for revolutionary socialists: which ends would justify which means? And how will you avoid what has happened so many times before, when the belief that "counter-revolutionaries" must be dealt with using "extraordinary measures" has led to an escalating cycle of paranoia over who the counter-revolutionaries are? I'm certainly not reassured by those who dismiss free speech as a bourgeois liberal value, or who think it applies to everyone but fascists yet lack a clear theory for determining who is or is not a fascist. (Since I could easily be classified as a supporter of "free speech for fascists," I could be seen as an enabler of fascism, and therefore no better than them.)

"How will you keep this idea that sounds perfectly reasonable from becoming a total disaster once implemented?" is an extremely serious question. I distrust anyone who doesn't think seriously about the potential consequences of various ideas. And Stephens is right that the history of communist states needs to be taught more (that would also, of course, include the 20,000,000 Soviet citizens who died in World War II and who we tend not to pay much attention to). Any leftism that justifies or downplays atrocities is not for me. It's important to be clear, consistent, and principled. (Likewise I am sure Stephens, who believes that Soviet atrocities indict socialism, holds the principled and consistent belief that U.S support for the killing of 500,000 Indonesian communists indicts American capitalist democracy.[12])

There is no difficulty whatsoever in being an anti-authoritarian socialist. Everyone should be one. You should believe in freedom and equality, not just one or the other. Freedom without equality means low-wage servitude, while equality without freedom means living in a police state. Conservative critics are right that it's hypocrisy for any leftist to condemn mass murder while justifying mass murders committed in the name of the working class. But that's a problem of hypocrisy, not of leftism. You won't find me giving excuses for the Shining Path or the GDR. But there is no logical reason why that should lead us to endorse the callous policies of the American right. Instead, we should be offering a set of ideas that are genuinely humane, compassionate, and socialistic.

Social Studies

Could Death Be a Bad Thing?

MY POSITION ON DEATH IS CONTROVERSIAL: I am against it. Most people I know are in favor of it. Not me. I think death is a thoroughly bad thing, and I oppose it entirely. What's more, I can't understand why nearly everyone else seems to disagree. Oh, they *say* they agree that death is a bad thing. But they don't. Not really. When you press them, most people think death is a natural part of the life cycle, one we must all resign ourselves to. I do not subscribe to this belief. I think it is perverse. There seems nothing "natural" about death to me. Living is what seems natural.

What fascinates me is the difference between what people insist they believe about death and what they actually believe. When I say that I find death bad, and I am opposed to it, people think I am saying something incredibly obvious and trivial. But when I discuss the implications of this, namely that life extension research would be a thoroughly good thing, it turns out that it isn't quite so obvious and undisputed that death is bad. In fact, many people hold the extreme position that "without death, life has no meaning." They believe that is not only an unavoidable fact of human existence, but that it actually confers a benefit on us, because long lives would somehow be unnatural or unbearable. In fact, when I actually discuss it with people, it ends up proving extremely difficult to convince people of the proposition that supposedly everyone already believes, namely that death is bad.

I have never wanted to die. And I have never wanted any of my friends or relations to die. (Nor have I even wanted my nemeses to die.) So long as I am in good health, as I hope to be, I can't see that situation ever changing. And yet I am consistently told that I must die. That's because death is inevitable and necessary, and without it life would not be life. And when I ask why more people don't see death as something that ought to be eliminated, people either say this is impossible (even though we do not know that) or that doing so would be going against nature (even though we go against nature constantly, and the distinction between the "natural" and the "unnatural" is an arbitrary construct).

From my perspective, believing that death is bad, life extension research seems not only *good* but *morally necessary*. That's because my view on death stems from my view on human freedom generally: people should get to decide for themselves how their lives will go. Death, presuming a person doesn't *want* to die, reduces a person's capacity to choose the direction of their life for themselves. Thus death is an abridgment of human freedom, and getting rid of as much of it as possible should be part of our broader effort to make people freer and freer from the restrictions on their autonomy imposed by both nature and other people. I believe that everyone should get to live as they please. That means I believe they shouldn't have to die, not if they don't want to.

But life extension research has never been a particularly popular social priority. Its public proponents are limited to a few fringe figures like Aubrey de Grey of the Methuselah Foundation, who seems intent on undermining his public credibility by sporting the beard of a biblical prophet.[1] "Life extension" isn't what we think about when we think about medical research; we don't think about preventing "death" but about preventing specific diseases that cause death.

I think we would do well to consider "death" as a problem in and of itself. Yes, people die from cancer, heart attacks, car accidents, falling pianos, old age, and snakebites, and those things are in no way the same. But something is gained by seeing death as a problem in and of itself: we begin to recognize the common principle, which is that we are trying to free people of being involuntarily deprived of their ability to choose how to live. What every cause of death has in common (with the possible, though highly debatable, exception of suicide) is that nature or another human being has stolen a person's free choice over their destiny.

That's why I think death is an urgent problem in *every* form. And I don't believe it gets much better if a person gets to live to an old age. I find it terribly sad that perfectly lucid elderly people are forced to come to terms with the fact that, regardless of how they feel about it, they will soon be killed. "Killed" seems the wrong word, because vaguely implies an intentional actor or an injustice, but whatever the cause the experience is the same for the person who must die. Nobody should ever have to be told "I'm sorry, regardless of how you feel about it, your life will soon be taken from you." We live in a world where everyone is told that. We should do everything we can to change that.

One reason I'm so anti-death is that I think life is such a truly extraordinary thing. I love life; it is everything. It is the precondition for every single other thing that a person can have or do. To take it from them, or allow it to be taken from them, is to deprive them of *everything they have*. It is the ultimate crime, which is why we punish it so highly. But if we value life, we should be trying to give people as much of it as possible.

Of course, no matter how much we increase the *capacity* to live, people might still choose to end their lives. Nobody should be forced to live, just as nobody should be forced to die. But the point is that there ought to be a choice; a moment's empathy should convince us that one of the most horrible positions to be in is that of the person who wants nothing more than to live but knows they are about to die. When we talk about "ending death" we are not so much referring to an infinite lifespan as to a "choice" of lifespan; the freedom to decide just how long one's life should be, and a commitment to constantly expanding the range of choices so that people can live as long as they feel they would like to live. Personally, I would not like to live forever. Instead, I would like to live for as long as it takes me to complete all of the projects I would like to do, and have all the experiences I would like to have. That will take a long time. Probably several thousand years. But currently, it is not an available option.

It goes without saying that it is only worth extending lives if we simultaneously maintain the quality of life. A long life spent in agony or in a state of mental decay may not be worth living. If we are to decide between keeping lifespans as they are and greatly improving the quality of life people have within those spans, or increasing lifespans without improving quality (or decreasing average quality), then quantity will obviously not be the top priority. Yet it remains true that, conditional on being able to give people the sort of lives they would actually enjoy, longer possible lives are always better. Nobody will be made to choose a longer life, but respecting individual desires means making sure they actually have the choice.

WHEN I HAVE PRESENTED MY POSITION on life extension to people, I have been shocked at just how willing people are to endorse depriving others of life. Some people think that even if research into immortality seemed promising, we should not pursue it, because "death is what gives meaning to life." Life is defined by the fact that there is death at the end, and if death were not there, neither would meaning be. I find that position shocking, because it amounts to being willing to force other people to die in order to make sure everyone follows your conception of significance. When I hear the sentence "death gives meaning to life," I feel as if I have found myself in the village of a suicide cult, who chant "death gives meaning to life" over and over as they force me to drink poison. Why should your perverse conception of meaning be everybody else's?

I believe that people give meaning to their own lives. If someone believes that only death can supply meaning, then they can opt to die. But it seems to me like the consensus position should be in favor of autonomy: people should get to decide how their lives will have meaning, which means that people should get to live a long time if they so choose. That means that everybody should support life extension, because even if you believe that "death gives meaning to life," you should still support increasing the ability for people who do not share your personal conception of meaning to extend their own lives.

The "naturalization" of death, another common argument, simply seems to me to be an error. Death is no more "natural" than salmonella, the New York subway system, or cottage cheese. Distinctions between that which is "natural" and that which is "unnatural" are based on mere assertion, rather than any actual meaningful principled difference. Death exists, we know that. But if life extension technology existed, it would be no less natural than death, because existence is existence.

Some in the pro-death crowd carefully dance around the issue with poetic phrases about how we should humbly accept our essential mortality. "Radical life extension smacks of an intemperate claim to have unlocked the fundamental mystery of life," said Roger Cohen of the *New York Times*.[2] But Roger should say what he means. In practice, what he means is that given a choice between massive quantities of death and zero death he would take the former, because of some nonsense poetry about temperance. I find this position a bloodthirsty kind of madness, and I resent Roger Cohen for wanting me to die.

EVERY DISCUSSION OF LIFE EXTENSION must deal with two core objections: the population problem and the inequality problem. The first holds that however desirable life extension would be in principle, it would create a population crisis on earth and would therefore lead to either (1) mass misery and resource depletion or (2) totalitarian restrictions on childbirth in the manner of China's infamous one-child policy. The inequality objection holds that life extension will inevitably be unequally distributed by class, and will simply result in rich people becoming immortal while the poor's existences remain nasty, brutish, and short.

As to overpopulation, first, I do not think it is a particularly serious concern. Population fears from Malthus to *The Population Bomb* have always been drastically overblown. As countries develop economically, their birthrates drop drastically, to the point where they eventually level off and achieve relative population stability. Innovating ways to more efficiently use resources, combined with curtailing the lifestyles of waste and excess encouraged by capitalism, could significantly increase the earth's capacity to support human life. Yes, the absolute elimination of death would ensure perpetual population growth. But the elimination of death is not actually practically likely to occur. (Although certain jellyfish seem to have achieved immortality easily enough.[3]) Instead, what we are talking about in practice is reorienting ourselves to see death as a problem in and of itself, and to take steps to reduce its occurrence as much as we can. We are, realistically, speaking, not actually going to create full immortality anytime soon, and if we ever did succeed in doing so, we would simply have to set ourselves to work on solving a new problem: spreading life elsewhere in the universe, either through finding other habitable planets or through terraforming uninhabitable ones. No, it wouldn't be easy, but we are speaking about long-term goals. In the meantime, attacking the problem of death should simply be done in conjunction with efforts to spread prosperity and birth control access, and to eliminate the hideous and environmentally destructive waste created by a lifestyle grounded in consumption.

There is also something of a moral problem to believing that population fears should cause us to turn away from life extension research. If the moral argument in favor of life extension is liberty-based, namely that people should be free to live as long as they please due to their autonomous control over their own destinies, then the idea that we should deprive them of that freedom in order to make room for new people (who do not yet exist) is highly debatable. If, as I suggest, there is very little distinction between "declining to invest resources in efforts to prevent death" and "inflicting death on people against their will," then we are faced with the question of whether a person's right to create new life trumps an existing person's right to continue to live. Since I believe the right to remain living is crucial, I tend to think restrictions on birth are far more justifiable than the refusal to eliminate death. (Though as I say, I doubt things will come to that.)

THE INEQUALITY PROBLEM IS A FAR MORE SERIOUS ONE. Many of the most prominent people who have showed an interest in life extension are Silicon Valley billionaires.[4] Nobody wants *those* people to live forever; inhabiting the same planet as them even for a short time is already a trying experience. Any successful life extension technology would be far more accessible to the rich, which might create an unprecedented and horrible new kind of feudal division, between those who die quickly and those who never die at all. And if death truly is as terrible as I believe it to be, the poor are then disproportionately saddled with something horrific that the rich can simply buy their way out of. There is already a divergence in average lifespans across classes in the United States, with life expectancy differing by as much as 20 years depending on whether you are on Native American reservation in the Dakotas or in a wealthy suburb in Colorado. By some measures, this divergence is getting worse, with some poor people's life expectancies actually shrinking even as the overall national average life expectancy increases. The better we learn how to prevent old age, the worse this will become.

It's difficult to get around the inequality problem. One could simply *justify* the inequality, and I am sure there are some utilitarians (and some utilitarian Silicon Valley billionaires) who would do so. Yet a situation in which billionaires never died but the rest of us did would be one of the most horrifying kinds of dystopias, one that must be avoided—even if avoiding it means that *nobody* gets to have their lives extended. The important point here, however, is that the inequality is a practical problem rather than a principled one. It's a problem because of the economic system we happen to live under. But it wouldn't be a problem under a different economic system, one without differences in access to life-saving medical treatments.

The elimination of differing health care access by social class seems, to me, to be a prerequisite to pursuing life extension. The first priority is to make sure that poor people have access to the same opportunities for (what are presently classified as) long lives as rich people. *Then* we can try to extend lives at the top end. In other words, first we should make sure everyone is living to 80 rather than dying of treatable illnesses at 50. After that we can talk about how to raise the average to 85 or 90 or 15,000.

In practice, then, my commitment to life extension comes after my commitment to creating a just economic system, because having a just economic system is the only way to ensure that life extension won't be implemented in a way that is horrendous. But since I strongly believe that life extension is an urgent moral imperative, I believe that creating a just economic system is an even more urgent moral imperative, and I would like us to get one quite quickly, so that we can eliminate death with all possible haste. We must solve life before we solve death. But also, we must solve death.

Whenever I discuss the problem of death with people, I end up feeling like a madman. To me, it is so obvious that life extension is an important human priority, that involuntary death is always a very bad thing and that everyone should agree that we should be trying to eliminate it as much as we possibly can. But people so easily accept the necessity and inevitability of death, they so quickly make up justifications for it, and they are so blasé about our need to stop it.

> *"But where is the ship actually headed?" I managed to ask, deliriously. "Do we know?"*
>
> *"Oh yes. It is on a fixed trajectory straight towards the center of the nearest large star."*
>
> *"But if the ship sails into a star, won't it instantly be incinerated?"*
>
> *"Oh, yes, absolutely. In a nanosecond!"*
>
> *"Why on earth are we heading into it then?"*
>
> *"We have always been heading for it. For the entire history of this ship, this has been its destination."*
>
> *"Can we change the ship's direction?"*
>
> *"It is unlikely."*
>
> *"But do you know for sure?"*
>
> *"No."*
>
> *"Is anybody trying to navigate the ship onto a different course?"*
>
> *"Oh, no. That would be tampering with nature. The ship's trajectory is what gives its journey meaning. We define ourselves as The Ship On Course For Collision With A Star. If we were not to collide with the star, we would no longer be that ship. Do you see?"*
>
> *I did not see at all.*

In discussing death with people, I often feel as if I have woken up on a spaceship heading for the center of the sun, where the crew seem to be making no effort to keep us from being destroyed. In response to my wondering why we don't try to steer the ship in a different direction, why we are accepting our trajectory as inevitable and natural, they come up with explanations for how plunging into the sun will give meaning to our voyage, or they explain why efforts to change the situation would be doomed to failure even though nobody has tried them. But for some reason I cannot resign myself; I cannot stop myself from thinking, over and over: "Why aren't we trying to steer the ship away from a path toward certain destruction of our lives? Why are we simply resigning ourselves and then jerry-building a narrative as to why this is both inevitable and desirable? How did I end up in this madness, and why am I the only one to whom it even appears as madness?"

I am a strong believer in the right to life. I believe we should all have as much life as we possibly can. And so the idea of opposing life extension research, in fact, of not seeing life-extension research as a top human priority, is to me pro-death. I see it as an essential issue for human freedom, perhaps the essential issue. Billions of people have lost their lives when they would not have chosen to. Because life is the most important thing we have, we must do everything to make sure that future people do have this choice, that they can have as much life as they please. I believe in maximizing human capability and the control we have over our own destinies. Thus I cannot accept the fundamental absence of this control represented by death.

I am very strongly anti-death. Why isn't anybody else?

The Climate Change Problem

LET ME MAKE A CONFESSION to you. I don't believe that human-caused climate change is a serious problem.

Now let me be clear: when I look at the empirical evidence, I am *very much* convinced that it is a serious problem. In fact, every time I dig into the facts, read the reports of experts, try to understand the problem for myself, I become terrified. And yet I still don't believe in climate change. I know I don't believe in it, because if I believed in it, I would be acting differently. If I truly believed that Florida was going to sink into the sea, and that urgent action needed to be taken in order to stop this from occurring, I wouldn't be editing a magazine. And I certainly wouldn't have spent any of the past six months reading books or watching YouTube videos. If I believed climate change mattered as much as I am supposed to think it matters, my every waking effort would be put toward calling urgently for political action. I am not doing this. Therefore, I think I believe less in the importance of climate change than I say I do.

Here is one reason I think many people reject the apocalyptic forecasts of climate change "alarmists": they don't actually seem very alarmed. Yes, when climate scientists tell us about the problem, they tell us that if we do not radically reverse course on emissions immediately, we will boil ourselves alive and create an overheated hell of drought, displacement, and despair. But then why aren't those climate scientists out in the streets? If the academic community believes climate change is a serious problem, there should be climate scientists going to every town in America, holding listening and teaching sessions at churches, libraries, and schools. They should be educating the public, fielding any and every skeptical question people might have. They should not just be giving quotes to newspapers, in which they tell us we're all going to die, but they should give free and open lectures around the country, debating skeptics and embarking on a massive project to shift public opinion and end apathy. If climate change is going to be as bad as climate scientists say it is, they need to work to alter the national mood. Barack Obama should be spending his days talking about it constantly. It should be his number one issue. After all, if the claims made by scientists are true, then this issue should essentially come before all others, because it threatens the survival of the species.

Supposedly, liberals believe the claims made by scientists, yet they do not treat this as an issue that comes before all others. Why didn't Hillary Clinton respond to every single question at the presidential debates by insisting on talking about climate change? Surely she affirms the scientific consensus. That scientific consensus implies that this is the number one issue. But it wasn't Clinton's.

I have a suspicion that the failure to act as if the scientific consensus is actually true fuels doubts that it is true. "Rising sea levels" is not something we actually take seriously, it's just something we say. After all, if liberals really took it seriously, it would be at the top of the *New York Times* every day. They'd never shut up about it. It isn't the top story, though. The top story is usually something Trump did.

Imagine scientists discovered an asteroid hurtling toward earth. And they tried to warn people that unless urgent action was taken to blow up the asteroid, everyone would perish. But "asteroid denialism" set in. Blowing up the asteroid would require raising taxes and would disrupt the orderly operations of capitalism. Republicans would insist that the entire asteroid idea was a scheme cooked up by elitist liberal eggheads designed to scare Middle America into voting Democratic and bringing about a feminist Marxist dictatorship. But honestly, if the people voicing concerns about the asteroid were penning occasional op-eds, rather than constantly doing everything they could to persuade people to be-lieve in the asteroid, I wouldn't be sure that they really believed there was an asteroid at all. If they spent their time going to conferences and eating brunch, I would think that perhaps the Republicans were right. After all, people who think an asteroid will kill us all unless people are persuaded to stop it do not sit around eating brunch. After all, it's a fuck-ing *deadly asteroid*.

The situation with climate change is much like the asteroid. Every good progressive affirms on an intellectual level that climate change is not just a problem, but *the* problem. Yet if it's really true that unless we act in the next few years, a series of very bad things will happen that may take many, many lives, nobody should be acting the way many contem-porary progressives act. Certainly nobody should be watching Netflix. Unless you convince people that they are about to suffer terribly, then climate change will not prevent them from voting for a denialist like Donald Trump. So you'd better be out convincing people...

CLIMATE CHANGE ALSO RAISES some very important issues about what constitutes a "rationally" held belief. Strangely enough, I think most people on the left believe in climate change for irrational reasons. They believe in it because scientists say it matters, or because the *New Yorker* says that scientists say it matters. But they haven't actually spent months carefully combing through the arguments made by skeptics, and figuring out what the flaws are. They haven't actually buried them-selves in mountains of climate data in order to verify to their satisfaction that the scientific findings are sound. In fact, it may be impossible for non-scientists to hold scientific beliefs "rationally." We have to trust that science is a rational process and that we are being told the truth.

That's a paradox of (good-faith) skepticism: by refusing to accept the claims of scientists on a trust basis, skeptics are demonstrating a kind of rationality. I am a "skeptic" of a certain kind, in that I am very uncom-fortable defending a "scientific consensus" that I cannot prove myself. If someone approached me with a series of pseudo-scientific arguments supposedly proving that climate change was not occurring, I would not know how to prove that it was. (George Orwell once pointed out how few of us, even those who paid attention in high school physics, would be able to respond effectively to the arguments of an especially wily Flat Earther.) I couldn't suddenly become an amateur climate scientist and defend the position rationally. I have to defend it with an appeal to authority, namely the authority of scientists.

This point about knowledge is important, because it means that ordinary people who are skeptical of climate change should not be treated as irrational and backward. In fact, it is perfectly healthy to be skeptical of the authority of experts. We can say that if I am not an expert in a field, I should not doubt the claims of those who are. But that position doesn't hold. After all, I am not an expert in Scientology or alchemy. Should I trust the claims of Scientologists or alchemists? From the inside of a scientific field, the difference between fraud and reason might be obvious. But from the outside, for people who are not trained scientists, the difference is not obvious. It's very difficult, when I am not an expert, for me to decide whom to trust among two people claiming to be experts. A Princeton physicist tells me that global warming isn't real.[1] The Intergovernmental Panel on Climate Change says otherwise. An oil executive tells me yet another thing. All of these people know more than I do about energy and the environment. Sorting out whom to trust is therefore hard. It's easy if you already know how to do it. But most of us don't know how to do it.

Yes, when 99% of scientists believe something, it's probably wise to believe it. But recognize that unless you teach people the underlying scientific facts, this is still asking them to believe based on faith. "Scientific consensuses are true" is a statement that can be believed for either rational or irrational reasons depending on whether you've worked it out for yourself or believe it for the same reason you might believe "what the Koran says is true."

Those concerned about climate change are therefore asking people to indulge in an act of faith: to believe, without understanding the underlying science very well, that the scientific prediction of an asteroid-type disaster is true. This is a major ask. It requires people to make a large amount of sacrifice for something that they are taking based on trust, trust that experts would never mislead them and are not deluded. It's no wonder people prefer the comforting denials of a Trump, the insistence that experts are full of it and that everything will be fine.

I must admit, I don't trust experts much myself. I think they're frequently arrogant and self-deluding. I also don't know anything about climate science, and I don't have time to learn. In this respect, I am like most people. The question here is how, if most people are like this, they can be moved to support the necessary serious political action on climate change. The answer, I think, is that they need reasons why expertise can be trusted. They need experts to be trying to persuade them, rather than just dismissing skepticism as ignorance. They need experts to act as if their prophecies are true, rather than going on with their quiet and comfortable lives in coastal enclaves. A crucial lesson for Trump-era progressives is this: *it's not enough to be right. You have to persuade people you're right.*

Here in Massachusetts, I think a large swath of my neighbors affirm that climate change is the number one threat facing humanity. And yet they have never done so much as bring it up with me in conversation. If this really were a problem of asteroid-magnitude, don't you think we'd at least be mentioning it with some regularity? If we think it's going to happen, shouldn't we speak about it?

If the science is right, we may be in the last few years where it is possible to do anything to stall the effects of emissions on the planet. That means it's a moment of extraordinary urgency. For every single progressive who believes that this is in fact true, it needs to be treated as the crisis it ostensibly is. Otherwise, why should anyone take the leap of faith required to produce serious action? A vast political movement needs to be built if there is any chance of reversing existing trends. Doing so is going to require more than just having the facts. It's going to require figuring out what it takes to get people to truly believe the facts, and then behave as if those facts are true.

Why Is The Decimation of Public Schools a Bad Thing?

THE SAME WORDS can have very different connotations to listeners on the right and listeners on the left. When Donald Trump told his supporters that he would soon be sending Hillary Clinton to jail, liberals were appalled. They insisted Trump was behaving like an "authoritarian strongman"[1] who promised to "actively subvert democracy."[2] Trump's threat to prosecute Clinton was the stuff of banana republics, where leaders put their political opponents in prison merely for the crime of dissent.

Yet Trump's promise sounded like something quite different to his base. To them, promising to pursue criminal charges was not a subversion of democracy and the rule of law. Instead, it was a promise to uphold them. Trump's pledged prosecution did not come across as a strongman's belief that the political opposition should be in jail, but rather as a declaration that even politicians are not above the law. To them, Clinton had committed a crime, thus she should be in prison. Whether you hear the (now-dropped) prosecution threat as a "tyrant's punishment of opponents" or "a promise to apply laws fairly and equally" depends on whether you believe Hillary Clinton did something wrong. And your perception of whether she committed a crime is strongly influenced by your pre-existing political preferences.

People therefore—stop the presses!—interpret political language through ideological lenses. What sounds obviously outlandish to one person may seem totally unobjectionable or even desirable to another. People on the left, however, often fail to comprehend this fact. They condemn "marginalization" and "inequality" as if everyone already agrees that those are bad things. (A lot of people don't.[3]) The same is true of "privilege" and "neoliberalism," which are treated as self-evidently undesirable even though many people do not know what those things are, let alone share a hatred of them.

This problem frequently occurs in progressive condemnations of school privatization schemes. When Donald Trump appointed billionaire Betsy DeVos to lead his Department of Education,[4] the general reaction from the left has been horror and disgust. The consensus view was that DeVos is something like the Education Secretary from Hell (a view I happen to share). This is because DeVos is a longtime advocate of both charter schools and voucher programs, and has spent large amounts of money helping transform Michigan's public schools into a heavily charter-based system. DeVos apparently believes, like many others in the "school choice" movement, that the government should not really be in the business of running schools, but should hand out credits to parents and have private schools and charters compete over students.

As progressives have correctly pointed out in response to her selection, DeVos's ideas would fundamentally change the way education is offered in this country. According to her critics, DeVos "wants to dismantle public education"[5] and is "trying to gut public schools"[6] Many strong critiques of DeVos have been written, and almost all of them spend their time vigorously denouncing her lack of commitment to preserving the country's public school system in its current form.

BUT HERE IS A CRUCIAL POINT: these critiques only sound bad to progressive ears. To conservatives, they sound very different. After all, the conservative line is that our public schools are a crumbling, bureaucratic, inefficient waste of money, a handout to the teacher's unions. Why *shouldn't* they be decimated? The argument of voucher and charter proponents is that voucher and charter systems are better than public schools. So unless you are already a committed progressive, there's nothing persuasive about pointing out that Betsy DeVos plans to "end education as we know it."[7] Of course she does. Education "as we know it" is ruining children's lives. The sooner it's ended, the better. Thus anyone trying to persuasively argue that Betsy DeVos's ideas are bad needs to go beyond simply repeating that they are an "assault on public schooling" or that they would "privatize the nation's schools." In proving these points, one will only convince the convinced. Instead, one needs to make a clear and convincing case about the social consequences of DeVos's beliefs.

First, let's consider what the conservative argument on schooling actually is. It goes like this: government-run institutions tend to function poorly. They are not efficient, like businesses are, because they do not have incentives to perform well. Businesses, because they must compete for customers in a market environment, must offer the best products if they want to stay profitable. Governments, on the other hand, can offer crappy products, and because they are state-imposed monopolies, there is no way for consumers to go elsewhere. School choice will improve schools, because instead of forcing students to attend whatever school the government happens to offer, choice allows parents to decide which school they prefer. Schools will have to strive to be better and better, because parents can pull their students out and go elsewhere if they don't like them. Introducing a profit motive into schooling offers a powerful incentive for schools to offer a great product. If there is money to be made on being a good school, you can bet businesses will want to provide great schools. Thus private, for-profit schools with vouchers are a highly efficient way of delivering the best-quality education.

One can therefore see why saying that DeVos wants to "dismantle public schools" is not an effective argument against the conservative position. If privatization makes better schools, then we *should* dismantle public schools. DeVos has argued that she is "driven by compassion for the less fortunate rather than any covert theocratic or elitist agenda." If charter and voucher proponents are right about the effectiveness of choice and competition, then that isn't a crazy position. And the pro-privatization position does not, on its face, sound ludicrous. After all, government is pretty inefficient, and many public schools do somewhat suck. Understanding why DeVos is the Education Secretary from Hell therefore requires examining a more basic set of principles, to understand just why the persuasive-sounding conservative case on education is actually deeply horrifying.

LET'S START WITH THE DANGERS OF PROFIT. In Michigan, where DeVos' education reform efforts have been concentrated, many charters are operated for profit, meaning that private companies can enter the schooling business just like any other business. To the right, "profit" isn't a dirty word. If we can pay people to offer great education to kids, why isn't this win-win?

But introducing profit into the school system is very dangerous, for a simple reason: it creates a terrible set of incentives. If we hand a voucher to a for-profit private school, or give a large grant to a for-profit charter school, there is a strong incentive for the school to give students as close to nothing as they can. After all, since a for-profit corporation exists to maximize value to shareholders (*not* value to students), for-profit schools should try to spend as little money educating students as possible, in order to reap the largest financial gains. If you don't have to spring for new lab equipment or new textbooks, you have no reason to do so merely because it would benefit the students. A for-profit school is no longer concerned with the interest and well-being of those who attend it. It is just a means through which money is redistributed from state governments to CEOs and shareholders. Adding a profit motive to things that are necessarily highly unprofitable, like helping the poor, makes it very tempting for companies to take the government's money and provide little in return. The existence of for-profit online charter schools shows the nightmare this can turn into.[8] Pay a company to set up a school, and they may just stick the student in front of a computer screen all day. By creating a system in which there is money to be made by figuring out how to create the *appearance* of education without actually providing it, you are sending out an open invitation to con artists and profiteers.

Privatization advocates have a compelling response to this argument. They reply that it misses the full picture. Yes, corporations have an incentive to maximize shareholder value. But they can't do that without satisfying their customers. The interests of shareholders and consumers are brought into alignment through the existence of choice. In the case of schools, because parents have a voucher, if the school is not prioritizing its students, parents can simply go elsewhere. Nobody is making them send their students to this particular school. The theory of school choice is about choice, and choice creates competition, which creates quality. A school that simply funneled money to its executives and shareholders would not long maintain its enrollment.

But the theory of choice here is a romantic fiction. In reality, parents will not have many options among which to choose (there are only so many schools within a feasible distance of one's home, after all), and moving schools can be an extraordinarily disruptive and complicated process that hurts the child. We can also see how, even in theory, it is easy for a privatized school system to simply enrich the wealthy, while making schooling for poor children worse. In a public school system, all money is spent on the schools. In a for-profit school system, at least some portion of that money is directed instead toward the pockets of shareholders (if it wasn't, the for-profit schools couldn't continue to exist). And if we have a school district comprised in total of three for-profit elementary schools, and all of them simply pocket most of the voucher money while failing to educate the children, then no matter what "choices" among schools parents make, they won't be able to improve the quality of the schools. One might expect new operators to enter the market, but if the only way to make any real money on the children is to neglect them, then new operators won't be any better than the old ones.

This gets at the fundamental mistake of free-market economic thinking, which is the fallacious belief that the choices we make in a market situation necessarily meaningfully reflect our "preferences." But what my choices say about my preferences depends on what those choices are to begin with. Defenders of free markets argue, for example, that people's "choice" to work in unsafe conditions shows that they prefer unsafe jobs with high pay to safe jobs with low pay.[9] But choice does not occur in a vacuum. Choices only tell us something significant about preferences to the extent that they are meaningful choices. "Would you rather be stabbed or shot?" is not a meaningful choice. Sophie's Choice was not a meaningful choice. Thus in order to understand how much meaning to attribute to choices, it's necessary to understand how choices are structured. If we create a private, for profit, school system, I might have to choose between sending my child to FedEx Junior High to have them train to pack boxes, or Burger King Junior High to have them train to flip Whoppers. If I decide to pick FedEx, that doesn't mean we have a school system that reflects my freely-made choices. My real choice would be to have taxpayer money paying for arts programs, English classes, and math, rather than being handed directly to the CEO and shareholders of FedEx. But that choice hasn't been made available to me on the free market. The poorer and more desperate a person is, the less meaningful their choices are. If I am rich, and I can easily move wherever I please and enroll my children in any school I like, then my choice of some academy in Switzerland is strongly indicative of the fact that I think it is the best school. But if I am poor, and live in Detroit, my choices are curtailed by my conditions and my capacities.

Free market capitalists do not understand how a lack of money can operate as a form of coercion. Thus they can make arguments (as made by the organization DeVos is a board member of) that child labor is a good thing, because they see the choice to go to work as freely made, failing to see how people's levels of economic despair can cause them to make "choices" that they very much do not want to make.[10] My decisions are only freely made to the extent that my other options are realistic. If my choice is to send my child down a mine or have my family starve to death, then I will send my child down a mine. *But I still don't want to send my child down a fucking mine.*

There are other serious problems with the "gutting" of public schools. For example, converting public schools to a voucher system makes education operate similarly to food stamps.[11] After all, SNAP benefits operate roughly the same way: instead of giving people food, we give them the equivalent of money, which they then use to go and buy food. A voucher program does the same for schooling: instead of giving them schools, we give them a voucher, which they can use to go and find a private school. But look what happens with food stamps: the moment you start handing out a "voucher," conservatives start seeing it as some kind of unearned "handout." Pressure then develops to cut the handout. Is there any reason to think that "education stamps" would be subjected to less cost-cutting political pressure than food stamps? A serious problem with voucher programs is that they erode the idea of education as a fundamental right, instead making it seem like a privilege that one does not necessarily deserve. But education should be a right, because children cannot help the circumstances of their birth, and should therefore not be punished for their parents' poverty.

Privatization schemes are also heavily dependent on the existence of highly astute parents, who have the time and inclination to carefully study schools. The most vulnerable children are unlikely to have such parents. And we can imagine a system in which private schools offer parents $100 out of the voucher money if they agree to enroll their children. Desperate or uncaring parents might snap up the cash, with the neediest children ending up in the most vicious, uncaring, profit-grubbing schools.

Betsy DeVos is a hellish choice for education secretary, because her ideology will create a hell for children. But that's not because she's in favor of the "private" rather than the "public." It's because the things needed by poor people, if done well, will never be money-makers. Introducing an incentive to make money will necessarily mean exploiting and neglecting the poor, whose "choices" are constrained by their circumstances. I fear privatization not because of some mystical devotion to the inefficiencies of government but because I fear the erosion of the idea of education as something that isn't win-win, that we give to children because they deserve it rather than because we can gain financially from it. I worry that the sort of people who run things "like a business" do not really care about children very much, and are motivated by the wrong incentives. I am concerned about what would happen if they ever faced a choice between doing the right thing and doing the lucrative thing. It seems a fragile and fantastical (almost religious) hope to think that a market for schools will produce good schools rather than simply a new means for parasitic corporations to engorge themselves on government money. However bad our public schools may be, I will always trust those who see children as an ends above those who see them as a means. And people like Betsy DeVos, who think of the world as a series of mutually beneficial business opportunities, strike me as the sort who should least be entrusted with the awesome responsibility of caring for and educating needy children.

A Public Option For Food

I KNOW IT IS A CONTENTIOUS POSITION these days, but I have always been in favor of public schools. I went to a public school. I enjoyed myself there. I believe it taught me some things. I've also always been suspicious of privatization schemes. I can't help but think that they will lead inexorably in the direction of giving children iPads rather than teachers.

Once, though, when I voiced my dubiousness about "voucherization," a gentleman challenged me.[1] Why, he said, did I think private schools with vouchers had to be worse than public schools? We entrust other areas of life to the private sector and they work just fine. Consider, for example, grocery stores. We don't have government-run grocery stores like we have government-run schools. And yet most people in the country seem pretty happy with their grocery stores. They can get whatever they want there, and if they can't afford it, we subsidize it with a "voucher" (i.e. food stamps). The profit motive hasn't led to a rapacious system of exploitation. In fact, it has given consumers the ability to get an astonishing variety of goods for incredibly low prices. Why are you uniquely suspicious of what the private sector would do to education, when it provides us so efficiently with our food?

The gentleman's argument was a strong one. I will confess that I felt a bit stumped by it. He was right. Every week I go to the grocery store and I get relatively tasty things for relatively low prices. And so I found myself tempted by his idea that education could be provided by "learning stores" just like nutrition is provided by grocery stores.

THEN I REMEMBERED THAT nutrition in America is a total disaster, that ⅔ of the country is obese or overweight,[2] and that half of the country either has diabetes or is at high risk of having diabetes soon.[3] If we start providing education like we provide nutrition, then God help the little children...

Food is actually the perfect example of a system in which the presence of a profit motive is having incredibly destructive human consequences. That's because it introduces a terrible incentive: to sell people the products they'll get addicted to rather than the products that are good for them. Americans live on junk food; they have terrible diets, with too much sodium, too many calories, too much sugar, and too few fruits and vegetables.

And as food companies seek to increase their revenue, the problem is spreading internationally. The *New York Times* recently reported that "multinational food companies like Nestlé, PepsiCo and General Mills have been aggressively expanding their presence in developing nations, unleashing a marketing juggernaut that is upending traditional diets from Brazil to Ghana to India."[4] Nestlé, for instance, hired legions of Brazilians to sell its products door to door, and regularly sent a barge down the Amazon river offering pudding, cookies, and candy. The result, according to the *Times*, has been "more obese Brazilians," with "a new epidemic of diabetes and heart disease." In places that "struggled with hunger and malnutrition just a generation ago" there are now "soaring rates of obesity," with "the growing availability of high-calorie, nutrient-poor foods" causing more people to be "both overweight and undernourished." In poor Brazilian towns, one can find 17-year-olds who weigh 250lbs and suffer from hypertension, problems once unknown in the developing world.

We know precisely why this happens. Bob Drane, the former Kraft Foods executive who invented Lunchables, described the logic of the industry:

Discover what consumers want to buy and give it to them with both barrels. Sell more, keep your job! How do marketers often translate these 'rules' into action on food? Our limbic brains love sugar, fat, salt... So formulate products to deliver these. Perhaps add low-cost ingredients to boost profit margins. Then 'supersize' to sell more... And advertise/promote to lock in 'heavy users.'[5]

Lunchables themselves were the result of this logic. They're bad for kids, since they're largely comprised of baloney and cheese, but Oscar Mayer realized that parents with little time would snap up something that eliminated the need to make lunch, and kids would crave them because it came with a big block of fatty cheese. (Experiments with healthier Lunchables were called off due to poor sales.)

Food and beverage executives are fairly open about how they think. "Half the world's population has not had a Coke in the last 30 days," said the president of Coca-Cola International. "There's 600 million teenagers who have not had a Coke in the last week. So the opportunity for that is huge."[6] According to the *Times*, a former Coke vice president said that "the goal became much larger than merely beating the rival brands; Coca-Cola strove to outsell every other thing people drank, including milk and water. The marketing division's efforts boiled down to one question... 'How can we drive more ounces into more bodies more often?'" Coke has specifically targeted poor areas around the world. Coke's former North American president, Jeffrey Dunn, was horrified by what he saw when he toured one of the impoverished districts the company was targeting: "A voice in my head says, 'These people need a lot of things, but they don't need a Coke.' I almost threw up." But when Dunn raised his concerns and tried to change the business, he encountered "very aggressive" resistance and was fired.

The usual response here is to blame the consumers: if people get fat and die from eating garbage and drinking poison, perhaps they shouldn't be buying it. If companies are selling products loaded with sugar and fat, it's because people really like sugar and fat. This is is always the way the industry responds. At a meeting of food executives in which a Kraft vice president tried to convince his peers to step up on nutrition, discussion came to a close when the CEO of General Mills vigorously defended existing practice. As the *Times* summarized:

> [Consumers were fickle.] Sometimes they worried about sugar, other times fat. General Mills, he said, acted responsibly to both the public and shareholders by offering products to satisfy dieters and other concerned shoppers, from low sugar to added whole grains. But most often, he said, people bought what they liked, and they liked what tasted good. "Don't talk to me about nutrition," he reportedly said, taking on the voice of the typical consumer. "Talk to me about taste, and if this stuff tastes better, don't run around trying to sell stuff that doesn't taste good." To react to the critics, Sanger said, would jeopardize the sanctity of the recipes that had made his products so successful. General Mills would not pull back. He would push his people onward, and he urged his peers to do the same.[7]

The former CEO of Philip Morris (since amusingly renamed "Altria" to convey a sense of innocence and benevolence), which owns Kraft, affirmed this, adding that it partially arises from the pressure of a highly competitive market:

> People could point to these things and say, 'They've got too much sugar, they've got too much salt... Well, that's what the consumer wants, and we're not putting a gun to their head to eat it. That's what they want. If we give them less, they'll buy less, and the competitor will get our market. So you're sort of trapped.[8]

This has been the consensus view. Those within the industry who have pushed for reform have gotten nowhere, and it's obvious why: as the Philip Morris CEO points out, a company that unilaterally decided to make its products healthier would not actually make the world healthier. It would just watch its market share plummet. So long as a company is concerned primarily with revenue and profit, asking it to care about nutrition is asking it to stop caring about its entire institutional purpose. It is like asking a drug pusher to sign on to an initiative to make heroin less addictive. Good luck.

It's long past time to discard the idea that companies just give people "what they want," and that blame for the popularity of inferior products rests with consumers. First, it's easy to understand why there needs to be a conceptual difference between "what people buy" and "what people want." That's because people *don't* want to die of heart disease, and yet they buy things that make them more likely to die of heart disease. And it's not enough to say that they must simply prefer "eating badly" to "not dying": if you ask them, they'll tell you they'd much rather *not* have diabetes. But they do. And part of the reason they do is that an entire multibillion dollar industry is dedicated to finding ways to make sure they keep eating poorly.

Companies don't just aggregate consumer preferences and try to satisfy those preferences. They also try to shape those preferences through expensive scientific research. Consider the Cheeto. The Cheeto is specifically designed to trick the human body through its "vanishing caloric density," which means that "if something melts down quickly, your brain thinks that there's no calories in it... you can just keep eating it forever."[9] People do not just eat piles of Cheetos because they are "dangerously cheesy," or because Chester Cheetah told them to. They eat piles of Cheetos because Kraft Foods consciously took advantage of an error in the way the human brain decides whether to keep eating something. As reporter Michael Moss says, "it's not just a matter of poor willpower on the part of the consumer and a give-the-people-what-they-want attitude on the part of the food manufacturers. What I found, over four years of research and reporting, was a conscious effort—taking place in labs and marketing meetings and grocery-store aisles—to get people hooked on foods that are convenient and inexpensive."

Moss found an internal Frito-Lay memo from 1957, which described the "fears and resistances" that were causing people to steer clear of potato chips, e.g. "You can't stop eating them; they're fattening; they're not good for you." But Frito-Lay was not focused on making sure people *could* stop eating potato chips, they wanted to find a way to make sure people felt *okay* with not stopping eating potato chips. So, for example, they stopped referring to their chips as "fried" and started referring to them as "toasted," because this made people feel less guilty about eating them. We can see here that consumer preference isn't being satisfied in any meaningful sense. The "preference" stated by the consumers was for potato chips to be less fatty and addictive. Instead of "giving the people what they wanted," companies found ways to fool them into thinking they were getting what they wanted. People are not asking for "a chip that seems healthier than it is," they're asking for "a chip that is healthy," so consumers have actually *not* been given what they want.

You could try to say that consumers still bear the responsibility for figuring out whether they're being deceived. But that's (1) more difficult than it sounds, (2) incredibly time-consuming, and (3) oblivious to the biological reality. First, large amounts of money are spent figuring out the answer to the question: "How can we make something that seems healthy but is actually addictively tasty (and thus not actually healthy)?" Yogurt has taken off in part because the industry realized it could be branded as a health food, but loaded up with sugar in a way that made people keep craving more of it. From a revenue perspective, the optimum food is the food that *seems* both tasty and healthy, which will often involve a lot of deception.

I'VE FALLEN DIRECTLY INTO THIS TRAP BEFORE. For a while, I ate Raisin Bran for breakfast, and I thought I was choosing a nutritious cereal. (It has fiber! And protein!) Nope: Raisin Bran has more sugar than Lucky Charms.[10] I'd also been proud of myself for eliminating sodas entirely. Instead, I drank Minute Maid's "Cranberry-Apple-Raspberry Juice" with my lunch. The label has pictures of leaves and fruits, and it looks so *natural*, so very unlike Coca-Cola. Unfortunately, it also contains 57 grams of sugar, more than root beer.

Now, you could blame me here. These products had labels (thanks only, by the way, to strict government requirements). I could have looked at them, and instead I made an assumption. But I refuse to accept all of the responsibility. It was not because I am stupid that I thought Raisin Bran was healthy. It's because the Kellogg's company *wanted* me to think that. They spent a lot of time thinking about the various ways that they could leave people with the impression that Raisin Bran is good for them without resorting to outright fraud. So it says "Heart Healthy" prominently on the box. It says "Real Fruit" and "Whole Grain." It says "Delicious Raisins Perfectly Balanced With Crisp, Toasted Bran Flakes" rather than "Delicious Sugar-Coated Raisins," which is what they are. And this is all designed so that I will do exactly what I did for a period of months: gobble Raisin Bran every morning, and think to myself "Wow, I can't believe Raisin Bran tastes so good, even though it's healthy. I guess because it's good for me, I can eat another bowl," without noticing that the whole *reason* it tastes so good and I want to eat another bowl is that a heap of sugar has been dumped into it.

It's tough to eat healthily, even when you want to, because you're fighting a massive industry that's trying to deceive you. Hacking your way through the thick web of manipulative branding techniques takes a lot of time and psychological energy. Figuring out how to eat well is not actually especially easy. You've got to spend a lot of time examining and comparing nutrition facts, and even those aren't designed as intuitively as they could be. (Imagine if fat and sugar content were on a color-coded scale instead of listed in raw numbers.) Industry lobbying has kept the FDA from listing sugar quantities in "teaspoons" rather than "grams," because hearing that something contains "five teaspoons" of sugar might make you far more likely to avoid it.[11] Providing consumers with the information they actually *need* in order to make their decisions well, e.g. giving them a more obvious and meaningful sense of what's in the products they're buying, would impact the revenues of companies that rely on people not asking too many questions. (If we really believe that consumer "preferences" should be satisfied, we should include warnings on certain processed foods the same way we include warnings on tobacco. The more informed consumers are about reality, the more defensible it is to say they have made a choice.)

The "consumer choice" defense also ignores the biological reality of what is going on. Cravings are not manifestations of human choice. They are biological urges that are extremely difficult to resist. "Once you pop, you just can't stop" is not a slogan, it's a fact. It is incredibly difficult to stop eating Pringles once one has started. I have tried and failed many times, and I am a person of uncommon stubbornness and willpower. The Pringle has been specially engineered to make me not just want to eat it, but need to eat it. Nutritionists and food scientists take very seriously the idea that food can have addictive properties. That's not surprising, because the industry tries so hard to make sure that it does. Yet the "individual responsibility" ethic prevails.

The harms of a corporate food system do not affect everyone equally. Instead, they fall disproportionately on the poor, who have less time for food preparation and information gathering, and thus default to fast food for its convenience. Disparities in health consequences reflect that fact: less well-off people have worse diets and suffer obesity, heart disease, and diabetes in greater numbers. A privatized system of nutrition delivery, predictably, delivers the worst outcomes to those with the least money.

EXAMINING THE FOOD SYSTEM IN DETAIL is instructive because it reveals a lot about how free markets work and don't work. We can imagine how things would play out if the same system were relied upon to deliver education: a few big companies would end up running most of the schools. Individuals could go to whichever school they could pay for. But since school companies would be competing with each other, and trying to maximize profits, they would be incentivized to spend as little as possible educating students, while deceiving parents into thinking their children were learning more than they actually were. Just as food companies do better not when they offer health but when they offer the appearance of health, school companies would adopt branding techniques that made them appear high-quality (use of the word "academy," fancy seal, uniforms, etc.) while trying to spend as little money as possible on actually educating the child. For-profit education will be as "educational" as for-profit products like Coca-Cola are "nutritional."

My friend Sarah likes to describe capitalism by comparing it to the "paperclip maximizer." The paperclip maximizer is a thought experiment used to warn about the potentially deadly effects of artificial intelligence. It's about how a machine given the wrong instructions will produce the wrong results. You have an intelligent robot, and you'd like him to collect paperclips. So you program the robot with the following instruction: "Maximize the number of paperclips in your possession." Then you set it loose. The robot first goes around the world collecting all the existing paperclips. But once it has them all, it still isn't finished. After all, it must *maximize* the number of paperclips it has. So it begins turning everything it finds into paperclips. Soon, the entire planet is nothing but a wasteland of paperclips. Eventually, the universe itself will be a vast cosmic heap of paperclips. A seemingly benign instruction, carried out with precision and efficiency, destroyed the world.

Corporations can operate similarly. The Coca-Cola company follows a mandate: "raise revenue by selling drinks." It sounds innocent. But the result is perverse: the company simply tries to get "as many ounces as possible into as many bodies as possible." Every additional Coca-Cola sold is an additional dollar of revenue. There is no upper limit, then. "Growth potential" is all that matters, regardless of other consequences. And the lives of people only matter to the extent that keeping them alive longer will allow them to drink more Coke. I'm not exaggerating here. Those are the words of the Coca-Cola executives. And they flow perfectly rationally from the structure of the institution.

Capitalism is very effective at increasing production. Even Karl Marx was impressed with its achievements. But it also only works to the extent that the institutional incentives will, when followed, produce good results. People who defend capitalism do think it produces good results, because the incentive is to sell as many goods as possible, and that means selling the products that people want to buy. But, like the paperclip maximizer, "sell the goods that people will buy" is a benign rule that leads to a perverse result. A company that takes a poll of the things people want in a snack, and sells a snack with those qualities, will probably do well. But a company that researches ways to trigger biological cravings, and uses subtle branding cues to trick people into thinking the product is better than it is, will do even better. The theory of a free market works at the "lemonade stand" level. Yet the paperclip robot, too, works at first: it's what happens when the imperatives are carried to their endpoint that is so destructive. Capitalism, carried to its endpoint, will devour the earth, because that's what its programming requires.

So it would be best if the school system did not operate like the food system. But perhaps we should be thinking about the opposite as well: what if the food system operated more like the public school system? What if there was a "public option" for food?

Public schools are an "option" because they already exist within a market for schools. If you'd like to, you can opt out of the public school system and send your children to a private school. Even Britain's single-payer health service, the NHS, is a public "option" of a kind, because people can still pay for private health insurance and private hospitals if they choose. (Because most people are satisfied with the NHS, however, only a fraction do this.) A public option is useful because it doesn't have to think about profit, it can just think about providing the public with what they need.

Let us imagine a public option for food. It is a state-funded restaurant called the American Free Diner. At the American Free Diner, anyone can show up and eat, and the food is free. It's designed to be as healthy as possible while still being pretty tasty. It's not going to be tastier than McDonalds fries, but the aim of the American Free Diner is not to get you to hooked on having as many meals as possible, it's designed to get you to have a satisfying and nutritionally complete meal. And there are options. For breakfast you can have eggs and (veggie?) bacon with fruit, oatmeal, avocado on toast, or a smoothie. Lunch is soups, salads, and sandwiches. Oh, and you can also always stop by and grab free fruit or other snacks. Now, you have to eat your meal during the time you're in the restaurant, so there's no smuggling food away and selling it. Anyone can have up to three meals a day there; you sign up with an ID and then you get a card. If you ate at the American Free Diner for every meal, you'd be meeting every possible recommended nutritional guideline. Every town has an American Free Diner in it. The music is great and there's a buzzing neon sign. But it's nothing too fancy.

Our "public option" for food does not mean people can't go elsewhere, just as our public school system doesn't mean that people can't enroll in private schools. But it does ensure that anyone who wants to can turn up and get a high-quality meal for free, without having to have much information on their own, without having to have any money, and without having to *do* very much. Now, the question is: what would happen? I think you'd see a lot of people taking their meals at the American Free Diner. That's because the food is *free*. And that would be a very good thing indeed, because every meal eaten there is a healthy meal. Who *wouldn't* eat at the American Free Diner? Well, rich people wouldn't eat there, because they can afford even nicer food. But rich people also enroll their children in private schools. They're not the target population here. What we're trying to do is make sure that everyone has access to a baseline level of nutrition, just like everyone should have access to a baseline level of education.

Personally, I think the Free Diner is our best way of solving our national nutrition crisis. Currently, we try to provide nutrition to the poor with a "voucher" system. That has a couple of problems. First, people don't know what to buy, so they are highly susceptible to being manipulated. Second, buying groceries and making meals at home is incredibly time-consuming, which is one reason people tend toward fast food. The Diner solves these problems. It doesn't restrict your choices, you can still buy whatever you want on the free market. But it does offer you one more choice: eat free, healthy meals at the Free Diner.

One of the reasons people will be skeptical about the Free Diner is that they have little confidence in the state to do anything right. There is a tacit acceptance of the basic idea of "public choice theory": that state actors are just as much selfish maximizers as anyone else, and that the only difference between the state and a corporation is that the state doesn't have to be as accountable to its consumers. But this view only captures part of the truth: sometimes states are selfish, sometimes they are not, just as human beings themselves are sometimes avaricious and sometimes benevolent. Which motive is acted upon will depend on who is in charge and how the institution is set up.

There's nothing inherent about a public school being public that requires it to be crappy. As I say, I went to a fantastic public school. But a few things are necessary for a public institution to run well. It needs to be free of bureaucratic constraint. It needs to have a clear mandate. It needs to be run by the right people. And it needs to be well-funded. When people think of the state offering food, I think they probably recoil: they think of Soviet canteens, perhaps, and government cheese. But there's no reason things need to be this way. I know at least a dozen people who could run a nutritious, delicious, and decidedly non-dreary nonprofit diner given a sufficient budget.

Frankly, I don't see many other easy ways out of our collective nutrition crisis. You could try to legislate the activities of companies like General Mills and Coca-Cola, restrict their advertising and regulate their product more. But ultimately, this won't change their incentives. You could try to publicly campaign to get people to make better nutrition choices. But this is probably doomed, since lack of desire/willpower is only a minor part of the reason why people eat bad food. You could try to restrict what people can spend food stamps on. But that only helps people who are on food stamps, seems invasive and nannying, and will be difficult to enforce. A better idea is to just open restaurants, and incentivize people to go there by making them free, and by deploying the same marketing/branding techniques that companies use presently to get people to make *bad* decisions. (It's called the American Free Diner to conjure patriotic associations.)

I used to think grocery stores were a good argument against public schools. Now, I think public schools are a good argument against grocery stores. The American diet is killing us, and people are making money encouraging us to continue eating badly, tempting us with pudding barges. It's time to introduce a public option for food. It's time for an American Free Diner.

This Little Rock and All Who Sail On It

ONE OF THE MOST (ONLY?) SENSIBLE OBSERVATIONS Ronald Reagan ever made has always been seen as one of his most absurd statements. In a speech to the United Nations, Reagan brought up the possibility of the world being overtaken by extraterrestrials:

> *Cannot swords be turned to plowshares? Can we and all nations not live in peace? In our obsession with antagonisms of the moment, we often forget how much unites all the members of humanity. Perhaps we need some outside, universal threat to make us recognize this common bond. I occasionally think how quickly our differences worldwide would vanish if we were facing an alien threat from outside this world.*[1]

It was not the only time Reagan mentioned the alien threat. He even explicitly asked Mikhail Gorbachev if the USSR would be willing to forget about the Cold War if and when the aliens invaded.[2] (Gorbachev agreed.) For some of Reagan's detractors, the president's ongoing interest in flying saucers (he claimed to have seen multiple UFOs, and may even have believed an alien told him to enter politics)[3] was further evidence of his own questionable judgment and, well, general spaciness. But, except for the truly kooky bits, that's not really fair. His UFO sighting claims may have been delusional, but the passage from Reagan's UN speech is exactly correct. It's a refreshing departure from the usual nationalist rhetoric to hear a president talking about the common bonds that unite humanity, and the cosmic insignificance of all our intraspecies conflicts.

Of course, it's somewhat hard to take seriously rhetoric about beating swords into plowshares when it comes from a president who was at that moment providing material support to Latin American death squads.[4] But personal hypocrisy doesn't affect the truth of a speaker's words. Reagan also may have been wrong that all human division would suddenly cease upon the event of an alien invasion: far more plausible is the situation from *The Day The Earth Stood Still*,[5] in which the countries bicker among themselves endlessly and the U.S. ends up shooting a gentle alien who turns out to have come in peace. It's still true, though, that thinking about the vastness of space and speculating on the existence of alien races is an effective way to make yourself feel embarrassed about all the time human beings spend trying to massacre and exploit one another. The cosmic scale is very good at making much of what we do look silly and futile.

Space is why I hate politics. I've never been able to shed a childlike fascination with distant stars, and a desire to find out who our neighbors are. I feel, sitting on the shore of the Great Cosmic Sea and looking at all its many distant lights, as if it's quite obviously desirable to figure out as much as possible about the universe, and to try to get off our own tiny island and venture out into the unknown. Obviously, that seems impossible now. But our species has been around for 200,000 years and we only invented satellites within the lifetime of presently-living people (heck, we only invented the doorknob a few generations ago[6]). If we could avoid destroying ourselves, we'd have a few million years to thinking about how to navigate our way through the universe. To me, it's *exciting* to think about what an animal that only came up with the internet 30 years ago could do with that time. And being on the edge of the actual "final frontier," but not knowing what it holds, is like living in the centuries before Earth was fully mapped. I'm sure plenty of people then didn't waste much time wondering what was off in the uncharted distance, and treated the outskirts of their towns and villages as the edge of the observable universe. But the curious impulse to *explore the unknown* (if not the often-simultaneous human impulse to *subdue and privatize the unknown*) is among the best of our traits.

Unfortunately, I don't get to think much about space, about what wonders and horrors are to be found across the galaxies, because spending time in space isn't morally defensible in a world filled with avoidable suffering. Missions to Mars should be considered unaffordable luxuries until everyone has adequate shelter, nutrition, and healthcare, and is free from violence and exploitation. It's not good thinking about the next phase of human ambition until we've successfully managed to sort this one out. Before getting to put our energies toward the search for other life, and the better understanding of the universe, we have to avoid boiling the planet alive or vaporizing each other in a nuclear holocaust.

Gil Scott-Heron's brilliant and disturbing poem "Whitey's On The Moon" neatly exposes the perversity of going to space in a time of poverty and racial inequality:

> *A rat done bit my sister Nell*
> *with Whitey on the moon.*
> *Her face and arms began to swell*
> *and Whitey's on the moon.*
> *I can't pay no doctor bill*
> *but Whitey's on the moon.*
> *Ten years from now I'll be payin' still.*
> *while Whitey's on the moon.*
> *The man just upped my rent last night.*
> *'cause Whitey's on the moon.*
> *No hot water, no toilets, no lights*
> *but Whitey's on the moon.*
> *Was all that money I made last year*
> *for Whitey on the moon?*
> *How come there ain't no money here?*
> *Hm! Whitey's on the moon.*

When you think about poor medical care, crumbling public housing, and resource-starved urban school districts—and then about poverty and disease around the globe—human triumphs in space exploration begin to seem shameful and somewhat sick. Of course, then it's difficult to know where to stop: once you start treating every dollar not spent on alleviating suffering as a dollar being squandered, everything above bare subsistence begins to seem like unjustifiable indulgence. Maybe it *is* unjustified, though. To me, that doesn't mean I'm going to stop frittering away bits of my meager income on pastries and floral-patterned cravats. But it does mean that until we fix systemic social problems, I'm going to feel bad about that, and so I'd like to fix systemic social problems as quickly as possible.

I subscribe to the Buckminster Fuller view: we all live aboard "Spaceship Earth," a pleasant little rock hurtling through the universe.[7] Fuller said that our spaceship was so well-equipped and well-devised "that to our knowledge humans have been on board it for two million years not even knowing that they were on board a ship." The trouble is, he says, that it didn't come with an operating manual, and so the seven billion of us who have found ourselves deposited here face a formidable challenge. We somehow have to organize ourselves successfully in order to maintain our health and that of our little spaceship earth.

People who are fascinated by the universe are often "humanists" or "universalists." These terms are often used to denote a lack of formal religious belief, but they also describe those who see human beings as a unified community, and reject divisions of nation, tribe, class, race, etc. The universalist looks forward to a time when there will be a mutually-felt brotherhood/sisterhood of all human beings. Not that we'll treat each other like actual family, or that there won't be certain individuals we just can't stand spending more than 10 seconds in a room with. But by realizing that we all share one unusual thing in common, namely the experience of being a conscious being in an unfathomably vast and absurd universe, we might see ourselves as united in the project of trying to figure out *what the hell this mysterious thing called life is.*

It all sounds impossibly naive and utopian, but it's the perspective that has been held by many of our most brilliant thinkers. Albert Einstein, who shares with George Orwell the quality of being constantly revered but never listened to—"Why is it that everybody likes me but nobody understands me?" Einstein once asked—lamented the way that human beings failed to understand the degree to which they were mutually dependent on one another, and all bound together by their common experience of mortality. Each person is mostly the same, in the sense that all of us have popped into existence on a strange planet for a brief time for no clear purpose. It is as if we have suddenly woken up with a group of strangers on a remote patch of land, without any sense of where we are or how we got here. The rational approach to such a situation is to work with everyone else to find the answers, rather than seeing yourself as an individual in competition with the others.

Einstein's perspective on the ties that humans shared made him a committed socialist and internationalist. "I look upon myself as a man," he said.[8] "Nationalism is an infantile disease. It is the measles of mankind." And he didn't just loathe nationalism, but militaries themselves. He condemned "that worst outcrop of the herd nature, the military system, which I abhor," going so far as to say:

> *That a man can take pleasure in marching in formation to the strains of a band is enough to make me despise him. He has only been given his big brain by mistake; a backbone was all he needed. This plague-spot of civilization ought to be abolished with all possible speed. Heroism by order, senseless violence, and all the pestilent nonsense that goes by the name of patriotism — how I hate them! War seems to me a mean, contemptible thing: I would rather be hacked in pieces than take part in such an abominable business.*

Militaries, then, are a useless misapplication of the natural gift of intelligence. They only exist because of a vast, wasteful intercontinental prisoner's dilemma, one that could be solved if people would only learn to see themselves as they really are, rather than dividing themselves into artificial competitive units like nations. (Note that while Einstein said he'd rather be chopped to bits than participate in a war, you can actually hold the fundamentals of this perspective to be true without becoming a strict pacifist.) He dearly wished we could abandon our pessimistic (and inaccurate) belief that "human nature" destined us for violence and mutually assured destruction, insisting that "human beings are not condemned, because of their biological constitution, to annihilate each other or to be at the mercy of a cruel, self-inflicted fate."

Einstein was equally critical of capitalism, because he saw in it the same kind of erosion of human solidarity.[9] It caused people to see themselves as competitive units instead of allies. The "crisis of our time," he said, was that we were incapable of seeing ourselves as united in a collective endeavor, and preyed on each other rather than pooling our resources:

> *The individual has become more conscious than ever of his dependence upon society. But he does not experience this dependence as a positive asset, as an organic tie, as a protective force, but rather as a threat to his natural rights, or even to his economic existence. Moreover, his position in society is such that the egotistical drives of his make-up are constantly being accentuated, while his social drives, which are by nature weaker, progressively deteriorate. All human beings, whatever their position in society, are suffering from this process of deterioration. Unknowingly prisoners of their own egotism, they feel insecure, lonely, and deprived of the naïve, simple, and unsophisticated enjoyment of life.*

For Einstein, "the economic anxiety of capitalist society" was "the real source of the evil." He "regard[ed] class differences as contrary to justice" and was frustrated by a system that worshiped "the cult of the individual," in which "production is carried on for profit, not for use." There was "only one way to eliminate these grave evils, namely through the establishment of a socialist economy, accompanied by an educational system which would be oriented toward social goals." We must "abandon competition and secure cooperation," and establish an economy in which "the means of production are owned by society itself," else we shall "face certain disaster." (Note that Einstein, like Orwell, was not an authoritarian socialist, and believed that it was crucial never to sacrifice liberty and democracy in our pursuit of equality. An important question in creating a fairer society, he said, was "How can the rights of the individual be protected and therewith a democratic counterweight to the power of bureaucracy be assured?")

There was a strong link between Einstein's belief in human fellowship and his belief in the pursuit of scientific knowledge. Making the world better requires comprehending it better, and the curious and humble attitude that the scientist takes to the universe is the one that we should all have in our dealings with one another. "We must learn to understand the motives of human beings, their illusions, and their sufferings," he said, "in order to acquire a proper relationship to individual fellow-men and to the community." "Understanding" is both a social goal and an empirical goal.

PERSONALLY, I HAPPEN TO THINK Einstein wasn't an idiot. I'm sure many people dismiss his political writings by observing that plenty of those who are geniuses in one field are foolish in another. Richard Dawkins may be a brilliant biologist, but he's a nincompoop on Twitter.[10] There's nothing about understanding relativity that necessarily gives you insight into the optimal organization of our economic system.

But Einstein's fusion of the "socialistic" and the "scientific" is both consistent and appealing. I don't think it developed accidentally. The more you contemplate the human place in spacetime, the bizarre accident of our being here, the completely impossible and probably meaningless questions like "Why me? Why this planet? Why now?", the more you wish we could just solve poverty, war, and despair as quickly as possible and set our finest minds toward the task of telling us what is going on. One reason I feel such a strong urgency to get social problems fixed is that I want us to *get to the good stuff*, i.e. the part of our history where we meet aliens, and I really want to be around to see what remarkable thing human beings do next. (My selfish desire to find out how the human story ends is one reason I would like to see a lot more resources put toward the question of how to stop death. Although on that, too, I can't justify life *extension* until we've actually made the lives people already have more free and fair.) And I hate politics because they're just a means to an end, and I'd like to get to the end rather than having to expend unnecessary energy on the means.

The *Star Trek* future is the one I like: exploring strange new worlds, seeking out new life and new civilizations, going boldly and all that. Of course, until we learn to control our worst impulses, we probably shouldn't venture forth, as we'd be a danger to those around us. (That is, by the way, the reason for the alien's visit in *The Day The Earth Stood Still*. He has been sent to give us a warning: the alien races have collectively concluded that unless human beings stop combining technological progress with extreme militarism, we will be deemed to pose an interplanetary threat and will have to be destroyed for the good of the community.) If capitalist humans went planet-hopping to extract as much wealth as possible, we'd quickly turn every wondrous new place into a wasteland. Donald Trump is bad enough as a U.S. president, let alone as an intergalactic dictator. Socialism first, space later.

Unfortunately, the delightful *Star Trek* future-world seems increasingly implausible. Science fiction these days is often bleak and dystopian, possibly because it's easier to imagine the end of the world than the end of capitalism, and without the end of capitalism, every conceivable high-tech future would be feudalistic and miserable. I mean, hell, when a violence-obsessed nihilist like Quentin Tarantino is hired to helm an R-Rated *Star Trek* film,[11] the franchise is not exactly likely to maintain the humane communistic spirit endowed upon it by Gene Roddenberry. But Tarantino *Star Trek* certainly accords with the sci-fi zeitgeist, which assumes that everything in the future is just going to be fucking terrible until we all shoot each other.

When you look at the old pulp sci-fi magazine illustrations, from the '30s through the '50, you get a sense of wondrous excitement about the fascinating and scary worlds we may uncover as we poke around. I love the warmth, enthusiasm, and imagination, the *romance* that used to be associated with journeying into the cosmos. I sense that a lot of that has vanished, even some of it in my lifetime. (Space used to be cool when I was a kid. Is space cool now? Do young people like space?) I don't doubt that that's largely because the universe became demystified: we discovered that the barriers to sending humans beyond the boundaries of our solar system were seemingly insurmountable, we discovered that the only reason to visit Mars or Venus was to be instantly frozen/boiled to death, and we discovered that the most exciting things you'll come upon in the interplanetary void are rocks, and even those will only be encountered extremely intermittently. The moon wasn't cheese, so we didn't go back.

Then again, nothing was really "demystified." In fact, the universe is a more mysterious place than ever. But major breakthroughs in understanding and exploration require greater and greater amounts of resources. And, well, it's definitely true that space is no longer much of a priority, as we can see from the continued downward trajectory of the NASA budget (and the continued upward trajectory of the military budget). Because I subscribe to the "Whitey's on the Moon" philosophy that you probably shouldn't be footling around with space shuttles while black people in rural Alabama are contracting parasitic hookworm,[12] I don't actually see this as a bad thing. If we had seen the extra fraction of the federal budget redirected toward free medical clinics in poor counties, I'd be overjoyed. Instead, of course, we build fighter jets, a type of plane that literally exists *to fight other planes.* Defense-related spending has gotten, shall we say, quite substantial.

And that's not to mention all the other money that goes toward what economist Samuel Bowles calls "guard labor,"[13] e.g. police, security personnel, and corrections officers, who exist to maintain order and safeguard rich people's things. I can't imagine what poor Einstein would think if he saw the sheer amount of resources that now go toward activities he considered inherently wasteful and destructive.

LOOK, I'LL CONFESS THAT I'M QUITE CHILDLIKE in many of my attitudes. I never got over my fascination with stars and planets. And I never found talk of aliens to be ridiculous; in fact, it seemed very hard *not* to believe that in a universe as large as ours, there are plenty of other outposts of life. In order to believe that we're alone, you have to think we're *incredibly* special. It also entails believing that *the most sophisticated lifeform in the entire universe*—a universe consisting of at least 100 billion galaxies with 100 billion stars in a galaxy—made Donald Trump the most powerful of all its individuals. That is a world too absurd for me to believe in. I cannot, or will not, believe that a universe so vast and strange could peak with something so pitiful and fumbling as humankind. (And no, the Fermi Paradox has never bothered me. Why would anyone want to come *here*? It's like asking why nobody has visited a particular blade of grass in the middle of Montana. They're not here because *we're not special.*)

Like I say, every night sky feels like looking into an ocean teeming with life, without being able to touch or see any of it. And I don't understand why more people aren't curious as to what it contains. Yes, obviously, if we contact the aliens they may enslave or devour us. They may even have (God forbid) Trumps of their own. But our species is partway through a unique adventure, and we have to pursue it to its endpoint. We have found out so much, but we know so very little. We're in an enviable position, though: all of us happen to be members of the first group of humans to experience exponential technological growth, with its accompanying exponential possibilities. That's thrilling, even though some believe it means we're on the cusp of creating Frankenstein-like artificial intelligence that outsmarts and then kills us. We might well bear witness to some truly astonishing breakthroughs.

That does involve avoiding the suicide of the entire species, though. And the prospects there don't necessarily look good. I am not a pessimist—or rather I am with Antonio Gramsci: "pessimism of the intellect, optimism of the will." (That is: don't allow the fact that you know your endeavors are probably futile to keep you from pursuing them with gusto.) I don't actually know how hopeful to be, though the fact of that uncertainty means it's not yet worth giving up. I do know, however, that Einstein was right: if we are to survive long enough to properly understand and explore the universe we have found ourselves in, human solidarity is imperative. A world of individual competitive units is a world without the collective energy necessary to pilot Spaceship Earth to wherever it's going. Human divisions, of the kind reinforced by nationalism and capitalism, must disappear if we are to accomplish anything truly impressive together. Figuring out what we are, and what we're capable of, is going to require all of us to work together.

Ghouls

All of Your Attempts to Redeem Martin Shkreli Will Fail

FOR SOME REASON, a number of writers seem to have taken it upon themselves to salvage Martin Shkreli's reputation. Previously, there had been a rough consensus that Shkreli, the oily, simpering pharmaceutical executive who raised the price of HIV drugs by 5000 percent before being indicted on fraud charges, was one of the most cretinous human beings alive.[1] This seemed utterly uncontroversial, in fact so self-evident as to render debate unnecessary.

But a miniature genre of article has sprung up: the Martin Skhreli Is Not As Bad As You Think hot take. From *Vanity Fair* to *The Washington Post* to *The New Yorker*, authors have issued the provocative thesis that, far from being the mealy, smirking, patronizing little snot he appears to be both at a distance and up close, Shkreli is anything from a blameless cog in a vast dysfunctional apparatus to a sweet and tender do-gooder unfairly disparaged by a society too stupid and hateful to appreciate his genius.

The former type of portrayal is the least outlandish, though perhaps the more insidious. Some have conceded that while Shkreli might indeed be a greedy heartless reptilian AIDS profiteer, his behavior is enabled by a broken system of drug approval and pricing, and the public's ire should be directed away from Shkreli and toward that system. James Surowiecki gave a typical example of this argument in *The New Yorker:*

The Turing scandal has shown just how vulnerable drug pricing is to exploitative, rent-seeking behavior. It's fair enough to excoriate Martin Shkreli for greed and indifference. The real problem, however, is not the man but the system that has let him thrive.[2]

The Atlantic's James Hamblin echoed this, saying that Shkreli's existence is "a product, not a cause," with an innovation-stifling regulatory structure far more to blame for Shkreli's scheming.[3]

The thrust of these arguments is easy to buy: by focusing on the acts of a single individual and his noxious personal qualities, instead of on the legal framework in which he operates, we entirely fail to advance any solution to the actual problem of drug price hikes. While it may be satisfying to hurl abuse at Shkreli, he is merely a scapegoat. *Business Insider* noted that Shkreli was "right" in insisting that he needed to maximize shareholder value, and went so far as to say that he may be "the villain we need to get our healthcare system in action."[4] One doctor mirrored Shkreli's own insistence that because what he did was legal, it wasn't wrong, saying:

> *Remember, he is not doing anything illegal. The media is portraying him as an unsentimental money maker. I couldn't care less if he boiled his neighbor's bunny. The demonization distracts us from the most important question, which is not why Shkreli is raising the price of Daraprim by 5,500 percent, but how.[5]*

But here is where I profoundly differ with these people: if Martin Shkreli boiled his neighbor's bunny, I'd be disgusted, not indifferent. I mean that quite seriously: nobody should have attention deflected away from their harmful, immoral behavior simply because it occurs within the context of more pressing structural issues. What these arguments encourage us to do is to shift blame away from Shkreli and onto our laws and policies. But by treating individuals like Shkreli as mere inevitable consequences, rather than human beings who make deliberate choices for which they should be held morally accountable, they effectively exonerate heinous behavior.

It's completely accurate, of course, to say that our *time* is better used trying to devise a fair drug market rather than sitting around despising Martin Shkreli. However, in apportioning *blame* for the Daraprim hike, Shkreli bears complete responsibility. It is no defense of anything to say that it is "legal" or made possible by the market. And if he believes that limiting patient access to medications is compelled by his mandate to maximize shareholder value, then Shkreli should find a job whose mandate does not require one to hurt people.

This is significant, because it reflects the way businessmen are often spoken of: as if they cannot be expected to act differently. Marxists are just as guilty of this as free-market libertarians; they believe it is senseless to "moralize" about the rich, who after all are the product of inevitable historical forces; to blame them is akin to blaming the moon for the tides. But I disagree strongly: I believe that humans have free will, and that it is both right and necessary to detest the world's Shkrelis, because unless morally shameful behavior is treated with scorn, it no longer remains shameful. Those who willingly maximize profits at the expense of the sick, regardless of whether they are behaving predictably or legally, should experience intense public ire. "Don't Hate Martin Shkreli, Hate the System That Made Him," we are told. But nothing stops us from hating both; nobody is required to choose.

But beyond the "focus on the system" angle, there is another class of Shkreli-defense out there, one far more extreme in its propositions: the "Martin Shkreli is actually a good guy" defense. A number of articles actually attempt to make the case that Shkreli is decent, sensitive, and misunderstood.

The general thrust is that once you get to know him, Martin Shkreli turns out to be a more "complex" and human person than his irritating public persona would have us believe. "When speaking for himself, instead of battling crass media characterizations, Shkreli is an endearing chap," said *Yahoo Finance*'s Rick Newman, in an article entitled "Martin Shkreli is Actually A Great Guy."[6] *Vanity Fair* and *Vice* have both run humanizing profile stories based on lengthy interviews. The *Vanity Fair* profile contained the following lines:

He's such a perfect villain when viewed from afar that it's almost impossible not to like him more up close. He swerves seamlessly among obnoxious bravado, old-world politeness, purposeful displays of powerful intelligence, and even flashes of sweetness.[7]

And the *Vice* profile, while questioning a number of Shkreli's claims and containing numerous criticisms, calls Shkreli a "finance wunderkind" and "a Horatio Alger story" and sympathetically relays Shkreli's claim that his unapologetically money-grubbing attitude is merely an exaggerated caricature that he plays for the public to entertain himself.[8] The *Vice* reporter sees Shkreli as an enigma because:

On one hand, Shkreli can wax poetic, as he did to me, about the "puzzle of medicine" and his desire to help people. On the other hand, he told Vanity Fair that he switched to biotech because hedge funds weren't lucrative enough.

Let's be clear: these reporters are dupes. The behavior Shkreli displays, veering wildly between charm and amorality, is not a sign of complexity, but of sociopathy. Seen up close, Shkreli does *not* become more likable, but more disturbing, because it becomes clear that he is willing to put on any facade necessary to get what he wants out of people. Ordinary, morally healthy human beings do not do this.

I am not simply exercising my imagination here. One of Shkreli's ex-girlfriends has confirmed that he is a manipulative, psychologically abusive habitual deceiver with zero capacity for empathy. As she explained:

It soon became obvious that Martin was a pathological liar, would pretend to cheat on me and brag about it to raise his value in my eyes, so I'd always feel like I was hanging on by a thread, could be replaced, would vie for his approval and forgiveness.[9]

Shkreli's ex-girlfriend also displayed screenshots of conversations in which Shkreli offered to pay her ten thousand dollars for sex, a proposition that revolted her. Again, ordinary people do not do this.

His menacing behavior has been noted elsewhere: he has been accused of waging a harassment campaign against an ex-employee, writing in an email that "I hope to see you and your four children homeless and will do whatever I can to assure this."[10] The "Old World politeness" that so impressed the *Vanity Fair* correspondent appears to be hauled out for the benefit of journalists, only to vanish once they leave.

Both reporters know this, though. As *Vanity Fair* notes:

> *"Sociopath" is a not uncommon description of him. "Malicious" is the word another person uses... Shkreli says that the harsh words don't bother him.*

Note how the "sociopath" designation functions here: not as an enormous red flag that should make a reporter worry she or he is being manipulated, but as "harsh words" from a hostile public. Surely, though, if people tend to refer to someone this way, it should be seen as a warning rather than a badge of honor. Once again, ordinary, morally function people are rarely mistaken for malicious, destructive sociopaths. Another writer, who went on a Tinder date with Shkreli and reported on it for the *Washington Post*, was also taken in by his disarming manner, even as he displayed exactly the same crass self-absorption we would expect:

> *He seemed the most genuine when he was acting like the guys I hung out with in high school (I dated the president of the chess club); that's probably why I felt so comfortable on our date. We finished our food, and Martin flagged down the waitress and ordered the $120 tea. This was the most surprising and jarring moment of the night. I know he's a multimillionaire, but I thought we were on the same page about this tea. He asked if I wanted a cup, and I couldn't bring myself to say yes. When Martin finished his tea, I asked how he liked it. "I'm not really a big tea drinker," he replied. What? I thought of all the good I could do with that money—donating it to charity, buying a new winter coat, buying myself 20 Venti iced*

soy vanilla chai lattes. He might as well have eaten a $100 bill in front of me.[11]

Shkreli deliberately purchased the most expensive tea on the menu and drank it in front of this woman despite the fact that he doesn't like tea. This is twisted behavior. Yet the *Post* writer remains sympathetic, concluding that Shkreli is "a lot more interesting and complex than I would have imagined." Again, "complexity" here is used to refer to "that peculiar combination of calculated charm and total lack of moral feeling that characterizes sociopathic individuals." There's no mystery as to what we're seeing.

Another writer who interacted with Shkreli on Tinder also came out with warm feelings about him:

> *I do believe that Martin Shkreli believes he is doing good for the world, or else he wouldn't have engaged with me. And even though Martin Shkreli is the current face of all that is wrong with capitalism, I do have sympathy for the guy. After all, even questionably sociopathic pharma bros deserve to get laid.*[12]

There are several problems here. First, it is peculiar to conclude that "because he engaged with me," Martin Shkreli "believes he is doing good for the world." What if, implausible as it may sound, Martin Shkreli simply cannot resist an opportunity to attempt to prove his intellectual superiority over others? We can apply a variation on Occam's Razor here: why assume the more complicated explanation (hidden benevolent soulful core) when the more intuitive one will do (he's an argumentative asshole)?

But even assuming Martin Shkreli *does* "believe he is doing good for the world," what sort of defense is this? Hardly anyone believes their own actions to be evil, least of all evil people. To the contrary, everyone from the IRA to the Klan believes they are doing good for the world, that their worldview is the correct one. A person's sincerity in no way excuses them; Donald Trump may sincerely believe that Muslims are a pox and Mexicans are rapists and that ejecting them all would be doing good for the world, but the honesty of his delusion doesn't make it a shred more justifiable.

Second, what is this about sociopathic pharmaceutical executives deserving to get laid? Perhaps under a Bernie Sanders administration the right to coitus will at last be construed as a basic human social entitlement. But until such time, why *on earth* would we grant the idea that Martin Shkreli deserves so much as a sultry flutter of the eyelashes directed toward him, let alone that he should have the expectation of genuine human affection? *If you're unpleasant, people will not want to have sex with you.* That should be the rule, lest unpleasant people begin to think unpleasantness pays unlimited carnal dividends. Referring to the importance of literary curiosity, John Waters once said that if you go home with someone, and they don't have books in their house, "don't fuck them." A similar principle should apply here: if you go home with someone, and they turn out to make their living profiting from the desperation of sick people, perhaps reconsider rewarding them sexually for their crimes.

BUT THE WORST PART OF THE Shkreli redemption-stories is that they give credence to Shkreli's lies about his price gouging. Each allows Shkreli to pour out all manner of self-serving horse manure about how much he cares about AIDS patients, saying things like: "It's our holy mission to make great drugs. And what we did with Daraprim is what it is. At the end of the day, the effort and the heart is in the right place." He compares himself to Robin Hood, says he has "altruistic" motives and that nobody who needs the drugs will go without them.

Nothing he says can be trusted. He promised to lower the price of Daraprim in late September of 2015. By the next February it remained $750 a pill.[13] He said insurance companies rather than patients would bear the cost; patients have been hit with co-pays up to $16,000. He insisted that the income from the price hike would be swiftly put back into new drug research; but in personal correspondence wrote that "almost all of it is profit."

The facts on the ground suggest that real people are being hurt by Shkreli's actions:

> *David Kimberlin had one month to get his hands on some Dara-prim.*[14] *His patient, a pregnant woman infected with toxoplas-mosis, was due to give birth in September. But in August, the 52-year-old doctor, who works at the University of Alabama in Birmingham, learned of the drug's price hike: a treatment that used to cost him $54 a month was now running at least $3,000. Babies born with toxoplasmosis need to be treated for about a year, with the total cost of treatment approaching $70,000 at the bare minimum. Fortunately, after a trip to the outpatient pharmacy, his pharmacist found a supply of the stuff already on the shelves—a break Kimberlin says saved the baby's life.*

During Shkreli's Reddit "Ask Me Anything" session, a Daraprim user worried about how he would pay for the medication:

> *If they don't follow through on their promises to provide it for free for patients like me for longer term, or if my insurance rejects the $27 per pill price, then I'll be significantly affected. I am not a wealthy man by any stretch, and will struggle to afford the $27 price without finding a way to convince my boss to give me a raise or borrowing money for the next year. I don't exactly have dispos-able income. I spend everything I make on my treatment.*[15]

Bear in mind, the commenter is worried about the $27-per-pill price that Skhreli promised. In actual fact, the medication remained at the astronomically higher rate of $750-per-pill. There's no word on how this user has fared, but all of Shkreli's showy professions of compassion are plainly fabricated. Again, not because of "complexity," but because this is typical behavior for someone incapable of empathy and willing to tell whatever lies necessary to get what he wants, in this case favorable press coverage portraying him as thoughtful and many-sided.

But by far the most over-the-top defense of Shkreli came from the *New Yorker*'s Kelefa Sanneh.[16] Sanneh made some of the usual points about the drug industry being the real culprit and so forth, but then got so wrapped up in Shkreli-love as to endorse Shkreli for the New Hampshire primary:

> *Last fall, Trump said that Shkreli "looks like a spoiled brat"; in fact, he is the son of a doorman, born to parents who emigrated from Albania. Look at him now! True, he has those indictments to worry about. But he is also a self-made celebrity, thanks to a business plan that makes it harder for us to ignore the incoherence and inefficiency of our medical industry. He rolls his eyes at members of Congress, he carries on thoughtful conversations with random Internet commenters, and, unlike most of our public figures, he may never learn the arts of pandering and grovelling. He is the American Dream, a rude reminder of the spirit that makes this country great, or at any rate exceptional. Shkreli for President! If voters in New Hampshire are truly intent on sending a message to the Washington establishment they claim to hate, they could—and probably will—do a lot worse.*

This is plainly ludicrous. Holding everyone around you in disdain is not "never learning the art of pandering." Trolling people on Reddit is not "having thoughtful conversations." And Martin Shkreli only embodies the American Dream to the extent that the American Dream is to start with nothing and work your way up to becoming as much of an enormous rich asshole as possible. (Actually, come to think of it, this is not far from how the American Dream is usually portrayed.)

But one can understand the pressures that would lead a writer like Sanneh to publish something so stupid. In the world of online writing, spewing indefensible opinions is financially incentivized. In a #SlatePitch-driven media, writers are constantly competing to best each other for the most "counterintuitive" opinion. So we get a whole mess of articles like "The American Revolution Was Actually a Bad Thing."[17] Or, from *Slate*'s own Matthew Yglesias: Actually, Deadly Bangladeshi Factory Collapses May Be A Good Thing.[18] (Yglesias eventually reached the logical endpoint of this reasoning, suggesting that the Nazis "may have had some good ideas.")

These articles come about for obvious reasons; "It Is Bad When Factories Collapse and People Die" is not nearly as provocative as its converse. Fewer people would click on an article entitled "Wasn't the American Revolution Nifty?" But here again, explanation is not justification. To take up immoral positions for the sake of Facebook and Twitter shares is to dishonor the responsibilities that come with being a writer (or rather, being a person generally.)

The simple truth is that some positions should not be defended. The Nazis did not have good ideas, factory collapses are tragic and must be stopped, and Martin Shkreli is neither interesting nor good, but a run-of-the-mill specimen of Wall Street vermin, albeit slightly more callous and two-faced than is standard even in America's financial sector. The desire to find a novel journalistic angle should never outweigh one's duty to acknowledge basic facts of the universe. Some things are simply true, with no contrarian angle to be taken, and that's perfectly alright.

It therefore remains worthwhile to hate Martin Shkreli, and to hate him intensely. Forget the questions over drug pricing; what we have serendipitously found in Shkreli is a convenient public example of everything a human being should strive not to be. Shkreli may have ignited a debate about access to medication, but his real social function is even greater: he displays all of the traits that our species must exorcise if we are to build a just and decent world. He is greedy, smug, and vulgar. He is a liar and a braggart. He treats women abominably. He is contemptuous of those he considers his lessers. His literary curiosity stops at Ayn Rand. (Actually, the Cliff's Notes to Ayn Rand, according to the reporter who looked at his bookshelf.) He doesn't just wish to amass pleasures for himself, but to deny them to others (witness his purchase of the sole copy of a $2 million Wu Tang Clan album and subsequent threat to destroy it.) He toys with people for his own amusement. He can be charitable, but only when it pleases him, for what motivates him is not the desire to maximize human good but to maximize his own power over others.

In short, even the people who have most loudly denounced Martin Shkreli have insufficiently appreciated just what a blight he is. Never mind "Shkreli is not the real problem." Shkreli is, in fact, the *only* problem, for once we can eliminate every little bit of Shkreli from ourselves, human beings will have reached perfection. We should teach about him in schools, cautionary sermons should be preached against him. Mamas, don't let your babies grow up to be Shkrelis.

All of these attempts to redeem Martin Shkreli must fail, then, so long as there is a glimmer of mercy and decency in the world. Of the many problems with the drug industry, Martin Shkreli may only represent only one of them. But of the many problems with humanity as a whole, Martin Shkreli represents essentially all of them.

Why Is
Charles Murray Odious?

FROM HIS EARLIEST DAYS, Charles Murray was—to put it charitably—a shockingly oblivious human being when it came to matters of race. As a teenager in the 1950s, he and some high school friends staged a cross burning on top of a hill.[1] Murray claims he was stunned when the residents of his Iowa town instantly thought the flaming cross was somehow racist. "It never crossed our minds that this had any larger significance," he insisted. Forty years later, with the publication of *The Bell Curve*, Murray would once again profess himself surprised that people could view him as a racist. "I'm befuddled by it... I don't know what to make of it," Murray said when even old acquaintances began calling his book dishonest and bigoted.[2] Murray wondered why he was being "punished" for producing perfectly valid social science research on a matter of public import.

One thing that has always fascinated me about Charles Murray is just how incapable he is of understanding why people do not like him. He seems to believe that if someone thinks him a racist, it must be because that person has not actually read Murray's work. They must be irrationally accepting caricatures of him from the press. They certainly cannot possibly have seriously engaged with his writings, for, in his mind, nobody who has done so could possibly come away with the idea that Murray is some kind of white supremacist.

Murray's self-perception as a persecuted truth-teller, who uses *real facts* that the *politically correct* simply don't want to hear, is reinforced by the fact that many people who hate him *haven't* read his work. Press coverage of Murray *has* distorted his positions, and it's frequently true that people label him a "white supremacist" or "eugenicist" without knowing what he actually says about race, genetics, and intelligence. Plenty of writings about Murray, such as the Southern Poverty Law Center's long file on him, are sloppy or biased, failing to engage seriously and fair-mindedly with his various claims.[3] This has allowed Murray, and those who appreciate his writing,[4] to claim that there are two *Bell Curves*, the book that people believe exists, and the book that actually exists.

But while this is partially correct, it's nevertheless extraordinary that Charles Murray can believe the negative reaction to him must be irrational and politically motivated. For while it is true that people unfairly attribute positions to Murray that he does not hold, the positions he actually *does* espouse in his work are just as extreme as even the most unsympathetic public portrait of him has depicted. People who see Charles Murray being violently hounded off college campuses might wonder what the fuss is about, and why left-wing protesters become so viscerally *angry* with Murray rather than dealing with his arguments. But while I am strongly opposed to the tactic of shutting down speakers on campus, it's important to realize that the *rage* at Charles Murray is entirely justified. For it can be very easily proven that Murray is a man with a strong racial bias against black people, insofar as he fails to respect them as equal human beings and believes them to be, on average, inferior to white people in matters of intelligence, creativity, and inherent human worth. Any serious inquiry into Charles Murray's actual body of work must conclude that, if Murray is not a racist, the word "racist" is empty of meaning. I do not necessarily believe Charles Murray *thinks* he is a racist. But I do believe that a fair review of the evidence must necessarily lead to the conclusion that he *is* one. Efforts to keep him from speaking on college campuses are, while in my opinion wrong both in principle and strategically, are entirely understandable. For Murray's intellectual project *does* involve passing off bigotry as neutral scholarship, and people who worry about "legitimizing" prejudice by giving it a platform should very much be worried about giving Charles Murray a platform.

It is crucial to distinguish between the things Charles Murray actually does argue, and the things he is said to have argued. Murray often gets the better of his opponents because they stretch the case against him beyond its limits, allowing him to correctly point out that they are misrepresenting him. Let us be clear, then: Charles Murray does *not* conclude that the black-white gap in IQ test scores must entirely be the product of genetic inferiority, nor that black social outcomes are entirely genetic in origin. *The Bell Curve* is not, strictly speaking, "about" race and IQ. And Murray does not argue in favor of a program of eugenics (though the error is easy to make, as Murray speaks positively of the work of previous eugenists and seeming to lament that the Nazi "perversion of eugenics... effectively wiped the idea from public discourse in the West"). Nor should Murray necessarily be called, as so many label him, a "pseudoscientist." His writings are above-average in their statistical scrupulousness, and he uses no less logical rigor than many highly qualified social scientists do. The problem is far less in his use of the scientific method than in his normative values and conceptions of the good, which affect the uses to which he puts his science.

However, having made clear what Murray does *not* say, let us examine what he does. The following claims are defended in Murray's writings:

1. Black people tend to be dumber than white people, which is probably partly why white people tend to have more money than black people. This is likely to be partly because of genetics, a question that would be valid and useful to investigate.

2. Black cultural achievements are almost negligible. Western peoples have a superior tendency toward creating "objectively" more "excellent" art and music. Differences in cultural excellence across groups might also have biological roots.

3. We should return to the conception of equality held by the Founding Fathers, who thought black people were subhumans. A

situation in which white people are politically and economically dominant over black people is natural and acceptable.

Taken together, these three claims show Murray to be bigoted, ignorant, and ignorant of his own bigotry. They more than justify the conclusion that he is a racist. And they make it extraordinary for anyone to be surprised that Murray's acceptance as a legitimate mainstream scholar causes a reaction of raw fury and disgust. Charles Murray would likely dispute that the above three points are made in his work. But the textual evidence is conclusive.

First: "Black people tend to be dumber than white people." *The Bell Curve,* which Murray co-authored in 1994 with Richard Herrnstein, is a book about the role of "intelligence" in society.[5] Murray and Herrnstein wished to prove that intelligence, as measured by IQ scores, played a crucial role in determining a variety of social outcomes, and that as a result a new kind of "cognitive elite" was arising. Murray and Herrnstein did not *endorse* the preeminence of the cognitive elite, and in fact worried over the effects of the change.

A core premise of the book is that intelligence is a meaningful and important concept, and that it is captured by IQ scores. As they write, "IQ scores match whatever it is that people mean when they use the word *intelligent* or *smart* in ordinary language." And the opposite of being "smart" is, they seem to believe, being "dumb":

♦ *"What are this person's chances of being in poverty if he is very smart? Very dumb?"*

♦ *"Statistically, smart men tend to be more farsighted than dumb men."*

♦ *"...fertility patterns among the smart and the dumb, and their possible long-term effects on the intellectual capital of a nation's population."*

The Bell Curve ignited a multi-decade controversy not due to its core thesis about class structure, but because of a multi-chapter detour into questions about ethnicity and intelligence. Murray and Herrnstein report the (undisputed) empirical finding that black scores on IQ tests are—as a statistical average—lower than white scores on IQ tests. They then speculate on some possible reasons for this difference (both genetic and environmental), while being careful to avoid solid conclusions.

Here, Murray's opponents occasionally trip up, by arguing against the reality of the difference in test scores rather than against Murray's formulation of the concept of intelligence. The dubious aspect of *The Bell Curve*'s intelligence framework is not that it argues there are ethnic differences in IQ scores, which plenty of sociologists acknowledge. It is that Murray and Herrnstein use IQ, an arbitrary test of a particular set of abilities (arbitrary in the sense that there is no reason why a person's IQ should matter any more than their eye color, not in the sense that it is uncorrelated with economic outcomes) as a measure of whether someone is smart or dumb in the ordinary language sense. It isn't, though: the number of high-IQ idiots in our society is staggering, and very academically accomplished people frequently turn out to be dunces. Now, Murray and Herrnstein say that "intelligence" is "just a noun, not an accolade," generally using the phrase "cognitive ability" in the book as a synonym for "intelligent" or "smart." But because they say explicitly (1) that "IQ," "intelligent," and "smart" mean the same thing, (2) that "smart" can be contrasted with "dumb," and (3) the ethnic difference in IQ scores means an ethnic difference in intelligence/smartness, it is hard to see how the book can be seen as arguing anything other than that black people tend to be dumber than white people, and Murray and Herrnstein should not have been surprised that their "black people are dumb" book landed them in hot water. ("We didn't say 'dumb'! We just said *dumber*! And only *on average*! And through most of the book we said 'lacking cognitive ability' rather than 'dumb'!")

Next, Murray and Herrnstein argued that black people's dumbness was probably partly responsible for their differing economic and social outcomes. The central argument of *The Bell Curve* is that, given the structure of American society, IQ is a core determinant of where one will end up in life. When it comes to ethnicity, Murray and Herrnstein use the fact that blacks, Latinos, and whites who have the same IQ scores will have roughly similar economic outcomes to argue that it is IQ differences, rather than racial oppression, that cause differences in those outcomes:

> *If one of America's goals is to rid itself of racism and institutional discrimination, then we should welcome the finding that a Latino and white of similar cognitive ability have the same chances of getting a bachelor's degree and working in a white-collar job. A black with the same cognitive ability has an even higher chance than either the Latino or white of having those good things happen. A Latino, black, and white of similar cognitive ability earn annual wages within a few hundred dollars of one another. Similarly, the evidence presented here should give everyone who writes and talks about ethnic inequalities reason to avoid flamboyant rhetoric about ethnic oppression. Racial and ethnic differences in this country are seen in a new light when cognitive ability is added to the picture.*

Murray and Herrnstein firmly believe that "flamboyant rhetoric about ethnic oppression" ignores the fact that America is largely "stratified according to cognitive ability" rather than race, i.e. there are rich black people and poor white people, but the rich black people tend to be smart and the poor white people tend to be dumb, and as America continues to stratify its economy by intelligence, the thing rich people will tend to have in common is not that they're white but that they're smart, though that will still mean they are disproportionately white because white people are disproportionately smart. It should therefore be uncontroversial to point out that Murray and Herrnstein are arguing: (1) that black people tend to be dumber, (2) that they are not disproportionately poor because they are oppressed, they are disproportionately poor because they are disproportionately dumb. They stress that they are not saying this is a *good thing* (they're worried about it!), they are just saying that this is how it is.

We should be clear on why the Murray-Herrnstein argument was both morally offensive and poor social science. If they had stuck to what is ostensibly the core claim of the book, that IQ (whatever it is) is strongly correlated with one's economic status, there would have been nothing objectionable about their work. In fact, it would even have been (as Murray himself has pointed out) totally consistent with a left-wing worldview. "IQ predicts economic outcomes" just means "some particular set of mental abilities happen to be well-adapted for doing the things that make you successful in contemporary U.S. capitalist society." Testing for IQ is no different from testing whether someone can play the guitar or do 1000 jumping jacks or lick their elbow. And "the people who can do those certain valued things are forming a narrow elite at the expense of the underclass" is a conclusion left-wing people would be happy to entertain. After all, it's no different than saying "people who have the good fortune to be skilled at finance are making a lot of money and thereby exacerbating inequality." Noam Chomsky goes further and suggests that if we actually managed to determine the traits that predicted success under capitalism, more relevant than "intelligence" would probably be "some combination of greed, cynicism, obsequiousness and subordination, lack of curiosity and independence of mind, self-serving disregard for others, and who knows what else."[6]

For a person of left-wing values, what any correlation between IQ and success means is that the structure of rewards in society should be readjusted so that they do *not* disproportionately favor people who have some particular random arbitrary characteristic (like being good with numbers), just the same as a society in which the elite is comprised solely of people who are good painters would also be unfair. The controversial aspect of *The Bell Curve*, then, is not its core thesis about IQ and class. Rather, it is that Murray and Herrnstein are contemptuous of the idea that racial oppression plays a significant role in American society, and attempt to attribute black-white economic differences to factors *intrinsic to black people.*

The most notorious way in which they do this is in their speculation about the role of genetics in the ethnic IQ gap. In their conclusion on the subject, Murray and Herrnstein were explicit that they were agnostic on the extent of the genetic component:

> *If the reader is now convinced that either the genetic or environmental explanation has won out to the exclusion of the other, we have not done a sufficiently good job of presenting one side or the other. It seems highly likely to us that both genes and the environment have something to do with racial differences.*

Note, however, that the agnosticism is on the *amount* of genetic contribution to ethnic IQ testing differences; the fact that there *is* a genetic contribution they find "highly likely." Murray and Herrnstein attempt to bolster the case for a genetic component by offering evidence that the gap persists even controlling for socioeconomic status, and that people in Africa also have lower IQs than white Americans.

But why did this claim actually make people so angry? It is, after all, an empirical hypothesis rather than statement about moral value. Murray and Herrnstein professed not to be able to understand what difference it would possibly make whether the gap was genetic or the result of environmental factors. As they wrote:

> *Imagine that tomorrow it is discovered that the B/W difference in measured intelligence is entirely genetic in origin. The worst case has come to pass. What difference would this news make in the way that you approach the question of ethnic differences in intelligence? Not someone else but you. What has changed for the worse in knowing that the difference is genetic?... We cannot think of a legitimate argument why any encounter between individual ethnicities and blacks need be affected by the knowledge that an aggregate ethnic difference in measured intelligence is genetic instead of environmental.*

In this statement, one can see why many people felt *The Bell Curve* to be a "dishonest" book. Murray and Herrnstein suggested that nobody should be *upset* by the question of genes, race, and IQ, because unless we assign some normative worth to IQ, the answer should make no moral difference. (Leave aside the fact that Murray and Herrnstein *did* slip into normative language about IQ.) Why would a genetic answer make a difference, *unless you were a racist?* If you believe all people are equal, surely you believe that this would hold regardless of what their genes turned out to be.

But this statement buries the fact that there *are* very important moral implications to the genetic question: the more the difference can be proven to be genetic in origin, the less responsible white people are for the disproportionate poverty affecting black communities. The massive black-white wealth gap, and the million black people in prison, aren't the lingering effects of multiple hundred years of brutal oppression: they're the inevitable and intractable results of something to do with black people themselves.

This is the aspect of the book that makes *me* the angriest, and that I sense is responsible for a lot of people being unwilling to take Murray seriously: he pretends not to even realize that his thesis allows white America to feel exonerated for the condition of black America. He says that it would make *no difference* whether the IQ disparities (and therefore economic differences) were genetically caused. But it would make a *massive* difference: it would relieve white people who think intelligence means merit from having to feel guilty about reaping the benefits of living in a society built on racial discrimination. His thesis is not just an academic question about nature and nurture: it would also provide grist for the argument that *slavery didn't matter very much* in the creation of present social outcomes; the reason black families have, on average, 1/10 of the wealth of white families, has little to do with the fact that they were prevented from accruing assets for over half the history of the United States, during which time they were kept in chains, beaten, raped, and murdered. Rather, it's because of *them* and the fact that they just inherently lack the "cognitive ability" to catch up. And that lack of cognitive ability has little to do with the fact that for hundreds of years, if a black child was caught with a book, white people would whip them. (As they say, since "the African black population has not been subjected to the historical legacy of American black slavery," and Africans are even less intelligent, "the hypothesis about the special circumstances of American blacks depressing their test scores is not substantiated by the African data.") The question may be empirical, but there *are* potential social ramifications here, and anyone discussing the issue could at least try to demonstrate a marginal awareness of them.

It's Murray's flippant treatment of this history that makes some scholars so angry at his work. He doesn't even take the widespread existence of racism seriously *as a hypothesis*. After all, a black-white IQ score difference, combined with evidence that IQ is in some degree heritable, is actually consistent with the idea that black people are genetically *superior* to white people in intelligence, and that their scores are depressed by early exposure to a society that devalues them from the earliest years of their lives (recall Malcolm X's teacher responding to his aspiration toward being a lawyer by telling him carpentry was more realistic). To put it differently: Black people could inherit average IQs of 110, while white people inherit average IQs of 100, but the disadvantages of living in a racist society from birth could mean that by a young age, black people end up with average IQs of 95 and white people stay at 100. As Ned Block explains, there is a hidden premise that a role for genetics must necessarily disadvantage blacks, but that's not necessarily the case.[7]

Murray evidently considers the hypothesis of black genetic superiority too laughable to be worth disproving, even though the only reason for ignoring it is if one has already assumed the conclusion one is seeking to demonstrate; namely that racism doesn't matter very much. The only reason why you wouldn't even entertain the hypothesis of black genetic superiority is if you felt it *couldn't* exist, something you would only think *before* examining the evidence if you were... a racist. (And no, Murray's scanty and unsystematic data on Africa doesn't help. People in the Congo, for example, probably had a difficult time holding their pencils to take IQ tests after the Belgians cut off all their hands. If you haven't considered the history of colonialism, war, and starvation in Africa, you haven't even *begun* to control for the variables necessary for any conclusion about genetics.)

Thus I suspect people are offended and appalled by *The Bell Curve* just as much for what is not in it as what is in it. Murray treats seriously the hypotheses that attribute black poverty to things about black people (both cultural and genetic), but casually dismisses hypotheses that suggest a strong role for the massive, centuries-long crime that was perpetrated upon black people (a crime that is hardly mentioned or examined). As Orlando Patterson put it, for 248 of the 377 years of U.S. history before *The Bell Curve*'s publication, black people were "an enslaved group, physically, economically, socially, legally, sexually, morally, and psychologically, subjected not only to the exploitative whim of individual white owners but at the violent mercy of all whites, under the encouragement and protection of the predatory dominant whites."[8] For Murray to not take that seriously as even a *hypothesis* in explaining contemporary racial disparities suggests both a lack of empathy and a lack of social scientific neutrality.

In fact, however, too much has been made of *The Bell Curve*'s discussion of race and IQ as evidence for why Charles Murray is a racist. As Murray has pointed out, the book is now two decades old (although he stands by it completely), and most of its contents were *not* about how black poverty was partly the fault of black stupidity. A far more illuminating piece of evidence about the Murray racial worldview is found in his little-read 2003 book *Human Accomplishment*, the text that substantiates point 2 on the above List Of Racist Charles Murray Beliefs: *Black cultural achievements are almost negligible.*

Human Accomplishment is one of the most absurd works of "social science" ever produced.[9] If you want evidence proving Murray a "pseudoscientist," it is *Human Accomplishment* rather than *The Bell Curve* that you should turn to. In it, he attempts to prove using statistics which cultures are *objectively* the most "excellent" and "accomplished," demonstrating mathematically the inherent superiority of Western thought throughout the arts and sciences.

Human Accomplishment is actually *funny* in how poorly reasoned it is. It is full of charts purporting to show that Europe has produced the most "significant" people in literature, philosophy, art, music, and the sciences, and then posits some theories as to what makes cultures able to produce better versus worse things. The problem that immediately arises, of course, is that there is no actual objective way of determining a person's "significance." In order to provide such an "objective" measure, Murray uses (I am not kidding you) the frequency of people's appearances in encyclopedias and biographical dictionaries. In this way, he says, he has shown their "eminence," therefore objectively shown their accomplishments in their respective fields. And by then showing which cultures they came from, he can rank each culture by its cultural and scientific worth.

You can see instantly where this falls to pieces: however possible it might be to rank scientists by citation count, how on earth does this work for music and art? First, by using encyclopedias, aren't you stacking the deck against cultures without written traditions? By counting *individuals*, aren't you favoring individualistic cultural achievements rather than communal ones? But even worse, how can you even produce an "objective" measure of achievement in music and art to begin with? Every aspect of a definition must be circular: the significant people are significant because they have significance. The classical values of Western thought are correct because they are the classical values of Western thought.

When Murray does actually attempt to defend his underlying values for artistic excellence, the results are a mess. He simply declares that objectivity exists, and that the alternative is refusing all judgment, and since this is impossible, there must be such a thing as objectively better art. He speaks derisively of "multiculturalism," of course. Most of his defenses of objectivity are mere assertion; there's no actual *argument* for why we should accept any of it. They amount to yet more circularity: *My values are objectively correct because there are objective things and my values are the things that are objective.* If you respond "Okay, prove it," Murray has nothing. Instead, he simply says that if "experts" believe it, it is objectively correct:

> I hold to a statistical understanding of objective: given a large
> number of expert opinions about a dozen specific qualities of a

work of art, we will not see a random set of responses, but ones that cluster around a central tendency.... The relationship of expertise to judgment forms a basis for treating excellence in the arts as a measurable trait.

Art and music pose a particular problem for this perspective, though, since Murray hates everything produced since 1950, even though experts in art and music disagree with him. If he permitted anything from the last half-century to intrude into his canon of human cultural accomplishments, he might end up having to include something *postmodern* (or worse, art made by blacks and women). Murray resolves this question by declaring that art and music since 1950 *simply do not count*; his list of achievements and methodology explicitly exclude anything after this date. That's because these things are postmodern, and postmodernism cannot produce excellence no matter what the experts say, even though "what the experts say" is the only coherent measure of excellence that Murray has actually offered. But the arbitrary time cutoff doesn't matter anyway, because:

> *In the arts, it is not clear that cutting off the inventories at 1950 involves the loss of much material at all. No doubt some art, music, and literature created from 1950 to the present will survive, but it is hard to imagine that the last half-century will be seen as producing an abundance of timeless work.*

Very well, then, the last half century objectively sucked. (Sorry, *Sgt. Pepper,* you're not a "human accomplishment.") Let's just concede that. What do Murray's statistical analyses of artistic accomplishment actually produce? Well, let's take music. Only Western music is considered, because non-Western music does not constitute Accomplishment. And what do you know, shockingly enough, out of hundreds of significant figures in Western music, there are almost no black people on the list. (Duke Ellington makes it.) Now, remember, this is a list of the *objectively highest human accomplishments* in music, and it doesn't cut off until 1950. Let's just remember, then, what happened in music in the time leading up to 1950.

Before 1950, black people had invented gospel, blues, jazz, R&B, samba, meringue, ragtime, zydeco, mento, calypso, and bomba. During the early 20th century, *in the United States alone*, the following composers and players were active: Ma Rainey, W.C. Handy, Scott Joplin, Louis Armstrong, Jelly Roll Morton, James P. Johnson, Fats Waller, Count Basie, Cab Calloway, Art Tatum, Charlie Parker, Charles Mingus, Lil Hardin Armstrong, Bessie Smith, Billie Holliday, Sister Rosetta Tharpe, Mahalia Jackson, J. Rosamond Johnson, Ella Fitzgerald, John Lee Hooker, Coleman Hawkins, Leadbelly, Earl Hines, Dizzy Gillespie, Miles Davis, Fats Navarro, Roy Brown, Wynonie Harris, Blind Lemon Jefferson, Blind Willie Johnson, Robert Johnson, Son House, Dinah Washington, Thelonious Monk, Muddy Waters, Art Blakey, Sarah Vaughan, Memphis Slim, Skip James, Louis Jordan, Ruth Brown, Big Jay McNeely, Paul Gayten, and Professor Longhair. (This list is partial.) When we talk about black American music of the early 20th century, we are talking about one of the most astonishing periods of cultural accomplishment in the history of civilization. We are talking about an unparalleled record of invention, the creation of some of the most transcendently moving and original artistic material that has yet emerged from the human mind. The significance of this achievement cannot be overstated. What's more, it occurred without state sponsorship or the patronage of elites. In fact, it arose organically under conditions of brutal Jim Crow segregation and discrimination, in which black people had access to almost *no* mainstream institutions or material resources.

Yet in Charles Murray's "objective" measure of the worth of Western musical creations, none of this appears. Instead, in addition to the usual heavyweights like Bach and Wagner, we get a slew of minor, forgotten English composers like John Jenkins, Nicholas Lanier, and Matthew Locke. This is (and I am not kidding) because Murray believes that their work better fits the Aristotelian standard for transcendent human feeling, with a "rootedness in human experience, seriousness of purpose, and intellectual depth." (I would, by the way, trade the entire musical output of all three of the aforementioned British composers for a single measure of a single song from Louis Armstrong's Hot Fives and Sevens sessions. It is my position that any book on *Human Accomplishment* that does not include Louis Armstrong is actually a book on human mediocrity. But I do not claim to be objective.)

Do I have to explain why Murray's framework is racist? Because Charles Murray thinks classical English composers were rooted in human experience and had intellectual depth (which we know, because they showed up more in the encyclopedias he picked), while black American composers (for that is what they are) were not. He's committed to that proposition by his framework, which claims to prove that the music on his list is objectively more accomplished. He's not just *more interested* in old English music, he literally thinks black music is worse, and that it's inarguably worse. He thinks this while seemingly never having actually engaged with or attempted to appreciate black music. Because he thinks human accomplishment is a measure of the fulfillment of the potential of the human mind, he thinks black culture is less sophisticated, less deep, and less intelligent than white culture. And he thinks he has proved it using science.

Of course, Murray being Murray, biology is involved as well. He determines—again, using *math*—that "no woman has been a significant original thinker in any of the world's great philosophical traditions." (This might, of course, be because much philosophical writing throughout the history of the world has been masturbatory nonsense, which women are less inclined or encouraged to produce, a hypothesis Murray does not consider.) And he is persuaded that "disparities in accomplishment between the sexes are significantly grounded in biological differences." Of course, accomplishment is defined as *the things that men have historically done* (philosophy, science) because *the things that women have historically done* (everything necessary to make those other activities possible) are not considered objective manifestations of excellence.

Human Accomplishment is a far more offensive book than *The Bell Curve*, and also far more persuasive as evidence that Charles Murray has no interest in doing serious social science (which is not supposed to consist of graphs showing why the art you like is clearly the best art). It's also a good book for countering Murray's assertion that his critics fixate on the contents of a single chapter of *The Bell Curve*. *Human Accomplishment* shows that Murray has a long obsession with racial difference, and with using statistics to prove the lesser intellectual gifts of black people.

BUT WHAT OF THE THIRD Racist Charles Murray Belief: *We should restore the conception of equality held by the Founding Fathers, who thought black people were subhumans.* Here, we return to *The Bell Curve*. Murray is right; people *do* get stuck on the "Ethnic Differences in Cognitive Ability" chapter and neglect the rest of the book. It's a shame, because the infamous chapter isn't actually the worst chapter. The worst chapter is actually the last: "Chapter 22: A Place For Everyone," which makes a normative argument about how people are to be kept in their proper places.

In "A Place For Everyone," Murray and Herrnstein finally give their actual recommendation for the philosophical foundation on which society should be organized. Given the empirical realities they have just claimed to demonstrate, that people differ in their intellectual capacities and that this affects social outcomes, how should we think about equality? Murray and Herrnstein recognize that their findings *could* be used in defense of social democracy, to say that rewards should *not* accrue to people on the basis of their intellect. But this is not the route they take. Instead, they say, they will defend "an older intellectual tradition" and a wiser one. They tell us how Confucius, along with the Greeks and Romans, believed everyone had a certain designated *place* in society. "Society was to be ruled by the wise and virtuous few," with "the most menial chores left to the slaves." After all, "neither the Greek democrats nor the Roman republicans believed that 'all men are created equal.' Nor did the great Hindu thinkers of the Asian subcontinent, where one's work defined one's caste." Murray and Herrnstein then quote John Locke, who believed that "there is [such] a difference of degrees in men's understandings, apprehensions, and reasonings... that there is a greater distance between some men and others in this respect, than between some men and some beasts." (For example, Locke wrote, "Amongst children, idiots, savages, and the grossly illiterate, what general maxims are to be found? What universal principles of knowledge? Their notions are few and narrow." Herrnstein and Murray inexplicably do not cite this passage.)

Murray and Herrnstein show that this political philosophy, which saw human beings as fundamentally *unequal* and deserving of particular individual stations like Hindu castes, was also held by the Founding Fathers. They cite Thomas Jefferson's belief that there should be a "natural aristocracy" of "virtue and talent." As they say, Jefferson "thought that the best government was one that most efficiently brought the natural aristocracy to high positions," and he wrote that the "best geniuses" should be "raked from the rubbish annually." The Founders, Herrnstein and Murray write, "were fully aware of how unequal people are [and] they did not try to explain away natural inequalities." Instead, they simply instituted a formal system of *political* equality, in which there could be gross social and economic inequalities but government would be open to all who were wise.

This is the conception that Murray and Herrnstein endorse. They say that it was the one held by Aristotle, who thought that some equality was good, but that "the question we must keep in mind is, equality or inequality in what sort of thing." (For Aristotle, there couldn't be complete equality, because some men are "as different [from other men] as the soul from the body or man from beast—and they... are slaves by nature... For he is a slave by nature who is capable of belonging to another—which is also why he belongs to another." Note the "man and beast" distinction between those fit for equality and "natural slaves," directly echoed in the Locke quote that Murray and Herrnstein cite approvingly.) They sum up their position on human difference:

> *In reminding you of these views of the men who founded America, we are not appealing to their historical eminence, but to their wisdom. We think they were right.... The egalitarian ideal of contemporary political theory underestimates the importance of the differences that separate human beings. It fails to come to grips with human variation.... It has become objectionable to say that some people are superior to other people in any way that is relevant to life in society.... Discrimination, once a useful word with a praise-*

worthy meaning, is now almost always used in a pejorative sense.
Racism, sexism, ageism, elitism—all are in common parlance, and
their meanings continue to spread, blotting up more and more
semantic territory.

It is essential, according to Murray and Herrnstein, for us to stop attempting to impose equality on a world of natural inequality. They recommend ending affirmative action; after all, it attempts to impose equality instead of letting inequality take its course. They reject "the idea of compelling everyone to help produce equal outcomes by race," and are "comfortable with the idea that some things are better than others—not just according to our subjective point of view but according to enduring standards of merit and inferiority." They believe instead of being granted social equality, everyone should find their proper *place*.

I wonder if Charles Murray has ever considered what it would be like for a black person to read Murray's praise of the "Jeffersonian" conception of equality. It's truly puzzling to me that he could be surprised that people react to him with rage, given that his book endorses (without qualification or reservation) the conception of human difference espoused by (1) Aristotle, whose idea was that some people were naturally fit for slavery, (2) the thinkers behind the Hindu caste system, (3) John Locke, who believed that "savages" lacked sophisticated mental capacities, and (4) Thomas Jefferson, whose "natural aristocracy" existed because he thought that black people were "inferior to the whites in the endowment both of body and mind," had a "strong and disagreeable odour" and had never once "uttered a thought above the level of plain narrative."

When Murray fondly praises Jefferson's idea of human social difference, he neglects to mention what Jefferson believed the human social differences actually *were*: he believed that black people smelled bad and were incapable of reason. How, in a book that is *literally* about people's greater and lesser reasoning capacities, and that *literally* claims black people are less endowed with such capacities, can you harken back to Jefferson, leaving his racial views unmentioned, and then act shocked when people think you're a racist? How can you not *be* a racist? How is there any way?

Nor can one simply historicize Jefferson, and suggest that his prejudices were merely ill-considered products of his time and might have been fixed if he had been exposed to our modern conceptions about race. Jefferson was actually *told* his views were heinous, *by a black person*. Benjamin Banneker was an ex-slave who had taught himself to read and write, and who had become a land surveyor and astronomer. He was highly skilled, building clocks and predicting eclipses. Banneker compiled a notable almanac, which he sent to Jefferson along with a letter. The letter, which made a stirring case for the equality of races and begged Jefferson to cease owning slaves, is one of the most remarkable documents in all of American history. (If the country really cared about teaching its history, Banneker's note would be required reading for every schoolchild.) He wrote:

> *We are a race of Beings who have long laboured under the abuse and censure of the world, that we have long been looked upon with an eye of contempt, and that we have long been considered rather as brutish than human, and Scarcely capable of mental endowments... I apprehend you will readily embrace every opportunity to eradicate that train of absurd and false ideas and opinions which so generally prevails with respect to us, and that your Sentiments are concurrent with mine, which are that one universal Father hath given being to us all, and that he hath not only made us all of one flesh, but that he hath also without partiality afforded us all the Same Sensations, and endued us all with the same faculties, and that however variable we may be in Society or religion, however diversifyed in Situation or colour, we are all of the Same Family, and Stand in the Same relation to him...*[10]

Banneker called Jefferson out on his hypocrisy, for writing so eloquently of liberty while keeping Banneker's fellow people in chains:

> *This Sir, was a time in which you clearly saw into the injustice of a State of Slavery, and in which you had just apprehensions of*

the horrors of its condition, it was now Sir, that your abhorrence thereof was so excited, that you publickly held forth this true and invaluable doctrine, which is worthy to be recorded and remember'd in all Succeeding ages. "We hold these truths to be Self evident, that all men are created equal, and that they are endowed by their creator with certain unalienable rights, that among these are life, liberty, and the pursuit of happyness."... Sir how pitiable is it to reflect, that altho you were so fully convinced of the benevolence of the Father of mankind, and of his equal and impartial distribution of those rights and privileges which he had conferred upon them, that you should at the Same time counteract his mercies, in detaining by fraud and violence so numerous a part of my brethren under groaning captivity and cruel oppression, that you should at the Same time be found guilty of that most criminal act, which you professedly detested in others, with respect to yourselves.

Jefferson wrote Banneker a brief reply, thanking him for the almanac and wishing the best for his race. (Later, in a letter to a friend, Jefferson disparaged the almanac's quality.) He continued to own slaves until his death, even though he was ridiculed by contemporary abolitionists. ("If there be an object truly ridiculous in nature, it is an American patriot, signing resolutions of independency with the one hand, and with the other brandishing a whip over his affrighted slaves."[11]) Nor was Jefferson a benevolent slavemaster.[12] He "punished slaves by selling them away from their families and friends, a retaliation that was incomprehensibly cruel even at the time" and "advocated harsh, almost barbaric, punishments for slaves and free blacks." And he didn't even free his slaves upon his death, as many of his contemporaries did, instead sending 200 of them to the auction block. This is not to mention the fact that he began having sex with (i.e. raping) Sally Hemings when she was 14 years old, and did not even free her in his will. He was, in nearly every respect, a thoroughgoing bastard.

ALL OF THIS IS CRUCIAL CONTEXT for understanding why people call Charles Murray a racist. To many black people, "Jeffersonian equality" cannot be separated from Jefferson, a man who continued to beat and rape black slaves despite the most eloquent pleas from black abolitionists. Murray is a racist in part because he doesn't think American history from the black perspective even *counts*. It doesn't even need mentioning. One can simply dismiss those who are horrified by your "Aristotelian/Hindu caste system/Jeffersonian" notion of "inherent human inequality." They must be irrational. They must simply be spewing *politically correct dogmas*. They must be some of those "beasts" unfit for the "natural aristocracy" of the talented, virtuous, and wise.

I do not see, then, how if the word "racism" has any content, Charles Murray is anything other than a racist. He has argued: (1) that black people are dumber than white people, (2) that black culture is objectively less accomplished and worthwhile, and (3) that the Founding Fathers' conception of social equality, an inherently racist vision in its every aspect, is worth reviving. Of course, I do not know whether Charles Murray *knows* he is a racist, just as I do not know what was in his mind when he burned a cross on a hill. But, when we put aside all of the distortions and exaggerations about his work, and examine its text closely, I do not see how we can escape the conclusion that Charles Murray thinks black people are inferior to white people, and that having them in socially, economically, and politically subordinate positions is acceptable. (And let me be clear: this is about black and white. Murray often praises Asians in order to prove that he is not a white supremacist. But with racism, the question is not: "Do you think you are the best race of all the races?" It is: "Do you hold bigoted and unfair perceptions of a particular race, and endorse their social subjugation?" There is a unique white bias against *blacks* in particular, as a result of the color line that has run through the entirety of American history.)

Some people may say that I have taken Charles Murray too seriously here. His work, so the argument goes, is self-evidently worthless and racist, so why bother dealing with his claims rigorously or carefully? Doesn't a serious examination of Murray's work "legitimize" him? By parsing his texts in detail, and making sure to be fair to them, I am spending more time than this man is worth. But while I understand this perspective,

I do not share it. Charles Murray, like it or not, has already been legitimized by his very public presence. He is supported by a major think tank, his books are put out by mainstream publishers. I believe his body of work is socially worthless and filled with a vile anti-black bigotry, and that anyone who publishes his books or invites him to speak is complicit in spreading prejudice. But avoiding confronting his claims directly only helps bolster his case to the public that he is being persecuted by people who cannot deal with his arguments. Murray says that *The Bell Curve* is "relentlessly modest" and "mainstream science cautiously interpreted."[13] Unless one proves otherwise, people might be tempted to believe him.

Throughout American history, each generation has had its Charles Murray types. During the era of the founding, there were those like Jefferson who believed that since black people's "griefs were transient," one could break up their families and destroy their bodies. There were those who measured "negroid" skulls to prove black inferiority, those who believed, like Murray, that in a system of "natural" inequality everyone should find their place, and that some people's places were in cotton fields or minstrel shows. And when, after centuries of being shackled, black intellect was finally set free to produce the most extraordinarily diverse body of musical composition in the history of sound, there were those who, terrified at the subversion of their dominance, scoffed at the supposed immorality and simplicity of "jungle music." That particular ugly strain in American thought, the trivialization and dismissal of black genius, lingers in books like Murray's *Human Accomplishment* and among those who use "multiculturalism" and "postmodernism" as derisive synonyms for black art.

Fortunately, the story of America is also the story of a defiant black resistance to these relentless attempts at diminution. It is not just the story of Thomas Jefferson, but the story of Benjamin Banneker, the scientist and ex-slave, whose ringing words made sure that Jefferson's racism did not go unrefuted, and made sure that nobody could say Jefferson "didn't know" the extent of his own monstrous crimes. Today, as Charles Murray attempts to revive Jeffersonianism, he should be met with an army of Benjamin Bannekers, ready to expose, with superior eloquence and moral force, the vicious lie of racial hierarchy and the flimsy idiocies of the "natural aristocrats."

The Political Sociopath: Ted Cruz in His Own Words

FOR SOMEONE WHO IS so thoroughly disliked by anyone who ever meets him, Ted Cruz has done inexplicably well at the political popularity contest. Political campaigning is supposed to be the art of winning people over, yet in his ascent to the U.S. Senate Cruz somehow managed to gain public approval despite a total lack of charismatic warmth. Bill Clinton always had to be the most well-liked guy in the room; Ted Cruz will almost certainly be the least-liked guy in any room he ever enters.

It's almost impossible to overstate the Texas senator's off-putting qualities. Cruz's senate colleagues unanimously despise him, and Sen. Lindsey Graham once made a "kidding-but-not-kidding" remark that if you killed Ted Cruz on the Senate floor, and the trial was held in the Senate, not a single Senator would vote to convict you.[1] Cruz's college roommate from Princeton has been asked to explain why he didn't take the opportunity to smother Cruz in his sleep, and a neurologist has attempted to posit a biological theory for why Cruz's face is so unsettling.[2] Seemingly, the only real debate around Ted Cruz's personal qualities is whether he's better described as a "creep" or an "asshole." Those who went to college with him knew him as a creep (it was the word most frequently offered when *The Daily Beast* interviewed his old classmates), citing his habit of lurking in the women's hallway in his paisley bathrobe.[3] On the other hand, those who worked with him on the Bush campaign in 2000 seemed unanimous in thinking him an asshole. Pro-files of Cruz are filled with first-person accounts confirming his unpleas-antness. Consider a few:

♦ *"A classmate confided in Ted Cruz that her mother had gotten an abortion. Ted called her mother a whore."*

♦ *"We hadn't left Manhattan before he asked my IQ...When I told him I didn't know, he asked, 'Well, what's your SAT score? That's closely coordinated with you IQ.' It went from, 'Nice guy,' to 'uh-oh.'"*

♦ *"Ted's style was sneering, smirking, condescending, jabbing his finger in your face—a naked desire to humiliate an oppo-nent. No kindness, no empathy, no attempt to reach common ground."*

None of this is especially noteworthy in itself; the Ivy League and the Senate are swarming with the condescending and cretinous, though it must take a special kind of arrogance to make one's self stand out as being uniquely insufferable among the Princeton undergraduate class. The real question is how someone this toxic could end up winning friends and influencing people. How could a man so downright *eely* (as Matt Taibbi memorably called him)[4] get people to spend time around him, hand him money, and fill out ballots with his name on them? How could he get volunteers going door to door in support of him, people who have lives and families and surely some other things they could do than advance the career of a man so personally repellent?

This is a mystery that goes beyond Ted Cruz. Plenty of politicians are terrible people; this is universally acknowledged. But the voting public actually selects these people to be in charge. Nobody in Texas was forced to vote for Ted Cruz. George W. Bush, who makes a policy of never speaking ill of another Republican, was moved by the existence of Cruz to break his affability pledge for the first time, saying "I just don't like the guy." Indeed, nobody does. Yet Cruz won a Republican senate pri-mary against Texas's Lieutenant Governor, then a general election. The question, then, is how people that nobody likes can become extremely successful. We might predict that such people would be "losers"; *because Ted Cruz is arrogant and nobody likes being around him, he has few friends and nobody wants to hire him to work with them.* But the opposite is often true: they not only win, but rise and rise indefinitely. How do they do this? By what process does raw ambition subvert the ordinary rules of social success? Why do losers win, why do assholes finish first?

Ted Cruz's autobiography is as useful a place as any to begin the search for clues, to figure out how he has managed to make people give him whatever he wants without making any effort to get them to like him.[5] To be sure, it's a propaganda book, written specifically to aid his campaign for the presidency, but it's clear that it wasn't ghostwritten, and it therefore contains a number of useful insights into how Ted Cruz thinks about and presents himself. The first striking thing is how open Ted Cruz is about his prioritization of personal ambition over any kind of deeply held moral conviction. Cruz doesn't speak very much about the formation of his conservative worldview. He does not portray himself as being concerned with the issues first and himself second. Instead, he sees aspirations toward humility as essentially dishonest:

> *Anyone considering running for office, as I was at the time, is supposed to act totally disinterested in the political process, to pose as the reluctant public servant only answering the call because the people need him or her so desperately. But that wasn't the truth. Not for me.*

For Cruz, then, ambition is a given; the only question is whether you're going to pretend you don't have it, or honestly admit that you do. Cruz gives himself points for telling the truth, but it's notable that his worldview doesn't allow for the existence of a genuine public servant, one who isn't "posing." Cruz cannot even conceive of the idea that someone would genuinely wish to serve others, would care about politics as something useful to society rather than the mere pursuit of personal success. This view of the world, in which everything is a game and the aim is to win, has been with Cruz since the beginning:

> *Midway through junior high school, I decided that I'd had enough of being the unpopular nerd. I remember sitting up one night asking why I wasn't one of the popular kids. I ended up staying up most of that night thinking about it. 'Okay, well, what is it that the popular kids do? I will consciously emulate that.'*

Of course, Cruz doesn't seem to have done a good job of emulating popularity, but it's again notable how cynically he thinks about it. Popularity is desirable, thus you should ape the popular, then you will have the desirable thing, and thus you will have won. There's not a moment's thought that friendship is something intrinsically enjoyable, that people might like each other for reasons that go beyond their pursuit of particular self-interested ends.

So even as a teenager, Cruz's only motivating force was political ambition. The 18-year-old Cruz spoke on camera of his desire for "world domination," and he listed his life goals as: go to Princeton, go to Harvard Law, start a successful law practice, enter politics, become the President. Not a word about actually making the world better, understandable since Cruz thinks anyone professing a desire to serve others is lying.

The lack of talk about values in the book is almost stunning. Cruz describes what he has done, and how he did it, but he almost never talks about why he did it. Most politicians use the opportunity of a campaign book to explain and justify their principles; Cruz seems to believe that such an exercise would be dishonest. Indeed, if you don't actually believe anything, it certainly would be.

So one of the most surprising aspects of Ted Cruz's book is that he doesn't actually come across as being particularly conservative, at least not in the sense of believing that being a conservative is about holding a particular set of moral convictions that one thinks are beneficial to society. In fact, as he describes the world, he can offer facts that make him sound almost like a left-winger. Consider the way he talks about his grandparents' indenture in Batista's Cuba:

The store gave the families credit, and the sugar mill paid their salaries through the general store, which then took the money to pay their debt and (in theory) give them any remaining money. But, of course, no money ever remained, and the arrangement led to perpetual servitude.

Or the hope offered by America to his destitute immigrant father:

It is difficult for many of us to fully comprehend what a beacon of hope this country offers the rest of the world. There is no other place on earth that would have welcomed so freely to its shores a man like Rafael Cruz. He was eighteen, penniless, and spoke no English... Barack Obama, noting his own rise from humble beginnings, has observed that 'in no other country on earth is my story even possible.' My family can relate to that sentiment. In no other country would Rafael Cruz's story even be possible.

The framing of these anecdotes is strange. In the first, Cruz describes a scenario in which ostensibly free market employment relationships created "perpetual servitude" for workers. In the second, Cruz speaks positively of America allowing poor, uneducated Hispanic immigrants to freely enter the country. Yet this is a man who supports untrammeled capitalism and massive new restrictions on immigration. Cruz's official immigration platform proposes to evaluate potential new entrants to the country so as to "prioritize the interests and well-being of Americans," with an immigrant more likely to be admitted based on their "language skills," "formal education," "resources to create jobs," "ties to the United States," and "lifetime earning potential." It's hard to see how Rafael Cruz, a broke teenager who spoke no English, would ever be admitted under such a regime, yet Cruz the younger is proud that America made his father's story possible.

Such paradoxes occur repeatedly. Cruz's background, as the child of an immigrant raised in a home with some family difficulties, has infected him with the kind of personal experiences that turn one left-wing. Yet he is committed to a rigid conservatism that prohibits him from allowing these facts to change his mind.

Consider an especially bizarre example of the tension between Ted Cruz's knowledge and his behavior. Here, Cruz describes the sexism his mother experienced as a female computer programmer in the 1950s:

> *One need not be a devotee of Mad Men to understand what faced working women in the 1950s. Coming out of college, my mom deliberately didn't learn how to type. She understood that men would stop her in the corridors of the Shell offices and ask her 'Sweetheart, would you type this for me?' With a clear conscience she could answer 'I'd love to help, but I don't know how to type!... I guess you're just going to have to use me as a computer programmer instead.'*

Later in the book, Cruz relates an anecdote from his time working alongside his wife, Heidi, on the Bush presidential campaign:

> *One day [Heidi] went into the office of Robert Zoellick, who was serving as Jim Baker's de facto chief of staff. Sitting at his desk with his glasses perched on the tip of his nose, Bob peered up, and Heidi said 'Bob, I just wanted to see, is there anything I can do to help?' He said, 'Yes. Grapefruit juice. I want grapefruit juice.' And with that he went back to work. Heidi came into the office where I was working hopping mad. 'Damn it,' she said. 'I've got a Harvard MBA. I've worked on Wall Street as an investment banker. And his request for me is grapefruit juice!?' After a moment, she asked me, 'What do I do?' I sympathized with her completely. Then I said, 'Sweetheart, here are the car keys. Go get him grapefruit juice, right now.'*

Cruz isn't an idiot; he knows from what happened to his mother that being called "sweetheart" and told to perform some mindless task is miserable and demeaning. And yet he can talk about "what faced working women" in one passage, and participate in the replication of that very same behavior later on.

Isn't this bizarre? Well, not really. It's actually not much of a paradox at all; it just requires you to accept the twin premises that Ted Cruz is (1) quite perceptive and (2) not very nice. That should be easy enough to admit, and is in fact confirmed throughout the text.

The thing about the autobiography, as others have noted, is that *as a book* it's really not bad. It's well-constructed and it isn't boring. Cruz is a good writer, insofar as writing consists of selecting appropriate words and combining them into pleasingly rhythmic sentences. But that only serves to reinforce the point: Cruz is an intelligent person whose pathological ambition and ego keep him from allowing that intelligence to do any good. He should know better, but because he was born incapable of feeling inclinations other than self-interest, he will never follow his observations through to their implications if doing so might unsettle his convictions and cause him to stray from his path.

All of the observations of classmates and colleagues confirm this. Cruz at Princeton is described as someone who arrived with a sense of purpose and never strayed from it; he wanted to win, and he would do anything it took in order to do so. A reporter who met him during the Bush campaign said Cruz "was all pure unbridled ambition," coming across as "a guy who would use whatever means necessary to get on top." All of that makes Cruz much more repellent than a sincere conservative.

If you want snapshots of Cruz the asshole, you'll find them in the book. Consider the following account of the birth of his child:

> *As she lay in the hospital bed, in labor, Heidi was typing furiously on her Blackberry, still tending to the needs of her clients. I admired her tenacious work ethic—it's one of the many qualities that made me fall in love with her—but this was too much. I gently pulled the Blackberry out of her hands. "It will be here later," I said. She had more important things to do. To be fair, when it came to leaving work at the hospital steps, I wasn't completely innocent. During much of the time were there, I was studying cases*

for an oral argument before the U.S. Supreme Court scheduled for two days later. I was appearing in support of a Louisiana law that allowed capital punishment for the very worst child rapists... So just hours after Caroline was born, I said a prayer of thanksgiving, kissed my beautiful wife and baby daughter, rushed to the airport, and flew to Washington to argue the case.

So he made his wife feel bad for checking her work messages after the birth of their child, then immediately ditched her because he felt his own work was more important. (In fact, throughout the book one is astonished at how somebody so successful and attractive as Mrs. Cruz could tolerate a lifetime of being entwined with such a man. The Universe seems to have attempted to send her a warning; her first date with Ted was at a restaurant called "The Bitter End.")

But if Cruz is an "asshole," made of pure self-interest and guile, we must wonder the extent to which he has any real political convictions. His ex-college roommate, who loathes him, has insisted that Cruz believes nothing, and that his every attempt to insist otherwise is calculated. But it's impossible to see inside Cruz's brain, and figure out the extent to which he is driven by conviction versus self-aggrandizement. What we can ask is a hypothetical: if Ted Cruz were given the choice between enacting a conservative utopia (while sacrificing his political career in the process, becoming a powerless nobody), and becoming the President of the United States (but guaranteeing that a conservative utopia would never come about), which would he choose? Again, we can't resolve it, but based on the evidence presented in Ted Cruz's book, in which his life seems to consist of the pursuit of success (as opposed to the pursuit of good conservative outcomes), it's hard to think that he'd turn down the Presidency for the sake of realizing his ostensible ideal political outcome. For Cruz, there is only one ideal political outcome, which is "world domination" (to quote 18-year-old Ted) by Cruz himself.

These traits, however, are widely shared among political elites. Ted Cruz is extreme but not aberrational. We can look at others, even with ostensibly different beliefs, who have a similar concern with electoral advancement over principle. Hillary Clinton, for example, is not Ted Cruz. Nor is she much like Ted Cruz, in any of the obvious ways. But she is a person about whom it is instructive to pose that same question: do we believe that, given the choice between becoming the President and enacting a liberal utopia (but being forgotten), Hillary Clinton would choose power or principle?

Clinton's supporters have long insisted that her reputation for being underhanded and power-craving is unwarranted. The charge, they suggest, is sexist; it creates an image of Clinton as a conniving shrew, when any fair-minded examination of her record reveals this isn't true. But it's certainly the case that Clinton shifts her professed principles in accordance with the political needs of the day. Even a Clinton-supporting newspaper columnist admitted that her stance on trade had shifted to better align with the populism of Bernie Sanders:

> *When it comes to campaign trail flip-flops, Hillary Clinton delivered a doozy this week. On Wednesday she announced her opposition to the Trans-Pacific Partnership free trade deal reached between the United States and Asian nations. Clinton says that any new trade deal must "create good American jobs, raise wages, and advance our national security"—and this one doesn't. Clinton, however, has long been a proponent of the TPP, particularly when she was secretary of state just a few years ago (by one estimate, she expressed support for it 45 times). It's doubtful she has suddenly become a protectionist or that, as president, she won't find some way to support a different version of the TPP. So let's be honest, this isn't about jobs; it's about one job, president, and Clinton's desire to be the next one.*[6]

Clinton's stances on other matters have shifted similarly. After defending gun rights in her race against Barack Obama, and pitching herself as a defender of the 2nd Amendment, Clinton used guns as a way to make herself seem more progressive than Bernie Sanders, going after him for coddling the 2nd Amendment. Her views on gay marriage seemed to change in accordance with its popularity among the public. After steadfastly insisting for years that marriage should be between a man and a woman, Clinton suddenly became a major gay marriage supporter when it seemed to be a nationwide inevitability. Clinton even wavers on women's rights; she will steadfastly defend Planned Parenthood to progressive audiences, but will then suggest that conservative sting videos against the organization offer "disturbing" evidence. She has been consistently inconsistent, morphing herself skillfully to fit each political circumstance. Is she a friend or an enemy of Wall Street? The answer seems to depend on whether she is standing on a stage next to Bernie Sanders.

In this respect, Hillary Clinton is a kind of mirrored opposite of Ted Cruz. Each of them is driven by ambition over principle, but each has chosen a different orientation: for Clinton, it's to adopt any position necessary to get votes. For Cruz, it's never to let the temptation toward compromise and harmony get in the way of the quest for domination. Yet both of these figures clearly wake up in the morning attempting, above all else, to win. Their goals are about them. Even right out of law school, Hillary Clinton was bragging that Bill would be the president. Once Bill did in fact reach the highest office, he and Hillary devised a plan for the presidency: "8 years of Bill, 8 years of Hill." It's hard to see this kind of strategizing as in the service of progressive goals; it seems much more like a Machiavellian quest to maximize one's time at the top. There's something very strange indeed about people like Cruz and the Clintons, who even in their 20s were openly plotting their political dominance.

Which brings us back to the original question: why do ambitious people succeed to begin with, if they depend on the support of others to achieve that success, and if those others know perfectly well that the ambitious people are lying about their beliefs and only in it for themselves? Yes, such people are "climbers," but they are enabled at every stage by the people who voluntarily hand them the power they seek.

One problem is that truly humble people rarely step forward, precisely because that humility is genuine. Ted Cruz is right to identify something suspicious in the "reluctant" public servant; for being so reluctant, they often seem quite eager. When most of us think of the truly decent people we have met, they are rarely in politics. They are teachers, social workers, public defenders, counselors, nurses, janitors, and aid workers. They are not in the public spotlight, precisely because they would refuse it if it were offered to them. There is nothing false in such people's apparent lack of ego; it's just how they are.

The old saws about politicians, then, contain some truth: nobody should be elected President who wants to be the President, for there is something astonishingly egotistical in wanting to become the President of the United States. The reason all of our politicians are so sociopathic and self-obsessed is that it takes a sociopathic and self-obsessed personality to seek political power over others. The success of a person like Ted Cruz is a function of the structures that determine social achievement. In politics, as in business, you are rewarded not to the extent that you bring about decent outcomes, but to the extent that you screw the other guy. The people who float to the top of such a system are therefore destined to be the people most willing to jettison thoughtfulness, moral rectitude, and selfless compassion when they get in the way of one's goals. Thus individuals who are thoroughly disliked, friendless even, like Ted Cruz or Richard Nixon, get rewarded with high office. Until we readjust our mechanisms for allocating success, and consign such people to the obscurity and ostracism they deserve, the political sociopath will continue to win the game. Until we allocate rewards on the basis of how decent and principled they actually are, rather than how well they can feign decency and principle, Ted Cruz will continue to win popularity contests despite being universally disliked.

Who Are The Real Nazis?

WHAT IS SOPHISTRY? It's a kind of slick pseudo-logic, a set of arguments that are superficially persuasive but deeply and dishonestly flawed. The hallmark of sophistry is the contrast between how much sense it *seems* to make and how little sense it actually does make when you stop to think about it. Someone making a sophistical argument seems incredibly logical and rational. Even as the arguments they make are revealed under scrutiny to be patently absurd, an uncritical listener might easily be tempted to believe them.

Dinesh D'Souza is a sophist, and a good one. Most people on the left probably won't appreciate just how good he is. Seeing the title of his new book, *The Big Lie: Exposing the Nazi Roots of the American Left*, they'll snort derisively. A book like this, they'll say, is so self-evidently absurd that there is no need to even bother with it. Even to call it sophistry is to pay it too great a compliment. Sophistry is subtle and persuasive. Calling the left Nazis is not persuasive, and it certainly isn't subtle.

One of the many harmful tendencies on the political left, however, is the failure to understand how things appear to people who are not already leftists. This is what prevented so many people from appreciating the threat posed by Donald Trump: actions that looked like PR catastrophes or disqualifying embarrassments to a progressive simply did not look the same to non-progressives. They'll treat *The Big Lie* the same:

too silly, don't even engage with it. Thus, even though according to *Publisher's Weekly*, D'Souza's book is currently the #1 bestselling political book in the country, the only major media outlet that has reviewed it has been the *U.S. News and World Report*, which wrote it off as "dull" and "dumb."

A major reason not to take *The Big Lie* seriously is D'Souza himself. By mainstream standards, D'Souza's career has been a comical embarrassment. D'Souza first found notoriety while an undergraduate at Dartmouth, where the student publication he edited outed members of the Gay Student Alliance. He became a prominent conservative pundit with his book *Illiberal Education*, but by the 2000s he had, in the words of *Vanity Fair*, "eaten away at his respectability in intellectual circles" with extreme and often bizarre claims.[1] He blamed 9/11 on Hollywood liberals, saying that Osama bin Laden was primarily motivated by a hatred of Western sexual decadence, an argument that put off conservatives with its implication that bin Laden shared their values.[2] His *The Roots of Obama's Rage* argued that Barack Obama was a conduit for his father's radical anti-colonial politics, with the "philandering, inebriated, African socialist [Obama, Sr.] now setting the nation's agenda through the reincarnation of his dreams in his son."[3] Even the conservative *Weekly Standard* called this "lunacy."[4] Further embarrassments followed. In 2012, he was forced to resign as president of a Christian college after allegations of adultery.[5] In 2013, D'Souza recorded an infomercial for pop-up Christmas trees.[6] And in 2014, he pled guilty to a felony campaign finance violation, spending 8 months at a halfway house. (D'Souza alleged political persecution by the Obama administration, tweeting: "MLK was targeted by J. Edgar Hoover, an unsavory character; I was targeted by the equally unsavory B. Hussein Obama.")[7]

Importantly, though, while D'Souza was discrediting himself more and more among the elite intellectuals who had once treated him as a serious thinker, he was building an audience elsewhere. D'Souza was embraced by Evangelical pastors like Rick Warren and made a fortune on the megachurch circuit. His books became bestsellers. His polemical documentaries, like *Obama's America* and *America: Imagine a World Without Her*, attracted huge audiences despite being critically panned. As with Trump, the fact that mainstream institutions declared him an "embarrassing failure" by their standards didn't make him one by everybody else's standards. It's easy to call him "fringe." But a lot of people live on the fringes, and they buy Dinesh D'Souza's books.

THE ARGUMENT OF *THE BIG LIE* is that you have been lied to all your life. Since you were a schoolchild, you have been told that Nazism and fascism were "right-wing" ideologies. You have been told that left-wingers hate fascism, that they reject racism, totalitarianism, militarism, and all of fascism's other constituent ideological parts. But this has been a calculated falsehood. In fact, the progressive left have always been the real Nazis. And they have covered it up by using Adolf Hitler's infamous concept of the Big Lie, the lie so "colossal" that nobody would believe anybody "could have the impudence to distort the truth so infamously." The progressive left calls the other side Nazis to disguise the fact that they, themselves, are Nazis. Every time a progressive accuses another party of fascistic behavior, it will be the progressives themselves who have acted like fascists. They call President Trump a fascist to disguise their own fascism. But fascism has always been fundamentally left-wing, and American conservatives must get serious about eliminating the threats posed by the Nazis in our midst, i.e. the left.

So far, so barmy. The book's thesis can be boiled down to the statement: "No, *You're* The Nazis" (which, frankly, I think ought to have been the title). It's obvious why hardly anybody on the left thinks this worth bothering with. Its thesis is politically childish and historically ignorant. It is a fundamentally *stupid* book. Once again, though, note the parallel: Trump, too, is childish, ignorant, and stupid. But he was also, to some people, persuasive, and he is now the President of the United States.

People who choose not to read *The Big Lie* will miss something: it's actually somewhat persuasive. It's wrong and deranged, but the ongoing conflation of "being right" and "being persuasive" is one of the reasons people believed nobody as wrong as Donald Trump could be so successful at winning support. *The Big Lie* is sophistry, and like all good sophistry, the ordinary person who reads it will come away, if not convinced, at least slightly unsettled and unsure of themselves. And while it's possible to refute most of the book in under a paragraph (stay tuned), it would be unwise to assume that just because D'Souza is delusional, this is a badly-written book. It is a well-written book, persuasive and carefully-sourced. It may be difficult for some people to accept that any book with *The Big Lie*'s thesis could have these qualities. But it does, and understanding that it does is important for leftists, who shouldn't laugh off people like D'Souza.

Let me go through and give you a potted version of *The Big Lie*. You will probably find it ridiculous for any one of ten zillion reasons. But instead of mentally arguing with the propositions, and identifying fallacious reasoning, I'd like you to focus on something else, namely how the argument as a whole might be persuasive to someone, and why it works rhetorically.

Nazism, D'Souza says, is leftist, and leftists have been trying to cover this up. But, in an important rhetorical move, D'Souza acknowledges that the reader probably finds this proposition difficult to believe. He says, however, that this is because the reader has been brainwashed. And he asks the reader to set aside their preconceptions about the argument, to allow D'Souza to present the evidence and then to judge the case on this basis.

We start with the history of Italian fascism and German Nazism. Benito Mussolini began as a socialist, heading the Italian Socialist Party. Even when Mussolini replaced his old class analysis with a belief in the primacy of the Italian nation, he was a communitarian who believed that fascism was a "true socialism" that countered "plutocratic elements." Likewise, while leftists have always tried minimize the "Socialist" aspect of "National Socialism," Hitler himself said: "We are socialists. We are the enemies of today's capitalist system of exploitation... and we are determined to destroy this system under all conditions." Hitler condemned the United States as "a country where everything is built on the dollar." At its root, both fascism and progressivism are concerned with the same goal: empowerment of the state and the subjugation of the individual.

It may seem crazy to compare Hitler and Mussolini with American progressives, D'Souza acknowledges. But the affinities have always been more significant than the left would like to admit. Nazi philosopher Martin Heidegger has been a favorite of radical leftists. And when we look at some of the "progressive heroes" among U.S. presidents, we see racist and totalitarian tendencies. Let us take, for example, Wilson, FDR, and Kennedy. Woodrow Wilson was an unabashed white supremacist who segregated the civil service and screened *Birth of a Nation* at the White House, touching off the rebirth of the KKK. He also launched an unprecedented crackdown on civil liberties, jailing critics of his war policies. When John F. Kennedy came back from a visit to Nazi Germany, he wrote in his diary that "I have come to the conclusion that fascism is right for Germany and Italy," and that "the Nordic races appear to be definitely superior to their Latin counterparts."

As for Roosevelt, he almost became an outright dictator. Mussolini himself said that he "greatly admired" Roosevelt, whose singular control of the government was "reminiscent of fascism." Roosevelt hosted Mussolini's aviation minister, Italo Balbo, at the White House and presented him with the Distinguished Flying Cross (the *New York Times* said Balbo left the White House "with his face wreathed in smiles," and Balbo wired Mussolini to say "the existence of anti-fascist sentiment abroad is a myth... exploded by the enthusiastic welcome my air squadron has received in America.") Roosevelt called Mussolini that "admirable Italian gentleman" and wrote that "I am much interested and deeply impressed by what he has accomplished."

Roosevelt was odious in other ways. He maintained segregation in the armed forces and New Deal agencies, placed more than 120,000 Japanaese Americans in what he himself called "concentration camps," and cooperated with racist Southern Democrats in their efforts to block anti-lynching legislation. Roosevelt appointed a former Klansman, Hugo Black, to the Supreme Court, and Black recalled that Roosevelt had been fine with his KKK membership: "President Roosevelt told me there was no reason for my worrying about my having been a member of the Ku Klux Klan. He said some of his best friends and supporters he had in the state of Georgia were among members of the organization. He never indicated any doubt about my having been in the Klan nor did he indicate any criticism of me for having been a member of that organization." When the Supreme Court overturned the National Recovery Act as unconstitutional, Roosevelt threatened to pack the courts with compliant ideologues. His aide Harry Hopkins said "we have lawyers who will declare anything you want to do legal." What could be more totalitarian?

Liberal American intellectuals were also sympathetic to fascism. The *New Republic*'s editor had warm words for Mussolini, for "arousing in a whole nation an increased moral energy." Gertrude Stein said Hitler should get the Nobel Peace Prize. Left historian Charles Beard called fascism "an amazing experiment in reconciling individualism and socialism." Columbia University economist William Pepperell celebrated the New Deal as a kind of "Fabian Fascism." Columbia itself "maintained friendly relations with Nazi academic institutions and representatives of Nazi Germany." When a Harvard alumnus, Ernst Hasnfstaengl, became the head of the Nazi press bureau, the *Harvard Crimson* called for him to receive an honorary degree "appropriate to his high position" in a "great and profound nation." A number of Harvard faculty attended a gala at the docking of a Nazi warship in Boston, and a Harvard delegation attended a 1936 celebration at Heidelberg University, which the British had boycotted for being a Nazi propaganda event.

But, D'Souza contends, nobody should be surprised by this. For the history of progressivism and the Democratic Party is a history of vicious racism, dating back to the beginnings of the Democrats under Andrew Jackson. Jackson was a brutal slaveowner, proud of his reputation as an "Indian killer." He massacred Creek refugees, writing to his wife that "it was dark before we finished killing them." Jackson "used a combination of trickery, threats, and murder to evict native Indians from Florida, Alabama, Mississippi, and Tennessee," was responsible for the

Indian Removal Act and the Trail of Tears, and declared that "the whole Cherokee nation ought to be scourged." Jackson's administration was brutal in its treatment of Indians, and treated them as less than human, with Secretary of State Lewis Cass declaring that "the Indian is a child of impulse" who is "unrestrained by moral considerations."

From the Jacksonian Democrats to Wilson's progressives, the Democratic Party remained racist to its core. The KKK was for many years, according to left historian Eric Foner, "the domestic terrorism arm of the Democratic Party." Republicans were the party of abolition and Reconstruction, while Democrats were the party of slaveowners and segregationists. In the early 20th century, the "progressive" movement added another type of racism to the mix: eugenics. Turn-of-the-century progressives were enthusiastic eugenicists, with birth control advocate (and Planned Parenthood forerunner) Margaret Sanger even giving a speech on eugenics to a meeting of the KKK, and in 1933 Sanger's *Birth Control Review* magazine published an article by Nazi eugenicist Ernst Rudin.

In fact, the Nazis were directly inspired by the actions of the Jacksonian Democrats and the progressive eugenicists. Hitler "praised to his inner circle the efficiency of America's extermination—by starvation and uneven combat—of the red savages who could not be tamed by captivity." Hitler was impressed by the writings of American eugenicists, and called environmentalist Madison Grant's *The Passing of the Great Race* his "Bible." He reported to have "studied with great interest the laws of several American states concerning prevention of reproduction by people whose progeny would in all probability be of no value or injurious to the racial stock." American progressive eugenicists, and American race laws from the Democratic South, directly inspired the Nazi Nuremberg laws.

Thus, D'Souza concludes: the idea that Nazism was "right-wing" and progressivism is "left-wing" is a fabrication, designed to obscure the fact that fascism, Nazism, communism, and Democratic ideology are united by a common commitment: to the totalitarian state, and to disguising racism beneath the rhetoric of social improvement. And today, when progressives criticize Donald Trump as a "fascist," the same thing is going on. In fact, *they* are the fascists: they are the ones who believe in silencing other people, by shutting down conservative speakers. They are the ones who believe in racism, through affirmative action and the continuation of eugenics through abortion. Conservatives are for individual liberty, Democratic progressives are for the totalitarian state, and thus just like Wilson and FDR, it is the left who are the fascists.

Alright, so we can see how everything goes off the rails when D'Souza tries to talk about the present. In these parts, the arguments really are of the "Hitler was a vegetarian" type. At one point, D'Souza even says that because Nazis were interested in race, and Democrats are interested in race, Democrats are Nazis. D'Souza also tries to conclude, from the argument presented, that we should reduce taxes on the wealthy and repeal Obamacare, because it's the only way to fight fascism. The explanation, to the extent it can be discerned, is that because Mussolini controlled the economy, and because FDR liked Mussolini and also wanted to "control the economy," all government intervention in the economy makes you Mussolini. This reasoning... does not hold up.

The rest of this is easy enough to decimate, too. D'Souza's tactic is to show that in the past, a number of people who have used the word "Democrat" to describe themselves have done horrific things. First, of course, today's Democratic Party might share the name of Andrew Jackson's Democratic Party, but that does not make today's Democrats Jacksonians. But, more importantly, if you define yourself not as primarily as a "Democrat" but as an "opponent of horrific things," D'Souza has proved nothing whatsoever about your politics. If your loyalty is not to a label but to some consistent set of principles, you have nothing to fear from D'Souza exposing the history of the Democratic Party as a history of slavery, eugenics, and terrorism. Yes, it's true, if you're invested in proving that Woodrow Wilson and FDR were admirable, a lot of the facts in the book may make you uncomfortable. If you want to salvage the reputation of Harvard and the *New Republic*, you're going to have a tough time. But if your starting point is "Racism, slavery, murder, and totalitarianism are bad things," then this book's criticisms do not affect your kind of leftism in the slightest.

The funny thing about all of this is that half of it could have been written by Howard Zinn or Noam Chomsky. *The Big Lie* is unusual for a conservative book in that it doesn't try to whitewash the history of slavery or the genocide of Native Americans. D'Souza calls it genocide, and he goes into detail comparing life on slave plantations to life in German concentration camps. He shows how the history of America contains a long track record of lynchings, forced sterilizations, and massacres. He admits that the Nazis took direct inspiration from U.S. laws, and says that even the Nazis found the American "one-drop rule" for determining "black blood" to be too strict. But for D'Souza, none of this indicts "The United States." It indicts "Democrats" and "progressives."

It's kind of a novel argument, honestly. I've certainly never heard it before. Usually conservatives seem to want to justify the internment of the Japanese, or to emphasize that most Indians died from diseases rather than direct killing. They wouldn't be terribly comfortable with the idea that American laws inspired the Nazis, because they like to think of America as, on the whole, pretty racially fair with the regrettable exception of slavery. Not D'Souza. He admits all of it, but says it was the liberals who did it.

As I say, logically speaking, this is not an effective maneuver, because it only works against someone who is trying to rehabilitate early 20th century Democrats. If you're a libertarian socialist like Zinn or Chomsky, and you are a committed opposer of every kind of tyranny, whether it calls itself progressive or not, D'Souza has just proved your entire case for you. If you are like George Orwell, a socialist whose socialism is defined in part by its skepticism of state power, it means nothing for anyone to prove that Hitler said he was against capitalism. (Although Hitler also clarified in 1930: "Our adopted term 'Socialist' has nothing to do with Marxian Socialism. Marxism is anti-property; true socialism is not" and said that socialism in the leftist sense was "a Jewish conspiracy.") If you are like the endless numbers of socialists who have despised racism and totalitarianism, and *haven't* flirted with state-worship, every argument in this book can instantly be proved worthless.

Why, then, do I think the book is effective? Because the argument is still a well-crafted piece of sophistry, backed with some solid, though dishonestly selected, historical sources. (I say "solid" because he relies on mainstream liberal historians like Eric Foner, Ira Katznelson, and Timothy Snyder, and "dishonestly" because D'Souza selects everything that could support the idea of a "liberal" sympathy for fascism and ignores all evidence of a right-wing sympathy for fascism; he plays up the "socialist" element in National Socialist even though this was trivial, while ignoring the "national" aspect, which was the center of the doctrine. He has to, because leftists have historically been defined by their skepticism of nationalism: "Workers of the world, unite!") And a lot of people *do* identify themselves more by labels than principles, downplaying the crimes committed by their "side" and highlighting those committed by the other side.

So, yes, the book is full of silly arguments, using endless "guilty by association" type fallacies, selecting its evidence prejudicially, and relying on the ludicrous idea that if ever a "Democrat" did something, then Barack Obama can essentially be held responsible for it. But the book is deeper than it looks: D'Souza has done some research, and has long discussions of the proto-fascist syndicalism of Georges Sorel and Lenin's ideas about imperialism. It's sophistry, but sophistry works. Certainly, D'Souza's book is better than large amounts of nonfiction that comes from our side, which is not nearly this accessible or clear. He actually responds to anticipated counterarguments, and has clearly read a lot of left writing, which is more than can be said for leftists who comment on the right. I don't wish we wrote books this dishonest, but I do wish we wrote books this readable.

It's time to start taking this stuff seriously. Historians have got to respond to books like D'Souza's, and they have to do so in depth. They need to concede the points that are right, and vigorously contest the points that are wrong. It may seem like this is "beneath criticism," but nothing is beneath criticism if large numbers of people believe it. And while Dinesh D'Souza may appear a laughingstock from the vantage point of the academy and the press, his books continue to quietly sell hundreds of thousands of copies.

And that's scary. Because this book isn't innocuous. D'Souza's ultimate conclusions are downright frightening. Just as certain parts of the left believe that if someone is a "fascist," they no longer have rights and you can do as you please to them, D'Souza calls for all-out war on the left, which he says is necessary to stop "Nazism": "This will require, from the Right, a new creativity, a new resolve, and a new willingness to use lawful physical force. Anyone who says physical force is out of bounds does not know what it means to stop fascism." People should be "duct taping Antifa thugs to lampposts," D'Souza says, and "we should not hesitate to unleash the law and the police on these leftist brownshirts." He even advocates using every arm of the government as a means of political repression, saying that Trump should "deploy the IRS, the NSA, and the FBI against the Left" and should stuff the Supreme Court with as many openly ideological justices as possible. All of this is justified, he says, because it is exactly what the "left" does, and anything is justified in beating them. It's a chilling conclusion. But it's all the more reason not to ignore the people who purchase books like this. Like fungi, ideas like these can grow in the dark, and by the time you notice them, it may be too late to stop them. I don't know who the "real" Nazis are, but I certainly know I don't want to be on the receiving end of whatever is directed against those who end up tagged with the label.

Hugh Hefner: Good Riddance to an Abusive Creep

HUGH HEFNER WAS NOT A GOOD PERSON. From the accounts of its residents, Hefner's Playboy Mansion functioned a lot like an internment camp. Hefner exercised absolute control over his "girlfriends": they had a 9pm curfew, and if they violated it Hefner would burst into tears and tell them they should move out. He instituted a strict set of bizarre rules, including forcing each girl to wear matching pajamas. ("If you do something wrong, you'll get an email. There's a strict code of conduct."[1]) He "would constantly create drama and infighting among his girlfriends by randomly changing his long-held positions or household policies to favor one over the rest of them." He would selectively belittle girls ("You look old, hard, and cheap"), talked down to them and "frequently made them cry."[2] He pushed Quaaludes on the girls, referring to the drugs as "thigh-openers."[3] According to Holly Madison, who spent years living with Hefner, he was manipulative, cold, and totalitarian. He refused to use condoms or be tested for STDs, and would require depressing group sex at regularly scheduled times.[4] Each week the girls would have a pre-set time to go to Hefner to receive their "allowance," and he would threaten to withhold their payment if they had dissatisfied him or broken a rule. As Madison writes:

> *We all hated this process. Hef would always use the occasion to*

bring up anything he wasn't happy about in the relationship. Most
of the complaints were about the lack of harmony among the girl-
friends—or your lack of sexual participation in the "parties" he
held in his bedroom. If we'd been out of town for any reason and
missed one of the official "going out" nights [when Hefner liked
to parade his girls at nightclubs] he wouldn't want to give us the
allowance. He used it as a weapon.[5]

Madison became severely depressed over her years in the mansion,
after she realized the security gates were there to keep her locked in,
and began thinking suicide might be her only way out. Two other
girls who spent time in the Mansion were clear: it was "like being in
prison."[6]

Hefner, then, was a domestic abuser. That's the name we have for this
type of person. What kind of person imposes a curfew on their "partner" and locks them inside a mansion, dictating their clothes, regulat-
ing their personal interactions, and chastising them for breaking his
"rules"? This is tyrannical and horrifying.

If you read the obituaries for Hefner, though, you won't really get a
full sense of the man the *Boston Globe* describes as "the pipe-smoking,
Pepsi-quaffing founder of Playboy magazine, whose cheerfully pruri-
ent vision of the good life made him a founding father of the sexual
revolution." The *BBC* begins:

Hugh Hefner created a fantasy world for millions of men but
unlike most of his readers, actually got to live the dream. He suc-
cessfully tapped into a new generation of Americans who were
enjoying rising standards of living in the boom years of the 1950s
and 60s. A political activist and philanthropist, he produced not
just a magazine, but a whole lifestyle. And in Playboy's famous
bow-tie-wearing rabbit he launched one of the most recognised
brands of the 20th Century.[7]

The *Washington Post* tells us:

As much as anyone, Hugh Hefner turned the world on to sex. As the visionary editor who created Playboy magazine out of sheer will and his own fevered dreams, he introduced nudity and sexuality to the cultural mainstream of America and the world. For decades, the ageless Mr. Hefner embodied the "Playboy lifestyle" as the pajama-clad sybarite who worked from his bed, threw lavish parties and inhabited the Playboy Mansion with an ever-changing bevy of well-toned young beauties.[8]

And the *New York Times*:

Hefner the man and Playboy the brand were inseparable. Both advertised themselves as emblems of the sexual revolution, an escape from American priggishness and wider social intolerance. Both were derided over the years—as vulgar, as adolescent, as exploitative, and finally as anachronistic. But Mr. Hefner was a stunning success from his emergence in the early 1950s. His timing was perfect. He was compared to Jay Gatsby, Citizen Kane and Walt Disney, but Mr. Hefner was his own production. He repeatedly likened his life to a romantic movie; it starred an ageless sophisticate in silk pajamas and smoking jacket, hosting a never-ending party for famous and fascinating people.[9]

One of the most remarkable tendencies in American media is its capacity to whitewash the misdeeds of truly horrible people, whether it's the *New York Times* talking about what Henry Kissinger wears to lunch at the Four Seasons,[10] or the *New Yorker* raving about George W. Bush's paintings without mentioning the fact that 500,000 Iraqis died in a war he launched.[11] Multiple women have said that Hugh Hefner essentially imprisoned them in his house and demanded sex from them. Holly Madison says she nearly killed herself because of his treatment. Apparently, though, this just makes him the "embodiment of the Playboy lifestyle."

Of course, the "controversies" about Hefner do get mentioned. Here's the *New York Times*:

> *Mr. Hefner was reviled, first by guardians of the 1950s social order—J. Edgar Hoover among them—and later by feminists. But Playboy's circulation reached one million by 1960 and peaked at about seven million in the 1970s.*

Look at this remarkable passage. Feminist criticism of *Playboy*, which centers around its embrace of the very kind of disgusting treatment of women that Hefner himself practiced, is lumped in with the persecutions of J. Edgar Hoover. "Sure, buzzkills like the Feminazis and Hoover came after it, but the circulation was incredible."

The feminist criticism of *Playboy* has always been obviously correct. Hefner literally reduced women to little bunnies who existed entirely to suck his penis. Of course, there's plenty of mention in the obituaries of Hefner's "highbrow" aspirations. In his words, "we enjoy mixing up cocktails and an *hors d'oeuvre* or two, putting a little mood music on the phonograph and inviting in a female acquaintance for a quiet discussion on Picasso, Nietzsche, jazz, sex." But it was always clear that the intellectual side of *Playboy* was strictly for men: he refused to discuss politics or literature with any of his girlfriends. They were there for him to have joyless unprotected sex with whenever he pleased.

Hefner's *Playboy* was committed to destroying the idea that women were people. As the *Times* quotes, Hefner demanded his writers go after feminism in the magazine's pages:

> *These chicks are our natural enemy. What I want is a devastating piece that takes the militant feminists apart. They are unalterably opposed to the romantic boy-girl society that Playboy promotes.*

That "romantic boy-girl society" was the "dream" Hefner frequently said he lived. It was little more than the dream of tyrannizing over women while wearing a bathrobe.

The world of *Playboy* was a profoundly sad one. In photos, Hefner never looks particularly happy, and he was a recluse who didn't even seem to enjoy the copious amounts of sex he had. ("There was zero intimacy involved... No kissing, nothing.") Hefner's fantasy lifestyle was *inhuman* in every way. It was sex as something mechanical and lifeless, something one did because it was the thing that made you a Playboy, rather than because of true passion. That's the dark secret about Hefner: he wasn't even a *hedonist*. A hedonist pursues pleasure. Hefner didn't care about pleasure. He cared about the taming and conquest of women.

There's an important critique of libertarian morality to the Hefner story, too. Hefner was an advocate for freedom from all kinds of government restraint, a champion of the First Amendment and abortion rights (as every obituary has reminded us repeatedly). He was a "passionate libertarian."[12] Hefner also believed he was changing American morality, saying: "What it really comes down to is an attempt to establish what has been called a new morality... really think that's what this thing called the 'American sexual revolution' is really all about." (This is taken from the *NYT's* charming compilation of Hefner's "Most Memorable Interview Moments."[13]) Here we see exactly what happens when "freedom" is taken to be a moral philosophy in itself. Like many libertarians, Hefner wanted to be free, but he wanted to be free from government tyranny only so he could exercise a kind of unaccountable private tyranny. As with libertarianism always, "freedom to be a dick" seems to be the goal. He wanted to establish a "new morality" that would simply let him do as he pleased to women, without any ethical constraints. "Liberty," while essential, is meaningless unless it is also coupled with a set of standards for how people should actually behave toward one another.

I am not actually celebrating Hugh Hefner's death. It's sad when people die. By "good riddance," I don't mean that I take personal pleasure in his death, but that the world will be better once it rids itself of Hefner's values. And since Hefner himself was an evangelist for those values until his last days, we are better off without him. (I felt the same way when Antonin Scalia died. I didn't want him to *die*; I would have preferred that he had remained alive and simply renounced his horrible beliefs and become a good person. But he never did, so we had to settle for death.)

The Cool Kid's Philosopher

IT'S EASY TO LAUGH, as some of us do,[1] at the phrase "conservative intellectual." When the most prominent public spokesmen for the right's ideas include Milo Yiannopoulos, Charles Murray, and Dinesh D'Souza, one might conclude that the movement does not have anything serious to offer beyond "Feminism is cancer," "Black people are dumb," and "Democrats are Nazis." (Those are, as I understand it, the central intellectual contributions of Yiannopoulos, Murray, and D'Souza, respectively.)

But according to the *New York Times*,[2] it would be a mistake to write off Conservative Thought so hastily. For we would be overlooking one crucial figure: Ben Shapiro. Shapiro, we are told, is "the cool kid's philosopher, dissecting arguments with a lawyer's skill and references to Aristotle." The *Times* quotes praise of Shapiro as a "brilliant polemicist" and "principled gladiator," a quick-witted man who "reads books," and "takes apart arguments in ways that make the conservative conclusion seem utterly logical." Shapiro is the "destroyer of weak arguments," he "has been called the voice of the conservative millennial movement." He is a genuine *intellectual*, a man who "does not attack unfairly, stoke anger for the sake of it, or mischaracterize his opponents' positions." He is principled: he deplores Trump, and cares about Truth. Shapiro's personal mantra, "Facts don't care about your feelings," captures his approach:

he's *passionate,* but he believes in following reason rather than emotion. Shapiro, then, represents the best in contemporary conservative thinking. And if the cool kids have a philosopher, it is worth examining his philosophy in some depth.

I will confess, I had not spent much time listening to or studying Ben Shapiro before reading about him in the *New York Times.* That might be a damning sign of my own closed-mindedness: here I am, a person who considers himself intellectually serious, and I have written off the other side without even engaging with its strongest arguments. So I decided to spend a few wearying days trawling through the Shapiro oeuvre, listening to the speeches and radio shows and reading the columns and books. If Shapiro had arguments that Destroyed and Decimated the left, I wanted to make sure I heard them. I consider myself a bit of a leftist, and I like to know when I've been decimated.

I'll admit that I was not immediately dazzled by the force of Shapiro's intellect. I started with his controversial recent Berkeley speech.[3] Toward the beginning, he addressed Antifa protesters, whom he called "communist pieces of garbage": "You guys are so stupid... you can all go to hell, you pathetic, lying, stupid jackasses." According to the *Times,* there is a wide gulf between Trump/Yiannopoulos-style vulgar conservatism and Shapiro-style Logical conservatism, but I just am not sure that I see in "Go to hell, you communist piece of garbage" the kind of "polemical brilliance" that Shapiro is reputed to demonstrate. The rest of the speech, when it got beyond making Botox jokes about Nancy Pelosi, was strong on insults ("pusillanimous cowards," "hard-Left morons," "uncivilized barbarians") and light on actual argumentation and substantive factual claims. Shapiro did say that the alt-right are full of "bullshit" and that the left overstates the threat posed by Shapiro's speeches. (Both true.) The main thrust of the speech, though, is that America is the greatest country in the world, that there are no real injustices facing black people, women, and poor people, and that if you don't do well economically here it's entirely your fault. As he says:

This country is an amazing place full of opportunity. Nobody, by and large, cares enough about you to stop you from achieving your dreams. That includes you, people who are shouting out there in the audience. No one cares about you; get over yourselves. I don't care about you; no one cares about you... That means, in a free country, if you fail, it's probably your own fault.

Shapiro scoffs at all claims that racism is a serious problem facing black people. This is in part because "I wasn't an adult when Jim Crow was in place... and I would bet you money that the people in this room haven't acted in a racist manner, that they haven't held slaves, or voted for Jim Crow." He says the idea that black people's disproportionate poverty has anything to do with racism is "just not true," and tosses out a few points to prove that the importance of race is overstated: First, Asian Americans are wealthier than white people, which would be impossible if racism determined economic outcomes. (Shapiro doesn't mention that the vast majority of Asian American adults are immigrants,[4] and they are disproportionately from the wealthier and more highly-educated segments of their own countries.) Second, he says, people of any race who work full time, are married, and have high school diplomas tend not to be poor, meaning that poverty is a function of one's choice not to do these things. (In fact, this theory, widely cited by conservatives, turns out to be vacuous[5]: of course people who have full-time jobs usually aren't in poverty, the problem is that black people disproportionately can't get jobs.[6]) Next, Shapiro says that because black married couples have a lower poverty rate than white single mothers, "life decisions" are what creates poverty. (Actually, even when two black people pool their wealth in a marriage, "the median white single parent has 2.2 times more wealth than the median black two-parent household."[7]) Finally, Shapiro says that the disproportionately black population in America's prisons say nothing about racism, because black people simply commit more crimes, and "if you don't commit a crime, you're not going to be arrested for it" because "the police are not going around arresting black people for the fun of it." (I have some black men in Louisiana I'd like Shapiro to meet so that he can explain his theory that people do not get arrested for crimes they haven't committed. But I'd also like to hear him explain why black men receive 20% longer sentences for the same crime as white men with similar backgrounds.[8])

What dispirited me about Shapiro's approach is that he's clearly not actually very interested in Facts at all. The role that race plays in American life is a serious sociological question, one that isn't answered easily. But Shapiro plucks only the statistics that suggest race doesn't matter, and pretends the statistics that suggest it *does* matter don't exist. Nobody can trust him, because if he comes across a finding showing that incarceration rates more closely follow crime rates than racial demographics, you can bet it will appear in his next speech. But if someone shows that a white man with a criminal record is far more likely to receive a job callback than a black man without a criminal record,[9] you'll never hear it mentioned. It would be perfectly reasonable for Shapiro to critique these findings; sociologists critique each other all the time. Instead, he selects only the parts of reality that please him. Just look at his reply when he was asked about the black-white wealth gap: "It has nothing to do with race and everything to do with culture."[10] That's a strange thing to say, because the wealth gap has existed continuously since the time of slavery: average black net worth has *always* been lower than white net worth, and there were massive structural obstacles to the black accumulation of wealth well into the 20th century, as we can see in Ta-Nehisi Coates' writings on the lasting impact of housing policy.[11] Family wealth is passed down intergenerationally, and so it's hard to conclude that the fact that the average white family has $13 of wealth for every $1 of wealth held by a black family is the sole result of spontaneous contemporary black cultural choices, with no historical component whatsoever.[12]

The impact of human decisions on outcomes, and the factors that shape the available range of choices, are difficult topics in social science with no simple answers. But one thing we do know is that, since black people were enslaved for 246 years (and free for 152), and Jim Crow was in operation *during the time of people who are still alive* (thereby being a core determinant of both their life outcomes and the capital that they were able to pass onto their own children), anyone who says "culture is everything" and "race is irrelevant" is not actually seriously interested in trying to figure out how the world works.

In investigating Shapiro's works, then, the first sign that he might not be a "philosopher" was that he didn't seem especially interested in the central task of philosophy, namely the critical scrutiny of your own beliefs. Shapiro's worldview is fixed and immovable. Watch the video of his answer on the racial wealth gap: when his black co-panelists laugh at his answer about culture, he does not think to himself "Hm, perhaps they know something I don't know about what it is like to be black." He thinks "They must be irrational and in need of my wisdom."[13] He doesn't listen to anyone, he just confronts them.

My initial impressions were also soured by Shapiro's casual bigotry. That may not be the wisest observation to lead with: I'm sure Shapiro would be very pleased with himself to hear me call him a racist. (Though Shapiro always[14] looks somewhat pleased with himself.) Nothing could better *prove his point*: the left has no arguments, so they resort to calling people they dislike "racists." And since he explicitly says that he *isn't* a racist, what am I doing if not using the classic left-wing "bullying" tactic of dismissing your opponent as a nasty, bigoted individual?[15]

But, well, I don't know what else to call a statement like this: "Israelis like to build. Arabs like to bomb crap and live in open sewage."[16] (Shapiro followed it with the hashtag #SettlementsRock.) *Arabs like to bomb crap and live in sewage*. Perhaps I'm crazy. Perhaps there's a definition of the word "racism" that wouldn't include a statement like that. But since the statements "Black people are violent and want to live in sewage" or "Jews are violent and want to live in sewage" would both sound... somewhat racist, I don't see how the conclusion can be avoided. What do you call a crass pejorative generalization about an entire ethnic group? I know one word, but I'm open to others. (By the way, it's amusing that Shapiro can see Gazan children swimming in sewage[17] and think "Wow, Arabs must just really have a thing for sewage," a train of reasoning roughly akin to "Wow, Haitians must really love dying in earthquakes, since a lot of them seem to have done it." Though I am reliably informed that Shapiro is a master of logic, so I am sure there is more to this than mere simple-minded prejudice.)

Shapiro's other thoughts about Arabs are all along similar lines. Usually conservatives are careful to draw a distinction: they are not condemning an ethnicity, but rather adherents to an ideology, namely Islamism. Not so with Shapiro: for him, the problem is not Islamism or even Islam writ large. It's *Arabs*: "The Arab-Israeli conflict may be accurately described as a war between darkness and light. Those who argue against Israeli settlements—outposts of light in a dark territory—argue for the continued victory of night."[18] Arabs "value murder" while Israelis "value life," and "where light fails, darkness engulfs." Arabs are therefore, as an undifferentiated unit, a people of darkness. Palestinian Arabs are the worst of all: they are a "population rotten to the core... Palestinian Arabs must be fought on their own terms: as a people dedicated to an evil cause."[19] The "Arab Palestinian populace... by and large constitutes the most evil population on the face of the planet." Since they're "rotten to the core," there's no such thing as a good Arab: your evil is defined by your ethnicity, by being a member of the People of Darkness and Murder rather than the People of Goodness and Light. Again, it may just be my failure to understand Facts and Logic, but I am having trouble understanding how population-level generalizations about the moral characteristics of particular ethnic groups can be anything other than bigotry. Shapiro has been clear about the implications of his view of Arabs as a dark and murderous people. He has said that "Secular Zionism[, which] requires that Arab citizens of Israel be guaranteed equal rights," "has always provided the seeds of [Israel's] destruction."[20] Instead, "God's road map requires the Jews to kill those who seek to kill them." Since Arabs universally "value murder," I can't see how this is anything other than a philosophical justification of genocide. Shapiro has said that Arab nefariousness could be stopped without resorting to genocide, and is offended by anyone who tries to invoke the g-word to describe his beliefs.[21] But since he has said (1) that Arabs are inherently murderous and bent on destroying Israel and (2) God permits Jews to kill those who seek to kill them, it's hard to see how he could disagree with anyone who *did* advocate genocide, except on pragmatic grounds.

Shapiro once explained his actual preferred solution to the problem of the dark Arab hordes: mass expulsion.[22] As he said, bulldozing Palestinian houses and subjecting them to curfews are insufficient "half-measures": the only solution is to drive every last one of them forcibly from their homes and take their land:

> *The Arab enmity for Jews and the state of Israel allows for no peace process. The time for half measures has passed. Bulldozing houses of homicide bombers is useless. Instituting ongoing curfews in Arab-populated cities is useless... Some have rightly suggested that Israel be allowed to decapitate the terrorist leadership of the Palestinian Authority. But this too is only a half measure. The ideology of the Palestinian population is indistinguishable from that of the terrorist leadership. Half measures merely postpone our realization that the Arabs dream of Israel's destruction. Without drastic measures, the Arab dream will come true... If you believe that the Jewish state has a right to exist, then you must allow Israel to transfer the Palestinians and the Israeli-Arabs from Judea, Samaria, Gaza and Israel proper. It's an ugly solution, but it is the only solution... It's time to stop being squeamish.* (Odd that the *NYT* didn't choose to quote this passage in its profile.)

Every last Arab—even those who are Israeli citizens—must be deported, Shapiro said, because their ethnicity means that they harbor a murderous "Arab dream." But to anyone who thinks this sounds like the textbook definition of "ethnic cleansing," he has a firm response: "It's not genocide; it's transfer. It's not Hitler, it's Churchill." Shapiro is referring to the Allied expulsion of German-speakers from Polish territory immediately after World War II, in which "Anywhere from 3.5 million to 9 million Germans were forcibly expelled from the new Polish territory and relocated in Germany." Shapiro favorably quotes Churchill's desire that "There will be no mixture of populations to cause endless trouble ... a clean sweep will be made."

There is only one problem with the precedent cited by Shapiro: it is actually a forgotten historic atrocity, which was characterized by mass rape, torture, and murder, and left at least 400,000 people dead.[23] Germans were interned in concentration camps and endured horrific journeys in which pregnant women froze to death. As Tara Zahra explains in a review of R.M. Douglas's *Orderly and Humane: The Expulsion of the Germans After the Second World War:*

> *After the Nazi defeat, the Volksdeutsche fled or were expelled to the West, and were stripped of their citizenship, homes and property in… "the largest forced population transfer—and perhaps the greatest single movement of peoples—in human history." Douglas amply demonstrates that these population transfers, which were to be carried out in an "orderly and humane" manner according to the language of the Allies' 1945 Potsdam Agreement, counted as neither. Instead…. they were nothing less than a "massive state-sponsored carnival of violence, resulting in a death toll that on the most conservative of estimates must have reached six figures." …Ironically, then, the postwar population transfers completed a process of segregation and ethnic cleansing that Hitler himself had begun…. Interned women throughout Czechoslovakia and Poland were subject to rampant sexual abuse, rape and torture. Germans were also forced to wear armbands or patches marked with the letter "N" for Nemec (German)—collective payback for the humiliation that the Nazis had inflicted on populations in the East. When they were finally transported west, the expellees traveled by cattle car, sometimes going with barely any food or water for up to two weeks. One victim recalled that each morning, "one or more dead bodies greeted us…they just had to be abandoned on the embankments."… Douglas concludes by calling the expulsions a "tragic, unnecessary, and, we must resolve, never to be repeated episode in Europe's and the world's recent history."[24]*

This is the model that Shapiro believed should be applied to the murderous Arabs. (Perhaps Israel could even have them wear patches with little "A"s on them. But that might seem a little racist, and Shapiro is firmly against racism.[25]) Shapiro has since suggested that his position on ethnic cleansing has evolved (without admitting that he ever endorsed it), in part because large-scale population transfer is simply impractical.[26] His position on the inherent evil of Palestinians, however, does not appear to have softened.

As I say, I realize I am playing right into Shapiro's hands by invoking the r-word to describe his belief that Arabs are bomb-throwing sewage-dwellers who deserve to be ethnically cleansed. But I happen to think Shapiro is a bit inconsistent on this. His standard of evidence for what constitutes ethnic prejudice seems to vary based on who the target is. When it came to George Zimmerman, Shapiro concluded that "there's no evidence of Zimmerman's racism."[27] Bear in mind that Zimmerman: approached a stranger because they had a Confederate flag tattoo so he could brag about killing Trayvon Martin,[28] got thrown out of a bar for calling someone a "nigger-lover,"[29] ranted about his girlfriend sleeping with a "dirty Muslim,"[30] tweeted that the lives of "black slime" don't matter,[31] labeled Barack Obama an "ignorant baboon,"[32] posted memes comparing Michelle Obama to Chewbacca,[33] and literally had a Confederate flag profile picture and sold paintings he did of said flag.[34] (Oh, and he also murdered an unarmed black teenager and proudly posted a photo of the boy's corpse on Twitter, but Shapiro has made it clear that he believes Trayvon Martin deserved to die.[35])

From that, we might conclude that Shapiro has an extremely high threshold for evidence he will consider sufficient to deem someone a bigot. But it doesn't apply universally: Shapiro seems rather quick to accuse his opponents of anti-Semitic prejudice. That could be because they have described him as a "neoconservative," which Shapiro considers an anti-Semitic slur.[36] Or they could, like the "Nazis" at PETA,[37] have diminished the relative value of Jewish lives by elevating the importance of animal lives. But nobody is quite as bad as Barack Obama, who Shapiro believes harbors a deep hatred of Jews. As president, Obama was a "philosophical fascist"[38] whose anti-Semitism was "clear-cut."[39] To support the "fascism" charge Shapiro cites evidence like Obama's "dictatorial demands ('I want a jobs bill on my desk without delay')," the "scornful looks and high-handed put-downs directed at his political opponents," and the "arrogant chin-up head tilt he uses when waiting for applause." Shapiro says that Obama's vision for America is totalitarian, citing Obama's hope that "the American people [should have] a government that matches their decency; that embodies their strength."

Alright, well, we may disagree over whether pressuring Congress to pass a jobs bill makes you literally Mussolini. But Shapiro says the anti-Semitism part is *clear-cut*. Why? Well, the first piece of evidence is that when the Israeli military stormed an aid flotilla bound for Gaza, killing nine activists,[40] the Obama administration soon released a statement saying that "The United States deeply regrets the loss of life and injuries sustained." "How else are we to interpret [this] lightning-fast, knee-jerk anti-Israel response?" except as evidence of anti-Semitism, Shapiro asks.[41] But perhaps you're not convinced. Well, Shapiro has more.[42] In 2009, Rahm Emanuel went to speak at AIPAC and told the audience that U.S. efforts to thwart Iran's nuclear program would be conditional on successful resolution of the Israel/Palestine conflict. This, Shapiro says, showed that Obama harbored a deep animus against Jews, because he holds Israel to a higher standard than he holds anyone else. And while it may have turned out that Rahm Emanuel never actually said anything like this,[43] leading at least one other columnist to issue a correction,[44] Shapiro stood firm. Not only did he not amend the story, but he later called Emanuel (who held Israeli citizenship for nearly two decades, whose middle name is literally Israel, and who even Jeffrey Goldberg thought made the idea of Obama being anti-Israel seem "a bit ridiculous"[45]) a "kapo," i.e. a Jew who does the Nazis' bidding. Shapiro said that any Jewish person who voted for Obama was not really a Jew at all, but a "Jew In Name Only" serving an "enemy of the Jewish people."[46] They may "eat bagels and lox," but by supporting an "openly" anti-Semitic administration they are "disgusting" and a "disgrace," and the "twisted and evil" "self-hating Jews" who "enjoy matzo ball soup" and "emerged from a Jewish uterus" but nevertheless choose to "undermine the Israeli government" "don't care a whit about Judaism" and in fact hold "anti-Semitic views."[47] (Those may be snippet-length quotes but go and read the columns if you suspect me of excising context or nuance.)

You must forgive me, then, for being somewhat confused by Shapiro's conception of prejudice, which includes people who say "these deaths are regrettable" but excludes those who use the n-word and shoot black children in the face. But I realize I am missing the meat of the Shapiro philosophy. Nevermind Shapiro The Ethnic Cleanser, what about Shapiro The Destroyer Of Weak Arguments? Shapiro has built his reputation on his formidable ability to dismantle liberal orthodoxies, his dazzling use of logic to expose leftists as vacuous bullies who must stifle conservative speech because they cannot actually refute or debunk it.

I'd like, then, to closely examine how Shapiro *destroys* a liberal argument, in order to see his famous method at work. Let's look at how Shapiro "debunks transgenderism."[48] When a student questioner confronted Shapiro about his belief that transgender women should not be considered women, here's the argument he gave in defense of the position:

> *You're not a man if you think you're a man... As far as the actual psychological issues at play, it used to be called gender identity disorder; now they call it gender dysphoria. The idea that sex or gender is malleable is not true. I'm not denying your humanity if you are a transgender person; I am saying that you are not the sex which you claim to be. [I]f you're going to dictate to me that I'm supposed to pretend, I'm supposed to pretend that men are women and women are men, no. My answer is no. I'm not going to modify basic biology because it threatens your subjective sense of what you are.*

When the questioner replied to suggest that transgender people just wanted to fit in, Shapiro hit her with a burst of Stone Cold Logic. After asking her how old she was, he asked her why she wasn't a different age. Answer: *because age is a fact not a choice.* Then he asked her why she didn't just change her species:

SHAPIRO: *If I call you a moose, are you suddenly a moose? If I redefine our terms...*
YOUNG WOMAN: *That's a completely different thing.*
SHAPIRO: *Yes, that's right. Men and women are a completely different thing. This is true. Have you ever met a man or a woman? They are completely different.*

Shapiro's position on transgender people is very simple then. He rejects "the pseudo-scientific nonsense that a man can magically turn into a woman," because it is no different than thinking an undergraduate can turn into a moose. Shapiro says that "individuals who believe they are a different sex than that of their biology are psychologically ill—self-evidently so" and has compared the idea of being transgender to his schizophrenic grandfather who thought the curtains were speaking to him.

But for a man who loves Logical Argumentation and would never "mischaracterize his opponents' positions," Shapiro doesn't actually seem to grasp what the left argument about gender actually *is*, or what it is he's actually supposed to be disproving.

Here is the actual argument that is made: the traditional conception held by people like Shapiro has treated "sex" and "gender" as synonymous. You're either a *man* or a *woman*. Which one you are is defined by your chromosomes. And because chromosomes are part of biology, and can't be altered, you can—as Shapiro says—no more change your sex/gender through your state of mind than you could change your age. There are men and there are women:

The argument made by the left is that this simple story doesn't account for something important: in the real world, we don't form our understanding of whether someone is a man or a woman by their chromosomes. Instead, we form it by how they look and act. What people mean when they say that "gender is a social construct" is not that "chromosomes are a social construct" but that in practice, gender isn't reducible to chromosomes. In the two pictures above, the person on the left is actually a transgender man and the person on the right is actually a transgender woman. It would seem strange to call the person on the left a "woman" and the person on the right a "man," because the fact that we associate gender with "masculinity" and "femininity" rather than just "chromosomes" means those words don't seem to fit those people very well.

This is the reason why people started to draw a distinction between "sex" and "gender," with sex referring to the biological component and gender referring to those qualities that seem much more fluid. Transgender people do not "think they are a different sex." Instead, they realize that their "gender" doesn't match their sex. As a transgender person explained in response to Shapiro, "most of the trans people I know, including myself, are under no delusion about what we were born as or what biological sex we are, we just feel uncomfortable with the features of our biological sex and seek treatment, usually, to alter those features and minimize our dysphoria."[49]

The dysphoria is not the "delusional belief that you don't have a penis when you in fact do." It's the distress that comes from feeling like a member of the "female" gender despite having the "male" sex, or vice versa. The argument being made is that the existing way we classify sex/gender is not adequately describing the actual fact, which is that because gender captures more than just chromosomes, the traditional terminology causes confusion and needs revising. Scott Alexander has a poignant and funny essay explaining why categories like "male" and "female" are malleable and why we should adjust them depending on the goals we're trying to accomplish:

*In no case can an agreed-upon set of borders or a category bound-
ary be factually incorrect. An alternative categorization system is
not an error... Just as we can come up with criteria for a definition
of "planet", we can come up with a definition of "man". Absolutely
typical men have Y chromosomes, have male genitalia, appreciate
manly things like sports and lumberjackery, are romantically attracted to women, personally identify as male, wear male clothing
like blue jeans, sing baritone in the opera, et cetera. Some people
satisfy some criteria of manhood and not others, in much the same
way that Pluto satisfies only some criteria of planethood... For example, gay men might date other men and behave in effeminate
ways. People with congenital androgen insensitivity syndrome
might have female bodies, female external genitalia, and have
been raised female their entire life, but when you look into their
cells they have Y chromosomes. Most people seem to assume that
the ultimate tiebreaker in man vs. woman questions is presence of
a Y chromosome. I'm not sure this is a very principled decision,
because I expect most people would classify congenital androgen insensitivity patients (XY people whose bodies are insensitive to the
hormone that makes them look male, and so end up looking 100%
female their entire lives and often not even knowing they have the
condition) as women. The project of the transgender movement is
to propose a switch from using chromosomes as a tiebreaker to using
self-identification as a tiebreaker.*[50]

Shapiro thinks being transgender is a mental illness, just as he believes
homosexuality should still be considered a mental illness (and was only
taken off the list thanks to "pressure group influence"[51]). But mental illness is another situation where the classifications we choose are choices:
homosexuality does not "inherently" fit in the category of mental illness; a society decides what it wants to call "illness." And since there
seemed to be very little good to come from calling some perfectly ordinary human trait an "illness," all this did was create unnecessary stigma.
Likewise, it was decided that there was no reason to see "believing your

gender identity to be different than your biological sex" an illness, so the DSM was revised accordingly, to focus on what *did* actually seem a problem, namely the distress this can lead to.

Gender and sex are complicated topics. There are a lot of unanswered questions (e.g. What is identity? Should gender be entirely subjective? How are racial and gender identity different?) All of these, though, are attempts to work out how we should revise our categories in the way that best reflects the human reality and allows us to talk coherently. The traditional categories were just too simple to capture the more complicated facts of how gender works. (Actually, Shapiro himself inadvertently proved this. In discussing why he would never recognize Laverne Cox as a woman, Shapiro accidentally referred to Cox as "she" before quickly correcting himself.[52] Why did he slip? Because Laverne Cox *does* seem like a woman, based on how the category "woman" is applied socially, and it feels *weird* to call her a man. Even Shapiro's subconscious is telling him that transgender people should be referred to by the gender they present as rather than by their biological sex.)

Shapiro isn't interested in discussing any of this seriously. Just look at how he distorted his questioner's response about moose: he says "Why aren't you a moose?" and when she replies "That's different," he interjects "That's right, men and women *are* different." She clearly said that species and gender are different (which they are, in that there's a good argument for revising one of the categories but not for revising the other). But he tried to convince his audience that she had essentially conceded his point, by seizing on and spinning the word "difference." (We call this "sophistry" rather than "logic.")

At every turn, Shapiro shows that he simply wants to make his questioners look foolish, rather than present the facts fairly. Just look at his discussion of suicide and bullying:

> *The idea behind the transgender civil rights movement is that all of their problems would go away if I would pretend that they were the sex to which they claim membership. That's nonsense. The*

transgender suicide rate is 40%. And according to the Anderson School at UCLA ... it makes virtually no difference statistically as to whether people recognize you as a transgender person or not... It has nothing to do with how society treats you... The normal suicide rate across the US is 4%. The suicide rate in the transgender community is 40%. The idea that 36% more transgender people are committing suicide is ridiculous. [Note: Shapiro has misconstrued a statistic on suicide attempts as a statistic on successful suicide] *It's not true and it's not backed by any science that anyone can cite. It's pure conjecture. It's not even true that bullying causes suicide... There's no evidence whatsoever that the suicide rate in the transgender community would go down in any marked way if people just started pretending that men were women and women were men.*

I can't find a study from the Anderson School about transgender suicide. The one UCLA study I *can* find on the subject, the one I think he must be referring to, directly contradicts Shapiro's contention, concluding that "a higher than average prevalence of lifetime suicide attempts was consistently found among NTDS respondents who reported that they had been harassed, bullied, or assaulted in school by other students and/or teachers due to anti-transgender bias" and "the prevalence of suicide attempts was elevated among respondents who reported experiencing rejection, disruption, or abuse by family members or close friends because of antitransgender bias."[53] (Another study found that "social support, reduced transphobia, and having any personal identification documents changed to an appropriate sex designation were associated with large relative and absolute reductions in suicide risk."[54]) So when Shapiro says that there's "no evidence whatsoever" and it's "not backed by any science," it's actually backed by the exact study he has just cited. (That study also demonstrates why another Shapiro talking point, that transgender suicides can't be caused by prejudice because black people have low suicide rates, is false: a crucial determinant of suicide likelihood is people's level of family support, and if black people have strong support networks, similar levels of discrimination could lead to differing levels of suicide.)

For a man who cares about Facts rather than Feelings, Shapiro doesn't seem to care very much about facts. There are plenty of minor mistakes that cast doubt on the *Times* quote that Shapiro "reads books." Some are just the little slip-ups that come from careless writing, e.g. the U.S. abolished slavery in "1862," "atheistic philosopher Gilbert Pyle" [sic]. Others are suspicious unsourced generalizations, e.g. "Walk into virtually any emergency room in California and illegal immigrants are the bulk of the population."[55] But there are also major embarrassing bloomers, like Shapiro promoting the false rumor that Chuck Hagel received a donation from a group called "Friends of Hamas."[56] A *New York Daily News* reporter had made up the group's name, as something so ludicrously over-the-top that nobody could possibly believe it, but Shapiro was credulous enough to think the organization could exist, and published an article demanding answers.[57] When it was pointed out that there was no such group, Shapiro did not retract the story. Instead, he doubled down, insisting that because he reported that *sources said* there was a Friends of Hamas, and the sources did say that, his reporting was sound.[58] (Note: this is not how journalism works.)

There are plenty of other points at which Shapiro has showed that his command of Logic may not be terribly strong. He loves Facts, but will make statements like "monitoring mosques is the simplest and most effective way of preventing terrorist attacks" and cite "simple common sense" as his source.[59] He will look back fondly on the era of the Hays Code, in which movies that did not portray correct moral messages were censored, and state that it is "no coincidence" that many great films were made during this time.[60] (Someone ought to introduce Shapiro to the idea that just because two things occur at the same time does not mean that one of them was responsible for the other.) The ACLU's attempt to bring Abu Ghraib photos to light was "designed as a direct attack on American soldiers abroad."[61] (Again, there's no argument here, he just says it.) Hip hop is "not music," people only say it is because of "cultural sensitivity," and it is the product of a "disgusting" culture; again, one presumes these are just Facts, not Feelings.[62] (No, he didn't like *Hamilton* either, and spent part of a radio show playing *Hamilton* and *West Side Story* side by side, like a cool kid, in order to show that *Hamilton* has "forced rhymes that aren't actually rhymes" and has "no harmony, no melody, just rhythm, and this is my problem with rap generally."[63]) The Supreme Court's decision to uphold the Affordable Care Act was literally worse than *Plessy v. Ferguson* and the case that allowed mentally ill people to be sterilized.[64] (Shapiro believes the decision "said that the federal government can force you to do anything" because it can "tax nonbehavior," though since there is zero practical difference between providing "a tax penalty for not doing something" and "a tax credit for doing something," this framework means every tax credit is a form of totalitarianism.) Some of his arguments just make no damn sense at all: witness his contention that capitalism doesn't mean the greedy pursuit of self-interest, *corporatism* does, while capitalism just means... I'm not sure.[65] (Try to reconcile his statement that capitalism isn't about economic self-interest with his statement that capitalism values people by their economic usefulness.) Or his case that socialism is racism because in capitalism people are valued entirely in accordance with their market worth, irrespective of race.[66] (Shapiro has argued that shop owners who discriminate among customers would go out of business, which might be true if there wasn't a huge racial wealth gap and no consumers ever preferred to patronize racially segregated establishments.)

Shapiro mocked T.I. for naming his children "Zonnique and Deyjah."[67] (It's not clear what the Rational basis for disliking black names is.) When Barack Obama said that "we need to keep changing the attitude that punishes women for their sexuality and rewards men for theirs," Shapiro wondered why Obama thought anyone should "be rewarded for their sexuality."[68] (I am curious how Shapiro did on the Logical Reasoning section of his LSAT if he believes "Don't punish X or reward Y" means "reward X and/or Y.") He thinks that criticisms of those who seem to love wars but decline to fight in them are "explicitly reject[ing] the Constitution itself, [which] provides that civilians control the military."[69] (Go ahead and try to figure out the reasoning on that one.) He was strongly against a federal ban on using cellphones while driving, because it would take away drivers' freedom of choice, yet he believes it is "morally tragic" that we no longer use the police to stop people from making and watching pornography, because it follows the "silly" philosophy that "as long as what I do doesn't harm you personally, I have a right to do it."[70] (Shapiro said that if pornography is legal, there would be no logical reason not to legalize the murder of homeless people, without addressing the potential meaningful distinctions between "having sex" and "killing a person in cold blood.") Shapiro may be The Cool Kid's Philosopher, but on the rare occasions when he actually dips his toe into metaphysics, the results are catastrophic: he argues that atheism is incompatible with the idea of free will because religious people believe that free will is granted by God.[71] ("My beliefs say that your beliefs can't be true therefore they can't be true" is known as "assuming the conclusion.")

But separate from Shapiro's shaky ability to tell the truth and understand simple reasoning, I find his actual moral values somewhat horrifying. These can't be "debunked" or "disproven," of course: they're matters of differing instinct. But I don't share Shapiro's religiously-derived conviction that "any moral system condoning homosexuality" will lead to a "fluid, careless amalgam of values" that will cause America to "suffer the fate of ancient Rome."[72] (Nor do I see any Facts to support this hypothesis.) I'm especially troubled by Shapiro's stance on war. In defending the invasion of Iraq, Shapiro specifically praised imperialism, saying that for the United States, "empire isn't a choice, it's a duty." Nevermind "weapons of mass destruction": maintaining U.S. global power is an end in itself, even if 500,000 Iraqis had to lose their lives a result. Shapiro even endorsed invading countries that do not pose any immediate threat,[73] suggesting that almost any Muslim nation could legitimately be attacked if doing so served the interests of our "global empire":

Did Iraq pose an immediate threat to our nation? Perhaps not. But toppling Saddam Hussein and democratizing Iraq prevent his future ascendance and end his material support for future threats globally. The same principle holds true for Iran, Saudi Arabia, Syria, Egypt, Pakistan and others: Pre-emption is the chief weapon of a global empire. No one said empire was easy, but it is right and good, both for Americans and for the world.

(We could call this the "Better Kill Everyone Just In Case" doctrine.)

What's more, Shapiro doesn't believe that criticizing the American government during a time of war ought to be legal at all. The champion of Free Speech has literally called for reinstating sedition laws. When Al Gore told a Muslim audience that he believed the United States' indiscriminate rounding-up and detention practices after 9/11 were "terrible" and abusive, Shapiro called the statements "treasonable," "seditious," and "outrageous" and demanded that the law respond:

At some point, opposition must be considered disloyal. At some point, the American people must say "enough." At some point, Republicans in Congress must stop delicately tiptoeing with regard to sedition and must pass legislation to prosecute such sedition... Under the Espionage Act of 1917, opponents of World War I were routinely prosecuted, and the Supreme Court routinely upheld their convictions... During World War II, President Franklin D. Roosevelt authorized the internment of hundreds of thousands of Japanese-Americans, as well as allowing the prosecution and/or deportation of those who opposed the war... This is not to argue that every measure taken by the government to prosecute opponents of American wars is just or right or Constitutional. Some restrictions, however, are just and right and Constitutional—and necessary. No war can be won when members of a disloyal opposition are given free reign [sic] to undermine it.[74]

The Wilson administration's crackdown on critics of the war, and the imprisoning of dissidents, were actually a low point in the history of American liberty, and the legal decisions upholding these acts are now discredited. But Shapiro sees this, along with the even more disturbing mass internment of Japanese Americans, as a model for eliminating critics of America's wars. (Although elsewhere Shapiro has called the Supreme Court's decision upholding Japanese detention "evil and disgusting."[75] Consistency, as I have indicated before, is not his forte.)

Having surveyed Shapiro's work, and pointed out the various ways in which he is not terribly logical, not terribly consistent, and not terribly well-informed (in addition to being not terribly humane), it is worth asking why so many people think of him as a "principled" and "brilliant" dismantler of arguments. The answer, it seems to me, is largely that Shapiro is a very confident person who speaks quickly. If he weren't either of these things, he wouldn't seem nearly as intelligent. Because he doesn't care about whether he's right, but about whether he destroys you, he uses a few effective lawyerly tricks: insist that there's "no evidence whatsoever" something is true, demand the other side produce such evidence, and when they stammer "Buh-buh-buh" for two seconds, quickly interrupt with "See? What did I tell you? No evidence." Or, just pluck some random numbers from a study, even if they're totally false or misleading, e.g. "40% of transgender people commit suicide and the risk doesn't go down if they are treated better," which was nonsense but sounded good. Cross-examine people with aggressive questions that confuse them: Are you a moose? I said: *are you a moose?* No? I didn't think so. I rest my case. Use shifting burdens of proof: demand a wealth of statistical evidence before you will admit that black people face any unique hardships, but respond to every criticism of the Israeli government by calling the speaker a "proven" and "undeniable" anti-Semite. Disregard all facts that contradict your case, but insist constantly that the other side despises facts and can't handle the truth. Call your opponents "nasty," "evil," "brainless" "jackasses." All of these techniques work very well, and with them, you, too, can soon be Owning and Destroying your political opponents on camera. (I would probably lose a debate with Ben Shapiro quite badly, as my instinct in public conversations is to try to listen to people.)

Let me tell you why Ben Shapiro actually *aggravates* me. It is not his voice or demeanor, though I understand why others find these characteristics grating. Nor is it the way he inserts references to first-year law school doctrines even when they aren't actually relevant.[76] It is, rather, that Ben Shapiro is lying to his audience, by telling them that he is just a person concerned with the Truth, when the only thing he actually cares about is destroying the left. "Facts don't care about your feelings" is a fine mantra, albeit kind of a dickish one. But it's worthless if you're going to interpret every last fact in the way most favorable to your own preconceptions, if you're going to ignore evidence contrary to your position, and refuse to try to understand what your opponents actually believe. The *New York Times* actually quoted a sensible-sounding ex-Shapiro fan, who said he realized over time that Shapiro was just concerned with convincing other people he was right, rather than actually *being* right. Shapiro is annoying because he claims to love speech and discourse, to believe you should "get to know people... get to know their views... discuss,"[77] but if you're an Arab he's already convinced you're a secret anti-Semite, and if you're a poor black person he doesn't need to know *you* to know that you're culturally dysfunctional.

The encouraging news is that if Ben Shapiro is the sharpest thinker among millennial conservatives, millennial leftists don't have too much to worry about. You may feel as if Shapiro is a Vaporizer of Poor Logic, the Aristotle of our time. You may feel as if he has brutally torn apart every person who has crossed him in public, through his tried and tested technique of speaking extremely quickly until they give up. You may feel that he is brilliant and thoughtful and sincere.

But before you treat these feelings as real, remember that annoying little fact about facts: They don't really care how you feel.

The Press

The Necessity of Credibility

DESPITE HAVING DECISIVELY WON the presidential election by the only measure that counts, the Electoral College, soon afterward Donald Trump decided to call the legitimacy of the entire process into question. "In addition to winning the Electoral College in a landslide, I won the popular vote if you deduct the millions of people who voted illegally," Trump tweeted.[1]

There was instant widespread condemnation of Trump. The *New York Times* ran a headline declaring that Trump's claim had "no evidence." *ABC News* declared it "baseless," *NPR* went with "unfounded."[2] *Politico* called it a "fringe conspiracy theory." Those news outlets whose headlines about the tweet did not contain the word "false" were criticized for failing their responsibility to exercise journalistic scrutiny.[3]

The *Washington Post* swiftly sicced its top fact-checker on Trump. Glenn Kessler denounced Trump's "bogus claim."[4] Kessler gave Trump a lecture on the importance of credibility, writing that since Trump was now "on the verge of becoming president, he needs to be more careful about making wild allegations with little basis in fact, especially if the claim emerged from a handful of tweets and conspiracy-minded websites." Should Trump persist in wildly distorting the truth, he "will quickly find that such statements will undermine his authority on other matters."

The media demanded to know where Trump had come up with such a ridiculous notion. The day after the tweet, Trump spokesman Jason Miller was asked by NPR whether there was any evidence to support the idea that millions of people had voted illegally. But surprisingly enough, Miller did have a source: the *Washington Post*.[5]

In 2014, under the headline "Could non-citizens decide the November election?" the *Post* had run a piece from two social scientists, Jesse Richman and David Earnest, suggesting that illegal voting by non-citizens could be regularly occurring, and could even be prevalent enough to tip elections.[6] As they wrote:

> *How many non-citizens participate in U.S. elections? More than 14 percent of non-citizens in both the 2008 and 2010 samples indicated that they were registered to vote. Furthermore, some of these non-citizens voted. Our best guess, based upon extrapolations from the portion of the sample with a verified vote, is that 6.4 percent of non-citizens voted in 2008 and 2.2 percent of non-citizens voted in 2010.*

Richman and Earnest's thesis was extremely controversial, and was so heavily criticized that the *Post* ultimately published a note preceding the article, pointing out that many objections to the work had been made. But the *Post* never actually retracted or withdrew the piece. It was ironic, then, that when Trump tweeted about millions of illegal voters, the *Washington Post*'s fact-checker chastised him for relying on "conspiracy-minded websites." After all, the conspiracy-minded website in question was the *Post* itself.

After Trump's spokesman pointed out that the tweet was consistent with assertions from the *Washington Post*'s own website, the newspaper's fact-checking department became extremely defensive. They awarded Miller's statement an additional "four Pinnochios."[7] Without actually linking to the *Post*'s original article about voting by non-citizens, fact-checker Michelle Yee Hee Lee tried to claim that the study wasn't *really* in the *Washington Post*. Instead, she said, it: "*was published two years ago in* the Monkey Cage, a political-science blog hosted by *The Washington Post*. *(Note to Trump's staff members: This means you can't say The Washington Post reported this information; you have to cite the Monkey Cage blog.)*"

It was an embarrassing defense. The writers had explicitly said that a reasonable extrapolation from existing data was that 6.4 percent of non-citizens voted in the 2008 election. They had said so in an article that appeared on the *Washington Post*'s website, displayed in exactly the same manner as every single other piece of reportage. And the *Post* still hosted the article, and had only noted that the piece was highly controversial. Yet instead of apologizing for the *Post*'s role in spreading a dubious claim, Lee relied on ridiculous distinctions. She insisted that the *Post* had "hosted" rather than "published" the article. She attempted to enforce a made-up rule, that people *aren't allowed* to cite the article as coming from the *Post*, but must instead cite it as coming from something called the "Monkey Cage," which sounds far less credible. Yet on the article page itself, there is *no* such disclaimer to indicate a distinction between non-*Post*-endorsed "blog posts" and actual *Post* writing, and the words "Monkey Cage" appear in tiny letters beneath the ordinary full-sized *Washington Post* logo. There is nothing to make ordinary readers aware that the *Post* is not responsible for any claims made in these corners of its website.

This is not to say that Trump's claim of massive voter fraud is correct. It *is* false, or at least totally unsubstantiated. We don't have any reason to conclude that millions of people voted illegally. The original study that appeared in the *Post* was criticized for good reason. Attempts to conclude that millions of people voted illegally voted rest on shaky extrapolations, rather than actual positive proof. But it's noteworthy that the *Washington Post* so blithely joined the chorus of those treating Trump's claim as self-evidently bizarre and deranged, while refusing to acknowledge they had themselves helped to give legitimacy to the idea. Of course, it's understandable that the paper would be reluctant to make such a concession. While it doesn't make Trump any less wrong, it does undermine the idea that Trump is entirely reliant on conspiratorial and discredited sources—unless such sources include the *Washington Post*.

But however embarrassing it may be to admit, the imperatives of professional integrity require one to concede that Trump wasn't just making things up out of whole cloth.

THE VOTER FRAUD STORY IS INDICATIVE of a much wider problem with U.S. political media: its attempts to point out Trump's falsehoods are consistently undermined by the media's own lack of credibility on matters of fact. Especially with the rise of "fact-checking" websites, whose analysis is frequently shoddy and dubious, the political media contribute to the exact kind of "post-truth" atmosphere that journalists criticize Trump for furthering.

An interesting and illuminating example of this can be found in the controversy over so-called "fake news." A few weeks after the election, a series of critics lamented the role of "fake" stories during the election cycle. A study by *BuzzFeed* reported that "the top-performing fake election news stories on Facebook generated more engagement than the top stories from major news outlets."[8] A number of commentators saw this as a bad sign for the future democratic governance. Andrew Smith of *The Guardian* suggested that the proliferation of false stories on social media was eroding the very foundations of reality.[9] In the *New York Times*, Nicholas Kristof solemnly concluded that "fake news is gaining ground, empowering nuts and undermining our democracy."[10]

One of the most ominous and sinister warnings about the threat of fake news was found in (again) the *Washington Post*. In late November, the *Post*'s Craig Timberg produced a detailed report alleging that much of the "fake news" on the internet was, in fact, a carefully-crafted Russian propaganda effort designed to erode Western governments through the spread of damaging disinformation.[11] The *Post* cited a "nonpartisan group of researchers" known as "PropOrNot," who had "identifie[d] more than 200 websites as routine peddlers of Russian propaganda during the election season, with combined audiences of at least 15 million Americans." Many news stories on the internet, the *Post* suggested, were not news at all, but lies propagated by Russia in order to further its own state interests. The *Post* concluded that while there "is no way to know whether the Russian campaign proved decisive in electing Trump… researchers portray it as part of a broadly effective strategy of sowing distrust in U.S. democracy and its leaders."

The report landed like a bombshell. It was soon the most-read piece on the *Post*'s website, was covered by *NPR,* and was being promoted by prominent journalists and commentators as a crucial investigation.[12] But subsequent scrutiny of the *Post*'s reportage revealed that its evidence for a Russian conspiracy was thin. PropOrNot's "list" of "Russian propaganda" websites targeted a number of totally innocuous independent media outlets, including left-wing outlet *Truthdig* and popular financial blog *Naked Capitalism.*[13] It turned out that to be classified as a "Russian propaganda outlet," one needn't actually be associated with Vladimir Putin or the Russian government. For the purposes of making the PropOrNot blacklist, it was sufficient that a media organization be "useful" to the Russian state. By that expansive criterion, plenty of ordinary political criticism and analysis (such as that found on *Truthdig*) could be classified as "propaganda." After all, anything critical of the U.S. government *could* be considered helpful to the Russian government. The *Post*'s allegations therefore rested on a dangerous premise: the idea that if one can't prove one isn't helping the Russian government, then one is helping the Russian government.

Furthermore, the PropOrNot organization itself was highly mysterious and of dubious reliability. Its Twitter feed regularly accused its critics of being "fascists" and "Putinists." All of its "researchers" were anonymous, and it was unclear what credentials or expertise they had, or who they themselves might be funded by. Thus the *Washington Post* tarred a series of legitimate independent media outlets as tools of the Russian state, based on the word of an unknown anonymous source.

The *Post* received intensive criticism over the report. The *Nation* said it had "smeared working journalists as agents of the Kremlin" by offering up a "McCarthyite blacklist."[14] Adrian Chen of the *New Yorker* called it "propaganda."[15] Glenn Greewnald and Ben Norton of *The Intercept* said the *Post* had offered "obviously reckless and unproven allegations… fundamentally shaped by shoddy, slothful journalistic tactics."[16]

In *Rolling Stone,* Matt Taibbi called it an "astonishingly lazy report" and said that "most high school papers wouldn't touch sources like these."[17] (Though *Rolling Stone* may not have been the optimal venue for launching a denunciation of substandard reporting using unreliable sources.[18]) Yet confronted with evidence that it may have reported a story riddled with falsehoods, the *Post* (again) refused to admit error. "I'm sorry, I can't comment about stories I've written for the *Post,*" replied reporter Craig Timberg. ("Can't," as is so often the case, meaning "won't.")

The irony here was that in writing about the spread of so-called "fake news," the *Post* had itself produced fake news. After all, wasn't this entirely the sort of story about which journalists were panicking? A poorly-sourced series of outlandish allegations, that brought harm to people's reputations without actually providing proof of wrongdoing?

The *Post*'s catastrophically bad reporting on "fake news" illustrated an unfortunate tendency of the American political press. When it comes to news about Russia or Vladimir Putin, all the usual standards of skepticism and caution (as one might apply to claims made by Donald Trump) seem to disappear. In October of 2016, Franklin Foer of *Slate* wrote a story alleging that a Trump Organization computer server was sending secret communications to Russia.[19] (Amusingly, it turned out that the server was routinely sending the Russians spam promotional flyers advertising Trump hotels.[20]) *Mother Jones* published quotes from an anonymous former intelligence official, claiming Donald Trump was a secret Russian agent.[21] After Hillary Clinton's loss, Paul Krugman became especially paranoid and unhinged, tweeting that James Comey and Vladimir Putin had "installed" Trump as president,[22] and declaring that the FBI was essentially in "alliance" with Putin.[23]

Such language almost seems a throwback to the 1950s, likewise a time when sinister Russian conspirators lurked around every corner and beneath every bed.[24] Most of the "Russians are coming" stories were thinly sourced or based on unsupported quotes from anonymous government insiders. Consider this one from (...again) *The Washington Post* entitled "If you're even asking if Russia hacked the election, Russia got what it wanted."[25] The writer argued that the Russian government had a conscious strategy to disrupt Americans' faith in their systems of governance, and that:

> ...[the] strategy manifested itself in the Russians' strongly alleged involvement in promoting "fake news" and disseminating hacked emails stolen from the Democratic National Committee. These emails hurt Hillary Clinton's campaign and weakened Americans' trust in the Democratic primary.

Note the key phrase: *strongly alleged*. When it comes to Russian meddling, it doesn't matter whether the *proof* is strong. It matters whether the *allegation* is strong. Once we have a strong allegation that Russia is doing something nefarious, we can treat it as fact. The press's treatment of Trump/Putin stories was little short of deranged. One can ponder how much of this was driven by loyalty to Hillary Clinton among certain journalists, versus how much was the sensationalistic pursuit of eye-catching stories. Either way, whenever the subject of Russia comes up, the press has a tendency to blow even the flimsiest rumor into the stuff of airport espionage thrillers. "Vladimir Putin has a plan for destroying the West—and that plan looks a lot like Donald Trump," wrote Foer in *Slate*.[26] Headlines like "The secret to Trump: He's really a Russian oligarch"[27] and "The Kremlin's candidate"[28] abounded.

But the mainstream media's looseness with facts goes well beyond stories about Russia and Trump. It's also furthered by "explainer" websites like *Vox*, which blur the distinction between (liberal) commentary and neutral empirical analysis.[29] Particularly pernicious is the rise of "fact-checking" websites, which are ostensibly dedicated to promoting objective truth over eye-of-the-beholder lies, but which often simply serve as mouthpieces for centrist orthodoxies, thereby further delegitimizing the entire notion of "fact" itself. As *Current Affairs* has previously argued at length, websites like PolitiFact frequently disguise opinion and/or bullshit as neutral, data-based inquiry.[30]

This happens in a couple of ways. First, such websites frequently produce meaningless statistics, such as trying to measure the percentage of a candidate's statements that are false. PolitiFact constantly spreads its statistics about how X percent of Trump or Clinton's statements are rated false, declining to mention the fact that this statistic is empty of any content, since the statements that are evaluated haven't been randomly selected. The centrist biases of fact-checkers also affect their decision-making. Fact-checkers have, for example, insisted that it was wrong to say Hillary Clinton wanted to get rid of the 2nd Amendment. But this isn't a "factual" dispute at all. It depends on one's interpretation of the 2nd Amendment's essential meaning, something that varies based on one's personal political values.

Efforts to soften critiques of the Clintons were persistent features of fact-checks during the election. For example, fact-checkers have insisted that a factory in Haiti that the Clintons helped build was not a sweatshop, despite the fact that wages in Haitian factories are under a dollar per hour and workers have complained regularly of exploitative and abusive treatment.[31] Conservative writer Sean Davis similarly encountered the topsy-turvy world of Clinton Foundation "fact checking."[32] When Davis wrote an article about the small percentage of its funding the Clinton Foundation spends on charitable grants (as opposed to its own in-house programming), PunditFact argued that the claim, "while technically true" was nevertheless "mostly false." Davis was understandably puzzled by the idea that something could be rated false despite "technically" being true.

But this happens frequently on fact-checking websites. Fact-checkers claim that while claims may literally be true, they're nevertheless false for giving "misleading" impressions or missing crucial context. For example, when Carly Fiorina claimed that she had gone from being a secretary to being a CEO, her claim was given "Three Pinnochios" by *The Washington Post*, even though Fiorina had indeed (by the *Post*'s own admission) been a secretary before she was a CEO.[33] The *Post* reasoned that while Fiorina was literally telling the truth, her statement was nevertheless false since she had advantages in life that other secretaries did not have.

The fact-checkers might think that by going beyond the literal meaning of statements, and evaluating the impressions they leave, they are in fact doing a greater service to truth and reality. In fact, they are opening the door to a far more subjective kind of work, because evaluating perceptions requires a lot more interpretation than evaluating the basic truth or falsity of a statement. It thereby creates far more room for bias and error to work their way into the analysis.

A good example of the perils of fact-checking can be found in Donald Trump's claims over birds and wind turbines. Trump doesn't like wind turbines, and frequently rails against them on Twitter and in speeches.[34] One of his favorite points to make is that wind turbines kill birds, specifically eagles. At one point, Trump said the following:

> *There are places for wind but if you go to various places in California, wind is killing all of the eagles... You know if you shoot an eagle, if you kill an eagle, they want to put you in jail for five years. And yet the windmills are killing hundreds and hundreds of eagles. ... They're killing them by the hundreds.*

This invited a vigorous fact-check from PolitiFact, who rated the claim "Mostly False" and said that Trump was "inflating" wind turbine deaths.[35] Yet wind turbines *do* kill over 100 eagles per year in California, as PolitiFact admitted. Furthermore, eagle deaths from turbines are such a serious concern to animal welfare advocates. Save The Eagles International has reported "millions" of wind turbine deaths[36] and the Audubon Society has warned that wind turbines, while good for the environment, come with "hundreds of thousands" of unnecessary bird deaths.[37]

Here we see how bias can affect fact-checks. Trump was clearly correct that wind turbines are a serious threat to birds, including endangered ones. Rating him "mostly false" depends on giving the least charitable possible interpretation to his words, suggesting that he meant hundreds were dying *within California per year* (which he did not say). And since it's actually about 116 eagles *within California per year*, this would be a slight exaggeration. But note: Trump's underlying *point* is still clearly valid. Wind turbines kill lots of birds. The Audubon Society is concerned. Trump isn't making this issue up, it exists and it's serious, and his sources are perfectly sound. The context and implications of Trump's remarks make them true, even if his statistic is marginally off. But while context matters if it can help prove Carly Fiorina's point is invalid, it *doesn't* matter if it can help prove Trump's point is valid.

It's clear why the fact-checkers wouldn't want to admit Trump's point about birds and wind turbines is a good one. First, it sounds ridiculous, even though it happens to be true. Second, it's Trump, and sober-minded centrists don't like admitting that Trump is right about anything. Third, it unsettles Democratic centrist political convictions, because it seems to undermine the case for green energy. (Though of course it doesn't. One can argue that wind turbines are worth the cost in bird-lives. Or one can argue that wind turbines should both exist *and* be made safer, as the Audubon Society does. There is no reason to be afraid of the facts.) But by refusing to admit that Trump is ever right, or at least has something resembling a point, fact-checkers render themselves untrustworthy.

When recently asked about Trump's claims of voter fraud, Trump surrogate Scottie Hughes gave a statement about the nature of truth that shocked many people:

> *One thing that has been interesting this entire campaign season to watch, is that people that say facts are facts—they're not really facts. Everybody has a way—it's kind of like looking at ratings, or looking at a glass of half-full water. Everybody has a way of interpreting them to be the truth, or not truth. There's no such thing, unfortunately, anymore as facts. And so Mr. Trump's tweet, amongst a certain crowd—a large part of the population—are truth.*[38]

Politico reporter Glenn Thrush called Hughes' remark "absolutely outrageous." After all, Hughes was suggesting that there was no such thing as objective reality, that Trump's claims of voter fraud were just as legitimate as the claims of those who had "reason" and "evidence" on their side.

Indeed, Hughes' remark is somewhat terrifying. (Although it doesn't sound particularly conservative. In fact, it rather resembles a mainstream liberal belief: that ideas of "truth" and "facts" are matters of interpretation, shaped by our personal identities rather than any "objective" reality. Hughes almost sounds as if she has been reading Foucault, and is on the verge of concluding that truth is little more than a series of differing narratives reflecting existing power relations.) If Hughes' perspective were taken to its logical extreme, it would mean that every form of bigotry and error was just as legitimate as its opposite. Such a world is nightmarish.

But before getting too sanctimonious, journalists should question their own role in giving this perspective a boost. The garbage churned out regularly by CNN and *Slate* may be better than Trump's tweets, but it is not *that* much better. And by failing to show humility about their own ability to generate truth, and themselves being highly detached from the real world, talking-head pundits and biased "data-based" journalists may be helping to create the "post-truth" environment, by robbing words like "true," "false," and "fact" of their meaning. By conjuring phony statistics (like "percentage of false statements") and treating highly subjective and interpretive judgments as if they are Just The Facts, the press steadily erodes the credibility it will need in order to effectively hold Trump accountable. Kellyanne Conway was correct to point out that the single biggest piece of "fake news" was the story that Trump couldn't win.[39] It's very difficult for places like, say, *BuzzFeed* to hold forth on the necessity of accuracy in journalism, when *BuzzFeed* itself had reported in 2014 that Trump "plainly has no interest in actually running for office."[40] Trump has actually established some formidable credentials as a truth-teller against his critics in the press. After all, they were the ones telling him that his confidence of victory was a delusion.

In fact, *BuzzFeed* even published a lengthy profile mocking Trump-supporting commentator Bill Mitchell for being "post-truth" and "post-math."[41] To *BuzzFeed*, Mitchell was laughably divorced from reality for his belief that "enthusiasm" was a far more reliable predictor of electoral success than polls. Mitchell was treated with open contempt by data obsessives like Nate Silver, for his failure to understand "basic math."

But Mitchell turned out to be right. This raises an important question: if Trump and his supporters were labeled "post-truth" or "anti-facts" for the act of ignoring polls, but they turned out to be correct, then why should allegations of being "post-truth" or "anti-facts" be taken seriously? By using these phrases with overconfident abandon against Trump supporters, even when they don't necessarily apply, members of the press diminish the currency of words like "truth."

None of this is to suggest that the mainstream media is somehow "just as bad" as fake news from conspiracy theory websites. What's reported in the *New York Times* frequently does bear a general resemblance to the truth. (Though not always, and one should never forget the *Times'* uncritical repetition of government claims about weapons of mass destruction in the lead-up to the Iraq War.[42]) The point is, rather, that even a single falsehood or misrepresentation can permanently destroy one's credibility, and being trustworthy requires *always* being honest and self-critical. If phrases like "post-truth" are used cavalierly, they can become insignificant. If "fact-checks" are not really fact-checks, but centrist opinion pieces, the word "fact" comes to connote "the highly contentious views of people who call themselves fact-checkers" rather than anything about *reality* or *the world as it actually exists*.

Those who say Donald Trump dwells in a "post-truth" realm are not wrong. He lies a hell of a lot, and misrepresents a hell of a lot more. But in order for the "post-truth" charge to be taken seriously, one must be careful and reliable in calling out "lies." And one must be serious in understanding why people become conspiracy theorists in the first place. If the press *is* unaccountable, condescending, and secretive, it won't be believed, even if it's right. (Similarly, one of the reasons that so many wild conspiracy theories develop around Hillary Clinton is that— as even her supporters admit—she is extremely secretive.[43] As a purely practical matter, if you act like you've got something to hide, people will assume you do. And they're not irrational to make that inference.) If people are heading for fake news, then it is urgently necessary to figure out how to get them back. One won't do that by continuing to do the same thing, such as continuing to spew biased and speculative punditry.

This is a story about glass houses and stones: in order to convince people not to believe in disreputable sources, you must first give them reason to believe that you yourself are reputable.

For progressives, having a reliable and trustworthy media means not being afraid of uncomfortable truths. If wind turbines kill a bunch of eagles, let's have the guts to admit it. If the Clintons are actually pretty noxious, let's be perfectly honest about their failings. If Trump is right about something, then he's right. And if he is wrong about something, but he read it in the *Washington Post*, then let's admit that this reflects worse on the *Washington Post* than on Trump. The truth is a precious thing, and it should never, ever be distorted for partisan reasons. Being credible means being self-critical, and trying to build a press that people can depend on to help them sort truth from lies.

Having a media people can actually trust should be a fundamental goal of Trump opponents. Currently, people don't trust the mainstream media. And the first thing the media must do is acknowledge that part of that mistrust is entirely rational and reasonable. After that, building true credibility will at the very least require a major rethink of how ordinary political media do business. They will have to interrogate their assumptions more, defend or revise their work in response to criticisms, and get serious about truth, fairness, and accountability. They will need to abandon the assumption, commonly held, that if people on "both sides" are mad at you, you must be doing your job well. And they will need to be extremely cautious in their factual assertions. If I go around asserting that Trump's attitude toward polls is "post-truth," then report that Trump is a possible Russian spy, I will have few grounds to complain when Trump's supporters decide to get their news from alt-right conspiracy websites instead.

Yet it is telling that long after the election, the people who were most wrong during the campaign[44] are still producing voluminous commentary.[45] No outlet that wanted to regain trust and build audiences would be keeping such people on its staff. But "pundit tenure" is powerful. Thus is also likely that the quest for credible media will necessitate the creation of *new* media. *CNN* and the *Washington Post* have never shown a particularly encouraging capacity for introspection and self-improvement, and it's unlikely that they're contemplating major internal overhauls in their mission and accountability practices. Their institutional imperatives consist, after all, largely of seeking views and clicks. For them, the 2016 election was a success rather than a failure. A lot of people, after all, tuned in. Why should they do things any differently? Thus it would be useful to have fresh, truly independent outlets, ones that disclose their biases, are transparent in their methods, and are constantly trying to improve themselves rather than simply pursuing the same useless sensationalism and empty horse-race punditry. If one's only options are *Breitbart* on the one hand, and *The Washington Post* on the other, readers lose no matter what.

Can The New York Times Weddings Section Be Justified?

AT THIS POINT, the weddings section of the *New York Times* is almost beyond ridicule. It has been mocked endlessly for its Ivy-infatuated elitism. It has inspired a fake Twitter account ("The bride is willing to overlook her groom's public school education, saying, 'sometimes you take a chance–the heart wants what it wants.'"[1]) and even a full book of parodies.[2] Placing one's wedding announcement in the *Times* has become "a sacred and important ritual that rich people have been performing for years," something the newspaper itself has even acknowledged.[3]

David Brooks, in *Bobos in Paradise*, described the upper-crust values that saturate the Vows section:

> *When you look at the Times weddings page, you can almost feel the force of the mingling SAT scores. It's Dartmouth Marries Berkeley, MBA weds PhD, Fulbright hitches with Rhodes, Lazard Frères joins with CBS, and summa cum laude embraces summa cum laude (you rarely see a summa settling for a magna–the tension in such a marriage would be too great). The Times emphasizes four things about a person–college degrees, graduate degrees, career path, and parents' profession–for these are the markers of upscale Americans today...*[4]

Everyone knows, then, that the Weddings section is disproportionately stuffed with members of the elite. In fact, this can even be proven mathematically. The "Wedding Crunchers" search engine collects all of the data from *Times* Vows entries, allowing one to carefully break down the demographics of featured weddings.[5] With it, one can see "the omnipresence of the Ivy League, lawyers, and Wall Street," and changes in the composition of the upper class over time (the rise of tech companies, for instance).[6] The numbers confirm that a "gay Princeton grad from Davis Polk" has an unusually high chance of being featured in the *Times* relative to the number of gay Princeton Davis Polk attorneys in the general population.[7]

The intricate application procedure for the Weddings strongly implies what the *Times* is looking for.[8] The Vows department requests that those who wish to have their nuptials featured submit "addresses, schooling and occupations," plus "noteworthy awards the couple have received, as well as charitable activities and special achievements." The also require "information on the residences and occupations of the couple's parents." The section's editor has described the decision-making process: "the basic premise is that we're looking for people who have achievements. It doesn't matter what field these achievements are in."[9]

Interestingly, the editor's words imply a sort of egalitarianism. You can be in any field you like, so long as you have achievements. And indeed, as the Wedding Crunchers data confirms, this represents a shift from the old *Times* philosophy. Before, the weddings section was a "society page" for the WASP elite, heavily featuring alumni of the same few boarding schools. These days, featured couples are more diverse, especially in race and sexual orientation.

Yet it's clear that this equality is extremely limited. It's still the case that the weddings section disproportionately focuses on the wealthy and highly-educated. Rarely are couples without college degrees featured, and prestigious universities predominate. To argue that the page has diversified is tantamount to saying "Why, we feature lots of different kinds of people. There are transgender Harvard grads, Hispanic Harvard grads...."

Here's the important question: if everyone admits that the *New York Times* Weddings section is disproportionately weighted toward the wealthy and highly-educated, how can it possibly be justified? How is it actually acceptable for an ostensibly liberal newspaper to conclude that wealthy, well-educated people's lives are more interesting and worth more attention than non-wealthy, less-educated people? Everyone laughs about the Weddings section, even the *Times* itself. But joking aside, isn't it morally indefensible to treat people as newsworthy in accordance with their elite social status?

There are several replies the Vows editors might make. One is to return to that theme of "achievement." After all, they do not care which field you are in, so long as you have "achieved." But we should note, first, the use of the term "field." "We don't care which field you're in" means "we don't care if you're a psychologist, a hedge fund manager, or an American Studies professor." But implicitly, "fields" refer to the sort of occupations that require advanced degrees. Is "working in a bodega" a field? Unloading trucks? Thus the kind of things the *Times* counts as "achievements" follow particular, narrow definitions of meritocratic success. Getting a promotion at Target isn't an achievement. Getting your electrician's license isn't an achievement. Serving honorably in the military isn't an achievement. Being the first in your family to get your associate's degree isn't an achievement. By viewing "achievement" through the prism of elite values, the *Times* implicitly dismisses non-elite achievements as being without worth, thereby diminishing the lives of the non-wealthy.

A defense that the *Times* looks for "achievements," then, only further confirms that the paper has a narrow view of what constitutes accomplishment, and of whose lives are worth writing about. You're worth writing about if you grow up on Martha's Vineyard and get an advanced degree in theology at Boston College while wearing a three-piece suit.[10] If you work at a Walgreens, you are unworthy of note.

Again, everyone knows that the *Times* thinks this. But how is that acceptable? The *Times* weddings section might be a trivial piece of fluff, without any serious social consequence. But it's odd for the nation's paper of record to have a little feature at the back that just screams "rich people's lives are worth more."

The *Times* might point to its occasional inclusion of a non-traditional wedding announcement. But these are the exceptions that prove the rule. In 2009, the *Times* featured the wedding announcement of two former drug addicts who had met at a Narcotics Anonymous meeting. The paper immediately received negative feedback from readers "who said they regarded the weddings pages as a place for upstanding people with good educations who come from good families."[11] One wrote: "Are we telling young adults it is alright to waste half their lives in a drug stupor and somehow it will magically work out?" From both the *Times*' decision to include the announcement and the readers' reaction to it, we can see that a *Times* wedding listing is not simply a reporting of an average cross-section of people getting married, but follows a conception of worth.

The *Times* does insist that its announcements are more inclusive these days:

> As the announcements under Woletz have become more diverse, parents like a union electrician, a retired firefighter and even a courier have popped up beside orthopedic surgeons and authors.[12]

But the defense only confirms the objection. If "even a courier" is the way couriers are thought of, then we are still dwelling in a world that sees couriers as something odd and foreign, rather than a basic occupation that people have. The *Times* attempts occasionally to inoculate itself against the charges of elitism by sprinkling an "unusual" person here and there. But these are such obvious contrasts to the rest of the page that they only confirm its general character.

Of course, the *Times* could always fall back on that classic journalist's cop-out: we're just giving the readers what they want. But this defense should never be taken seriously. (It's often deployed to justify giving more coverage to atrocities committed against Westerners than to those committed against non-Westerners.) The existence of a market for something cannot justify its existence. To test the absurd extreme of the principle: if I start a magazine called *Kitten Stompers Monthly*, and someone objects to my publishing a magazine about stomping kittens to death, it is no defense for me to say "Well, I'm just giving my readers what they want." Of course I'm giving my readers what they want. But my readers clearly have despicable values, so why would that exonerate me?

The majority of New Yorkers (like the majority of Americans generally) do not have college degrees.[13] Yet almost without exception, those featured in the *New York Times* weddings section have attended college, often a highly prestigious college. Let's be clear what this means: a paper run by liberals, who would profess themselves averse to inequality, openly treats most of the population as insignificant. Now, perhaps this is not unexpected. Nobody, at this point, is surprised at the hypocrisy and elitism of the *New York Times*. But how do they defend it? How can they possibly believe themselves progressive while continuing to publish something that so openly views wealth and education as markers of virtue? How can they justify seeing "getting a Yale anthropology degree" as an accomplishment but not "working a physically-demanding job"?

My hunch is that the *Times* staff all implicitly do feel as if going to a prestigious university is more of an accomplishment than becoming a shift supervisor at a Costco. But my hunch is also that few of them would feel comfortable admitting that they feel this way. Yet if they really do believe it's acceptable to prioritize certain people's lives over others, they should be willing to say so, and openly state the reasons why, as well as their case for how this comports with their liberal values.

The ugly hypocrisy of the *Times* wedding page has been pointed out before. In 2002, journalist Timothy Noah called for its abolition, since it is "built on the false assumption that the weddings of wealthy non-celebrities constitute news."[14] (Noah's case was undercut by the fact that he admitted having lobbied heavily to have his own wedding included in the section.[15]) But for some reason, no amount of scorn seems to induce any amount of shame. Yet it is shameful. It's completely trivial. But it's shameful. And the *Times* should either justify the Weddings Section, by explaining why it's acceptable to be an elitist, or get rid of it entirely.

How The Economist Thinks

CURRENT AFFAIRS IS WELL-KNOWN for its signature "Death to *The Economist*" bumper stickers, which have greatly improved the expressive capacities of the American motorist when it comes to demonstrating a discerning taste in periodicals. But occasionally, members of the public send us adverse feedback on our vehicular adhesive strips. "What," they ask, "is your problem with *The Economist*? Why be so rude? How can you wish death upon a perfectly innocuous and respectable British political magazine?" *Current Affairs*, it is said, is behaving badly. We are being unfair.

It's true that death is an extreme consequence to wish on another magazine, even if the magazine in question is *The Economist*. And sometimes I do wonder whether the sentiment goes a bit too far, whether it would be more fair to wish something like "a minor drop in circulation" or "a financially burdensome libel suit" on our London competitor.

But then I remember what *The Economist* actually is, and what it stands for, and what it writes. And I realize that death is the only option. A just world would not have *The Economist* in it, and the death of *The Economist* is thus an indispensable precondition for the creation of a just world.

In his deliciously biting 1991 examination of the role of *The Economist* in shaping American elite opinion, James Fallows tried to figure out exactly what was so repellent about the magazine's approach to the seeking of truth.[1] Fallows puzzled over the fact that American intellectuals hold a disproportionate amount of respect for *The Economist*'s judgment and reporting, even though the magazine is produced by imperious 20-something Oxbridge graduates who generally know little about the subjects on which they so confidently opine. Fallows suggested that *The Economist*'s outsized reputation in the U.S. was partially attributable to Americans' lingering colonial insecurity, their ongoing belief that despite all evidence to the contrary, British people are inherently intelligent and trustworthy. (I have exploited this delusion throughout my life.) Fallows even dug up an embarrassingly snooty quote from Robert Reich, boasting about his sensible preference for British news: "I, for one, don't get my economics news from *Newsweek*. I rely on *The Economist*—published in London."

But the most damning case put by Fallows is not that *The Economist* is snobbish and preys on the intellectual self-doubt of Americans through its tone of Oxonian omniscience. (Though it is, and it does.) Fallows also reveals the core flaw of the magazine's actual reportage: thanks to its reflexive belief in the superiority of free markets, it is an unreliable guide to the subjects on which it reports. Because its writers will bend the truth in order to defend capitalism, you can't actually trust what you read in *The Economist*. And since journalism you can't trust is worthless, *The Economist* is worthless.

Fallows gives an example of how reality gets filtered as it passes through the magazine and reaches *The Economist*'s readers:

> *Last summer, a government man who helps make international economic policy told me (with a thoughtful expression) he was reading "quite an interesting new book" about the stunning economic rise of East Asia. "The intriguing thing is, it shows that market forces really were the explanation!" he exclaimed in delight. "Industrial policies and government tinkering didn't matter that much." By chance, I had just read the very book—Governing the Market by Robert Wade. This detailed study, citing heaps of evi-*

dence, had in fact concluded nearly the opposite: that East Asian governments had tinkered plenty, directly benefiting industry far beyond anything "market forces" could have done. I knew something else about the book: The Economist magazine had just reviewed it and mischaracterized its message almost exactly the way the government official had. Had he actually read the book? Maybe, but somehow I have my doubts... The crucial paragraph of The Economist review—the one that convinced my friend the official, and presumably tens of thousands of other readers, that Wade's years of research supported the magazine's preexisting world view—was this: "The [Asian] dragons differed from other developing countries in avoiding distortions to exchange rates and other key prices, as much as in their style of intervening. Intervention is part of the story—but perhaps the smaller part. That being so, Mr. Wade's prescriptions seem unduly heavy on intervention, and unduly light on getting prices right." These few lines are a marvel of Oxbridge glibness, and they deserve lapidary study. Notice the all-important word "perhaps." Without the slightest hint of evidence, it serves to dismiss everything Wade has painstakingly argued in the book. It clears the way for: "That being so . . . " What being so? That someone who has taken a First [at Oxbridge] can wave off the book's argument with "perhaps"?

Here, then, is the problem with the magazine: readers are consistently given the impression, regardless of whether it is true, that unrestricted free market capitalism is a Thoroughly Good Thing, and that sensible and pragmatic British intellectuals have vouched for this position. The nuances are erased, reality is fudged, and *The Economist* helps its American readers pretend to have read books by telling them things that the books don't actually say.

Now, you may think that Fallows' example tells us very little. It was, after all, one small incident. He spoke to one man, who had gotten one wrong impression from one faulty *Economist* review. Perhaps we were dealing with an exceptional case. Presumably Fallows encountered this kind of thinking regularly, but perhaps he's singling out the minor part of the magazine's otherwise-stellar reportage and reviews.

Let me, then, add a data point of my own. Until last week, I had not read *The Economist* since high school, where debate nerds subscribed to it in order to quote it to each other and prove themselves informed and worldly. But a few days ago, I was trying to compile a list of news outlets that *Current Affairs* staff should regularly glance at, in order to make sure we are considering a broad and ecumenical set of perspectives on contemporary geopolitics. I remembered *Current Affairs'* ostensible rivalry with *The Economist*, and thought it might be a good idea to at least read the damn thing if we're going to be selling bumper stickers calling for its execution. I am nothing if not open-minded and fair.

What, then, did I find upon navigating over to *The Economist*'s website? The very first article on the page was a piece called "A selective scourge: Inside the opioid epidemic," subtitled "Deaths from the drugs say more about markets than about white despair."[2] Its theme is classic *Economist*: the American opioid epidemic is not occurring because global capitalism is ruining lives, but is the tragic outcome of the operation of people's individual preferences. A quote:

> It has even been argued that the opioid epidemic and the Trump vote in 2016 are branches of the same tree. Anne Case and Angus Deaton, both economists at Princeton University, roll opioid deaths together with alcohol poisonings and suicides into a measure they call "deaths of despair". White working-class folk feel particular anguish, they explain, having suffered wrenching economic and social change. As an explanation for the broad trend, that might be right. Looked at more closely, though, the terrifying rise in opioid deaths in the past few years seems to have less to do with white working-class despair and more to do with changing drug markets. Distinct criminal networks and local drug cultures largely explain why some parts of America are suffering more than others.

25 years after Fallows wrote his *Economist* takedown, not a single

thing has changed. The 1991 *Economist* used the meaningless phrase "that being so" to dismiss an author's entire argument and conclude that markets should be left alone. The 2017 *Economist* concedes that "as an explanation for the broad trend," economic despair "might be right," but that "looked at more closely," drug deaths are not about despair. "Looked at more closely" functions here the same way that "that being so" did: it concedes the point, but then pretends it hasn't. After all, if despair might be the correct "explanation for the broad trend," what does it mean to say that "looked at more closely" the trend isn't the result of despair at all? It's either an explanation or it isn't, and if it doesn't hold when "looked at more closely," then it wouldn't be "right" as an explanation for the broad trend.

What happens when *The Economist* looks at opioid deaths "more closely" is simple obfuscation. The magazine shows that opioid use looks different in different parts of the United States, because the drugs themselves differ. For example, when it comes to heroin, "Addicts west of the Mississippi mostly use Mexican brown-powder or black-tar heroin, which is sticky and viscous, whereas eastern users favour Colombian white-powder heroin." Note the subtle invocation of "free choice" language: heroin users in the Eastern United States "favour" Colombian heroin. It's not just that this happens to be the available form of the drug; it's also that they have a kind of rational preference for a particular form of heroin. Every subtle rhetorical step is toward exonerating capitalism for people's suffering, and blaming the people and their own foolish choices within a free and fair marketplace.

The Economist's article on the opioid epidemic offers some legitimately interesting observations about regional variation in types of drug use. Increases in deaths have been concentrated more heavily in places where drugs are available in easier-to-ingest forms. The trouble is that *The Economist* argues that this implies the idea in the article's subtitle, that deaths from drugs "say more about markets than white despair." That's just a conclusion that doesn't follow from the provided evidence. The magazine's own charts show that drug use of all kinds has been rising, meaning that the differences between usage types can't account for the broad trend. The drug type differences can tell us why different places may experience differing levels of rises in opiate deaths, but they can't tell us why so many people are now drugging themselves who weren't before. And we can't answer that question without considering economic class; opiate addiction has disproportionately risen among poor white people, meaning we have to find a way to understand what specific race- and poverty-correlated factors are causing the change.

The Economist is not, therefore, an honest examiner of the facts. It is constantly at pains not to risk conclusions that may hurt the case for unregulated markets. This tendency reached its absurd apotheosis in the magazine's infamous 2014 review of Edward Baptist's *The Half Has Never Been Told: Slavery and the Making of American Capitalism*. The magazine objected to Baptist's brutal depiction of the slave trade, saying the book did not qualify as "an objective history of slavery" because "almost all the blacks in his book are victims, almost all the whites villains." When outraged readers pointed out that this is because the victims of slavery tended to be black, *The Economist* retracted the review. But as Baptist observed in response, there was a reason why the magazine felt the need to mitigate the evils of slavery.[3] Baptist's book portrayed slavery as an integral part of the history of capitalism. As he wrote: "If slavery was profitable—and it was—then it creates an unforgiving paradox for the moral authority of markets—and market fundamentalists. What else, today, might be immoral and yet profitable?" The implications of Baptist's work would have unsettling implications for *The Economist*. They would damn the foundations of the very Western free enterprise system that the magazine is devoted to championing. Thus *The Economist* needed to find a way to soften its verdict on slavery. (It was not the first time they had done so, either. In a tepid review of Greg Grandin's *The Empire of Necessity* with the hilariously offensive title of "Slavery: Not Black or White," the magazine lamented that "the horrors in Mr Grandin's history are unrelenting." And the magazine' long tradition of defending misery stretches back to the 19th century, when it blamed the Irish potato famine on irresponsible decisions made by destitute peasants.[4])

Why, then, have a "Death to *The Economist*" bumper sticker? Because *The Economist* would justify any horror perpetrated in the name of the market and Western Enlightenment values, even to the extent of rationalizing the original great and brutal crime on which our prosperity was founded. Its tone, as Fallows observed, is one "so cocksure of its rightness and superiority that it would be a shame to freight it with mere fact." And the problem with that is not that *The Economist* is cocksure (I of all people should have no objection to cocksureness in periodicals), but that it doesn't wish to be freighted with inconvenient truths. The fact that *The Economist* has a clear set of ideological commitments means that it will pull the wool over its readers' eyes in the service of those commitments, which saps it of intellectual worth. It will lie to you about the contents of a book by waving them away with a "that being so." Or it will reassure you that capitalism has nothing to do with opiate deaths, by asserting without evidence that when "looked at more closely," drug addiction is "less" about despair. It will fudge, fumble, and fool you in any way it can, if it means keeping markets respectable. And it will play on your insecurity as a resident of a former British colony to convince you that all intelligent people believe that the human misery created in "economically free" societies is necessary and just. It will give intellectual cover to barbarous crimes, and its authors won't even have the guts to sign their names to their work. Instead, they will pretend to be the disembodied voice of God, whispering in your ear that you'll never impress England until you fully deregulate capitalism.

The Hierarchy of Victims

MOST PEOPLE BELIEVE that the media is biased and untrustworthy. A Gallup poll taken last year showed that the percentage of Americans who believe the mass media can be trusted "to report the news fully, accurately and fairly" has been steadily dropping for 20 years.[1] Now only 32% of people have confidence in the news, with the number being even lower among certain demographic groups (such as Republicans, who are at 14%). That lack of confidence is simultaneously worrying and reassuring. It's worrying, because in a world where people shun mainstream information sources, they may be more susceptible to lies and conspiracies. Yet it's also reassuring, because it means people are being quite sensible. They're right to believe that the mass media has no credibility and is unreliable, because both of those things are true. Of course, they're wrong if they think Alex Jones is better. But hating CNN is a healthy and rational perspective.

Even though everyone can agree the media sucks and is biased, people still disagree on the *ways* it is biased. Republicans think it has a liberal bias (which is true, although since the spawn of FOX News, right-wing media has more than successfully made up for this). People who believe in chemtrails believe it has a bias in favor of covering government mind control projects. Donald Trump thinks it has an anti-Donald Trump bias (also partly true, though the media also loves Trump because he brings ratings). And those of us on the left correctly perceive that the news's real bias is generally toward sensationalist nonsense rather than toward a particular well-defined political agenda.

But one of the most easily provable forms of media bias, one that shouldn't really be up for serious debate, is its biased weighting of the importance of different people's lives. Throughout the mainstream media, people's suffering becomes news not on the basis of how bad it is, but on what the victim's demographic characteristics are. Some people's deaths are news, some people's aren't, and the question of who matters reflects nothing more than the purest kind of subconscious prejudice.

I don't think I am saying anything new here. Everyone knows about "missing white woman syndrome." Everyone knows that a missing Ivy League college student will be far more of a news story than a missing high school dropout. Everyone knows that two people getting shot on the floor of the New York Stock Exchange would receive far more coverage than five people getting shot on the streets of Baltimore, and that a much larger terrorist attack in London will be front page news while a terrorist attack in Baghdad won't be.

Yet even though this is universally understood, I don't think it's nearly discussed enough. To me, it seems totally morally reprehensible and without justification. Since I believe that all human lives are of equal worth, the idea of having worthy and less worthy victims horrifies me.

And the numbers are incredibly stark. Our World In Data recently discussed a 2007 study that looked at the relative weight afforded by news networks to different kinds of deaths.[2] The study looked at over 5,000 natural disasters and 700,000 news stories that ran on the major news networks such as ABC, NBC, and CNN. It concluded "that networks tend to be selective in their coverage in a way that does not adequately account for the severity and number of people killed or affected by a natural disaster." That's an understatement. In fact, the study found that the loss of 1 European life was equivalent to the loss of 45 African lives, in terms of the amount of coverage generated. Deaths in Europe and the Americas were given tens of times more weight than Asian, African, and Pacific lives. The study found that networks "cover less than

5 percent of the disasters in Africa and the Pacific." Africa was particularly neglected. This may partly have been due to the differing types of catastrophes that affect people in different continents; stunningly, the study found that it would take 38,920 deaths from a food shortage to generate equivalent coverage to a single death from a volcano.[3] The study's authors point out that there are serious implications to this kind of coverage disparity across types of people and types of deaths. Because the news shapes our opinions on what matters, what kinds of issues are urgent and what policies we should pursue, differently weighting different kinds of deaths leads to a skewed view of what is going on in the world. This is why we end up paying so much attention to terrorism and so little attention to disease, so much attention to mass shootings and so little attention to "everyday" violence. Even in the category of everyday violence, coverage is skewed. The word "Chicago" has become a stand-in for street violence even though it is far from having the highest murder rate in America (that would be St. Louis, followed by Baltimore, Detroit, and New Orleans. Even Memphis is higher than Chicago).[4] And violence around the U.S.-Mexican border is currently "worse than ever seen before,"[5] but almost entirely ignored even by the "liberals" in the press. And yes, of course, the Afghanis killed by U.S. airstrikes and the Yemenis killed by Saudi bombing are given far less attention than anything that happens to an American. The bias toward sensational events and away from high-status victims helps generate a completely irrational public understanding of the world.

The bias toward and against coverage of certain deaths, then, is both hideously racist/elitist *and* directly harmful to human lives. Trillions of dollars are spent on national security, billions on prisons, because we are far more terrified of dying from street crime or terrorism than from high blood pressure.[6] And because we don't appreciate other lives as having similar worth to our own, we are likely to pursue policies that disproportionately sacrifice the well-being of others for the sake of a small improvement in our own (such as the Iraq War, in which an entire country was destroyed and 500,000 people killed over a hunch that a man might have had a weapon that could someday possibly hurt us.) The media's hierarchy of victims is dehumanizing and reinforces our worst moral tendencies, in that it views Europeans as worth 45 times as much as Africans. But it also turns us stupid and causes a lot more people to die than would if we were presented with information on human deaths in a fair and even-handed manner.

Journalists have a bunch of pitiful excuses for differential coverage. First, they defend the concept of newsworthiness: a killing in Chicago isn't as newsworthy as a killing in Times Square, because the former happens far more often. Notice, however, that this is an indictment of the entire concept of "newsworthiness" rather than an actual defense of journalistic practice. It actually tells us that "news" is precisely what we *shouldn't* be interested in, because news is going to prioritize aberrations rather than things that are commonplace and ongoing. People think that reading the news is a good way to stay "informed." But it isn't at all, because it is tilted toward paying excessive attention to things that happen the least often. The entire concept of "newsworthiness" is in tension with giving people an accurate impression of the world, and journalists should ditch it and focus on trying to educate people on what matters in the world, "newsworthy" or not. Taken to its logical endpoint, would this radically alter the way we present the world, with just as much attention given to cancer, malaria, and traffic deaths as terror and freak accidents? It would. But that's exactly what we should be doing.

I've also heard journalists defend the disparate coverage of people in different places, by suggesting that what matters in Paris actually matters more to an American than what happens in Nigeria. I don't buy this. Frankly, what happens in either place is generally fairly limited in its direct consequences for what happens to me in Louisiana. But I don't see why Paris should matter to me more than what happens in Lagos. Journalists might justify this by saying that, as a matter of *fact* news consumers are more interested in Paris than Lagos, but this is just a defense of peddling prejudice because there is a market for it. And while the impulse to spend more time thinking about a dozen people being killed in a school shooting than 5,000 per day who die from dirty drinking water is understandable (one of these involves a more direct and brutal kind of violent trauma, something it's impossible not to react to),[7] the job of the news should be to help us curb our instinct toward caring more about those closer to us than those far away, or those killed violently versus those killed by disease (or by capitalism).

In fact, so many journalistic justifications for the profession's worst practices center around the preferences of news consumers. News organizations are strongly concerned with their popularity, and they pay far more attention to stories that they know people will be interested in. At some media outlets, this reaches extremes; page hit-counts are tracked in real time, with writers praised whenever they write things that bring the outlet a lot of hits and attention. Keeping eyes fixed to the screen is everything, and since the American public's preferences are colored by prejudice against poor people and non-Westerners, poor people and non-Westerners are simply going to be disproportionately left out.

It may sound absurd for me to talk about "producing things that people like to read" as if it's a bad thing. But it *is* often a bad thing. (Nobody could ever accuse me of it.) The more you defer to preference, the more you're going to end up simply reflecting whatever feeling people happen to hold already, rather than what you think is actually justified and necessary. This is often a problem with markets; they just give people whatever garbage they happen to think they want, or can be convinced to think they want, regardless of whether it's actually any good for them or not. If a media company decides to "give the public what it wants," and what the public wants is racist or trashy, then the company will end up producing things that are racist and trashy. It's actually important for an organization committed to informing people to remove itself from market incentives as much as possible (this is one reason why *Current Affairs* doesn't monitor its numbers of page views or carry advertising).

Mostly, journalists avoid discussing the rationale behind differing coverage of different victims. This is because it makes them profoundly uncomfortable; they are liberal in their sensibilities, and the idea that they are reproducing a bigoted and irrational view of the world is distressing. But when they do discuss it, many of them will defend it by pointing to differing levels of newsworthiness or public preferences. These arguments simply assume the conclusion: producing sensationalism for ratings is justified because news is inherently about drama and this is what the public wants. Those things are just a description of the problem, though. I wish journalists would conduct a lot more self-scrutiny rather than instantly leaping to defend their role in perpetuating an obviously bigoted and harmful hierarchy of human values. We need more detailed studies on exactly how victim differentials work and the variables that shape coverage, and then we need news organizations to totally reshape the way they determine what people ought to hear. (I am skeptical that this could ever happen until the profit motive is taken out of news.)

Everyone knows the media is biased, but this particular bias is both universally known and rarely discussed. It's past time that changed. All human beings are equal, and having a fair-minded and well-informed understanding of the world depends on not prioritizing those who happen to live on the correct continent or die in the most shocking and unusual way.

CNN Will Never Be Good For Humanity

IT SHOULD BE PERFECTLY OBVIOUS to anyone that there is no war between Donald Trump and CNN. It may look like there is. But there isn't. This is because Donald Trump and CNN share the exact same core objective: to put on a really good show.

I say this is "perfectly obvious." That's because it's an undeniable fact that CNN exists to serve the interests of the Turner Broadcasting System, which in turn exists to serve the interests of Time Warner, Inc., which exists to serve the interests of the shareholders of Time Warner, Inc. And Donald Trump exists to serve the interests of Donald Trump, whose primary interest is in appearing on television a lot and being famous and powerful. These two sets of interests are perfectly symbiotic, and there is no reason that there should be any serious conflict between them. Donald Trump wants to be on television. CNN wants people to watch television. And because people watch television when Donald Trump is on it, neither CNN nor Trump has any reason to make any effort to seriously undermine the other.

It's bizarre, however, that when I have mentioned to people the simple fact that Donald Trump and CNN have the same relationship as clown-fish and sea anemones, I have been treated like some kind of conspiracy theorist.[1] I am, it is suggested, positing some kind of worldview in which media and political elites gather in backrooms and conspire over cigars. I am being cynical, and implying that nothing is as it seems and that we're all stupified, zombified sheeple, unaware that the powers that be are laughing behind our backs while we obsess over a spectacle manufactured for consumption.

But in actual fact, I'm implying nothing conspiratorial at all, and it exasperates me endlessly that the idea should be perceived this way. I don't think Sarah Sanders and Wolf Blitzer meet for breakfast each morning and plot out the day's Trump feud. Rather, it's simply that by independently pursuing their own personal/institutional objectives, they benefit one another. This requires no shady collusion whatsoever. After all, the clownfish and the sea anemone do not have to work things out in a smoke-filled room. They don't even particularly have to like one another. They simply go about their business, and the same thing happens to be good for both parties. Thinking about how relationships emerge from rational self-interest doesn't make you Glenn Beck with his chalkboard; it's standard economic thinking.

I'll give you further evidence that I'm not offering a "conspiracy": you don't usually see conspiracies described openly in the pages of the *Hollywood Reporter*. And yet here we are:

> On the TV front, [network president Jeff Zucker] and CNN have ridden the Trump wave as adeptly as any outlet.[2] In the critical 25-to-54 demographic, CNN's daytime audience in January was up 51 percent year-over-year (Fox News was up 55 percent); it pulled in an extra $100 million in ad revenue (counting both TV and digital) last year compared with past election years. Profit for 2016 neared $1 billion, and the short-term outlook suggests the Trump bump will lead to another $1 billion haul. "It's going to turn 2017 into an even better year than we already expected to have," says Zucker.

Here's the *New York Daily News'* Don Kaplan:

> The feud between Donald J. Trump and CNN is like an iceberg:

There's so much more going on beneath the surface than anyone knows. At first glance, it would seem completely adversarial, but it's not... Those who know Zucker understand his ego is almost as outsized as Trump's, and given their history, the pair shares a special bond — one that entitles Zucker to a level of access other news executives do not enjoy. Zucker told New York Magazine the pair talked at least once a month during Trump's campaign for the White House.[3]

And *Politico*:

In fact, the presidential campaign and the first few weeks of the Trump administration have proven to be a boon to the bottom line for CNN and its competition. In many respects, Trump's vitriol toward the media and the tough coverage of his administration reinforce themselves, driving coverage forward.[4]

By all accounts, the rise of Donald Trump in American politics has been fantastically good news for CNN, which has seen an incredible ratings boost[5] and reaped a billion dollar profit from the campaign cycle.[6] And Jeff Zucker is an old friend of Donald Trump's, having launched Trump's television career by commissioning *The Apprentice* in 2004. (You can find lots of photos of them hanging out together.[7]) For the head of a network with an ostensibly adversarial relationship with the new president, Zucker has seemed remarkably pleased with the direction of things: "This is the best year in the history of cable news ... for everybody. We've all benefited." (The *New York Times* recently observed that "nibbling filet mignon in a private dining room overlooking Central Park, Jeffrey A. Zucker, the president of CNN, did not look like a man perturbed."[8]) According to *Politico*, Zucker and CNN recognized early on that "Trump would be a ratings machine," and deliberately gave him "quite a bit of coverage," including broadcasting many of Trump's rallies and speeches in full.[9] Faced with the fact of his own complicity in the rise of a terrifying and incompetent president, Zucker said he had no regrets, and reportedly "sleeps great at night."

All of this is completely at odds with the received idea that Trump and the network are in a fight to the death, with Trump undermining journalists, ushering in a post-fact era, and posing a serious threat to the freedom of the press. CNN contributors and correspondents declare that Trump poses an "existential crisis" for American journalism[10] and poses a threat to democracy and free speech.[11] But television executives don't seem to share that opinion. During the election CBS's Les Moonves seconded Zucker's perspective:

> *It may not be good for America, but it's damn good for CBS... For us, economically speaking, Donald's place in the election is a good thing... Donald's place in this election is a good thing... The money's rolling in, and this is fun. It's a terrible thing to say. But bring it on, Donald. Keep going.*[12]

Could anyone who actually had serious grave concerns about Trump speak like this? (Moonves later insisted he had been joking, though since what he said was true, it's unclear what the joke was supposed to be.[13]) Certainly anyone who thought that the future of the press was at stake, or recognized that millions of lives could potentially be destroyed through mass deportation (let alone nuclear war and climate change) you would have a hard time classifying anything about the election as "fun" or wishing Trump continued political success. Yet that's how the heads of CBS and CNN are feeling: they're not worried. They're downright pleased. For them (as opposed to everyone else), this is great. It is, as Zucker put it, "a very exciting time."[14] You don't have to speculate especially wildly, then, in order to be skeptical of there being any real "hostility" between Trump and CNN. All you have to do is listen to its chief executive's words.

Again, this doesn't necessitate believing that there is a conscious effort on CNN's part to help Trump. While overt media-political collaboration does happen (according to Cenk Uygur's internal account of working at MSNBC, the Obama administration had significant pull with executives there and shaped the network's tone[15]), the real question is simply whether it's possible for a profit-driven media to care much about serious journalism or moral values if ratings and profits lie elsewhere. Financial self-interest powerfully shapes us on a subconscious level, and it's easy to see why the optimal position for CNN at the moment is to feel like they are opposing Trump while not actually doing anything to seriously undermine him.

And that's precisely what seems to be happening. Yes, there were spats with Sean Spicer and Kellyanne Conway. These are entertaining; they even go viral![16] But after Donald Trump's first speech to Congress, in which he accomplished the spectacular feat of reading from a set of pre-pared remarks for the first time in his political career, CNN declared him "presidential,"[17] with even the network's progressive commentators gushing over Trump.[18] It was somewhat bizarre to see Trump's supposed bitter adversaries giving him totally undeserved praise for a transparently manipulative bit of agitprop. But as *The Atlantic*'s Derek Thompson explained, television news is a show, and shows demand narratives, and Trump steadily becoming statesmanlike is a great narrative, so there was no reason not to give Trump the story he wanted:

> *The fundamental bias in punditry is not toward "presidential" behavior or against "resistance." it is more simply pro-plot twist. Narrative shifts are great for television, so great that it is irresistible to manufacture them in the absence of actual shifting narratives.*[19]

(Journalistic symbiosis with Trump has a long history, by the way. Ever since the *New York Times* compared him to Robert Redford in 1976,[20] before writing in 1989 that *The Art of the Deal* made one "believe in the American Dream again,"[21] Trump has been offering the press great stories, and the press have dutifully printed them. Trump knows the ins and outs of media as well as anyone alive, and has been phenomenally successful at using the news to his advantage in order to build his celebrity and, ultimately, his power.)

Anybody who believes that CNN's rhetorical commitment to journalism is actually serious should read the *Hollywood Reporter*'s account of Zucker's plans for the network. Serious adversarial reporting such as Jake Tapper's has a place because Tapper successfully draws viewers. But the rest of the network's plans have barely any connection to anything resembling journalism. Its future is in stand-up comics (W. Kamau Bell) and TV chefs (Anthony Bourdain—I love him, but that's what he is.) They paid 25 million dollars to a YouTube vlogger named Casey Neistat, a man whose specialty appears to be giddily trying out incredibly expensive goods and services on camera,[22] and whose stated plans for how to use the $25 million were inscrutably vague and buzzword-laden.[23] To bolster their investigative reporting, CNN poached a team from *Buzz-Feed* who had "broken several major stories, including Trump's appearance in a soft-core *Playboy* video." (A consequential scoop if there ever was one.)

But while the network's preference for popularity over integrity would seem undeniable, CNN editorial VP Andrew Morse has insisted that it isn't what it looks like: "We are decidedly not in the clickbait business... We don't do cat videos, we don't do waterskiing squirrels." Morse might be a little more believable if the network's politics section didn't literally run headlines like "Haha Guys, This Bird Looks Like Donald Trump."[24] (He might also want to check the network archives before confidently declaring that CNN is free of cat and squirrel-based news stories; in fact, CNN is the perfect place to go for a "Squirrels Eating Potato Chips" video,[25] and in the weeks before the election they were literally running stories like "Here's The Whole Election In Cat GIFS."[26])

The point here is not that there is something wrong with providing access to amusing cat photos or clips of squirrels noshing on Pringles. It is simply that CNN is a company, not a public service, and it can be expected to act like a company. Its aim is to produce content that people will watch. Sometimes the public's taste will coincide with the public good. But not too often. And the rise of somebody like Donald Trump, who constitutes both a unique threat to human wellbeing and a unique opportunity for compelling television, heightens the tension between the journalistic and economic motivations of CNN. And since it's the economic dimension that directs most corporate action, especially when there are billions of dollars to be made, CNN has a lot to gain from being just antagonistic enough toward Trump to guarantee some good entertainment without being so antagonistic as to bring him down and have to return to C-SPAN levels of thrilling political discourse. Thus to use Moonves' formulation, in the Trump era, what's "bad for America" is great for CNN.

The fact that CNN will never be good for humanity is not really the fault of the people who work at CNN. After all, it's hard to see how they could do anything differently. (Though, to their credit, they have experimented with some impressively elevated programming, such as their town hall debate between Bernie Sanders and Ted Cruz on the future of the Affordable Care Act.[27]) Once your mandate is to get viewers, you've already got a pernicious conflict of interest, and the quest for viewers (or clicks) is endemic to contemporary American media. So much is driven by the pursuit of eyes on the page or screen, and anyone working within that system will struggle to do things that are morally necessary but don't really attract a viewership.[28]

This is a very old criticism, but I think in many ways it is a correct one. (The most clichéd sentiments are also often the truest sentiments.) When the production of media is motivated by profit, the temptations to sacrifice integrity are going to be great. In the case of Donald Trump, these temptations will be all but irresistible. An age that requires resistance therefore requires independent nonprofit media. Economics still runs the world, and behind the apparent war between CNN and the Trump administration is a relationship just as agreeable as that of the clownfish and the sea anemone.

What Is The Point Of Political Media?

IT'S TEMPTING, when you write about politics, to think that you are useless. And if the received view of political media is correct, you probably are: people choose the news sources that they agree with, thus you're speaking almost entirely to the already-converted. Financiers read *The Wall Street Journal*, liberal professors read *The New York Times*, alt-righters read *Breitbart*, racist uncles watch *Fox News*, democratic socialists read *Jacobin*, Trotskyists read *CounterPunch*, and insufferable policy nerds read *Vox*. Every media outlet just reinforces already-held beliefs, news consumers build themselves an echo chamber, etc. It might even be worse than that: Ryan Cooper of *The Week* says that "95% of journalism is infotainment for the upper middle class,"[1] meaning that even when the content is ostensibly "political," in its function it bears no real relationship to politics. It's just something for people to look at, with the *New York Times* serving roughly the same purpose for upper-middle class liberals that wrestling and motor racing serve for a different demographic.

There's certainly good reason to be skeptical that journalism does very much. The idea that we should read the news to "be informed" has always seemed strange to me, since the process of becoming informed is treated more as a ritual than as an act with any obvious utility. That's especially true because the entire concept of "news" is somewhat irrational. It's not just biased toward the sensational and toward treating some people's lives as more important than others, but it leads us to have a fundamentally warped view of the world, because it prioritizes sudden events over continuous facts.

But it's important to distinguish between the statements "media doesn't do very much *good*" and "media doesn't do very much." The fact that something is "infotainment" doesn't actually mean it doesn't have an effect, insofar as being drunk off infotainment can affect a populace. Every time I watch CNN I am conscious of the fact that I am not learning anything and am slowly having my brain deadened. That in itself, though, means it is doing far more than simply parroting back my own opinions and worldview. I am far more inclined toward the "manufacturing consent" view of media, which says that mass media functions to spread an ideology favorable to the economic interests of those who own it, rather than the "echo chamber" view, which seems to suggest that media entities simply reflect and reinforce people's existing inclinations.

It's important to adopt the view that media creates people's biases rather than reflecting them, because this has been precisely the philosophy guiding the creation of right-wing media, which has been incredibly successful in actually affecting its audience's worldviews. A study of the effect of FOX News on its viewers showed that it had an impressive power of persuasion. When FOX News was introduced into a local television market, it succeeded in turning people more conservative; the study authors found that "Republicans gained 0.4 to 0.7 percentage points in the towns that broadcast Fox News," concluding that "Fox News convinced 3 to 28 percent of its viewers to vote Republican, depending on the audience measure."[2] There's a huge gap between 3 and 28, of course, but actually shifting people's opinions to any measurable degree is an impressive accomplishment, and can make a difference in places where elections can turn on small margins.

Of course, we know that propaganda works, otherwise we wouldn't have the advertising industry. The American people wouldn't have spontaneously decided to support a war in Iraq in the absence of a campaign by the Bush Administration to persuade them that such a war was necessary. Woodrow Wilson's Committee on Public Information had massive success in turning a skeptical public into wholehearted supporters of U.S. entry into World War I. While there is mixed evidence about whether political attack ads work (and advertising executives obviously have an interest in convincing people that they do),[3] if we believe that people's opinions are shaped by factors external to themselves, then it's probably possible to at least marginally bump them in one way or the other.

The media provide people with the "talking points" that they use in their day to day lives. Even when a media outlet isn't persuading its *readers*, it's handing the readers a set of opinions and facts that they will then use in discussion with other people around them, sometimes persuasively, sometimes not. They're "rhetorical arms traffickers" who provide the weapons that people will use in polical conversation and argument. It could be that pretty much every person reading *Jacobin* is on board with single-payer healthcare, but that by handing those people a stack of facts about why single-payer makes sense, and where the criticisms of it go wrong, you strengthen those people's ability to be ambassadors for left policies as they go about their lives.

One moment when I realized just how powerful the media could be was when I heard two store clerks in a New Orleans jewelry store discussing Bernie Sanders. One said to the other something like "Yeah, but what about all the Bernie Bros? I mean the whole thing just seems to me to be the Bernie Bros." And the other person kind of floundered. I thought to myself "My God, is this going on all over the country?" Some guy writes a 1000-word article in *The Atlantic,* coining a silly pejorative term on the basis of absolutely nothing, and it spreads everywhere and shapes the very way that people talk about left politics. It was frightening, because it seemed as if little chunks of catchy rhetoric had significant power to get ordinary people talking about politics in different ways.

Because so many on the left are materialists, many of them are skeptical of the power of ideas. That seems like a mistake: even when you're just preaching to the choir, what you say to the choir will affect what the choir says to their friends, and political rhetoric can spread like a disease. Conservatives have realized that media is incredibly powerful: the Tea Party was born from the media, Trump was born from the media. Neither had true grassroots backing, they just had the power of television. But if you say a thing enough times it becomes true: Trump became viable because he said he was, Bernie Bros became a campaign issue because people said they were. The reason I'm in media is that I think its powers are actually underappreciated. The *National Review* helped revive the fortunes of conservative ideology by feeding ideas to a movement. *FOX News* turned many perfectly nice relatives intolerable. If the left is to reverse the effect, we need to think about how media works and how to use it for good.

Crime & Punishment

Mass Incarceration and The Limits of Prose

WRITING COMPELLINGLY about the prison system is nearly impossible. The challenge is to bridge the gulf between the readable and the necessary; true crime sagas are thrilling to read, mass incarceration statistics are moderately less so. Real trials never feel like John Grisham novels, and prisons themselves are often less the gritty gangland battlegrounds of HBO's *Oz* than an endless bureaucratic tedium. For those who believe American criminal justice is dysfunctional and unjust, this creates a frustrating paradox: many of the stories that most desperately need to be conveyed are those that are the most difficult to tell interestingly and well.

The task of persuasion remains crucial, though. Despite growing recent public awareness and scholarly attention given to the problem of mass incarceration, it has proven difficult to create the sense of urgency required to start bringing down walls and signing release orders. "A dozen books in recent years have addressed this problem without having much of an impact on policy or practice," laments Robert Ferguson in *Inferno: An Anatomy of American Punishment*. "Why has identification of the problem had so little effect? What is it about punishment that confuses people?" Everyone now knows about it, but mustering the will to stop it is another matter.

Ferguson himself believes the answer lies in an insufficient examination of the nature of punishment and the American punitive psyche. But the problem might be less to do with a lack of a certain kind of writing, and more with some inherent limitations of the subject matter. For, where a writer is concerned, prisons differ in an important respect from ordinary places: they are arenas where all sensation, all color and variety, has been deliberately extinguished. This spareness of stimulus does not easily lend itself to enticing or unique prose.

Literature on mass incarceration therefore easily becomes didactic. Writers about prisons, both inside and out, are faced with creating vividness from the mundane, and find themselves with a limited and clichéd vocabulary. "America's criminal justice system is broken," they say, in a sentence that has been written verbatim tens of thousands of times. Or they will resort to the familiar statistics; the third of black men that will pass through prison gates at some point, the millions entangled with the court system in some way. To stimulate intrigue, writers will call this system Kafkaesque, even though it really isn't. The Kafkaesque is defined by mystery. Who is doing this? What logic governs this thing? In the case of American prisons, we know the who, how, where, when, and why. It's a matter of public record.

One can contrast these difficulties with the successes that the Black Lives Matter movement has had in creating political pressure around the killings of black people by police. The names and lives of victims, like Walter Scott, Sandra Bland, and Eric Garner, make for powerful, wrenching narratives. Prisons themselves are a different matter. There is no single moment of tragedy; the injustice is stretched over years or decades. And it is not an individual story, but the story of multitudes. But harms that take place over long periods of time, and are perpetrated collectively, become abstract. Protests against policing can animate around discrete events, such as a tragic death or a non-indictment. Yet the prison system is not an event, but a constant. It doesn't build toward a sudden, violent climax. Instead, it operates perpetually in the background, a slow, quiet suffocation rather than a single deadly gunshot. Fruitvale Station can show us the devastating final hours in the life of a single individual, Oscar Grant. But how do you tell the story of millions being housed in cages for decades? What could a film about solitary confinement look like, except a blank wall accompanied by a scream?

A number of recent books have attempted to deal with this challenge, and to rouse the kind of passion necessary to activate real public opposition. None of them quite succeeds, since nothing ever can. But by placing them side-by-side, one can see the truth emerging in the gaps. Their varying approaches to crafting mass incarceration narratives, and what those approaches both capture and fail to capture, reveal how the limitations of prose affect our ability to communicate effectively about the prison system.

One of these is *Mr. Smith Goes to Prison*, which benefits from a unique angle.[1] Jeff Smith was a promising young state senator in Missouri when he lied to the FBI about a campaign finance violation, earning him a year long sentence in a federal penitentiary. As an ex-political science professor, Smith had long been interested in the criminal justice system, and the conviction afforded him with an unexpectedly in-depth experience of it. Ever the enterprising politician, Smith took advantage of his stretch to produce a detailed entry into the neglected genre of involuntary ethnography.

THE PRISON MEMOIR HAS NEVER BEEN an especially robust or popular genre, and it is not difficult to see why. Each must describe the same sensations: the routinization, the deprivation, the slow process of setting aside what it was like to be human. As a result, they tend to bleed together, the narrator's voice lost the moment her identity was stripped at intake. Claustrophobic and stark as the cell it is written in, the form is inherently hostile to the literary impulse.

Mr. Smith Goes to Prison avoids this pitfall, distinguishing itself by taking advantage of its author's strengths. Smith has a wry voice and absurdist humor that enliven his recounting of the experience, and a social scientific academic background that lets him make important big-picture policy observations. The risk was that Smith would simply write a "fish-out-of-water story," how he went from brokering appropriations bill negotiations to trading packs of cigarettes. And of course, he does tell that story, but Smith also aims to use examples from his observations to inform a wider systemic critique.

Smith is keenly observant of tiny details, from the kitchen's B-grade meat containers stamped "For Institutional Use Only" to the dated pop culture reference points of long-term inmates. He compiles a list of rules for survival (never accept a candy bar left on your pillow; it comes with major hidden strings attached) and translates prison slang ("dipping in the Kool-Aid" means barging into a conversation uninvited). He tells us how to steal peppers from the warehouse (always in the socks, since the pockets bulge too much). He explains the intricacies of racial hierarchy and segregation, and frankly discusses the issues of sexuality in prison, including rape. He carefully demonstrates the mechanisms of prison profiteering, from minor offenses like the mass theft of food supplies by correctional officers to major operations like the dollar-a-minute phone calls and the massive mark-ups on commissary goods.

Smith is especially good at showing the real-world implications of policy questions. His passages on solitary confinement are especially disturbing, discussing the ways in which it gives inmates "depression, rage, claustrophobia, and severe psychosis" with the lack of stimulation and interaction creating a "slow-motion torture." He points out how small things matter, like giving inmates access to weightlifting equipment. Dismissing safety paranoia, Smith says that bodybuilding is one of the most important ways that inmates learn to develop and be proud of their achievements, and that it gives them hope and dignity.

One might think Smith's experience somewhat narrow, because he spent his time in a minimum-security prison. But this turns out to be one of the book's most important points: contrary to what the public believes, the differences between minimum and maximum-security facilities have shrunk in recent years. No more Club Fed, with its tennis courts and spas. Minimum security is maximum security without the barbed wire; the conditions are just as stark and brutal, and the discipline is just as rigid.

Smith is exasperated by just how unnecessary so much of that rigidity is, and documents its harms to the well-being of both inmates and the communities into which they will ultimately be released. Storing inmates far from their families and making phone calls unaffordable breaks down relationships, and that lack of a support network increases their likelihood of re-offending. The cruelty of the correctional officers is often needless and builds mistrust and hostility. And the educational programming offered to inmates borders on the fraudulent, with some "classes" consisting of sitting silently in an empty room until an hour has elapsed. The only real skills training offered is a several-week course on "how to grow tomatoes in water."

All of this, for Smith, creates an unconscionable waste. He points out that inmates are intelligent, creative, and often remarkably entrepreneurial, but that their abilities are being squandered. The miniature economy that runs in a prison traffics largely in pornography, cigarettes, Mother's Day Cards, and peanut butter (for muscle building). But its operators are well-familiar with economic and mathematical concepts, even though they use "somewhat different jargon than you might hear at Wharton."

Smith is not the first one to note this; *The Wire*'s Stringer Bell used the formal economic knowledge he gained from reading *The Wealth of Nations* in order to master the drug market. But Smith is policy-oriented, and has recommendations for how these skills can be put to good use. Inmates are hungry for knowledge, he says. They have endless time on their hands and want the knowledge and connections that will help them stay in jobs once released. But the prisons consistently fail to provide even the most meager opportunities; even Smith's own repeated attempts to teach classes to his fellow inmates were instantly vetoed by the prison administration.

Like every memoir ever written by a politician, *Mr. Smith Goes to Prison* is partly self-serving. Smith frequently trumpets his long history of volunteer work and enjoys listing his political achievements. And though Smith does everything to come across a decent guy who made a regrettable error of judgment, it is nevertheless disturbing when he admits he planned to pin the campaign finance misdeed on a young staffer who had committed suicide.

Still, Smith's book is invaluable, since it manages to be both vivid and thorough in documenting America's prisons from the inside. It's regrettable that it takes a state senator to tell these truths, though. The "fish out of water" story is good at bringing the facts to life, but its premise also means the described experiences will inevitably be atypical. Smith does his best to remain focused on the lives of those he did time with, but he has a very limited access to their inner worlds. Everyone in prison is putting on an act in order to survive, and Smith admits he rarely manages to break through and find people's true selves. Smith's book is overflowing with useful observations and facts, but it remains an outsider's account.

BRYAN STEVENSON IS INTENSELY AWARE of this challenge in Just Mercy, recently released in paperback.[2] Stevenson, who has worked as a lawyer on behalf of the poor for decades, is foremostly concerned with conveying the experiences of his clients. The book is framed by Stevenson's own account of his work defending the indigent, and how he came to recognize the depth of the justice system's bias and cruelty, but he is careful to use these in the service of telling the stories of those he works for.

Stevenson has already received well-deserved praise for the emotional force of his writing and his skillful selection of devastating anecdotes. The people he meets are impossible to forget. There is Joe Sullivan, a mentally disabled thirteen-year-old sentenced to life without parole, sent to an adult prison where he suffers unspeakable sexual abuse and ends up in a wheelchair. Yet Sullivan still retains an upbeat spirit, asking Stevenson about cartoon characters and reciting a little poem about how nice life will be when he goes home. It is impossible not to be outraged by the hell Sullivan has been condemned to. Stevenson's depictions of tormented youths doomed to spend their entire lives suffering from horrors totally disproportionate to their crimes should make it difficult to justify the very idea of trying children as adults. (Stevenson managed to convince the Supreme Court to abolish mandatory life without parole for juveniles in 2012, but the only practical effect is that a hearing must be provided before giving a child life without parole.)

The story at the heart of Stevenson's book, though, is that of Walter McMillan, accused of a murder he couldn't possibly have committed. (Scores of people from his church were selling sandwiches with him in front of his house while it happened.) Yet while McMillan's case seems a slam-dunk for the defense, Stevenson shows how the specter of racism continues to haunt the justice system. McMillan is a black man who had relations with the white woman who was murdered, and in Monroeville, Alabama, this is enough to put him under suspicion in the community. In fact, it is almost enough alone to convict him; the actual testimony against McMillan is laughably unreliable and contradictory. But McMillan is sent to death row nevertheless, where Stevenson fights a lengthy battle to present the evidence that will exonerate McMillan. After six years watching those around him in his cell block being executed one by one, McMillan is finally released, but by this time trauma-induced dementia has set in. When Stevenson goes to visit McMillan in his care facility, he finds that McMillan still believes he is on death row. McMillan's story is a harsh reminder of the stakes, not just because of how patently unfair his conviction was, but because his tragic ending shows that many injustices can never be set right after the fact.

Yet Stevenson's choice of McMillan as the main case study also has a shortcoming: McMillan was innocent, and very obviously so. His case is thus a perfect illustration of just how little truth and justice can matter when it comes to defendants who are poor and black. But while cases like McMillan's are not infrequent, the main group of people on whom the injustice of mass incarceration is inflicted are not necessarily innocent.

It's understandable that Stevenson would pick the most sympathetic possible case to anchor his book. It shows just how little American constitutional protections can really matter in practice. Here we have a gentle, harmless man with a rock-solid alibi, and his life is nevertheless ruined because of his status in the racial and economic hierarchy. Nevertheless, the most common story of American prison life is not that of Walter McMillan. It is that of people who did commit crimes, often violent ones, but who nevertheless receive sentences vastly out of proportion with those crimes, and who are given none of the resources they need in order to build a stable life for themselves. Thus a fair criminal justice system will require building sympathy for more than just those who are already sympathetic.

This speaks to one of the central dilemmas in animating public support for prison reform. On the one hand, it is tempting to make the points that will most easily convince people: low-level drug offenses shouldn't carry long prison terms, fourteen-year-olds who tagged along when an older brother killed someone shouldn't get life without parole, the innocent should go free. All of these statements are true, all of them demand changing current American practice, and all of them can probably be supported by a good majority of people.

But America's prison system is so vast, so bloated and so cruel, that making it humane is going to require unpopular reforms as well as popular ones. The reform-minded often emphasize drug sentencing, because it seems an issue on which it is easy to build political consensus. Yet even fixing drug policy would barely put a dent in the number of incarcerated. And as Gilad Edelman puts it in the *New Yorker*, "having a fifth of the world's prison population would be better than having a fourth, but not by much." The real problem is sentences for violent crime, but as Edelman says, "acknowledging the need to cut down the number of violent prisoners is a tough sell."

BUILDING THE NECESSARY EMPATHY for violent criminals, and showing the way they too are victimized and locked into an inescapable cycle of imprisonment, is part of the project of Alice Goffman's acclaimed ethnography *On the Run*.[3] For eight years, Goffman attempted to immerse herself in the world of the guilty, young black men in Philadelphia who spend their lives in and out of various jails and prisons. The result is an extraordinary piece of work, logistically speaking, since Goffman is able to bring details from lives that are typically never seen or cared about by elite policymakers.

Goffman brings readers inside the lives of the men of 6th Street, whose entire lives seem defined by their interactions with police. They are ruled by fear and mistrust, the War on Drugs destroying any prayer they might have had of maintaining an ordinary existence. Goffman aims to help readers understand why Mike, Chuck, and the other 6th Street Boys act as they do. They are criminals, to be sure, but in Goffman's portrayal their lives seem almost inevitable.

Goffman's work has encountered some extraordinarily high praise as well as some fierce criticism. One criticism of the work, made by Dwayne Betts, is that its attempt to humanize backfires. In fact, Goffman simply "encourages outsiders to gawk," reducing these men to the sum of their crimes and their police encounters. She thus fails to portray the neighborhood in three dimensions, excluding its culture, its warmth, its relationships, and treating it solely as a dysfunctional symptom of the drug war.

Multiple reviewers have gone after Goffman for supposedly taking liberties with the facts. The most vociferous has been Northwestern University law professor Steven Lubet, who has repeatedly accused Goffman of dishonesty in the *New Republic*. Lubet says that Goffman's accounts of certain events, like her supposed visit to Chuck's deathbed, do not add up. But he also suspects something fishy in her narrative, especially a passage in which she discusses her readjustment to life outside 6th Street.

The factual challenges to Goffman have not gone particularly far. Gideon Lewis-Kraus of the *New York Times* and Jesse Singal of New York magazine checked them out, and her sources seem to confirm her reporting. But Lubet is right to hit upon Goffman's narrative of her return to Princeton as seeming particularly odd. In the "Methodological Note" at the end of her book, Goffman writes of arriving at Princeton after her time on 6th Street:

> *The first day, I caught myself casing the classrooms in the Sociology Department, making a mental note of the TVs and computers I could steal if I ever needed cash in a hurry... The students and the even wealthier townies spoke strangely; their bodies moved in ways that I didn't recognize. They smelled funny and laughed at jokes I didn't understand. It's one thing to feel uncomfortable in a commu-*

nity that is not your own. It's another to feel that way among people who recognize you as one of them...The Princeton students discussed indie rock bands– white people music, to me– and drank wine and imported beers I'd never heard of. They listened to iPods, and checked Facebook...Moreover I had missed cultural changes, such as no-carb diets and hipsters. Who were these white men in tight pants who spoke about their anxieties and feelings? They seemed so feminine, yet they dated women. More than discomfort and awkwardness, I feared the hordes of white people. They crowded around me and moved in groups.

The passage may seem an unusual one to single out, tucked as it is at the end of the book. But it's notable for its failure to ring true, given the facts known about Goffman's background. As Lubet points out, Goffman was raised in tony surroundings as the child of prominent academics. She attended a prestigious private school, and was at the University of Pennsylvania when she was researching the book. To think that somehow when she got to Princeton, she was baffled by the existence of the iPod, stretches the limits of the imagination. For a wealthy double Ivy Leaguer to be looking for TVs to steal in case she needed extra cash is hard to believe.

Her fear of white people is similarly implausible. Goffman says she was scared especially of white men, even though "on some level, I knew they weren't cops, they probably wouldn't beat me or insult me." On some level? This despite the fact that her adviser was a white man, and that no male sociologist in the history of Princeton has ever been mistakable for a cop.

But Goffman's failure interestingly reinforces the point about the difficulties of discussing mass incarceration. It appears as if Goffman's research was sound, but the narratives she laid atop it were faulty. Goffman attempts to use the "fish out of water" framing in order to make her personal story seem more exciting, but doing so requires her to distort her experiences and background in a way that harms her credibility. And she tries to tell a story about how the drug war has created a Wild West in which black men are forever on the run, but this isn't exactly true. The reality is, as it always is, more complex than that. While easily-summarized punchlines may sell books ("white Princeton sociologist enters a terrifying urban battleground and loses herself in the process"), when they imply things that aren't true, they damage our ability to understand and address the social problems they are supposedly concerned with. Yet in that old battle between the readable and the necessary, the readable continually wins out.

THE SAME TENDENCY toward narrative at the expense of truth applies equally to the classic text of the anti-mass incarceration movement, *The New Jim Crow*.[4] By invoking America's own apartheid, Jim Crow, Michelle Alexander wanted to forge a powerful image that would stir public sentiment. She tried to avoid simply presenting dusty statistics, using the segregation comparison to convey the severity and urgency of the injustice. But as critics have pointed out, the Jim Crow metaphor isn't precisely accurate. As law professor James Forman has explained, calling present-day criminal justice Jim Crow fails to explain the system's often equally devastating effects on Hispanics and poor whites. It also obscures the fact that mass incarceration was not imposed simply by whites, but also involved support from blacks fearful of crime. Thus even Michelle Alexander doesn't quite identify the problem precisely.

Smith, Stevenson, Goffman, and Alexander have all written powerful books, each using a different strategy to try to capture what criminal justice in America today is like. Each of them succeeds to a degree, and each ought to be read. Ultimately, though, none of these authors can do what they set out to do, because America's prison system tests the limits of prose. You can try to turn it into a story with a moral, a snappy metaphor or the cry of an innocent man accused. But it's too bleak, pointless, and devastating to be captured in any of these.

I REMEMBER WHEN I FIRST REALIZED how little there truly was to be said about what goes on inside a prison. I made a stupid, naïve blunder interviewing a client while working at a public defender's office.

"How are you?" I asked him with eager-intern chirpiness.

"I live in a tent with 80 men and there is no air conditioning. So that's how I am."

"Oh," I replied sheepishly, making a "whoops" face. "I'm sorry."

Monotony does not make for good stories, yet politics thrives on stories. *12 Years A Slave* must be about about man who escapes slavery instead of the scores who did not, because this is where the story is. As Stanley Kubrick described his fundamental problem with *Schindler's List*: "The Holocaust is about six million people who get killed. *Schindler's List* is about 600 who don't."

This is not to deny the countless horrifying incidents in the life of the American prison system. But so many of these tend toward the meaningless. I once worked on a class-action lawsuit against a prison in the American South, and I remember reading the statements that had been taken from the inmates. There was one man who was deprived of medical care as he slowly watched his testicle grow steadily larger and turn purple. Each day he would look at the testicle. Each day as the pain worsened, he would beg the guards to take him to the hospital, and each day they would tell him to shut the fuck up. Eventually, when the testicle had grown to the size of a baseball, he was finally brought to the doctor to be castrated. By that time, the cancer had spread. The end.

It is hard to imagine the film version of this scenario being successful. You can't readily adapt it for Netflix. Yet these are the stories that we are trying to tell. Stories without lessons, without resolution or purpose.

Literature is a key ally of social progress for its ability to induce empathy, but literature seems powerless when it comes to mass incarceration. This is unfortunate, because for no issue is the creation of empathy more crucial than in criminal justice. From the beginning, the task is to foster love for the most despised. Not only that, but with prisons being hidden away in countrysides, people must be made to feel something that they cannot see.

One reason the prison epidemic has been hard to excite public emotion against is that while it is easy enough to write about, is difficult to write about powerfully. The story of a prisoner is the story of a starved brain, a human being slowly going mad inside a box. The story of American criminal justice is the story of millions of such people, being placed in suspended animation and put away. What can be said about this? Where's the moral? When it comes to mass incarceration, words simply fail us.

Can Prison Abolition Ever Be Pragmatic?

"While there is a lower class, I am in it, and while there is a criminal element I am of it, and while there is a soul in prison, I am not free."
— Eugene V. Debs

THERE ARE A COUPLE of reasons why I love Eugene Debs' "I am not free" quote, spoken upon his conviction for violating the Sedition Act in 1918.[1] To begin with, it's a good first principle for leftism: so long as there is injustice and suffering in the world, you should feel deeply troubled by it. It also does something extremely difficult: it empathizes with the despised, encouraging us to care about all of humanity, even those who have done horrendous and cruel things. It's an exhortation to universal compassion: you have to care about everybody, without exceptions.

But Debs's statement also contains a radical, even extreme, view of prisons: so long as there is a single person left in prison, Debs feels that freedom is impossible. It's clear the kind of world Debs wants: a world without social classes, without a division between criminals and non-criminals, and without prisons. And Debs doesn't seem to believe this is some impossible dream: he wants it to actually happen, because it's the precondition of his own freedom.

"Prison abolitionism," the belief that prisons should not just be reformed but abolished entirely, has a long tradition within the left.[2] Early socialists believed strongly that because the causes of crime were social, a fair society could eliminate the existence of crime, and therefore the need for prisons. As Peter Kropotkin wrote in a pamphlet:

> *The prison does not prevent anti-social acts from taking place. It increases their numbers. It does not improve those who enter its walls. However it is reformed it will always remain a place of restraint, an artificial environment, like a monastery, which will make the prisoner less and less fit for life in the community. It does not achieve its end. It degrades society. It must disappear... The first duty of the revolution will be to abolish prisons–those monuments of human hypocrisy and cowardice.*[3]

Clarence Darrow actually gave an address to a group of inmates at the Cook County Jail in Chicago in which he called for the total abolition of imprisonment:

> *There should be no jails. They do not accomplish what they pretend to accomplish. If you would wipe them out, there would be no more criminals than now....They are a blot upon civilization, and a jail is an evidence of the lack of charity of the people on the outside who make the jails and fill them with the victims of their greed.*[4]

(Afterwards, it was reported that prisoners who were asked what they thought of Darrow's speech said they found it a bit too radical.) The prison abolitionist strain in left-wing thinking has continued: Angela Davis's 2003 *Are Prisons Obsolete?*, which laid out an uncompromising case against confinement, has attracted a following on the left,[5] and even CNN contributor Marc Lamont Hill has pushed prison abolition, concluding that "if the system was fair, there would be no prison."[6]

The arguments made by prison abolitionists are straightforward: prisons make the world worse rather than better. They are inhuman places, and in many cases do not operate very differently from conditions of enslavement. They do not address the root causes of crime, and they encourage recidivism by hardening criminals. Or, as Emma Goldman colorfully put it in "Prisons: A Social Crime and Failure":

> *Year after year the gates of prison hells return to the world an emaciated, deformed, will-less, ship-wrecked crew of humanity, with the Cain mark on their foreheads, their hopes crushed, all their natural inclinations thwarted. With nothing but hunger and inhumanity to greet them, these victims soon sink back into crime as the only possibility of existence.*[7]

The case made by prison abolitionists has rhetorical force, and I think a certain persuasive power. It makes both emotional and logical appeals: emotionally, it invokes the human love of liberty and hatred of coercion, while logically, it proposes that the costs of prisons outweigh their benefits.

IT ALSO, TO A LARGE MAJORITY OF THE POPULATION, almost certainly sounds completely insane.

As Gene Demby notes, while people agree that liberty is great and all, they quickly recall the "What About My Cousin?" question: they remember a person they knew who was genuinely violent and dangerous, and realize that they feel far safer knowing that person is locked up.[8] Then, they remember all of the crimes that were worse than those committed by their cousin, and the abolitionist position begins to seem even loopier. Nevermind my cousin, what about Ted Bundy? What about serial rapists and armed robbers and hedge fund managers? Are you saying that they should be left free to roam about society perpetrating their evil deeds on the unsuspecting and upstanding? How naïve can you possibly be?

And, indeed, I think the historical prison abolitionists have often been naïve, or at least misleading. In response to questions about the worst kinds of offenders, they point to the factors that drove such people to their crimes. Very few people on death row, for example, had ordinary, prosperous, and stable early lives. And those crimes that do not occur for obvious social reasons can be treated as manifestations of mental illness, with treatment rather than punishment being the goal. Prison abolitionists frequently point to restorative justice approaches that try to bring both victims and offenders together to figure out a way that the wrong done by the crime can be undone.

But none of this actually addresses the question. All of it sounds good in theory, but it describes an ideal society rather than the society in which we actually live. In the real world, there are people who have committed serious violent crimes, like serial domestic abusers. If those people were all suddenly freed one day, they would likely resume the pattern of abuse, because it's very hard to transform a person overnight. If you are concerned not just with the injustice inflicted on defendants by a brutal prison system, but on victims by violent aggression, then prison abolition just amounts to blindly focusing on stopping one injustice while ignoring the potential consequences for increasing the amount of another injustice. That's what's meant by naïveté: instead of asking the question "In which cases can restorative justice approaches work, and are there others in which they would not?" prison abolition adopts an extreme position, and says "Punitive justice is wrong and restorative justice is right, therefore we must end punitive justice." Prison abolitionists advocate all kinds of sensible measures, like decriminalizing marijuana use and sex work, increasing community services that help people find jobs, and having courts rely more heavily on creative forms of restitution and community service than prison sentences. That still doesn't get us a straight answer to the question, though, which is: when is prison justified and acceptable? If abolitionists really see prison as being akin to slavery, that question is absurd: it's like asking when slavery is justified. Holding the abolitionist position must mean that murderers would be set free, regardless of the possible consequences. We can see this kind of difficulty in the rousing tracts of people like Goldman and Darrow: both of them said jails were in and of themselves a crime, but neither was willing to confront the problems that flow from such a view.

Because prison abolition seems an untenable position, then, most progressive people are advocates of prison "reform" instead. They subscribe to a position like the ACLU's: decriminalize certain offenses, emphasize rehabilitation, improve prison conditions, and stop using the prison system to warehouse the mentally ill.[9] They believe that while there will always be some need for punishment, the goal should be to make the U.S. prison system a lot more like those of the Scandinavian countries: humane and reform-oriented, and with a focus on keeping the perpetrator from harming society again rather than exacting revenge on them by depriving them of comfort. (Florida's Department of Corrections, for example, proudly states that most of its state-run facilities are not air-conditioned, even in the blistering summer heat.[10] Louisiana has its mostly-black[11] inmates picking cotton.[12]) Recently, a socialist acquaintance who opposes prison abolitionism told me that he thought the left's aim should be for all prisoners to have conditions like those afforded to Norwegian mass murderer Anders Breivik. Showing me a photo of Breivik's comfortable, IKEA-furnished cell, he said that if we could make prisons look like that, it's hard to think there would be any serious injustice left.

I think many people would be tempted to agree. Anders Breivik murdered dozens of children. He did it with deliberation and planning, and he is totally unapologetic. Giving him conditions essentially no different from (probably better than) the average college dorm room instinctively seems totally unobjectionable, possibly even too lenient. And Norwegian prisons are, in general, intentionally not much different from living on the outside. As one prison governor said, they follow the "normality principle," meaning that "daily prison life should not be any different than ordinary life, as far as this is possible."[13] As a result, the lives of Norwegian prisoners sound almost idyllic:

> *Inmates on the prison island of Bastoey, south of Oslo, are free to walk around in a village-style setting, tending to farm animals. They ski, cook, play tennis, play cards. They have their own beach, and even run the ferry taking people to and from the island. And in the afternoon when most prison staff go home, only a handful of*

guards are left to watch the 115 prisoners.

If this is what prison life could be like, then why adopt an abolition framework at all? Surely, even if we are romantic utopians, the Norwegian system ought to satisfy us.

And yet: I cannot help but feel that the abolitionist principle is actually the right one. As I looked at the photo of Breivik's cell, at first I thought to myself "Well, there doesn't seem anything wrong with this. Surely this is the ideal." But then I realized that using the word "ideal" to describe what I was seeing seemed perverse. After all, the photo I was looking at existed because 77 people were dead. I was not just looking at a comfortable room. I was looking at the place where a racist mass murderer was kept, and being asked to evaluate whether it was a sensible and fair place to keep such a person. This is the question around which prison reform asks us to frame our discussions: what is the humane way to treat a person who commits an atrocity? And the answer, for seriously committed reformers, is in that photograph.

What I like about abolition, though, is that it rejects the premise of the question. It says that, if we are assuming that in our ideal society, the Anders Breiviks would be given IKEA furniture and ping pong tables, we are still assuming the existence of Anders Breiviks. But the kind of society we are aiming for should not be the one in which "criminals are well-treated." It should be a society in which we do not have white supremacists murdering dozens of children.

Now, once again this sounds profoundly naïve. I can feel the eyes rolling. "Well, of course we'd all love a world without crime, but that's not going to happen, which is why the important question is about what we do here and now." However, this misses the point: what the abolitionist is actually saying is that, while it's good to improve prison conditions, it's vital to remember that "prison conditions" are not the real issue, just as if we mainly targeted "improving conditions for prisoners of war" rather than "stopping war" or "improving support given to the families of people who die in mining accidents" rather than "stopping mining accidents," our focus would be too narrow in a way that led us to fail to appreciate the true problem.

Prison abolitionists, ironically enough, sometimes seem more committed to stopping crime than those who criticize them for being naïve about crime. Some approaches to criminal justice focus on things like improving public defender services, improving prison health care, ensuring freedom from police harassment. But what the abolitionists socialists have always said is that, while these are valuable and should be done, it's equally important to try to understand why crime happens in the first place. In Clarence Darrow's speech to the Chicago prisoners, he said:

> The only way in the world to abolish crime and criminals is to abolish the big ones and the little ones together. Make fair conditions of life. Give men a chance to live. Abolish the right of private ownership of land, abolish monopoly, make the world partners in production, partners in the good things of life. Nobody would steal if he could get something of his own some easier way. Nobody will commit burglary when he has a house full. No girl will go out on the streets when she has a comfortable place at home. The man who owns a sweatshop or a department store may not be to blame himself for the condition of his girls, but when he pays them five dollars, three dollars, and two dollars a week, I wonder where he thinks they will get the rest of their money to live. The only way to cure these conditions is by equality.

Now, Darrow might have been thinking simplistically in believing that nobody would steal if they were rich already (see, e.g., Wall Street). But note that he is thinking about how to get rid of crime itself. The reason he would be uncomfortable saying that "the goal is to make American prisons more like Norwegian ones" is that for Darrow, the elimination of violent crime is inextricably tied in with the entire point of socialism, which is to create a society in which people are prosperous and happy and don't hurt each other. Abolition is a useful way of thinking about things, because it says "The task is to make a world in which prisons are unnecessary" rather than "The task is to make a world in which prisons are comfortable."

Of course, people think such a world is impossible. Prisons will always be necessary, they believe, because some people will always be warped and cruel. But I object to this way of looking at things: it accepts an erroneous chain of reasoning often held by conservatives, namely that human nature is prone to violence and viciousness and this is an ineradicable part of us. The reason I call this view "erroneous" is that I don't think it's a correct inference: the argument is that because humans have always been a certain way, they must always be a certain way. This is no more logical than if, in 1900, I had said "there has never been a successful man-made aircraft, thus there will never be a successful man-made aircraft." Or, if I had said (as I did) in 2016, "America has never elected a president who has openly bragged about committing sexual assault, thus America will never elect a president who has openly bragged about committing sexual assault." When we assume we can judge the full range of possibilities for the future from the evidence we have about the past, we can end up cramping our ambition through self-fulfilling prophecies, or underestimating certain risks.

The truth is that we don't know the degree to which crime can be controlled by addressing social causes. We don't know it, because we've never seriously tried it. But we do know that there are cities in the United States that have incredibly low crime rates, where violent crime hardly ever occurs and property crime is incredibly infrequent.[14] We are far from understanding why that's the case. Since we know that it is the case, though, we know that it's possible to create places in which crime is almost nonexistent. Violent crime has consistently been dropping in the United States despite the public perception otherwise (not helped by Donald Trump's demagogic attempts to terrify people).[15] It is impossible to know how much further it could be made to drop. (Nor is that because we've been locking up all of the criminals. States with low crime rates can also have very low incarceration rates, whereas states like, for example, Louisiana have both incredibly high crime rates[16] and incredibly high incarceration rates.[17]) Since very low-crime societies are possible already, even when they consist entirely of perfectly ordinary human beings, it does not actually seem especially naïve to believe that both crime and prisons can essentially be eliminated from the world. I refuse to see Anders Breiviks as an inevitability; I believe he is the product of a perverse racist ideology, one that can be countered and eradicated.

Prison abolition and prison reform can actually be reconciled fairly easily. The ultimate goal is prison abolition, because in a world without hatred and violence there would be no need for prisons, and the goal is a world without hatred and violence. In the interim, prisons must be made better and more humane. It's not that you should, in the world we live in now, open the prison gates and give murderers probation. It's that you should always remember that even if you think prison is a necessary evil, that still makes it evil, and evil things should ultimately be gotten rid of, whatever their short-term necessity. You can be both pragmatic and utopian at the same time. One should always adopt the "utopian" position, because it helps affirm what our ideal is and serves as a guiding star. But you can simultaneously operate with the real-world political constraints you have. As Angela Davis says, "the call for prison abolition urges us to imagine and strive for a very different social landscape." It's useful because it gets us thinking about big questions, picturing what very different worlds might be like and then beginning to plot how we might get from here to there.

To me, one of the most moving pieces of writing on prison is Oscar Wilde's "Ballad of Reading Gaol."[18] I find it a far more persuasive indictment of the concept of prison than any number of abolitionist tracts or policy papers about restorative justice. Wilde, destroyed by an unjust and bigoted Victorian criminal court system, wrote that no matter how we felt about the justice of particular laws, the very existence of prisons was a stain on humanity:

> *I know not whether Laws be right,*
> *Or whether Laws be wrong;*
> *All that we know who lie in jail*
> *Is that the wall is strong;*
> *And that each day is like a year,*
> *A year whose days are long.*

But this I know, that every Law
That men have made for Man,
Since first Man took his brother's life,
And the sad world began,
But straws the wheat and saves the chaff
With a most evil fan.

This too I know—and wise it were
If each could know the same—
That every prison that men build
Is built with bricks of shame,
And bound with bars lest Christ should see
How men their brothers maim.

Eugene Debs's principle is an essential one, then. You can't rest until the prisons are gone, because only then will injustice have been banished from the world: While there is a soul in prison, I am not free.

Even When It Doesn't Save Money

IT IS FREQUENTLY TEMPTING to justify policies by pointing to the money that will be saved by implementing them. This is a mistake. Or rather, it's dangerous. Because if you suggest that the reason to do something morally good is that it saves people money, then you're stuck if it turns out that this morally good thing actually doesn't save people money, or turns out to cost quite a bit of money.

Cost-saving arguments are often made by people on the left in order to defend their policies. Giving prisoners college degrees, for example, is good because it ends up saving the state money in the long run by reducing rates of reoffending.[1] The death penalty is bad because it's extremely costly to actually implement, given the complex legal procedures necessary in order to successfully execute someone.[2] Drug-testing welfare applicants is bad because it costs a lot of money without yielding many results.[3]

Each of these arguments has something in common: they support a left-wing policy position without requiring a left-wing set of moral preferences. They try to show conservatives that one doesn't need to be on the left in order to support educating prisoners, ending the death penalty, and declining to give drug tests to welfare applicants. It's enough just to care about saving money. And everyone wants to save money!

But by making these kinds of arguments, people on the left both come across as dishonest and stake their claims on highly risky propositions.

There's something dishonest here because the real reasons why many people on the left support these things have nothing whatsoever to do with cost-saving. They don't like the death penalty because they find it barbaric, they think prisoners should have access to education because they believe everyone deserves an opportunity to better themselves, and they don't like drug-testing welfare applicants because they think it's intrusive and demeaning.

How can one be certain that it's not really "cost-saving" that motivates these positions? Well, because if it turned out that the policy in question didn't save money, or there was a way to save even more money by doing the opposite, many people advancing these arguments would become somewhat uncomfortable. The easiest response to the cost-saving argument against the death penalty is that the death penalty would become much cheaper if we just took people behind the courthouse and shot them immediately after they were found guilty. And what if we find an incredibly cheap, yet even more invasive, way of drug testing welfare applicants? Would an opponent's position waver even slightly? The truth is that most leftist positions are motivated by moral instincts, and everyone knows it. It's convenient that educating prisoners or ending the death penalty might be good for the government's coffers, but it's certainly not why we care about those things.

You're also doing something very risky when you make a big deal out of cost-saving arguments: you're depending on the facts to always back you up. The moment the economics change, the argument that was in your favor is now just as powerful a reason not to listen to you. Many pragmatic cases for liberal immigration policy are of this sort. People will say that immigrants grow the economy, or they put more into the system than they take out, or they don't decrease native-born employment. But if the facts change, and someday immigrants do take out more than they put in, would the advocates of liberal immigration policy then change their minds?

Many of them wouldn't, because immigration is actually a moral issue (people should be free to move about the world, especially when a land of prosperity has more than enough to go around) rather than a matter of pure economic self-interest.

The fact that these arguments are premised on appeals to self-interest is another reason why leftists should be careful about them. If we say that people should help prisoners because it is in their self-interest to do so, we are telling them that the reason they should care about prisoners has little to do with empathy and altruism. But that means that we're affirming the legitimacy of selfishness and callousness, instead of grounding our appeals in the moral imperatives that come with being human. The fact is that many of the things we believe in aren't going to be cost-savers. In fact, they're going to be very expensive. It's extremely costly, for example, to provide prisoners with good healthcare. If we want to follow the cost-saving criterion, we should just let prisoners die when they get sick. But that's abhorrent. And it's abhorrent because it shows a lack of willingness to sacrifice anything in order to ensure all people have the basics of life guaranteed to them.

The same type of problem plagues progressive arguments about economic inequality. Opponents of inequality frequently suggest that inequality is not just bad for those at the bottom. In fact, it's bad for everyone, including those who seem to benefit. Robert Frank suggests that people at the top are forced into a status competition that even they don't get anything out of,[4] while others have reported that health, happiness, and trust in a society can be worsened by high levels of inequality.[5] The Washington Center for Equitable Growth (WCEG), an anti-inequality think tank, seeks research on the various effects inequality might have on everyone[6]:

> *How, if at all, does economic inequality affect the development of human capital?... Do different levels or kinds of inequality impact the potential for talent to emerge across the income, earnings, or wealth distributions, and, if so, how? We are interested in proposals that investigate the myriad mechanisms through which economic inequality might work to alter the development of human potential across the generational arc, including children, young workers, prime-age workers, and older Americans.*

But note: many progressives are not against inequality because they believe it harms everyone. They are against inequality because they believe it harms the poor, but proof that it harms everyone would be a very convenient way to make a strong case for getting rid of it. After all, if you don't need people to be altruistic, but just need them to care about themselves, it's easier for you to persuade the rich that reducing inequality would be a very good thing.

WHAT IF INEQUALITY ISN'T BAD FOR EVERYONE, though? What if it's fantastic for everybody at the top? What if the only people who are seriously deprived are the huge numbers of people who lose out? Then what? If the case against inequality is that we're all hurt by it (somewhat counterintuitive, since it seems as if the wealthiest among us probably aren't hurt at all), then what happens if that case turns out to be shaky? If you've carefully avoided the moral appeal, you've got very little left. But it may well turn out to be true that some things are going to have to require sacrifice, period. They're not going to "help the rich as well." Not everything is win-win, and if you try to frame everything as win-win, you are avoiding making the honest and difficult moral demands upon people that are necessary to build a more just world.

This is not to take a position that the empirical findings showing the harmful effects of inequality are wrong. They may well be right. But it's clear that the WECG, which is, after all, committed to equitable growth, would very much like it if the research it produced turned out to give reasons why inequality is bad. It's true that in their call for proposals, the Center doesn't say that you have to find inequality has harmful effects on human capital. But I am not sure they want to end up producing a pile of research showing that inequality doesn't have wide-ranging effects. (The instinct to use purely neutral and technocratic arguments, as against explicitly moral ones, can lead you to some strange contortions indeed. The WCEG even has an article explaining how slavery was bad in part because it was bad for the slaveholders, by inhibiting "economic creativity" and innovation. If it had been great for economic creativity, would it have been justified?)

This doesn't mean costs are irrelevant, or that we shouldn't consider the effects of a policy on everybody before deciding whether it is a good idea. Instead, I am saying that our values should be presented honestly and frankly, and that we should be clear about just how much our position is actually being influenced by the empirical considerations of cost-saving. If you bury your morals, and talk as if you're just about the numbers, you'll quickly be exposed as inconsistent when you have to fudge or bury the numbers on an issue where they conflict with your morality. (For example, people on the left say that racial profiling doesn't work. But if it did, would it be okay, or would we end up trying to avoid or massage the statistics in order to continue to maintain that it didn't work? Legal philosopher Ben Eidelson has suggested that the real reason we should be against racial profiling is that it's a hideous affront to human dignity that singles people out based on a pernicious demographic characteristic.[7]) There is sometimes a tendency among liberals to be cowardly about their own supposed values, and to try to argue based on conservative premises ("we're the *real* patriots"), on the theory that Americans are mostly conservative in their instincts and need things framed accordingly. But Republicans will always make better Republicans than Democrats will, and when you appropriate someone else's values and disguise your own, you just sound cowardly and vermicular.

With Democrats losing at nearly every level of government, it's more important than ever for progressives to develop a clear and persuasive political message.[8] I am skeptical of approaches that do not offer an obvious coherent moral worldview. Cost-saving arguments risk muddying the values one is trying to express, because it becomes unclear whether one cares about the conservative principle of small government or the leftist principle of giving people help. And sometimes it's just going to be true that you can't have everything, that we are going to have to be asking some people to sacrifice or care about things for reasons other than self-interest. While it's not impossible to make multiple kinds of arguments in succession, all of which point toward the same end, it's also important to stick by your values, and tell people why you hold them, instead of pretending that you are just following their own values and their own logic. People just might respond better to some honesty. I don't like the death penalty because I believe in mercy, even when it's hard. I don't like inequality because it's an obscenity for some people to be billionaires while others can't pay for their children's cancer care. And I don't like drug tests or profiling because they are vicious and spiteful and rob people of their humanity. Saving money is a bonus. But when it's not why we care about what we care about, it's not what we should spend our time talking about.

The Autobiography of Robert Pruett

Oct. 9, 2017

IT IS VERY UNSETTLING to have a conversation with someone for the first time, just before they are about to be killed. A few weeks ago, I tried to get in touch with a man named Robert Pruett. A friend of his wrote back with an address, adding: "You might not want to lose too much time." She told me that this upcoming Thursday evening, the 12th, Robert is scheduled to be executed by the State of Texas. I had known that Robert was on Death Row. I hadn't realized he had about a month left on Earth.

I wanted to talk to Robert because for three years, I have been thinking about him. In 2014, I was prowling around one of the more depressing parts of the internet—a webpage with the life stories of Death Row inmates—and I happened across a link to a document labeled, simply, *Robert Pruett's Autobiography*. It had nine chapters, and a preface. I intended to skim over it lightly, arrogantly presuming I pretty much knew the trajectory of prison memoirs. Instead, I spent two days completely engrossed. I'd never read anything like it.

First, here are a few undisputed facts about Robert Pruett. He is 38 years old, and has spent every single day of his life in prison since the age of 15. The crime for which he was convicted at that age—the murder of a neighbor—was in fact committed by Robert's father, Sam Pruett. The prosecution's theory was that, even though the senior Pruett actually stabbed the victim, Robert was present and liable as an accomplice. At an age when many children have just finished middle school, Robert was given a 99-year sentence in the Texas penitentiary. Five years later, at the age of 20, Robert was accused of killing a correctional officer, Daniel Nagle, who had given Robert a disciplinary infraction for eating a sandwich in the hallway. While no physical evidence ever connected Robert to the killing, inmate-witnesses said they had seen the crime, and the torn-up disciplinary report was found next to Nagle's body.

Let me set aside, just for the moment, questions about Robert's innocence or guilt in the killing of Daniel Nagle. First, I'd like to talk about his life. I'd like to talk about his book, and the reason I've spent three years thinking about it.

One reason I couldn't stop reading Robert's writing is that he is deeply smart and reflective. His autobiography is more than just the facts of a prisoner's life. It is an effort by a man, incarcerated since before he could legally drive a car, to figure out how it all happened, to examine and collect his memories and figure out whether things could have been different. Robert is trying to deal honestly with the questions of nature, nurture, and individual choice: how much of his life was a result of the accident of his birth, and how much was result of his decisions? He knows, he says, that in his youth he did terrible things: stealing, fighting, using drugs. But when someone ends up in prison as a teenager for a crime committed by his father, it's hard to deny that things would have been very different if the same child had been raised by different parents.

Robert begins with the quote from Socrates: "The unexamined life is not worth living." To make his life worth living, Robert wants to examine it, as thoroughly as he can. He begins:

> *I often lie awake during the wee hours of the morning, staring at cracks in a white, concrete ceiling, pondering my life. Every crevice inspires a thought, every thought a memory; thus, an introspective journey begins, guiding me through scenes resembling an S.E. Hinton novel. From the dilapidated trailer parks of Houston to the*

Mayberry-like streets of Vidor, waves of memories come washing over me like the rising morning tide: riding a bicycle for the first time, jumping off a bridge into the river, playing a guitar, that first kiss, stealing candy from a store, laughing with my family, crying alone in a prison cell....As I replay clips from the past a question that has intrigued me for years resurfaces: Why are we the way we are? What causes human behavior? ... I believe we can understand ourselves and what influences us through an introspective process that includes an examination of our past experiences and the behavioral patterns in our families. Ultimately, we make our own choices in life, but it helps to know why we are inclined or predisposed to certain types of behavior.

To begin to figure out how his background made him, Robert starts by profiling his parents. His father, Sam, had criminal tendencies from a young age, and was told by his family—who beat him regularly—that he was a "demon child." Robert says his father was "the most violent man I have ever met," a habitual criminal who pulled a knife on anyone who angered him. Robert's mother and father married young, and soon after Robert was born his father was sent to prison after a cross-country string of robberies, leaving his mother alone to raise three children.

Robert tries to piece together everything he can remember about his early years. He starts:

Many of my earliest memories are blurry and discontinuous: rolling around on a thick carpet in a dimly lit room, Mom rubbing my legs to alleviate excruciating muscle spasms, gasping for air in the midst of an asthma attack, sitting on my mother's lap in a crowded room (probably a hospital waiting room or the welfare office)... Pressing my face against a warm car, lying on a soft couch, staring at a picture on a wall depicting dogs playing pool, my siblings as children—these are the images that flash through my mind when I rewind the hands of time. Trying to recollect and reconstruct some of these early events is like gazing through a windshield on a foggy day.

Soon, as he moves forward in time, things grow darker quickly. Robert's mother struggles to pay the bills, and they often cannot afford to eat more that one meal a day. Robert recalls opening the fridge to find nothing but a jar of jelly, and making a meal out of it. It was a life of transience: "the scenery changed more often than the weather back then. From trailer parks to apartments, Mom moved us to places conducive to our survival." Sometimes the children were dependent on their mother's boyfriends for subsistence:

Unfortunately, the few men that I remember her being with were scumbags. One man she was with was named James, sometimes called Bo. He was an angry soul who openly detested my brother and me. No matter how hard we tried, we could do no right in James' eyes. He kicked Steven in the groin once, showing that he had no compunction about using his extremities to "discipline" us. When I was about five years old, I left some toys on the living room floor and he spiked me like a football, then commenced to punch. Exhibiting obstinacy early on, I screamed through tears, "Wait until my dad gets home, he'll kick your ass!" He hit me again and pointed at me.

"Your daddy's a punk and he's getting ass fucked right now. Don't you know what happens in prison?"... My brother and I slept in the same room and we stayed up many nights talking about James and how much we wished our real dad would come home. "Bubba, when dad gets home will he kick that punk's butt?"

"Yeah, our dad is one tough dude," he assured me.

"I can't wait until he comes home."

After a moment of silence I asked, "Who can beat up our dad?"

"The Incredible Hulk."

"Who can beat up the Incredible Hulk?"

"He-Man, the most powerful man in the universe!"

"Who can beat up He-Man?"

Deepening his voice he roared, "Almighty God!"

I was impressed, but I pressed on, "Who can beat up God?"

He placed me in a headlock and exclaimed, "Only I!"

We wrestled around until we heard our mother warn us to keep it down. We had our own way of dealing with problems.

My mother sometimes talked about our father. She spoke of him with reverence, affectionately describing him and telling my siblings and me stories about him. Most of this was for my benefit because they knew him, but they enjoyed our moments together and listened attentively. I grew to love the man my mother talked about and I longed for him to return home. "When will dad be home, Momma?"

"Pretty soon."

"When's 'pretty soon?'"

"It's not too far away."

My five-year-old mind conceptualized "pretty soon" as being a time of the year, like after Christmas or before Easter. I wasn't sure when it was, but I knew that all would be righted in the world "pretty soon."

When Robert is seven, his father is finally released from prison. Robert recalls meeting him for the first time:

At the airport I stood in between Mom and Steven as passengers exited the plane. I hadn't seen a picture of my father, so as I studied each face, I was relying on Mom's description: an older man with a bald head An elderly man fitting that description appeared walking with a cane. "Is that him?!"

They both laughed and Mom said, "I sure hope not."

A moment later a man emerged with a thick ZZ Top beard and a bald head, a cup in his hand. He stopped in his tracks when his eyes rested on us and he stared for a second. Tears began to stream down his wrinkled face. He tossed his cup into a trashcan and closed the distance separating us in long strides. He and my mother embraced, then she waved Steven and me closer so the four of us could huddle. In the midst of one of the most loving and memorable moments of my life, I cried and thought, I have a father.

But the return of Robert's father also brings trouble. Sam Pruett is impulsive and violent. He doesn't hesitate to whip Robert with a belt for misbehaving. The family moves frequently, sometimes because of lost jobs and sometimes because Sam is fleeing the law after stabbing someone.

Robert's memoirs contain plenty of experiences typical of a Texan childhood in the late '80s and early '90s. He scrounges quarters to play Super Mario Brothers at the arcade. He tries his first Whatchamacallit bar, and finds it transcendently delicious. He catches tadpoles and crawfish in a drainage ditch, gets lost in the forest with his dog. When he visits a wealthy relative, he gets to ride a horse. With his friends, he discovers a remote pond, where they swim every afternoon until realizing it is infested with water moccasins. Robert admits that he liked Vanilla Ice's music, but insists that everyone did back then and that anyone who denies it is a liar. He rides bikes, climbs trees, flirts with girls, and goofs around. (He also meets his grandmother, who hisses at him and calls him Satan.)

Robert's father and brother rarely hold down jobs for long, and the jobs they do get are low-paid; brother Steven works digging holes at a salvage yard, and at one point, his father's job is to sleep in a bar to make sure it isn't burglarized, an assignment for which he is paid largely in beer. But the family periodically enters the tree-trimming business together, a collective enterprise Robert looks back on fondly:

> *When I close my eyes I can still see my brother John—before he got too fat—up in a tree, yelling down instructions to the ground hands, systematically bringing a tree down piece-by-piece. I can still see Junior in his cutoff shorts and long-sleeved button-down shirt holding my brother's rope because, "Well, someone's gotta hold the fucking rope, smart ass!" (Yeah, but holding the rope was all his lazy ass ever did!) I remember rolling logs and hauling limbs to the truck and trailer, unloading and loading them. I can still smell freshly-cut pine and oak trees mixed with chainsaw smoke and oil gas. I can still hear the buzzing of saws or a tree cracking as it falls.*

I grew stronger lifting logs and dragging bush, chopping and stacking wood, loading and unloading debris, [but] what I was best at was landing jobs. My dad bragged that I was the best salesman he had. Being just a kid but very well-spoken and charismatic, I had many homeowners eating out of my palm after delivering my sales pitch. I'd ring a doorbell to a house with a dead tree. "Excuse me, I'm Robert Pruett with Pioneer Trees." I'd extend my hand for them to shake. "I noticed that you have a dead and rotting tree threatening your nice home here. Would you care to have a free estimate for a full removal and haul off?" Potential customers often thought I was cute and more often than not I got them to commit to paying for tree work. (As good as we were, sometimes accidents happened. We've dropped logs on doghouses, swimming pool water pumps and fences, and an occasional branch busted a window.)

The innocence doesn't last, though. For every moment of boyish adventure and father-son wood-chopping, there is a corresponding scene of violence or drug use. Robert gets high for the first time at age 5, when a stranger encourages him to sniff gasoline from a tractor. His parents both smoke pot constantly, and let him join in when he is still in elementary school. (Though they strictly forbid tobacco.) Robert's father takes him hitch-hiking across Texas to deliver a suitcase full of marijuana, on the theory that a man with a child will never be suspected of drug trafficking. Even Robert's most positive memories are often colored by the presence of drugs: he fondly recalls duetting with his dad on a rendition of Cheech and Chong's "Up In Smoke."

Many events are disturbing. Robert's brother, Steven, is molested by a family member and a camp counselor. His mentally-challenged sister is raped and CPS places her in a foster home. She enters a romantic relationship with a cousin, with whom she huffs paint and becomes addicted to cocaine, and has her own children taken away from her. Various relatives are always in and out of jail, and seemingly everyone around Robert is a heavy drug user. The family gets evicted from numerous trailer parks and motels, often because Robert has broken something or gotten in a fight. Robert's father is constantly violent. He threatens to kill the repo man who takes their truck. When Robert gloats after defeating him at a Nintendo game, he throws the controller and shouts "get your goddamn ass out of here before I beat you to death, boy!" He hits Robert's mother in an argument over money. Robert insists throughout that his father loved the family dearly, but was incapable of controlling his rage.

Robert tells us that he was once a promising student, and from the quality of his writing it's easy to believe him. He remembers his pride when a teacher praised his counting skills and moved him up to the advanced class. But by a very young age, Robert is becoming like his father. He gets into fights. He smokes pot constantly, even as a preteen. He begins to steal things, first shoplifting candy bars and porno magazines, before moving on to bikes and money. Robert's father hits him whenever he is caught stealing, but mostly seems upset that Robert has allowed himself to get found out, and thereby caused trouble for the family. "Don't shit in your own backyard," he tells Robert, which Robert interprets to mean that he should never steal from people who live nearby.

School becomes a disaster. When a teacher discovers that Robert is high, he is sent home, where his mother pretends to be upset. Soon, he is expelled from the 7th grade, and sent to an alternative school, where he continues to get smoke weed and steal things. Bad habits become worse habits: his older brother Steven allows him to try cocaine, which he soon begins using regularly. He goes from using drugs to selling drugs, and thinks nothing of burglarizing a neighbor's trailer.

Finally come the events that will end Robert's childhood and his life outside. It is 1995. Robert and two friends steal his friend's dad's Ford Granada, break into a house, and take television sets, VCRs, and a dozen rifles from a gun rack. They are spotted by the homeowner, and chased back to their trailer park. The police arrive, and Robert is put in handcuffs and taken away.

Robert manages to receive probation. But he is still an angry young man, addicted to drugs. When he arrives back at the trailer park, he believes a neighbor named Ray has secreted away some of the rifles from the burglary. Confronted, Ray denies it. Robert rants to his father about Ray. Sam Pruett becomes enraged on his son's behalf. When Ray walks through the park at night looking for a lost dog, loudly swearing, Robert mistakenly believes Ray is shouting at him, and tells his father the family is being disrespected. The Pruetts approach Ray and an argument escalates into a fight. As he has done many times before, Sam Pruett suddenly draws a knife and fatally stabs Ray.

All three Pruetts—Sam, Steven, and Robert—are arrested. Not yet 16, Robert finds himself charged with murder. At the Juvenile Detention Center, he has a breakdown:

> *I begin to panic. I bang on the door [over and over] and a chief returns with the doctor. The doctor is stern with me, orders me to stop banging and calm down or I'll remain on observation. I work myself into a frenzy and become hysterical. "Please! You don't understand! I'm not supposed to be here! They made a mistake! Please, just let me go home! I can't stand it in here anymore! I'm only 15! Please! Let me go!!" Over the next few days I remain in my room on observation, screaming and sobbing all day, begging to be released, unable to fathom my situation. The doctor and chiefs say it's out of their hands... I feel so frightened, so sad, so alone. The walls feel like they are closing in on me, I wheeze until I start hyperventilating, unbothered by the snot and tears running down my face. I curl into the fetal position in the corner of my room and moan for hours and hours, beg God to have mercy on me and let me out. I repeatedly tell Him how sorry I am for being such a bad kid. I think about how stupid I have been and punch myself in the head and face, then bang my head on the floor until a chief catches me. Soon my room is filled with chiefs and the doctor. I'm handcuffed to the bunk. Just as they begin to leave I ram my head into the bunk and they quickly restrain me until a football helmet is strapped to my head. The doctor promises I'll remain there until I calm down. I curse him and the chiefs and lose all control, scream and thrash about violently until I feel the sting of a needle prick my backside. Darkness overtakes me.*

Soon, Robert calms down, and begins to introspect:

Alone in my room, facing charges of murder and the fear of an unknown future, I reflected on my past. I thought about all the people I had hurt in my life. How did a homeowner feel when he returned home to find his place violated and his possessions stolen by me and my friends? I had no right to take from people who had worked hard for what they had. I had no right to take from anyone. I realized that the drugs and my addiction to the fast life clouded my judgment, rendered me extremely selfish and didn't allow me to empathize with the people I had robbed or hurt with my behavior. I was ashamed of myself, the person I'd been, and I desperately wanted to change. I didn't want to hurt or steal from people anymore. I was beginning to understand that stealing and robbing wasn't just wrong because you'd go to jail, but more importantly, it was wrong because it hurt innocent people. Away from all the negative influences and off of drugs for the first time in years, my conscience was awakening... During that first week, while I was freaking out, I thought of my father killing Ray and mumbled incoherent prayers for Ray and his family. I begged Jesus to forgive me for being the catalyst that brought it all about.

It is too late, however. Robert and his father are given 99-year sentences, while Steven receives 40 years. Robert is transferred from the juvenile facility to the penitentiary, along with several other children who have been certified as adults:

The bars and wire mesh cages, along with the angry and aggressive jailers, cast an immediate oppressive and dismal ambience. A tall and muscle-bound black jailer set the tone for us. "You boys are not in daycare anymore. You will follow orders here and conduct yourselves like men, 'cause that's what the courts say you is, and if you give me or any of my deputies problems we will not hesitate to beat your ass and make your life miserable." If that speech didn't con-

vince us, the bloody beatdown that another deputy unleashed on a mouthy trustee a few hours later certainly did. We talked amongst ourselves in the first holdover and tried to exude courage and confidence, but inside we were all trembling.

As a small 16-year-old in a prison full of brawny adult convicts, he faces immediate threats of predatory sexual violence. Robert recalls arriving at the prison, wondering when the violence would come. It did not take long:

The bright South Texas sun illuminated the razor-wired fences and made them sparkle as we pulled into the Garza West compound. The Garza West and East Units are built on the old Chase field Air Force base. Like all TDCJ units, guard towers surrounded the double fences. The inmates all wore white; the guards wear grey.... Each dorm had two large fans on either side of it, but they only circulate the extreme heat and humidity, making it feel like an oven inside. As soon as I stepped through the door I felt all eyes on me, checking out the 'new boots.' Grown men of every race, but mostly black and Hispanic, were playing dominos and chess, watching TV and exercising.... My heart raced and sweat poured from every pore as I carried my mattress and property to my bunk....Regardless of what you have ever heard, read about or seen on TV, nothing can prepare you for what it's really like inside prison. All of my father's war stories, as well as everything the deputies and older inmates from the county jail had said, had me on edge and mentally prepared to fight. I knew it was coming, just didn't know when, where and who....Once the guard did a channel check on the TV and left the dorm, a young black dude who'd watched every move made since I entered the building welcomed me to prison with an ultimatum: "Say, White boy. Watcha gone do? Fight, fuck or bust a $60?" Translation: I had the choice to fight him, let him have sex with me or pay him commissary for protection.

Because he is young, Robert has to quickly develop his fighting abilities to avoid being raped. Every day the threat of violence hangs over him. Correctional officers are physically abusive and inmates must perform intensely physically demanding labor all day in the heat. Faced with the knowledge that he will likely never see the outside world again, he lapses into anger and despair:

> *My hatred for the system grew exponentially. It burned me up inside that they, the judges, prosecutors and politicians, could do what they had done to kids like me. Every order from a guard or rule I had to obey grated on my nerves. When I was called out into the fields I felt like a slave, that they were rubbing salt into my wounds, making me pound on dirt in the blazing South Texas sun. Every time a guard told me to shave, tuck my shirt in, or gave me any other order, I felt like they were slapping me in the face. Prison life began to gnaw at my psyche, wear me down and made me abhor waking up each morning.*
>
> *I was dying inside.*

Soon, Robert becomes suicidal and slashes his wrists. The attempt fails, and only makes his life worse: his scars are taken as a sign of vulnerability, and he covers his arms in tattoos to avoid revealing them to potential predators. As he finds himself engaged in fight after fight, trying to avoid showing weakness, he realizes that he seems to be following a path that was set for him a generation ago:

> *Violence is the order of the day in prison. Many of us were conditioned to respond aggressively to any perceived threat or disrespect. My father was a very violent man from decades of living that type of life. So much so that he carried it to the freeworld, reacted violently when he felt 'contested.' He had an edge about him that frightened me as a boy and I often wondered why he was so explosive and crazy. Then I came to prison and experienced this environment myself and I understood him a little better, what made*

him that way. Sometime around the middle part of 1999 I had a startling revelation: I was becoming my father. Part of me was proud that I commanded a great deal of respect amongst the convicts, that most knew I'd not only fight when forced, but I was a force to be reckoned with. It had become instinctive almost for me to lash out at dudes who crossed my boundaries. Violation of my personal space was unacceptable and it unleashed the monster in me. That monster was the only thing the predators seemed to respect. The moment I realized I was becoming my father, depression crept in. [He was] one mean sonofabitch. I didn't want to be that way; it brought tears just thinking about it, finally comprehending the inadvertent psychological conditioning that occurs in prison and its effect on me. Yet, to renounce violence in here is equivalent to losing all respect. Losing respect means to concede to the whims of the predators.

Robert's mind develops in different directions. He becomes a Christian, then begins to question the justifications for faith. Influenced by the strong current of white supremacy in prison, he becomes a racist, reading *Mein Kampf* and getting a swastika tattoo to intimidate people, before realizing how horrifying the ideology is and renouncing it:

I didn't realize it back then, but all of my anger and hate regarding race was misdirected and ignorant. I was so pissed off at the system for throwing me away that I needed somewhere to focus my negative energy. As the years passed I opened my eyes and matured, slowly growing out of that convoluted ideology on race. Today, I realize that there is no pure race; we all share DNA and we all sprang from the same source... I understand that more often than not socioeconomic factors play the largest role in how people are treated. The rich and famous have it made; while the poor outcasts from both the ghetto and trailer park have it rough. My hope is that as society evolves, we'll erase the things that separate and divide us such as race and class.

After an early life spent skipping school and doing drugs, Robert takes as many classes as he can, learning whatever he can about human beings in order to understand himself better:

> *Psychology 101 was one of my favorite classes. Human behavior intrigued me. After taking the class I read books on the pioneers of psychology like William Wundt, Sigmund Freud, Carl Jung, CJ Watson and BF Skinner. I then delved into books on population biology, behavioral genetics, sociology, anthropology, evolutionary psychology and anything related to behavioral sciences. I wanted to understand the general human psyche so I could better understand myself, where I came from, how I became the person I was and how I could become better....I began to grasp how growing up in poverty affected my behavior... I learned how some traits are genetically transferred, such as aggression and addictive personality disorder, but that genes don't issue tyrannical commands; we can learn to control our genetic impulses and alter our predispositions with the right conditioning. Psychology taught me so much about the human condition, our childhood traumas and complexes that need to be resolved, and it truly helped me understand why I behaved the way I did prior to my arrest. I had put myself, my ego, above everyone else. The environment I was raised in was conducive to my criminality. I used drugs to numb my mind and ease the burden of my existence, then became addicted and committed crimes to feed the destructive cycle that was my life. Obviously, my parents were ill-equipped and had no clue about child development as they let me get high with them. Yet, psychology helped me better understand them, their pasts and why they had such a hard go of it.*

And yet, though Robert studies hard, he continues to feel more and more hopeless. He is frequently denied access to prison courses because of disciplinary infractions. His fellow inmates are impressed with all of his new knowledge, but one of them teases him about how all the learning will "come in handy" during 99 years of working in fields. Robert laughs, yet realizes just how sad he is to think that he literally has no opportunity to get out of his situation, that he will very likely die in prison. All the while, even as he grows mentally, physically he is stuck in a world of confinement, violence, and hopelessness. Worse, the combination of the "tough" persona he has developed to survive as a teen among adults and the aggressiveness inherited from his father have turned him into an impulsive, high-strung, sometimes brutal person.

In 1999, age 20, Robert is accused of killing a correctional officer who writes him up for eating a sandwich in the wrong place. The officer, Daniel Nagle, is found stabbed, next to Robert's shredded disciplinary report. Other inmates, who receive deals in exchange for their testimony, claim to have heard Robert confess. A cut on Robert's hand, which he claims to have received in a weightlifting accident, is presented as further evidence. Robert is tried, convicted, and sentenced to death. Robert's case goes through a series of appeals, centering around the lack of any forensic evidence connecting Robert to the murder weapon, and he is given half-a-dozen stays of execution. Last week, the U.S. Supreme Court declined to hear Robert's final request for a stay.[1]

Ironically, in his autobiography, Robert says that life among the condemned men was far more peaceable and tolerable than life in the general population had been. Perhaps because of their shared fate, and a corresponding recognition of the futility of petty conflict, the residents of Polunsky Unit managed to forge a strong bond and amuse themselves with gallows humor:

One of the greatest times of my entire life were spent right here on the row, hanging out with Tiny, Jeff Prible, Bob Dylan, Richard "Psycho" Cobb, Boxcar, Pennywise, Bandit, Ghost and Third... We practically lived together as we stayed hooked up on the "mics" 24/7 (we discovered how to talk to each other through our radios on the "mics"). We listened to sports and music together, shared our deepest thoughts, darkest fears and all of the good and bad times of our lives. We played games like Risk, Monopoly, chess, checkers, trivia, hang-man and derivatives of them all. We went on mental excur-

sions together, turning out our lights and closing our eyes as we went out hunting, fishing, skateboarding, swimming, fighting in wars, and even heading out to the club to meet chicks. We invented a game called Death Row Idol in which we competed with songs, poetry, jokes, skits, and stories, then we all casted our votes to see who'd be voted off of the gurney. We laughed and cried together, sharing intimate memories, regrets, hopes and dreams. I grew to love those guys like brothers. Sadly, only Jeff fought his conviction. The rest of us had no hope of surviving this experience, so we just tried to enjoy our moments together until that fateful day arrives. Unfortunately, the order of the day here is death. The state has relentlessly snatched away so many. Tiny was killed on June 16, 2011... they got Kevin and Billy in May 2010... Woody seemed happy to go in September of 2007... Budders also high-stepped it outta here in September of 2011... Wolf reminded me that "as long as there's life there's hope" before he was taken in May of 2005 with Chi-Town... A few months before they killed Mark Stroman, who got here around the same time I did, he told me they'd killed over 200 people since we drove up. Images of these dudes and countless others flash through my mind at times; I can hear them laughing, remember things they did and said, and more often than not it just seems senseless that the state killed them.

This takes us up to the present day, as Robert still sits on Death Row, his appeals exhausted, seventy-two hours left before his life will be ended by the Texas Department of Criminal Justice, at 6p.m. on Thursday, with a fatal dose of pentobarbital.

Robert's autobiography is an incredibly difficult book to read. First, it is long, since it contains literally every memory Robert can think of from ages 0 to 30, though that makes it all the more remarkable as a document of his development. Second, it is disturbing: from its very first pages it is full of violence and cruelty, and as Robert goes from childhood to premature adulthood, a good deal of that violence is perpetrated by Robert himself. But the greatest difficulty is that of reliability: how does the reader know that Robert is telling the truth? In the book, Robert strongly insists that he is innocent of the murder that he is about to be put to death for. If we believe him, then a horrific injustice is about to occur in the State of Texas. But if we don't believe him, what then? The book is powerful in part because its narrator feels so *honest*: he wants to sincerely introspect about his life and the factors that caused it to unfold the way it did. He doesn't hesitate to take full responsibility for doing a number of truly horrible things: burglarizing houses, hitting people, stealing drugs, stealing guns, and precipitating his father's murder of Ray. Robert reflects intelligently on the balance between environmental determinism and individual choice. He quotes Randy Pausch: "we can't choose the hands we are dealt, but we can choose how to play them," and concludes that "for the most part, my father and I both played our hands in the worst possible ways." What he says, though, is that people "should be defined not by their mistakes but by whether or not we have learned from them and have become better people as a result." Yet the innocence/guilt question still looms large, because what judgment we come to about whether Robert committed the crime must inevitably color our entire impression of his self-analysis.

Here is the incredibly frustrating and complicated part of Robert's case: I do not think it is possible to determine his innocence or guilt based on the available evidence. The case against Robert feels compelling: there were witnesses, Robert was in the building with a cut on his hand, and the torn-up disciplinary report had Robert's name on it. *And yet:* the evidence against Robert is no more compelling than the evidence that has been brought against many people who have turned out to be innocent. In plenty of wrongful convictions, the evidence seemed like a slam-dunk. Robert's case does not seem like a slam-dunk: inmate-witnesses who receive deals have *incredibly* strong motives to lie, having a cut on your hand in prison isn't uncommon, and tearing up some other guy's disciplinary report is precisely what you would do if you wanted to deflect suspicion after having murdered a correctional officer. Robert claims Officer Nagle was widely despised, even by other correctional officers, and believes he was framed. And frankly, that's perfectly plausible: I wrote recently about John Thompson, a Louisiana man who was framed for murder by a career criminal.[2]

But it's precisely because it's so difficult to know what happened to Officer Nagle that nobody should feel comfortable with the execution of Robert Pruett. If the weapon had been tested and Robert's DNA had been found on it, that could have given us confidence. Instead, the testing found: nothing. Legally, that's not enough to reverse Robert's conviction. Rationally, however, it should deeply unsettle us. I don't know whether Robert Pruett murdered Daniel Nagle. But I am certain that the State of Texas doesn't know either, and that alone should be reason not to take Robert's life.

IF I AM BEING HONEST, THOUGH, the innocence issue has never been fundamental to my interest in Robert Pruett, and while I don't want to suggest it isn't important, I also don't want to dwell on it too much. That's not because I don't find Robert's defense persuasive, but because even if Robert Pruett didn't kill Daniel Nagle, the criminal justice system contains plenty of other "Robert Pruetts" who did commit the crimes they were accused of. And those people do not deserve to be put to death either. I am capable of understanding, knowing the facts of Robert's life, how someone in his position *might* have murdered someone like Nagle. Robert Pruett was literally born to the man who landed him in prison for life. In elementary school his parents were giving him drugs, and by his teenage years he was facing 99 years. It would be hideously poetical for the son to end up receiving the death penalty for the crime his father taught him to commit.

I would be sympathetic to a Robert Pruett who *had* killed someone because I understand that what happened to Robert at the age of 15 was a horrific injustice, and that what happened subsequently cannot be separated from that injustice. For the state to take a child, and throw him into an adult prison, where unless he becomes scarily violent he will be mercilessly raped, is to do everything possible to create a monster. One reason it's important not to focus on whether Robert committed the second crime is that it ignores the first crime: the crime committed by telling a teenager he will be caged with rapists for 99 years. If that crime had not occurred, if the Texas justice system had treated him rationally and humanely, instead of throwing him into the abyss, then Robert might be a psychology professor today, rather than a man whose life is about to end pointlessly at the age of 38. (And I do mean pointlessly. Della Nagle, sister of Daniel, says that not only does she not know whether Robert is guilty, but that "Because I don't believe in the death penalty, I have no desire to watch the state murder somebody... It's not going to make my family whole again, but it is going to make his family not whole and so I have no desire to go see him be killed."[3]) It's very difficult not to agree with what Robert says about the initial decision to put him away for life:

> *A jury isn't required to explain their vote. Apparently, they thought I was beyond rehabilitation, that the only solution was to throw me away. Think about it for a second. Society places many restrictions on minors because they aren't mature enough to make responsible decisions. Studies have shown that parts of the brain related to reasoning don't fully develop until the mid-20's. At 15 I wasn't old enough to be outside after the 11pm curfew, I couldn't watch R-rated movies without adult supervision, I couldn't smoke, drink, get a tattoo, own a gun or even drive a car. Yet I was mature and reasonable enough to make decisions that would impact the rest of my life? Old enough to spend the rest of my life in prison? It is still unfathomable to me.*

Giving up on a person at this age is especially cruel when you think about how little Robert Pruett was to blame for having been been born to Sam Pruett. And it's especially senseless when you think about how it disincentivizes a teenager from ever trying to make up for their mistakes. Yet despite spending more than half his life in prison, Robert is still a vastly different person than the middle-school hoodlum who broke into houses and sold pot in 1993. That kid disliked reading, punched his way out of problems, and had no qualms about hurting people. The Robert

Pruett of today has renounced violence and detests the person he was for many years. And despite ample evidence in his memoir that nearly everyone around him, both in his family life and in prison, had strong racial prejudices, he deplores racism:

> It wasn't until I got to death row that I realized my ignorant and hateful views on race were a reflection/projection of how I felt about myself, that I'd constructed a complex ideology totally rooted and parallel to the things I most disliked about me. I used to go on tangents about the criminality exhibited by the black youth of America, how it needs to be addressed and curbed, but the truth was that I was talking about myself the entire time and didn't even realize it. It's a truth that we project onto others the things we most hate about ourselves. Carl Jung said that our shadow selves, the part of our psyches that we store repressed emotional themes and the aspects of our personalities we dislike, is represented by what we hate/dislike in others. You are what you hate...

Paradoxically, it was Death Row that enabled Robert to realize this:

> Somehow, I believe it took me coming here, living the life of extreme adversity that I have, in order to conquer my shadow and grow in the ways I have... I needed to have my life ripped away from me, to face a hopeless situation and experience great loss and pain in order to finally break through and spread my own wings...

And yet Death Row's calming effect on Robert's psyche, its ability to melt away grievances and catalyze growth, can't possibly justify the act of execution itself. As Robert writes, once you change a person, you're no longer taking the life of the person who perpetrated the crime:

> The thing is, they aren't killing the same people who committed the crimes. It takes years for the appeals to run their course and in that time people change. Sure, some are just dangerous as the day they

arrived, and I'm not saying everyone's some kind of angel, but so many have grown and matured in here and found their true Self. Many have realized the errors of their ways and would be productive members of society if they were given the chance. Even with a life in prison, these guys had much to offer humanity, not to mention the loved ones left with the scars of their murders.

That applies to Mark Stroman, who Robert met before Stroman's execution. Stroman had committed a truly horrendous hate crime: in 2001, he shot three South Asian people, two of whom died, as "revenge" for 9/11.[4] But something remarkable happened after the tragedy: Rais Bhuiyan, the surviving victim, went on a pilgramage to Mecca and had a revelation. He corresponded with Stroman, who it turned out had been the "victim of extreme abuse and neglect as a child and became addicted to methamphetamine while in his teens." Bhuiyan forgave Stroman, and dedicated himself to saving Stroman's life, starting an organization called World Without Hate: "I'm trying to do my best not to allow the loss of another human life," Buiyan said. "I'll knock on every door possible. In Islam it says that saving one human life is the same as saving the entire mankind. Since I forgave him, all those principles encouraged me to go even further, and stop his execution and save another human life." As Bhuiyan worked to have him spared, Stroman realized just how harmful his bigotry had been. Days before his scheduled execution, he said:

> *For him to come forward after what I've done speaks volumes and has really touched my heart and the heart of many others... My friends and supporters [have been] trying to save my life, but now I have the Islamic community joining in, spearheaded by one very remarkable man named Rais Bhuiyan, who is a survivor of my hate. His deep Islamic beliefs gave him the strength to forgive the unforgivable. That is truly inspiring to me and should be an example for us all. The hate has to stop, we are all in this world together.[5]*

Stroman's repentance, and Bhuiyan's forgiveness, were an extraordi-

nary story about the possibilities for restorative justice. It didn't matter.
The State of Texas executed Stroman anyway. His last words were: "Hate
is going on in this world and it has to stop. Hate causes a lifetime of pain."

Mark Stroman wasn't innocent. He was guilty of, as he said, the unfor-
givable. But his execution was still an injustice, because it denied the
possibility of any kind of reconciliation or rehabilitation. As Robert
writes in his memoir, the death penalty is not just unfair because of the
risk of taking innocent lives, but because it is also an inhuman act of
revenge perpetrated upon the guilty:

> *What the state is doing here is completely wrong. Not only is the
> system flawed and more than a few innocent are killed, but it's a
> stain against humanity when society kills in the name of justice.
> How do you teach someone it's wrong to kill by killing? The death
> penalty is about vengeance, hate, and ultimately, fear. Hopefully
> one day the death penalty will be abolished. Until that day arrives
> all of us who are horrified and outraged by the primitive and bar-
> baric killings here should stand up against it.*

That's why I don't think the question of whether or not Robert should
be executed should hinge on whether or not Robert took a life. The
evidence of his guilt is woefully short of anything that could reasonably give us enough confidence to kill a man. But say Robert isn't telling
the truth. It's possible, because thanks to the unforgiving quality of the
Texas justice system, proving his innocence is the only possible route to
saving his life. Even if this were the case, though, *The Autobiography of
Robert Pruett* provides ample evidence that his death would be an indefensible tragedy. Not that these qualities should be necessary for mercy,
but Robert is brilliant and sensitive, and his memoir makes it clear that
in destroying Robert, society has squandered one of its most promising
assets. Certainly, Robert could have made different choices during elementary school, and we can blame that small child as much as we like.
Yet we also see how much couldn't really be helped. Pruett's autobiography is a kind of anti-*Hillbilly Elegy* that ends at Death Row instead

of Yale Law School, and shows us how difficult it can be to transcend a childhood of poverty and violence, without anyone helping you or encouraging you, when every surrounding influence is a bad influence driving you further toward a seemingly inevitable terrible endpoint. No life more conclusively shows that, whether thanks to divine jealousy or genetic happenstance, in this unforgiving world the sins of the father are visited directly upon the son.

March 4, 2018

I never did meet Robert. The Texas Department of Criminal Justice refused my requests to meet with him, citing a regulation that turned out not to exist. Robert was executed on October 12, 2017, at the age of 38. I spent the last several days of his life frantically trying to draw attention to his case, to the point of desperately trying to get ahold of the Pope thinking he might be willing to telephone the Governor of Texas, who is Catholic. (This could not have made a difference, but it was very hard for me to accept that there was no way to stop the state from carrying out this premeditated and unnecessary killing.) After Robert's death, I was sad, but far more than that I was angry. I felt furious that this country, and this world, could be so cruel and stupid as to allow a government to intentionally inject Robert Pruett with poison. I felt hatred, not just for every judge and criminal justice official who refused to elevate justice above law, but for everyone else as well for failing to stop the execution, especially myself for all the time I spent on comparatively frivolous things while Robert moved steadily closer to the end of his life. I hope I can atone a bit by continuing to tell his story.

I am told that, contrary to some press reports, Robert did not appear to suffer, and was placid and collected as he was taken into the death chamber.

Honesty About
The Death Penalty

THE DEATH PENALTY IS NOT A DETERRENT. The death penalty is racist. The death penalty is costly. The death penalty risks executing innocent people, and probably has. The death penalty is not used in nearly all other industrialized democracies. The death penalty probably won't bring victims' families real peace of mind.

Each one of these is an argument I believe about the death penalty. I've made them all before, to one person or another. I have them down cold: I can recite the statistics on how much likelier a person is to get the death penalty if their victim is white rather than black; I can tell you that it costs the state at least $1 million to execute someone, often ten times that, and that California has probably spent over $4 billion total on the death penalty[1]; I can tell you about men like Cameron Todd Willingham and Carlos De Luna who were executed despite strong evidence of their innocence,[2] and men like John Thompson,[3] who were nearly executed before being exonerated. I can give you half-a-dozen pragmatic, evidence-based reasons for opposing the death penalty.

And yet if I'm being truly honest with myself, and with you, none of these arguments means very much to me.

It's not that I don't think they're good arguments. They're all correct, or I wouldn't make them. It's just that they have very little to do with the reason I oppose the death penalty. That's because my opposition to the death penalty is entirely rooted in a visceral horror at the intentional taking of defenseless human life. I make those other arguments against the death penalty strategically, when I think they will persuade people. But they don't matter much to me, because if the facts were otherwise, it wouldn't change my position on the death penalty. If the death penalty were guaranteed not to kill innocent people, I would still oppose it. If there was no racial difference in the likelihood of receiving the death penalty, I would still oppose it. If other industrial democracies used the death penalty frequently, I would still oppose it. Even if it were a deterrent, I would still oppose it, because I don't think you can murder people just because doing so causes other people to think twice about murdering people themselves.

I oppose the death penalty because I believe it's almost always immoral to kill anyone who does not pose an immediate physical threat to someone else. And since practically speaking, here in 21st century America, it's possible to eliminate the threat that even the most hardened killer poses, I don't believe that we can ever justify killing someone for a crime they have committed. For me, that's the end of it. There's not really any other element to the calculus. It's a very strong instinct I have, it's not shared by most, and a lot of people would recoil in revulsion at it. But I can't get rid of it, because it's far too essential a belief.

Frankly, I suspect there are plenty of people who oppose the death penalty for similarly non-rational reasons, but who end up making all of the aforementioned arguments because they are persuasive to others, rather than because they are their own reasons. That is to say, I think plenty of people who use the argument about risks of executing the innocent are not interested in the *real* level of risk of executing the innocent, they are absolutists like myself who are disgusted by the spectacle of a person being lethally injected. But because it's hard to persuade someone else to be disgusted by something they're not disgusted by (since disgust is largely instinctual), we end up making the above arguments, even though we'd still be unhappy even if every single one of those problems were excised. Because I want to be honest, however, I feel it's important to be clear on why I oppose the death penalty. It's not because it's racist or risky or costly; it's because every single usage of it fundamentally assaults my sense of justice, even if that usage is non-racist, non-risky, and non-costly.

I know that we need to make innocence arguments in order to be persuasive, because "Can't you see how horrible this is?" only persuades the already-persuaded. It's also worth noting, however, that I think more people would be viscerally disturbed by the death penalty if it were made more real to them. Albert Camus, in "Reflections on the Guillotine," tells of his father, who strongly supported the death penalty after a prominent local case in which man was convicted of robbing and murdering an entire family.[4] Camus' father wanted to see justice done, so he went to watch the man be guillotined. (The French continued to use the guillotine until 1977.[5]) Camus says that when his father came home from the event, his face was distorted and he could not speak. Instead, he simply went to his bedroom, lay down, and suddenly began to vomit. Camus explains that his father could only support executing the murderer because he hadn't actually contemplated what that meant. But once he understood, he was horrified: "He had just discovered the reality hidden under the noble phrases with which it was masked. Instead of thinking of the slaughtered children, he could think of nothing but that quivering body that had just been dropped onto a board to have its head cut off."

A person may have committed a horrible crime, one in which they brutally abused other people. But when they are taken to be executed, they have always been turned powerless and almost pitiful. A prisoner in chains is weak compared to his captor, and there's something disturbing about committing violence upon a weak individual, irrespective of how tyrannical they may once have been. Muammar Gaddafi and Saddam Hussein, at the ends of their lives, were miserable specimens. They had once been killers themselves, but by the day of their deaths they had been reduced to little more than bodies in cages. Killing a person in a cage seems one-sided and sadistic, however emotionally compelling vengeance may be when talked of abstractly.

George Orwell says something similar in "Revenge is Sour."[6] He writes of seeing a former SS officer in a prisoner of war camp in 1945. The ex-Nazi was now a bedraggled nonentity, kicked and shoved about by his guards. As Orwell wrote, when he actually saw the man in the flesh, "the Nazi torturer of one's imagination, the monstrous figure against whom one had struggled for so many years, dwindled to this pitiful wretch, whose obvious need was not for punishment, but for some kind of psychological treatment." Orwell says there is a bleak contrast between our fantasies of revenge and its reality. "Who would not have jumped for joy, in 1940, at the thought of seeing S.S. officers kicked and humiliated? But when the thing becomes possible, it is merely pathetic and disgusting."

But in the contemporary United States, steps have been taken to ensure that people don't experience that feeling of disgust. We do not conduct public executions, because if we saw what we were doing, more people might react like Camus' father and simply begin throwing up. We have also, as many observers have noted, "medicalized" capital punishment through using lethal injection instead of the more viscerally unsavory methods. The contrast between lethal injection and the guillotine is illuminating, actually. Lethal injection instinctively feels more humane than decapitation; after all, it's just "putting somebody to sleep." But in reality, it can cause excruciating pain. As Amnesty International has suggested,[7] it only gives the appearance of being humane. In fact, the guillotine, with its near-instantaneous effect, might be far more humane for the person actually being executed. Yet it's inconceivable that the guillotine would be used in the contemporary United States, for the obvious reason that it would make us all sick to our stomachs. Anyone who is serious about their support for the death penalty, though, should be fine with public decapitations. (Interestingly, the Saudi government has made this point when criticized about their own controversial record of beheadings. A beheading, they say, is just a more honest and efficient way of doing what we already do in the U.S. It's a point that's difficult to respond to, unless you're just as horrified by our own record as you are by theirs.)

I understand, then, that it's always going to be hard to persuade people to feel an emotional hatred of the death penalty if it does not come naturally to them, and that my own feelings can't be *rationally* defended, just as a belief that we should all be decent to one another can't be rationally defended. But instead of just setting aside our emotional convictions, and trying to persuade people with intellectual arguments about deterrence, risk, cost, and fairness, I think we ought to be trying to make the reality of the death penalty more intelligible to people, to ensure that nobody can talk about it abstractly without thinking about what it actually means to strap a person down and kill them. I want people like Robert Pruett to seem like conscious human beings, which they are, rather than malevolent abstractions. It's easy to endorse doing violence to words; it's harder when we think about a "quivering body," a person sweating as they are laid onto a board to have a blade dropped, or a needle inserted.

Discourse

Thinking Strategically About Free Speech and Violence

WHEN IT COMES TO NEO-NAZIS, the most important thing is to stop them from gaining power. We know that, as brutal as they are are when wandering the streets beating black men with metal poles,[1] if Nazis ever again achieved control of a powerful state, the consequences would be inconceivably horrific for hundreds of millions, probably billions, of people around the world.[2] The growth of white supremacist ideology in the 20th century led to slaughter on an unimaginable scale. It must never, ever happen again.

When there are white supremacists in our midst, then, and we are deciding how to deal with them, the strategy question is of critical importance: what is the best way to actually undermine the political prospects of racist movements? The actions taken by leftists must be discussed in terms of their predictable consequences. The task is to stop the Nazis. A vital question, for any given left-wing approach, should be: "Does this help us, or does it help the Nazis?"

This seems like it should be too obvious to be worth saying. If you're trying to eliminate the existence of white supremacist ideology, you need to decide what to do based on whether it stops the spread of white supremacist ideology. But many conversations among left-leaning people end up focusing on somewhat abstract questions of moral justice without addressing the equally important question of pragmatic usefulness. For example, when the question of "whether to use violence" is addressed, many people dwell on the legitimacy of violence rather than the efficacy of violence, even though whether violence is justified depends in part on what it accomplishes. And when the question is "Should free speech rights extend to Nazis?" the conversation often centers around "whether Nazis deserve rights" rather than "whether curtailing Nazis' rights is an effective means of combating them." This lack of focus on long-term strategy and concrete consequences is dangerous. If one concludes, say, that "Nazis do not deserve rights" but has not carefully examined whether taking away Nazis' rights will help or hurt the Nazi cause, it might turn out that the seemingly justified course of action and the "most likely to stop the Nazis" course of action do not coincide.

The issues of "free speech" and "violence" are incredibly fraught and complicated. There are no easy answers to questions like: "At what point does speech become too dangerous to permit?" or "When is violence justified?" I am skeptical of anyone who believes they have an absolute resolution. But I do know that we should reject any answer that fails to seriously address the question "Realistically, what would be the predictable consequences of accepting this belief?"

When it comes to the issue of free speech, a lot of people on the left now seem to subscribe to a position roughly as follows:

> *The traditional liberal idea that "everyone has the right to speak" is a fantasy. In theory, this may be true, but in practice different people do not have an equal ability to speak. Far right voices have far more of a mouthpiece (e.g. Fox News) than the voices of marginalized and oppressed people. "Free speech" therefore does not mean that we should allow more speech from the far right, but that we should try to elevate the speech of those who are not heard. Furthermore, being free to speak does not mean that you are entitled to a platform. Nor does it mean you are entitled to be free of social consequences for your speech. Besides, "hate speech" or speech that causes harm should not be protected.*

This is related to, but distinct from, another emerging left-wing principle about justifications for the use of violence, increasingly relevant as "antifa" groups advocate using physical force against the right.[3] The position here is generally something like:

> When fascists are permitted to speak, they spread fascism. Fascism must not be allowed to spread. Thus fascists should not be permitted to speak. Fascists cannot be reasoned with. They must be physically resisted. White supremacist or genocidal speech is in itself violence or incitement, so physically stopping fascists from speaking is only a form of self-defense. Neo-Nazis should be punched when they appear in public, because doing so makes them afraid and makes it clear that their ideology is not socially acceptable. The only language such people know is violence, and they must be defeated with a superior show of "counter-violence."

Two post-Charlottesville opinion pieces capture the emergent left consensus fairly well. K-Sue Park, in a *New York Times* article entitled "The ACLU Should Rethink Free Speech," adopts the position that civil libertarians have adopted too narrow a conception of speech rights, in a way that has benefitted far right groups over disadvantaged and marginalized people.[4] Natasha Lennard, in a *Nation* article entitled "Not Rights but Justice: It's Time to Make Nazis Afraid Again," defends Antifa tactics, arguing that regardless of what protections far-right speech receives or does not receive from the state, it is crucial to "confront [neo-Nazis] in the streets" and make sure that "all far-right events will be bombarded and besieged."[5]

I actually find all of these arguments incredibly persuasive. In fact, their conclusions seem almost inescapable. They even feel logically compelled: (1) Nazis advocate genocide (2) Genocide is horrifically violent and must be prevented (3) Nazism is inherently violent (4) Defensive violence is therefore justified as a means of preventing the spread of fascism. Alternately, (4) can be: government restrictions on fascist speech are therefore justified, people found to have far right sympathies should be fired from their jobs, or universities should refuse to permit fascists to speak, etc. Whatever counter-measure is being defended, the violence of fascism seems to easily justify the proposed response.

But it's strange that a chain of reasoning should seem so compelling and conclusive when it doesn't actually address that all-important question: will whatever is being advocated in (4) actually be an effective long-term tool for undermining white supremacists? We have managed to produce a justification for the use of Tactic X to stop the Nazis that doesn't actually evaluate whether Tactic X stands any chance of working. Efficacy has to be part of any analysis of legitimacy, however. For example: if we are debating whether our country is justified in entering a war, whether we are justified depends in part on what we think will happen if we enter the war. It's easy to say something like: Country A encroached on our territory and killed our people, therefore we are justified in retaliating. But what if we know that our retaliation will cause a cycle of violence that will kill millions more people, and that there is a diplomatic solution available that would result in no more loss of life? Retaliation, in that case, wouldn't be justified. And yet so many of people's conversations about justifications occur this way, dwelling on whether we have legitimate grounds for this or that action rather than whether the action will actually have a positive effect.

The left critiques of free speech rights and nonviolent tactics frequently avoid engaging with the question of consequences. Look at the structure of these arguments: free speech doesn't entitle you to a platform. Free speech doesn't mean that people can't disrupt you. White supremacist speech is violence, therefore violence against it is self-defense. All of these justifications sound good, yet none of them actually respond to the most serious objection, namely that adopting these positions would not actually help the left.

Consider K-Sue Park's free speech article in the *New York Times*. Park believes that the ACLU's approach to speech is too limited, because by defending the rights of white supremacists, the ACLU is failing to address the various ways in which the ability to speak is unequally distributed:

> *The hope is that by successfully defending hate groups, its legal victories will fortify free-speech rights across the board: A rising tide lifts all boats, as it goes. While admirable in theory, this approach implies*

that the country is on a level playing field, that at some point it over-
came its history of racial discrimination to achieve a real democracy,
the cornerstone of which is freedom of expression....For marginalized
communities, the power of expression is impoverished for reasons
that have little to do with the First Amendment.

It should first be noted that one part of this is simply wrong. The ACLU's theory, that ensuring speech protection for people on the other side ultimately helps out side (the "rising tide" idea) in no way "implies that the country is on a level playing field." One can acknowledge that in practice, the ability to speak is unequally distributed while still believing that everyone benefits from the aggressive defense of First Amendment freedoms. Many people who support the ACLU's efforts to restrict state power to regulate speech are *also* concerned with the ways in which other factors limit certain people's ability to be heard, e.g. the role of money in determining whose voice is the loudest.[6]

More importantly, though, Park's argument falls into this category of "persuasive-sounding notions that don't actually work through what the implications of buying into them would be." Park says that the ACLU ought to "rethink" its position and become more "holistic." But what are we actually talking about? The ACLU's job, at the moment, is to resist attempts by the government to limit people's freedoms. It does this by taking cases whenever the government is exercising unjustified or unconstitutional power over someone. The reason that the ACLU doesn't care about the identity of the "someone" in question is that, as Park says, it believes restricting government power quite obviously helps everyone. Now, we can *say* that the ACLU should remove white supremacists from the category of people it helps. But we haven't addressed the question that raises: what if the organization shifts its focus away from an absolute defense of the First Amendment, and as a result a set of bad legal precedents ends up curtailing everyone's First Amendment rights? Park's critique doesn't actually address this. Instead of dealing with the argument that is actually made (a failure to defend the First Amendment in all cases of infringement will cede powers to the government that will be used against the oppressed), it simply dwells on the fact that the world is unjust and uses vague terms like "holistic" and "contextual" without saying clearly what this would actually mean for the future of speech jurisprudence and what potential effects this may have on those victimized by government overreach.

The same question needs to be answered when it comes to shutting down the events of right-wing speakers on college campuses. Leave aside the issue of whether there is a principled reason for allowing student groups to invite whomever they please to speak. Even if we assume that protesters are correct in seeing little meaningful difference between Milo Yiannopoulos,[7] Charles Murray,[8] and Adolf Hitler, the question of what to do is still a strategic one. That necessarily involves considering how left actions will be portrayed in the media and received by the public. When protesters leave a professor in a neck brace after a Charles Murray talk, this does not look good for the left.[9] When a teenager outside a Yiannopoulos event is beaten and covered in paint for wearing an American flag hat, this does not look good for the left.[10] Of course, one can say that the media coverage will be unfair, that the press will pay far more attention to the violence committed by left protesters at a Milo event than the worse violence committed by right-wing protesters.[11] But if you are are worried about consequences, it doesn't matter who is to blame, it matters what the effects of your actions are.

One oversight seems to be that acts are evaluated by their short-term success without regard to their role in a long-term strategy. For example, if we get our university to commit to banning hate speech, and they cancel a talk by a white supremacist, we may think we have scored a tremendous victory. But then, next month, our new rule may be invoked by pro-Israel groups to make the case that the Students For Justice In Palestine should be banned. Or we might punch a Nazi, and feel pleased and victorious as we watch him bleed and cry, not realizing that we have just made him 100 times more determined and vengeful, and have pushed his previously unsympathetic friends another inch closer to the far right position. The fist administered to Richard Spencer's face was justified on the grounds that humiliating white supremacists would reveal them to be weak and erode their support.[12] In the short term, that seems to have been the case;

Spencer said he didn't want to go outside anymore.[13] In the long term, predictably, he came back, this time with hundreds of supporters carrying torches,[14] and (by one measure) the alt-right continued to grow.[15] This is not to say that punching Richard Spencer caused him to organize the torch march, but that it's easy to think short-term successes are victories when they actually have either no effect or a counter-productive effect in the long run. And as Fredrik deBoer has put it, there's a natural instinct to want to engage in the fights we can win easily rather than the fights we actually have to win:

> Incidents like the black bloc protests at Berkeley or the punching of Richard Spencer grant people license to overestimate the current potential of violent resistance. Hey, Spencer got punched; never mind that the Trump administration reinstituted the global gag rule on abortion the next day. Hey, Milo's talk got canceled; never mind that the relentless effort to deport thousands, a bipartisan effort for which the Obama administration deserves considerable blame, went on without a hitch.[16]

It's also possible, in the celebration of anything that appears to harm white supremacists, to end up jettisoning principles that are ultimately important for protecting the left. For example, when it comes to speech on campus, one reason to embrace the absolute principle "everybody should be allowed to speak" rather than "everybody should be allowed to speak except X," even if "X" is just limited to "bigots," is that the addition of any qualifier whatsoever opens up room for greater and greater restrictions. The "slippery slope" argument is often called a "fallacy," but it's actually just an inquiry into what the limiting principle is that will prevent our category from expanding to cover a greater and greater number of cases. It's easy to declare that transphobic speech should be banned from campus. It sounds good, even unobjectionable. But that's the principle that led to pressure at Cardiff University to cancel a talk by anarchist feminist Germaine Greer, whose Second Wave feminist framework has led her to say some appallingly insensitive things about transgender people.[17] The abandonment of the principle that repulsive views should still be heard may well come back to haunt anyone whose views could be perceived as repulsive by anyone else.

Likewise, post-Charlottesville, there has been a gleeful rush to "doxx" white supremacists and get them fired from their jobs. This is seen as an especially effective tactic, because it inhibits the ability of white supremacists to live ordinary lives, and if it becomes hard to be a white supremacist and live an ordinary life, the theory is that fewer people will want to become white supremacists.[18] But there's a reasonable case to be made that one should be *very* careful about endorsing the tactic of getting people fired, even for holding white supremacist beliefs.[19] That's not because one deserves to be able to have genocidal views and also be warmly embraced by society, but because the left has always (correctly) stood for the principle that employers should have limited ability to deprive people of work for reasons that have nothing to do with their job performance. Igniting a "doxxing war" and legitimizing/encouraging the tactic of pressuring employers to fire people for non-work-related reasons not only has risks such as mistaken identity,[20] but contradicts a fundamental principle of the left approach to labor rights: what you do in your time off the job should be no business of your employer. Principles like these will always have exceptions (speech isn't unlimited, employment protections aren't unlimited) but it's important to at least understand why there might be some value in preserving them or keeping the exceptions to them well-defined and strictly limited.

The lack of engagement with "possible horrible/counterproductive consequences" is equally present in left justifications for violence, especially surrounding the actions of Antifa groups. Consider Natasha Lennard's article on "making Nazis afraid."[21] Lennard recognizes that having the government deprive Nazis of free speech rights might be ineffective, since countries that have banned neo-Nazis still, shockingly enough, have thriving neo-Nazi movements. (She does not, however, acknowledge the other possible harms that might come from empowering the state to adjudicate which forms of speech are acceptable, and even says that countries with greater state power to restrict hate speech are no less free than the United States, an assertion I do not agree with, because I believe that entrusting the state with greater power to decide what is acceptable inherently makes people less free.) But she says that even if we do not increase state power, Antifa disruptions of events by white supremacists are desirable and justified. She also voices no qualms whatsoever about the use of violence:

> *We are, to take some liberties with the words of Inglourious Basterds' inimitable Lt. Aldo Raine, in the fightin'-Nazis business. Antifa is a promise to neo-Nazis and their bedfellows that we will confront them in the streets; we will expose them online and inform their place of employ. We are not asking venues to deny space to far-right events; we are vowing that all far-right events will be bombarded and besieged.*

Already, this framing should raise concerns. I am not confident that someone who invokes the bloodthirsty and cartoonish language of a Quentin Tarantino character is interested in a sober-minded evaluation of the practical means by which racism can be defeated. Violence against Nazis, as we can see from this passage, carries a certain thrill and romance, and there is a danger that people will rationalize it because it gives the opportunity to engage in a noble moral struggle rather than because they have actually examined the various alternatives and concluded it is optimally helpful.

Lennard does acknowledge that "one of the major critiques of antifa" is that "physical confrontation can backfire by alienating moderates and centrists and provoking only further violence from the right." But her response to this serious critique is cursory and cagey. She says that:

> *The history of anti-fascism in 20th-century Europe is largely one of fighting squads, like the international militant brigades fighting Franco in Spain, the Red Front-Fighters' League in Germany who were fighting Nazis since the party's formation in the 1920s, the print workers who fought ultra-nationalists in Austria, and the 43 Group in England fighting Oswald Mosley's British Union of Fascists. In every iteration these mobilizations entailed physical combat. The failure of early-20th-century fighters to keep fascist regimes at*

bay speaks more to the paucity of numbers than the problem of their tactics. That is a lesson we can learn: Gather in greater and greater numbers.... White supremacy has never receded, because it was asked politely. The onus is on centrists and liberals to examine their own values if they would rather decry the counter-violence of those willing to put their bodies on the line against neo-Nazis than embrace a diversity of tactics in the face of the intractable problem of racism in America.

None of this answers the question: what is the likely effect of acts of violence (or, in Lennard's euphemistic phrase, "counter-violence") on the political fortunes of the American far right? "Embrace a diversity of tactics" sounds great. "Putting bodies on the line" sounds great. "Gather in greater numbers" sounds great. But we need to know whether the critics who say that violence will beget violence are correct. How similar to particular historical situations is the United States in 2017? Lennard's theory appears to be that the *only* way to prevent the rise of fascism is through violently attacking those who support it, and that if any violent anti-fascist group failed, it was simply because they did not have enough people committing enough violence. The solution is always, then, more violence. If you see white supremacist groups growing, you need greater numbers of people "besieging" them.

But what if this is wrong? What if, in fact, violent besiegings *do* contribute to an escalating cycle of violence? What if, here and now, they *do* serve as a formidable recruiting tool? I hope we're certain that this is not the case, because if we're *wrong* the consequences could be disastrous. I even see people on the left citing Hitler himself, who said that "only one thing could have stopped our movement—if our adversaries had understood its principle and from the first day smashed with the utmost brutality the nucleus of our new movement." But are we certain that we should be trusting Adolf Hitler as an authority on what to do about Nazis? Hitler believed in a world in which only "superior brutality" could ensure political success. And, certainly, it worked for him—it just also left tens of millions of people dead. Personally I believe we should make sure we have exhausted every other possible option before resorting to "utmost brutality" and I would like to know why people think we *have* exhausted the other options.

I'm not confident that Lennard is taking the difficult questions seriously. For instance, she says that "white supremacy has never receded because it was asked politely." But this is a facile and unfair description of those who question the utility of violence. Nobody is saying you should *ask white supremacy politely to go away.* The battle is not for the hearts and minds of white supremacists, but for the hearts and minds of the general public. Many on the left who take Lennard's position believe that those who call for nonviolence are suggesting you can "debate white supremacism out of existence." That's not the case, though. What they say is that you win more public supporters by making your case through a clear and well-organized communication of your ideas than through showing up to right-wing events and hitting people with clubs. "Nazis don't listen to reason," people scoff. No, but people who are *not* Nazis might listen to reason, and the important thing is to make sure that the Nazis are marginal by keeping the vast majority of people on your side rather than driving anyone else toward theirs. "Fascism cannot be defeated by speech."[22] But how the *hell* do they know this? *Nazi Germany* couldn't be defeated by speech. But a nascent and tiny group of fringe racists? I have more confidence than many on the left in the power of left-wing ideas to defeat pseudoscience and bigotry. And I'm always amazed that people give up on the value of communicating anti-racist ideas using reason and rhetoric even before they have actually tried it.[23] (Also, if we're being honest, some white supremacists *can* actually be convinced to drop their ideology. Former KKK "prodigy" R. Derek Black was slowly drawn away from his father's racist belief system thanks to patient and caring liberal classmates,[24] and recently wrote an essay on how shameful America's racial history is.[25])

Here is what I am worried about: I believe that unless the question of violence is treated carefully and responsibly, it could lead to something very bad indeed for the left. For example, say more people come around to Lennard's reasoning, and believe that fascists should not be permitted to speak publicly. And say they also blur the distinction between neo-Nazis and everyday Trump supporters, who are all lumped under the catch-all category "fascists." And since fascism is horrific, and the Antifa principle is that it must be stopped "by any means necessary," there is very little check on the permissible uses of violence. My fear is that, sooner or later, some blonde teenage girl wearing a MAGA hat,[26] or some disabled veteran in a Trump shirt,[27] is going to end up getting put in a coma. And when that happens, the left will face an almighty hellstorm of right-wing rage. I want to know why people are so confident that their endorsement of violent methods wouldn't lead to this. But all I hear are the same lines, over and over: You have to "nip Nazis in the bud," "fascism doesn't go away when it's asked politely," etc.

The usual talking points were repeated by Antifa supporter Mark Bray during a recent interview on MSNBC:

> *How do far-right movements grow? I say they grow by becoming normalized. By not being confronted. By being able to present them-selves as family friendly and respectable. ... By showing up and con-fronting it it prevents their ability to be presented as mainstream. [Furthermore,] you need to prevent them from being able to orga-nize. People involved in politics know that for movements to expand, they need to be able to organize and grow, and if you stop that, it prevents it. Historically, we can see that Nazism and fascism was not stopped by polite dialogue and reasoned debate, it had to be stopped by force. And unfortunately, self-defense is necessitated in the context we're seeing today.*[28]

Think about all the unanswered questions here. A sample: "If they grow when they are able to present themselves as family-friendly and respect-able, isn't there a PR risk with making our side look like the aggressors?" "What kind of 'confrontation' are we specifically talking about? The thou-sands of people who marched peacefully in Boston 'confronted' the right, but that seems different from showing up with clubs and beating them.[29] Aren't there essential distinctions between the efficacy of different kinds of confrontation?" "You say that if you 'stop' them from organizing, they stop growing. But if you stop them publicly and drive them back under a rock, won't they just organize in the shadows, like the alt-right have already been doing?[30] Do you really think that in the absence of actually *murdering* people with white supremacist beliefs, or inflicting a wave of truly extreme violence, you can stop them from meeting and spreading their message?" "When you say 'it had to be stopped by force,' this involved killing people; do you believe that in the contemporary United States, killing people for holding white supremacist beliefs is acceptable?" "What do you mean by 'self-defense'? Does that mean that if protesters are physically attacked by neo-Nazis they can fight back, or that physical attacks on neo-Nazis are themselves an act of self-defense?" Everything Bray says sounds compelling. And yet it doesn't tell us any of the things we really need to know. In fact, MSNBC's Chuck Todd followed up with Bray to try to get a more specific answer on one of the crucial questions, namely how Bray could be sure that violence wouldn't simply lead to more violence. Bray totally evaded the question:

> *Q: Are you at all concerned that violence begets violence?*
> *A: Self-defense is important. I'm more concerned—I mean, look at Cornel West. He said that the antifascists defended them from being run over and attacked. So I think the notion that people are seeing self-defense as being counterproductive is not entirely true. Self-defense is important, and fascism shows it is violence incarnate, it will come after us and we need to defend ourselves.*

Look at how dishonest this is. Bray is asked something very specific. How do we know that his endorsement of (unspecified) violent tactics will not simply fuel more violence from the right? He replies that "self-defense is important" and says that antifascists defended Cornel West from being run over. He then uses this fact to conclude that it is "not entirely true" that "self-defense" is counterproductive. Then he repeats that fascism is violence and people need to defend themselves. One does not need to reject the concept of self-defense in order to see that Bray is not taking the violence question seriously. In fact, he is trying to mislead the audience by using a term, "self-defense," that could cover many possibilities yet sounds impossible to argue with. This is literally the logic:

Q: "Won't the embrace of violent tactics lead to more violence?"

A: "Are you saying you want Cornel West to be run over? Are you saying people shouldn't get to defend themselves?"

But what kind of self-defense are we talking about? What are the acts that are being defended, and in what circumstances? Never trust anyone who speaks in abstractions and refuses to say exactly what it is they are justifying.

I don't see anything wrong with people advancing the argument that violence is justified as a tool against white supremacy. What does seem wrong, however, is the way the subject is frequently discussed on the left: without nuance or serious consideration of counterarguments. Recently, Noam Chomsky critiqued Antifa methods, suggesting that they actually ended up aiding the right.[31] Instantly, leftists called him "ill-informed" and dismissed his criticisms[32]; I even saw one commentator on social media compare Chomsky to a member of the Judenrat.[33] Instead of listening to and dealing with Chomsky's (very serious and important) criticism, they instantly branded as a traitor a man who has spent 50 years tirelessly working to support left causes.

I've even seen people react with hostility to those mentioning Martin Luther King's commitment to radical nonviolence and his belief that nonviolence was the most effective political tactic for achieving civil rights gains. Now, I actually understand why some people bristle at attempts to use King to chastise the left: even though MLK was an uncompromising anti-capitalist whose Birmingham Jail letter was a stinging critique of moderates who believed in slow, incremental change, these days he is often selectively quoted in order to tell radicals they are being too radical. Nothing is more infuriating than seeing a man who believed in deep and immediate change in the racial and economic hierarchy being invoked to justify the things he opposed.

Yet one cannot allow people's distortions and misuses of King to prevent a serious engagement with his philosophy. King said that he was "no doctrinaire pacifist" and held a "realistic pacifism," meaning that while war could sometimes be necessary, it was always a necessary *evil*, and needed eliminating from the earth.[34] He believed that nonviolence as a tool for social change was not just morally superior to violence, but that it was "one of the most potent weapons available to oppressed people in their struggle." If one of the greatest thinkers and most effective political tacticians in the history of social movements thinks abandoning nonviolence means giving up one of your most potent weapons, you should probably have very good reasons for dismissing his position.

Many of the arguments I've seen against nonviolence, however, have not been especially persuasive. Sometimes they're just sophistry: one *Washington Post* op-ed suggests that "violence was critical to the success of the 1960s civil rights movement, as it has been to every step of racial progress in U.S. history."[35] The author's justification for this statement is that Martin Luther King intentionally provoked violence *from police and white supremacists* in order to demonstrate the violence inherent in the U.S. racial hierarchy. But using this to say that "violence was critical" to the civil rights movement is odd, because it implies that the civil rights movement itself was violent, when it wasn't. One can blur distinctions, but the civil rights movement simply did not deploy aggressive violence against its opponents.

The usual response here is to invoke Malcolm X: Martin Luther King's nonviolence, it is said, only worked because whites preferred to deal with the nonviolent Martin rather than the non-nonviolent Malcolm. And that's true: King succeeded in part because of a tacit "good cop/bad cop" dynamic between himself and more radical black activists. Endorsing King's nonviolence without understanding the full range of tactics used in the pursuit of black liberation is a selective reading of history. But flattening Malcolm X into little more than a "scary, violence-advocating counterpart" to MLK is no less misleading. Something that is very rarely noted about Malcolm X is that while he is known for his *defense* of violence, he is not known for actually having *used* violence. In fact, in practice Malcolm X was generally no more violent than King. He was famously pictured holding an M1 carbine rifle, and openly criticized demands that black people refrain from fighting back even if attacked.[36] But Malcolm did not stage armed uprisings; he spoke of self-defense against aggression and a willingness to use whatever means would actually secure a person's rights and dignity. "I don't mean go out and get violent," he said, but rather exercising nonviolence *on the condition* that others remained nonviolent. "It doesn't mean I advocate violence, but at the same time, I am not against using violence in self-defense." The rifle-photograph actually illustrates Malcolm's attitude well: in it, he stands looking out the window, gun at the ready. He is not prowling around seeking racists to kill, he is standing firm and protecting his rights and dignity.

If someone is going to advocate "self-defensive violence" or "violence if necessary to achieve one's rights" it's very important to make clear what would and would not constitute self-defense, and what "necessity" is. Malcolm X was an incredibly disciplined and thoughtful individual, and he made careful distinctions between violence as a specific narrow tool for achieving one's liberty against another violent aggressor, and wanton, useless violence. One can even agree with everything Malcolm X says about the *legitimacy* of violence in self-defense and still believe that King's *strategy* of nonviolence is the optimum way to achieve certain social objectives. Personally, this is where I come down: I do not feel comfortable telling someone who is physically attacked that they should not defend themselves, but I also think King is right that radical nonviolence (never forget the "radical" part) is usually the best way of winning the public to one's cause, unless you are already in a situation where Hitler is about to take power and there is little left to do but fight.

If we're going to endorse "self-defense," though, it's important to be clear on what that is. In Charlottesville, the *New York Times'* Sheryl Gay Stolberg reported seeing "club-wielding 'antifa' beating white nationalists being led out of the park."[37] Is attacking people who are retreating a form of self-defense? The justification here is usually that fascist ideology is *itself* violence, meaning that it's not necessary for a person who holds such an ideology to actually be the one to initiate physical force in order for violence to be "defensive." But if we accept that, then simply walking up to a Trump supporter and stabbing them would seem to also be an act of self-defense, at which point... "self-defense" seems to mean something quite different from people's ordinary understanding of it. Mark Bray (a white Ivy League professor!) says it is a "privileged" position to criticize "self-defense."[38] Fine. But have we thereby justified every single kind of aggressive act toward anyone on the right, or are there some we haven't justified? The slippage, where once you've justified "any means necessary" in combating fascism, you have license to do anything to anyone that you've labeled a fascist, seems in part responsible for some of the more aggressive (and, to my mind, strategically unhelpful) acts by Antifa members.

Frankly, I think Antifa's confidence that any criticism of it is simply "privilege" and "defending Nazis" creates an incredible and embarrassing amount of arrogance. First, it gives them license to do whatever they please at protests, regardless of whether 90% of their fellow leftists would prefer the action remain peaceful (which makes them anti-democratic; they never seem to actually ask the communities they claim to serve what *they* think ought to be done, and the peaceful majority can end up being held responsible for the acts of a tiny violent minority). But it also leads them to stray from the actual message of the left, toward empty aggression. In one video from a Boston protest, an antifa member shouts "GET THE FUCK OUT OF MY CITY!" at a man holding an American flag and a P.O.W. flag (when the man is interviewed, he doesn't seem to be entirely all there, nor does he appear to be especially threatening).[39] In another, a crowd gathers around a man wearing a MAGA hat, with a masked Antifa member closing in on him and shouting "Fuck you! Fuck you! Fuck you!"[40] This is, first of all, inarticulate and stupid. ("Fuck you!" is a statement empty of any actual leftist content, it's just a grunt.) But I also don't see any principled, strategic, and disciplined anti-fascist action here. I just see aggressive, macho white guys being aggressive, macho white guys. And it seems to me as if they're enjoying themselves just a *little* too much. I certainly don't see either any "moral high ground" being claimed *or* any actual useful combating of Nazi ideology. (I do, however, see grist for new columns in *Breitbart* and the *National Review*.)

And yet: I also can't outright condemn Antifa. That's because I am concerned with consequences, and there were people in Charlottesville who gave persuasive accounts of the benefits that came from Antifa members stepping in to defend people from white supremacists when the police would not. Cornel West said that when peaceful clergy members were advanced on by members of the fascist groups, Antifa "saved our lives, actually. We would have been completely crushed, and I'll never forget that."[41] A similar account came from clergy member David Freeman.[42] Freeman says that before Charlottesville, he had "no patience with anyone advocating violence to advance social justice," for tactical reasons. However, he confirms West's story that were it not for the intervention of Antifa, a lot of nonviolent clergy members would have been brutally attacked:

> *I am still stalwart in my devotion to nonviolence but now, after Charlottesville, the story is more complex and nuanced. A group of Nazis advanced towards us. A band of AntiFa stepped up to defend the clergy, we asked them to step back and allow us to make our nonviolent stand. They respected our request and reluctantly backed off. ... After perhaps a hundred Nazis broke through our line we regrouped but an even larger Nazi force started towards us. The AntiFa rushed in and broke the Nazi charge. We did not ask for them. We were prepared to be beaten. However, we all respected that they defended us in love despite our disagreement on tactics. They certainly saved 19 clergy and me from a brutal beating and likely even death.*

Thus anyone who wishes Antifa had not been present in Charlottesville must reckon with the voices of the clergy who were thankful to have them there. Neo-Nazis are—unsurprisingly—inherently violent and often the aggressors, and if nobody is prepared to defend against them, innocent people will be hurt. Furthermore, it's wrong to draw false equivalencies between the far right and left (as Trump outrageously did). Racist violence by skinheads is not the same as someone throwing a water bottle at a Republican, the cause of racism is not the times as the cause of anti-racism, and since only one side in Charlottesville committed a murderous act of domestic terrorism, nobody should be talking about "violence" as some single nebulous category without drawing clear distinctions of scale, origin, and purpose. Anti-fascist violence consists of administering a righteous smack or two to guys who say the n-word and deny the Holocaust, while fascist violence consists of using a sports car to kill a kind-hearted Bernie Sanders voter.[43] Even if one believes all violence is wrong, some acts of violence are far more reprehensible than others.

I think this leads us straight back to the compromise position, though: evaluate everything in terms of its strategic usefulness, and don't be glib or ambiguous (like Bray and Lennard) in answering incredibly difficult questions. There is no good argument for a lot of what Antifa does. Going to a white supremacist rally and intentionally picking a fight, or trying to pepper spray Trump supporters in order to prevent them from going to a talk, seems to be, as Chomsky says, a "gift to the right." I am embarrassed to share a political orientation with someone whose idea of a protest for justice is to run after a man in a Trump hat shouting "Fuck you!" The need for self-defense is real, however, and I trust what the Charlottesville clergy members are saying. The solution seems to be that white supremacist actions should be met with massive nonviolent counter-protests that stand ready to defend themselves if they are attacked, but that do not actually initiate force against the far right. Nonviolence and self-defense are not particularly difficult to reconcile; one can mix Martin's commitment to countering hate with love and Malcolm's belief that people must be permitted to protect themselves if they are aggressed against.

I understand why people on the left have so easily become inclined to set aside the principles of free speech and nonviolence. Both of these concepts are used hypocritically these days in order to defend the status quo. Conservatives who chastise the left over "free speech" are entirely cynical and unprincipled. When events by racists like Charles Murray are threatened, it is a sign that college campuses have become "illiberal." But when Black Lives Matter supporter Keeanga Yamahtta-Taylor is forced to cancel a campus speaking tour over right-wing death threats, free speech conservatives go oddly silent.[44] My favorite example of how "free speech" has become an entirely meaningless term on the right is a recent *Wall Street Journal* op-ed in which the writer says that there are new "glimmers of hope" for free speech on college campuses.[45] As an example, she cites the fact that Pomona College fired the incoming director of its LGBTQ resource center because he had written tweets that said he was suspicious of white people.[46] To the *WSJ* writer, the fact that someone lost their job for holding a particular opinion was evidence that free speech was being *protected* and *defended*. For conservatives, the words "free speech" can mean little more than "anything that undermines the social justice left," even if the thing that undermines the left is... punishing people for their speech.

But I don't think it's obvious that the solution to right-wing hypocrisy is the abandonment of potentially vital civil libertarian and nonviolent principles. That's because these ideas are more useful than they initially appear, and it is easy to miss their power. "The best way to stop Nazis is to let them speak" seems flatly wrong at first. Yet the counterintuitive view might be the correct one; it might be more effective to spend your time recruiting people to your side than trying to put a stop to the recruiting efforts of the other side. Beware obvious answers, especially when the stakes are high. Likewise "the most effective weapon against hate is love" seems trite, sappy, and naive. But Gandhi and King weren't idiots. They thought deeply about all of the points that people raised against them, and still concluded that nonviolence was the optimal path. They believed that things that seem satisfying and effective in the short-run might actually not be the best course for achieving justice. And they knew it would be *hard* for people to suppress their instincts and impulses on this, but they also knew that nothing worth doing is ever easy. I am not sure if they were right, but I'm going to be very careful before concluding that they were wrong.

The argument that when Nazis are allowed to organize, their views become normalized and endanger people, seems to be more and more widely accepted on the left. I *nearly* buy it myself. But then I also hesitate, because I realize that there is another, unspoken flip-side: what happens when Nazis are *not* allowed to organize? Do they go away? Or do they fester in the dark? When Charles Murray speaks on campus, he is normalized. But what happens when Charles Murray *isn't* allowed to speak on campus? Does he cease to exist and be heard? Or does he develop martyr status and sell more books?

I can't resolve the difficult issues around speech, violence, "no platforming," and fascism. But what I can do is beg people to think about these things more critically and cautiously, to stop believing that observations like "Fascism is violence" can automatically settle strategic questions, and to recognize that *everything* depends on us getting this right, because if we happen to be wrong, the consequences will be catastrophic.

"Debate" Versus Persuasion

ONE COMMON ARGUMENT on the left runs as follows: one should not have an excessive confidence in the power of "rational debate" to solve political disagreements. There is, after all, no reasoning with some people. They are beyond argument, and thinking that you can reason with them is delusional. Any attempt to do so is likely to hurt your political fortunes, because it misunderstands how power works. Politics is not a university debating society, in which each side offers its premises and conclusions and the team with the tightest logic wins. It is "war by other means," a clash of interests that is won by gaining the ability to push your agenda through, not by showing the other side how reasonable you are.

This issue often comes up when someone on the left does something perceived to undermine free speech and open discussion. When a white supremacist gets punched in the face,[1] or a right-wing pundit gets shouted down on a college campus,[2] some moderate and civility-minded person will suggest that the best way to fight right-wing ideas is by debating them, not by shutting down the conversation entirely.[3] Inevitably, the response of those who do believe in shutting down "debate" is roughly as follows:

It's ridiculous to suggest 'debating' certain ideas, like fascism. You can't debate such a thing. You can only destroy it. It is laughable to propose that we should sit down and argue about whether white supremacism is a good thing.

A version of this argument is made by Richard Seymour.[4] Seymour says that "fact-checking" members of the far right is "beside the point." You can't "debate" someone like Donald Trump or Marine Le Pen. That's because a debate only works if both parties are interested in having one. But people like Trump and Le Pen aren't interested in debate. They use language as propaganda, rather than in a good faith attempt to find truth. Anyone who has watched a video of Adolf Hitler's spittle-spraying orations can instantly see the futility of "debate" against certain parties.

Seymour therefore counsels against ideas like, say, inviting Marine Le Pen onto your talk show so that you can grill her. You might think you can "expose" Le Pen this way, but you won't:

> *The basic idea that 'exposing' fascists is bad for them, that 'exposure' is something that they want to avoid, depends on the totally erroneous idea that they are there to free associate about their ideas, to converse, to logically defend various truth claims. If they were worried about being 'exposed' in that way, they wouldn't come on your television show, or go out of their way to court publicity.*

Discussion about the limits of debate is important. It has implications for questions of both free speech and political tactics: if dialogue is impossible, what's the point of attempting it? If right-wing speakers are not attempting discussion, but propaganda, why shouldn't you try to shut them down? And if political power is not built through debate, should we even be trying to convince people?

It's important, in considering these questions, to clear up what "debate" is to begin with. Many of the criticisms of "debating" people seem to assume a narrow definition of debate: they criticize those who think pure logic can successfully counter right-wing political points. The idea here is that "debate" consists of rational argumentation: I present my points, with evidence, you present counterpoints with evidence, I rebut your counterpoints, you parry my rebuttal with some more evidence, and one of us wins through superior logic. It is this form of debate that is impossible with Donald Trump. With Donald Trump, I present my points, with evidence, and he says I founded ISIS and then brags about having a billion dollars. You can't really meet this with "fact-checking" or even "logical argumentation," because facts don't mean anything to him.

But it's too simple to say this means you can't "debate" people like Trump or Le Pen. From the fact that you can't use a particular kind of debate (throwing facts at someone), we would be concluding that you can't debate them at all. That's not necessarily true, however. "Debate" is not strictly a contest of logical argumentation; it is a contest of persuasion, and the strict presentation of factual arguments and conclusions is only one of the ways in which this occurs.

Debates are about argument, but they're also about rhetoric, the art of discourse. "Rhetoric" has a negative connotation these days, but it shouldn't. It has a great tradition. Rhetoric is simply the use of spoken and written tactics of persuasion. The rhetorician calculates her words for the effect they will have on the audience. As classically conceived, this is opposed to the "dialectician," who uses words in an open-minded truth-seeking inquiry.

Richard Seymour is right. People like Trump and Le Pen aren't doing anything resembling open-minded truth-seeking inquiry. Instead, they are calculating their words toward a particular end, namely the end of getting people to support them. It's therefore not so much that you "can't debate" such people as that you can't bring logic to a rhetoric fight.

It may sound as if I'm encouraging the left to give up reason and embrace propaganda. But that's not quite what I mean. I think it's very important to seek truth, examine yourself, and figure out what the facts are. I just don't think that's necessarily what wins debates. Political debates are won by having the most persuasive messages. All I'm suggesting is thinking about trying to find some words that actually convince people, rather than trying to find the most logically precise words. In a public political contest, being too logical will make you sound lawyerly and difference-splitting. It won't carry the audience, and the audience are the ones who vote.

In making the decision as to whether to debate someone, and how, it's that effect on the audience question that should be crucial. It's all about the audience; you're never going to persuade your opponent, your job is to persuade the person watching. Yet Democrats often debate as if they're trying to persuade their opponents, which is one reason they fail. You shouldn't be trying to prove to Trump that he's wrong, or somehow grill Marine Le Pen on television until sheer force of reason causes her to abandon her lifelong political convictions. What you should be doing is trying to make these people look callous and foolish, which may or may not involve the use of pure logic.

I don't like to invoke the authority of the ancient Greeks, but Aristotle really did point out something quite useful in his treatise on rhetoric. He wrote that:

> *There are... three means of effecting persuasion. The man who is to be in command of them must, it is clear, be able (1) to reason logically, (2) to understand human character and goodness in their various forms, and (3) to understand the emotions-that is, to name them and describe them, to know their causes and the way in which they are excited.*[5]

Rhetoric consists of logos, ethos, and pathos—logic, emotion, and character. To be a skilled persuader you need all three. Make purely logical arguments and you'll flounder, because you also need to be able to use language in ways that touch people emotionally and that convince them you're a person of sound character who ought to be listened to. People come around to your views partially for logical reasons, but partially because they come to trust you, and to see you as reliable.

That's one key reason why people on the left lose debates. It's not because "you can't debate a fascist," it's because fascists think about how to actually win the audience. If you're not thinking about that, of course you'll lose.

There's something that sounds faintly dirty about encouraging people to think beyond purely rational forms of persuasion. But it's that refusal to get one's hands dirty with rhetoric that is the problem, not the willingness to use language rather than physical force as one's chief political weapon. The choice is not necessarily between "trying to reason logically with the other side" and "engaging in violent struggle." It could also be that for progressives, persuasion is usually best effected neither through violence nor formal deductive reasoning, but through effective messaging, telling people things that actually get them to support your politics. In other words, it's not just what you say, but how you say it and who you are.

Bernie Sanders offers a good illustration of what I mean about using language effectively by going beyond reason and incorporating character and emotion. I long thought Sanders would be particularly effective in a debate against Donald Trump, far more so than Hillary Clinton.[6] That was not because Sanders has a more acute command of debater's logic than Clinton; in fact, she's far better at this. Rather, it's because Sanders had those other two appeals: the emotional appeal and the character appeal. Sanders could very effectively describe meeting people without health insurance, and speak with moral conviction about the plight of the underclass, and he could fundamentally get people to trust him by having a kind of personal integrity that many people respected. (Hardly anybody respects the character of either Clinton or Trump.) Democrats need to not just be right on the facts, but to have candidates that can speak to people on an emotional level, and who seem to have the kind of human traits in which people can place their confidence. (This is why, political positions aside, it's probably a bad idea to run a slippery self-aggrandizing politico like Cory Booker or Andrew Cuomo in 2020.)

Thus I think giving up on argumentation, reason, and language, just because Purely Logical Debate doesn't work, is a mistake. It's easy to think that if we can't convince the right with facts, there's no hope at all for public discourse. But this might not suggest anything about the possibilities of persuasion and dialogue. Instead, it might suggest that mere facts are rhetorically insufficient to get people excited about your political program. You don't need to refuse to debate people. You need to stop trying to debating them simply by pointing out that their statistics are erroneous and their syllogisms faulty.

Again, let me emphasize quite clearly that while I believe in the power of persuasive communication, I do not believe in Trying To Reason With All The Trump Supporters. That would be stupid. For one thing, you're far less likely to persuade a serious Trump supporter than a person who is instinctively left-leaning but simply doesn't vote because they find all politics disgusting. And as Michael Kinnucan has pointed out in *Current Affairs*, it may also be unwise to focus on appeals to the (largely) mythical "swing voter" who hops back and forth between Republicans and Democrats depending on who makes the best argument in that particular cycle.[7] The vast majority of people who vote are pretty set in their ways, and time may be better spent energizing and politicizing the people who don't participate (but who have real grievances and would benefit from joining a political movement). Under this theory, effort is better directed at activating black voters in Detroit rather than flipping the small number of people in rural Michigan who turned from Obama to Trump. (I say this "may be" better because I am less certain than Kinnucan is that "swing voters" are hopeless, even if they are a small minority, and they can, after all, be a small minority that counts for quite a lot.)

So I don't share the belief that if we just sat down with people on the far right, and talked about our differences face to face, we would find that we all believe the same things deep down. This was Barack Obama's perspective, and it was colossally naïve. If you sit down with Republicans and try to "meet them in the middle," they will just sense that you are weak and eat you alive. It turns out that human beings don't all "believe the same things deep down." Some of us believe deep down that the free market should be permitted to work people to death without even a basic guarantee of subsistence. Others of us believe that the government should ensure everyone gets healthcare and housing. These beliefs cannot be reconciled, and most of the people who hold each of them are pretty committed to their perspective, so discussing them does not seem as if it will be especially fruitful.

But it's also true that you can't build political power without caring about discussion and communication, because it's impossible to coordinate human activity without these things. Every successful political movement has built itself in large part using words, because it takes words to convince people to perform acts. And political rhetoric, which incorporates factual reasoning but also goes beyond it, has a noble heritage, from the logical and emotional force of Martin Luther King's argument against piecemeal civil rights advancements[8] to the rousing words of the Internationale.[9]

Ultimately I worry that, in mocking the idea that you can "debate" fascists, some on the left also end up jettisoning the very idea of having to persuade people of your ideas, and end up thinking that the only way you can "debate" someone is by fact-checking them (and since we know that doesn't work, language fails us and we must retreat into violence). Yes, it's true, you can't just present the facts and evidence and assume people will agree with you and you'll win. But any good lawyer could tell that you don't just win a case through the force of the evidence, you also win it through the effectiveness of your presentation.

The other side understands this. Republicans know how to appeal to people's guts, to their feelings of bitterness, suspicion, and fear. If the left is going to respond, it needs a message of equal power. Not mere facts, though of course we want those. But something that appeals to the nobler emotions: to solidarity, and joy, and the spirit of human kinship. We have effective emotional appeals, we just need to use them.

There's nothing inherently shameful about political rhetoric. In fact, it's essential. You should be appealing to the heart as well as the brain. You should have a character people can trust, not just arguments they can agree with. And it's the only way you'll win.

"People You Disagree With"

I HATE THE PHRASE "people you disagree with," even though I'm sure I've written it more than once myself. First, it's now overused, and every overused phrase should be immediately discarded. But I am also frustrated by the way it's used in pleas for people to communicate productively about political and moral questions. Usually, anyone who mentions "people you disagree with" will be encouraging us to be more patient and understanding of those whose values are opposite from our own. Examples: a TED presentation on how you should "find out what's in the hearts" of people you disagree with, the innumerable how-to guides on keeping Thanksgiving dinners with people you disagree with from descending into brawls, and an app called "Burst" that deliberately begins conversations between people of differing political persuasions:

> Burst is an app that connects you to people you disagree with. We believe conflict can be resolved with conversation so we built a product to help people do that. Social networks put people in social bubbles. Our goal is to burst them.

The phrase, as you can see, is somewhat value-laden. Hardly anybody ever says that you *shouldn't* talk to people you disagree with, since that would sound ridiculous. There's an old test for whether a political statement is so imprecise as to be meaningless: if you said the opposite, would anyone conceivably advocate it? For example, "I believe our country should be strong and prosperous." —> "I believe our country should be weak and impoverished." Clearly, the underlying disagreement between the speaker and their opponents is actually about what *strong* and *prosperous* mean. A meaningful statement of a value, then, would be one like "I believe that a prosperous country ought to provide free college education." There are plenty of people who believe the opposite of this, and will say so. (This isn't really a "test" and doesn't always work, but it sure is fun to try out on political speeches.)

By encouraging us to "talk to people we disagree with," then, a person is making a statement that is inherently difficult to reject. But the phrase itself, "people we disagree with," is glossing over the nature of those disagreements, and collapsing very different kinds of human conflict into a single category: *disagreement.* The connotations of the word disagreement mean that the phrase is automatically diminishing the size of the gap between the two people's perspectives. A disagreement is frequently low-stakes: you and I disagree about whether *Short Circuit 2* is better or worse than the original *Short Circuit* film. (They're both terrible.) Perhaps we disagree on whether a particular wall is painted "turquoise" or "cyan." Or maybe we disagree about whether, as Ben Shapiro alleges, all Arabs are a murderous horde of anti-Semites.

You may notice that one of these Disagreements does not feel quite like it fits with the others. I mean, certainly, it's technically a disagreement, because my position on the question does not align with Shapiro's position. But one of the reasons that the "anti-free speech left" has gotten so exasperated with calls to "debate and discuss" with those they "disagree" with is that they do not see racism as a matter of "disagreement." Disagreement implies that there could be compromise. It also contains a subtle relativism: I say po-tay-to, you say po-tah-to, let's call the whole thing off. People who demean entire ethnic groups are not people I have a disagreement with. They are people whose value systems I find horrifying. I want to see those values disappear.

Ironically, given that it is supposedly an exhortation to mutual understanding, the phrase "people you disagree with" seems to display a limited understanding of what human conflicts are actually like to those who participate in them. Do Israelis and Palestinians "disagree"? Well, yes, they do. But also, to characterize it that way misses that the disagreement is built on a much deeper clash of interests. Did the Communists murdered in the 1979 Greensboro massacre disagree with the Klansmen who shot them? Do the Amazon workers who toil in warehouses stuffing boxes for Jeff Bezos disagree with him on how long a workday should be? Yes and yes. It's more than that, though. Seeing clashes of interest as "people disagreeing" is what we might call the "Obama view." Barack Obama's position was that while he may have *disagreed* with Republicans, he nevertheless believed they were well-intentioned people and hoped to be able to work out their differences. The Republicans, on the other hand, believed Obama was a poisonous socialist who needed to be destroyed at all costs. This disagreement was never going to be resolved harmoniously.

I don't, for example, "disagree" with Donald Trump. I don't even think he has any beliefs to disagree with. I think he is just a rapacious plutocrat who wants wealth, power, and fame and enjoys bullying others. I'd have nothing to say to him if I sat down in a room with him, because our dispute isn't an intellectual one. He acts based on his gut feeling that America should be an imperial power with him in charge, and I act on my gut feeling that this will make the world horrible and needs to be stopped.

It does feel somewhat ironic that I find myself opposing the "people you disagree with" framework. That's because I actually strongly believe that leftists should spend more time engaging with those on the other side, should address their arguments, should talk to Trump voters. I think a refusal to talk to anyone who doesn't already share your politics will doom you to irrelevance; you have to be persuading people, and persuasion involves dialogue. I'm in favor of the very "sitting down at the dinner table" approach that the "people you disagree with" people want to see, and I think we need more empathy for those whose beliefs or actions may horrify us. (I have to believe leftists should empathize with Trump voters, because I believe leftists should empathize with people on death row, many of whom have committed *murder*, which is at least somewhat worse than voting for Donald Trump.)

I don't see a binary choice, though, between "believing your political beliefs are polite 'disagreements' and thus being willing to have civil discussions about them" and "believing that politics is a fight to the death waged by competing interest groups and thus discussion is futile." I can find right-wing values not just *different*, but *appalling*, yet still believe that it's necessary to get along with and talk to people both (1) as a matter of ordinary human decency and (2) thanks to the practical necessity of having to convince people you're right if they're going to join your side. You can follow a "hate the sin, love the sinner" approach. But an important part of that is the *hatred* you feel toward the sin. The trouble with a lot of pro-civility rhetoric is that it is often actually a suggestion to tone down feelings of outrage and passion. But because I believe my convictions are important, outrage and passion are essential. I'm still able to converse with a conservative without keeping them from speaking, and I'm happy to review their books and explain why their arguments are all faulty. That still doesn't mean that the conflict in our values is like a disagreement over movies or wallpaper, and if you characterize it this way, it's hard to believe you actually care very much about your core convictions. (This is why I was always dubious about Ruth Bader Ginsburg's uncommonly chummy relationship with Antonin Scalia, whom she said was a "good" person with whom she happened to have differences. He was not, in fact, a good person.)

My colleague Briahna Gray has gone so far as to argue for engaging in dialogue with actual far-right white supremacists. But importantly, in doing so, she's not giving an inch to them, not implying their beliefs are "legitimate" or that white nationalism is just one of the many diverse viewpoints humans hold. She believes in talking to them because she recognizes that it may be necessary. It's a tough question, though, and "Why won't you talk to people you disagree with?" wouldn't be a persuasive response to a black person who didn't see any point conversing with someone who saw them as less than human.

In order to understand the world, you have to try to describe it accurately. Flattening politics into mere disagreement obscures just how intense and irresolvable conflicts of human values can be. If you're going to make the case for engagement with political opponents, it's too easy to frame the question as "whether or not you're willing to talk to people you disagree with." The more accurate, and thus more challenging, way of putting it, is "whether or not you're willing to talk to people whose values revolt you." I happen to think you ought to. But on that, I realize there's room to disagree.

Let The Kooks Speak

HOLOCAUST DENIERS HAVE NO ARGUMENTS. This is because, whenever they attempt to formulate arguments, they are destined to run headlong into the stubborn facts of the historical record, with its mountains of documentary and eyewitness testimony showing the full scope of the Nazi horror. For this reason, usually the best way to deal with a Holocaust denier is to allow him to hang himself with his own words. Because the historical reality of the Holocaust is among the most well-established of factual certitudes, anyone attempting to deny it will quickly be forced to resort to babble rather than reason. It is the simplest thing in the world to humiliate such people.

A strange thing happened in Brooklyn last year. Visitors to the Brooklyn Commons, a left-wing café and event space, noticed something horrifying on the bulletin board: a flyer advertising an upcoming event at the Commons, on "9/11 and our Political Crisis," with "investigative journalist" Christopher Bollyn.[1] From a distance, the flyer didn't look like much, but in small print it spoke of a plot by "neocons and their Zionist partners in crime" to dominate the world. Christopher Bollyn, as it turns out, is not only a 9/11 conspiracy theorist, but a raving anti-Semite who thinks the Jews assassinated JFK.[2]

Many were baffled by why the Brooklyn Commons would hold such an event.[3] Why on earth would a progressive café provide a platform for a blatant racist? It was yet another confirmation of the (true, and depressing) fact that in certain parts of the radical left, it's not terribly uncommon to find anti-Semitic conspiracy theorists.[4]

Outrage was quickly directed against the Commons, who were met with demands to cancel the event. Interestingly, a large part of this came from the radical left itself. Though often accused of being unwilling to purge anti-Semitism from their ranks, leftists quickly and vigorously condemned the Commons. Rabble-rousing journal The *Baffler* called the Commons' hosting of the event a "grievous misjudgment" and demanded its cancellation.[5] *Jacobin* magazine, which has worked with the Commons, expressed shock and seconded the demand. The Brooklyn Institute for Social Research, an organization that puts on left-wing teaching sessions, announced its decision to "remove all of our programming from the Brooklyn Commons despite the significant logistical and financial challenges that this decision entails."[6] On social media, the Commons was treated with contempt and disgust.[7]

Astonishingly, the Commons went ahead and let the event proceed. The Commons' owner, Melissa Ennen, defended the event on free speech grounds. In a statement, Ennen said that she allows anyone to book the space and hold events there, and does not investigate their views:

> *I did not research the speaker before accepting the rental. I do not have the time, resources or inclination to censor the hundreds of groups who rent the space. Since launching in 2010, the list of renters has included local Tea Partiers, conservative promoters of charter schools, explicitly anti-union corporations, elected officials who voted for the Patriot Act and wars in Iraq and Afghanistan.[8]*

Ennen made no defense of Bollyn's views. Instead, she said that she had a reason for allowing racists to book the space. As she explained: "I agree that all forms of racism should have no place in leftist spaces, but in my opinion, to get to the root of racist thinking, confrontation works better than censorship." Ennen finally quoted a story from a man named Paul Frantz, who in the 1970s had attended a talk by notorious eugenicist (and inventor of the transistor) William Shockley. Frantz explained that by listening to Shockley speak, he realized just how wrong Shockley truly was. Shockley's blatherings about genes and IQ taught Frantz that just because someone was a Nobel laureate, they didn't necessarily know what they were talking about.

On social media, Ennen's defense was mocked. One person called it a "ridiculous defense of an indefensible booking," others suggested it was a pathetic excuse, one that offensively invoked free speech and anti-censorship to justify giving a platform to a racist. "Racism is not like a vaccine," a commenter said. "We don't need to expose everyone to it to make sure they don't catch racism." Others laughed at Ennen's invocation of free speech. Free speech, they said, means the government can't censor you, not that you have to help racists spread their message.

Many of these arguments seem compelling on the surface. That the café could defend Bollyn's talk is almost inconceivable. But once we think through the actual implications of the criticisms, it becomes less obvious that the Brooklyn Commons was wrong to permit the event.

If we take the owner's words to be true, the Brooklyn Commons is set up, as the name implies, as a "commons." It's a space that anyone can rent, to put on any event they like. It's therefore designed to be "democratic," in the sense that every single person has an equal ability (presuming they can afford the rental fee) to gather there and give whatever kind of presentation they like.

Ennen says that she takes this principle very seriously indeed. (In fact, she refused to apologize, saying that she was willing to lose friendships over the issue because she feels so strongly about the question of censorship.) Thus, even though she herself is a progressive, Ennen has allowed groups she opposes including the Tea Party to use the space. According to her, when she say anyone can book the space, she means it.

If that's true, it is less clear that the Brooklyn Commons should have canceled the speech. People argued that the Commons was "hosting" and "providing a platform for" a racist. But "hosting" implies that the Brooklyn Commons invited the speake, when the Commons only "provided a platform" in the same way that it provides a platform to everyone. If

I set up a true Speakers' Corner, the entire point is to allow anyone to talk. The very moment I start introducing restrictions ("except racists"), it's no longer an open forum. The important question, therefore, is "should anti-Semites be given the equal freedom to book an open public event space?"

We can draw analogies. Say we introduce a community arts program, which offers free art supplies to starving painters. If one painter paints disgusting racist portraits, should we stop giving him paints? If we have a community typewriter-lending program, in which we rent low-cost vintage typewriters to hipster poets, should we refuse to lend typewriters to someone who writes misogynistic rap lyrics? Some people may feel that we should make these distinctions. But it's important to acknowledge what that entails: someone has to be empowered to assess a painter's art to determine whether it is racist or not.

This may seem like a sort of "slippery slope" argument. But it's not quite that. Instead it points out that the moment you start making content distinctions (of whatever kind), you have assumed the power to determine who should and shouldn't speak in a place. You might have very, very good reasons for thinking that a particular person has such hideous beliefs that they shouldn't speak (and you might be right). But it becomes your determination. Dissident scholar Norman Finkelstein, himself a victim of censorship,[9] tried to explain this fundamental principle of free speech in a recent lecture to the Communist Party of Great Britain.[10] Finkelstein, citing John Stuart Mill, asks the communists why they should be the ones to determine which speech to authorize. (Finkelstein also pointed out that if you're certain a speaker has nothing of value to say, it is all the more reason not to be afraid to let him speak.)

The authority point is extremely simple and very important. The reason for being a free-speech absolutist is not that all viewpoints are equally legitimate, but that deciding which viewpoints are legitimate involves assuming the power to start making speech distinctions. And unless that person is infallible, people will inevitably be wrongly censored sometimes. After all, it's easy to see how this could happen. If you've refused to rent to the anti-Semite, what about the Tea Partier? They're racists too! And what about the neoconservatives? They caused 600,000 deaths! Soon the entire notion of a "freely accessible public event space" disappears.

BUT WHY IS THIS ABOUT "censorship" or "free speech" at all? Whenever discussions like this come up, about the decisions of private entities to permit or not permit events, one common reaction is to point out that the First Amendment applies only to the government. Private entities, they say, are under no obligation to honor people's free speech rights.

Yet it's unclear why only government acts can qualify as restrictions on speech, in a world where the government is not the only entity capable of exercising power over people. If corporations control access to the means of speaking publicly, then "private censorship" can stifle public speech just as effectively as governments can. Consider Twitter. Twitter is a private corporation. The First Amendment does not apply to it, and it can get rid of whichever users it pleases. Because of this, when conservatives are kicked off Twitter and whine about being censored, liberals quickly point out that their free speech has not, technically, been violated.[11]

Yet because everyone is on it, Twitter has tremendous power to control public discussions. For journalists and writers, Twitter is an incredibly important professional resource, where connections are made and projects are hatched. Some people have built their entire careers on Twitter. Thus they must stay on Twitter's good side, because it has the power to vaporize their professional lives, as it did to one odious right-wing pundit, if they displease the corporation.[12] Thus far, they have generally limited their bans to defensible cases (though not always[13]) but there is no restriction on Twitter's ability to stifle its users, thus all are dependent on its continued benevolence.

These days, so much of the "commons" (if by this, we mean "the place where public discussions occur") is privatized. That gives corporations like Facebook a tremendous power to censor speech (as it did recently, in sending a haunting Vietnam War image down the memory hole, before meeting with public outcry).[14] These powers may be distinguishable from that of a government in principle (you can always go and start your own Facebook!), but in practice the power of corporations over people's lives is nearly unlimited.

So if we confine "free speech" to government acts, we are confining it to a very narrow realm. If parks are private, and social media is private, and event spaces are private, then this kind of "free speech" doesn't guarantee anything at all. It certainly doesn't mean being guaranteed the ability to speak. If one is not prohibited from speaking, but there is nowhere one can speak, then the idea that one is entitled to speak freely is meaningless. Some people say "the right to speak is not the right to be heard." But this only supports the Brooklyn Commons' position. Bollyn had the right to rent a space and set up a PowerPoint in it. He wasn't entitled to have anyone come to his event.

But in that case, does everyone have to let everyone speak all the time? Should racists be given television shows? Should crackpot climate change deniers be put alongside experts? Should there be no such thing as a safe space? Do we have to let misogynists speak at feminist events? Of course not. It's not that all viewpoints must be included all the time, it's that there should be freely-accessible common spaces in which all viewpoints can be heard. It's not that *Current Affairs* should publish every submission we receive, it's that everyone should have the equal ability to start a website (and if ISPs started blocking anti-Semitic websites, that would implicate free speech despite being non-governmental). Every corner need not be a Speaker's Corner, but there should always be a Speaker's Corner. And since there are very few true public "commons" spaces, it's admirable for the Brooklyn Commons to be one of those.

A crucial question is whether Ennen was telling the truth that the Commons is in fact a commons. If Ennen had previously refused any invitations on subject-matter rather than logistical grounds, her entire defense crumbles. If she would refuse a booking from the Klan or Dick Cheney, then it is hypocritical (and a minimization of anti-Semitism) to permit Bollyn. Some have suggested that the Commons' actions in whitewashing the event (and Ennen's own history with the 9/11 Truth movement) implied that they were more sympathetic to Bollyn than they let on.

But the wider point is less about the specific behavior of the Commons, and more about the arguments people made in opposing that behavior. Separate from the factual determination about whether the Commons' representations of its own motives are true, many on the left are skeptical of the commons principle in itself. They argue that racist speech has no value, and that "free speech" is about not having the police confiscate your printing press, rather than being entitled to particular kinds of public discussion spaces. But if "lack of value" is the relevant question, then someone has to determine that value. And if people are free to rent discussion spaces in theory, but in practice nobody will rent to them, then the "right" carries no real-world effect in enabling speech. (Again, this is not to imply that people should be required to rent to all comers, but that someone who did rent to all comers shouldn't be condemned.) If we solely conceive of "free speech" as a legal entitlement rather than a social value, that freedom will exist solely within the text of the law.

There is an important pragmatic argument here, also. Bigots may find their cause helped by efforts to censor them. As commenter Samuel Chance pointed out, by keeping yourself from hearing racists, you do not thereby eliminate racism. In fact, the opposite can be true. Chance wrote: "Bad ideas are best confronted rather than suppressed. If you deny ignorance a public forum, the ignorance doesn't die, it grows in private. When you later are forced to confront it, it might by then be stronger than you." It's important to argue with Nazis not because Nazis can be convinced, but because people who are not yet Nazis need to see why the Nazis are wrong. They need to see that the left's principles make sense, that we are doing more than just asserting that the issue is beyond debate. While those on the left tend to simply declare that debates are so settled that arguments do not need to be put forth, those on the right happily dispense voluminous literature on why leftist arguments are wrong. As a result, the politically naive can lack the critical intellectual tools necessary to keep themselves from being seduced by poisonous arguments.

There are several things one can do when an anti-Semite announces an event. It's true you could protest the event space, for not canceling the event. You could boycott it, and try to convince other groups not to hold events there. You could (at the extreme end) threaten to drive it out of business, or at least make it so toxic that few people wish to be associated with it. (Indeed, the Brooklyn Commons owner reported receiving emails "threatening dire consequences for The Commons.")

You could also take a different approach. Instead of targeting the event space, whose crime was not to distinguish among those to whom it rented space, you could target the anti-Semitic 9/11 Truther whose event poses the problem to begin with. You could hand out literature to all attendees, explaining why this man is odious and should be ignored. You could stage a massive protest outside, a protest against the event itself rather than the event space. You could even attend the event, and perform calculated symbolic disruptive acts.

You could go beyond even this. You could demand that the event space allow another event, this time a teach-in about the problem of anti-Semitism. At that event, you could perform an important self-examination on the question of whether the left has done enough to combat anti-Semitism. Is the problem that we are allowing them to rent event space? Or is it deeper?

I've been told that my view that "the solution to bad speech is more speech" is romantic and unrealistic.[15] The idea of civil public discourse is a fantasy; you don't reason with fascists, you destroy them. And I have to admit, all of that sounds very persuasive.

But let's look at the actual facts of what ended up happening in Brooklyn. The Commons didn't cancel its event, despite pressure. Protesters showed up, and mayhem ensued.[16] Bollyn did speak. But according to witnesses, he simply rambled incoherently for nearly two hours to a tiny group of bored misfits. An *AlterNet* writer who went said it was a "pathetic spectacle" with the "supposedly brave iconoclast, prevaricating for a half-empty room of gullible dimwits while dressed like a dad at a PTA meeting." The *Daily Beast*'s Jacob Siegel wrote that "not long after the talk started, people started to nod off," and that and that once you "strip away everything else... here was a middle-aged man dully clicking through slides."[17] So Bollyn gave his speech, and he was a failure who converted nobody.

Whatever theoretical skepticism people might have about letting racists speak, here we can chalk up a victory for open public debate. Bollyn didn't have his event canceled, he was allowed to say exactly as he pleased. Nobody in his lunatic fringe group could claim he was censored. The most destructive weapon against Bollyn was his own words.

I tend to think that left-wing critics of free speech are giving a gift to the racists. One of the most constant rhetorical themes of the American racist right is "they won't listen to our arguments, they just call us racists and try to shut us up." And because it's true that the left doesn't listen to their arguments, and just calls them racists and tries to shut them up, credulous people may think their views are right. This is precisely what happened in the debate surrounding *The Bell Curve*. Many people denounced the book without having read it. Then conservatives pointed out, correctly, that the critics hadn't even read the book they were criticizing. That makes it look like the left is in fear of the truth. But those that did read the book had an easy time showing its massive errors of statistical reasoning.[18] (And in fact, years before, Noam Chomsky had already diligently vaporized one of the co-authors' intelligence theories.[19])

Thus it's easy to win if you stay focused on the truth. I will have the debate on race and intelligence any day of the week, any time, any place. I will have it because the racists should have their bluff called. Of Bollyn, an attendee said that "the facts and conclusions he's reached are what these people don't want to hear."[20] But when they say that nobody wants to listen to the facts, they're wrong. Not me. I'd love to hear these supposed "facts." I say bring on the facts! What they want is for me to call them racists and keep them from speaking. What they really, really don't want is to have anyone actually examine their arguments. Once you let such people open their mouths, you hear how little they have to say.

In the Bollyn case specifically, we also saw some positive good come out of the event. The protesters who came to the event were far-left radicals, who detest anti-Semitism so much that they want its speakers to be prevented from renting space. The pictures of those radicals serve as an important rebuttal to those who associate leftist critics of Israel with anti-Semitism. If Brooklyn Commons had quietly refused the booking, we would never have had such public evidence of the left's hatred of anti-Semitism.

The question of "free speech for racists" is both incredibly difficult and incredibly important. The instinct to take the easy route, and make sure people with hideous beliefs cannot have platforms, is an understandable one. But you don't get rid of a belief by pretending it isn't there. The Bollyn event itself was outrageous. But what happened is exactly what should have happened. People organized against him, to show where they stood. The left did what it should do: insistently refused to put up with anti-Semitic bigotry. And, in the end, nobody ended up listening to Christopher Bollyn.

So let the kooks speak. Let them rent whatever spaces they like. There is no easier way to prove their insignificance than to let them have their say.

Money

Generation Wealth

A COUPLE OF YEARS AGO, the *Economist* published a brief article arguing that money was making Native Americans poor and lazy. The piece, entitled "Of Slots and Sloth," featured a photograph of a grinning Native man at a slot machine, and concluded that the distribution of casino revenue to tribe members ended up making them poorer by disincentivizing them from working.[1] Citing a study from the *American Indian Law Journal*, the *Economist* said that while Native American reservations were plagued by poverty, alcoholism, and poor health, the "biggest problem" of all might be the distribution of gaming money among tribes, since it created indolence and held back innovation. Tribes that shared their revenue among members remained in poverty; by contrast, a tribe that *didn't* distribute revenue had instead "used its casino profits to diversify into other businesses, such as harvesting huge mollusks for export to China." Mollusk-harvesting was thought, by the *Economist*, to be a far more responsible use of Native Americans' resources.

The *Economist*'s article was, of course, racist. But the problem wasn't that the magazine had suggested that cash payments made Native Americans slothful. That is, after all, a question to be answered empirically (though it is also laden with value judgments about the alleged shamefulness of slothfulness). No, as with so much bigoted social science, the *racist* aspect is less about the questions that are asked than the questions that are *not* asked. There has never been anything wrong with the theory that being given free money can disincline a person to work. What's objectionable is that this pathology is only ever detected in poor members of racial minority groups. Nobody ever proposes that the rich may be slothful thanks to the passive income that accrues from capital. Yet if a few hundred dollars a month from the reservation casino has corrosive effects on the work ethic of the destitute Indian, just imagine how fucked up the children of the wealthy must be. Why should there be so much investigation into what might be wrong with poor people, and so little investigation into what might be wrong with rich people? Dependency and dysfunction, if these are indeed useful sociological concepts, are surely just as present in those with money as in those without it.

This has been a recurring problem for sociology generally. We have endless studies of poor people, but very few of rich people. Bestselling ethnographies like Alice Goffman's *On the Run* and Matthew Desmond's *Evicted* examine the chaos and hardship faced by the American underclass, and there are plenty of diagnoses of the social and cultural ills of the deprived. But the affluent don't get treated as specimens for social scientific study in the same way. Of course, we may believe that it's good and proper for poorer people to receive the bulk of the attention; after all, to the extent that the lives of the poor give us insight into how poverty is generated, we might learn some lessons about how to stop it. But it's also odd that social science knows so much more about the private and personal lives of one class than the other. After all, if any group qualifies as specimens of dysfunction, it is the wealthy.

LAUREN GREENFIELD'S *GENERATION WEALTH* begins in Bel Air.[2] Greenfield attended high school in Southern California, and became fascinated with the way social status and wealth operated there. She has since spent three decades photographing the lives of both the affluent and the aspirationally affluent. *Generation Wealth*, a massive compilation of photographs and interviews from over Greenfield's career, is an attempt to provide a comprehensive look at the role of money, celebrity, and consumption in American life.

The Los Angeles tweens and teens we meet early in the book have become defined by the search for status through material acquisition. They buy multi-thousand dollar handbags to take to class. Other kids in their grade are given BMWs when they turn sixteen. They compete over whose family can afford the best designer clothes, the most elaborate bar mitzvahs, the biggest houses. We meet a 12-year-old whose working-class mother is bankrupting herself to finance the girl's love of Ed Hardy designer tank tops. The daughter knows she is putting great financial strain on her mom, and says she sort of feels bad about it, but explains: *"I want the world; I want designer clothes, I want eternal happiness, the fountain of youth. I want to be able to afford ritzy private schools. I want the best of everything. Money is most definitely important for everything on my list of what I want."* It is very difficult not to hate her.

We meet Emanuel, a sad-eyed teenager at the prestigious Harvard-Westlake high school whose family is not well-off, but who pressures his parents to buy him Cartier and Dior so that he can fit in at school. "I fantasize about being rich all the time," he says. He dreams of having enough money to buy anything he wanted at the Hermès store, where a light summer jacket can run nearly $15,000. Emanuel thinks more money might help his parents' marital tensions, which often arise from arguments over spending (and are possibly exacerbated by Emanuel's own penchant for Gucci sweaters).

Some of the kids we meet are impressively self-aware. They realize that the world they live in is shallow and ultimately unfulfilling. "Money has ruined me," says one thirteen-year-old. Emanuel knows it too:

> *I've seen kids whose lives have been ruined by money. One of my friends lives with his mother in this huge empty house in Bel-Air—it's like this skinny little lonely boy and his skinny lonely mom up in her bedroom. I was there four times, and I saw his mom once, for a passing moment. And I'm like 'Do you see her more than that?' And he goes 'No.' They talk through the intercom a lot, like, 'I'm going to dinner.' 'Ok, bye.' I felt bad for him. He's unbelievably lonely and depressed. I think that distance is created when you have a lot of money.*

Greenfield's Southern California is a world of ludicrous excess, where families have dog groomers, personal trainers, nutritionists, and nannies, and where one's worth is measured in jewelry, cars, and handbags. It is also a world of acute image-consciousness, where people spend unbelievable sums of money attempting to remain youthful. "I'm unhappy with my cuticles," says one 11-year-old who owns 32 pairs of designer jeans.

From L.A., Greenfield travels across the country, uncovering an American mania for consumption and excess. We meet Norbert Aleman, a septuagenarian cabaret proprietor who lives with five women and thirty peacocks in an Italianate Las Vegas mansion. There are the parents who pay an interior designer $40,000 to create a pink princess bedroom for their toddler. (The moment it is complete, the daughter announces that she doesn't like pink anymore.) We visit a nightclub where a flying "Champagne Fairy" dangling from a wire bounces from table to table delivering high-priced alcohol, with one bottle costing $250,000. There are galas, premieres, and balls. Women in ridiculous hats attend horse races, men in cufflinks brood behind ornate desks. People consume caviar and truffles. (I realized that I have never actually seen either a truffle or caviar in real life, and did not know that there were still people who ate them. I am grateful to Greenfield for documenting such things.) We meet the "old money": Harvard undergrads boozing in tuxes and sixth-generation members of the Newport yacht club. Then there are the gaudy *nouveau riche*, like luxury car rental tycoon "Limo Bob" in his furs and chains, or the McMansion-dwellers who stock their enormous libraries with books purchased by the foot. (One former model has elaborate built-in mahogany bookshelves filled entirely with hundreds of copies of a single volume: her own self-published collection of fashion photographs.)

Then *Generation Wealth* travels around the world, showing us how global mass media has allowed American hedonism and excess to be exported abroad. There is a Chinese real estate billionaire who lives in an exact replica of the White House complete with Oval Office, and who has built a ⅓ scale Mount Rushmore sculpture in his backyard. Also in China, a Harvard Business School graduate runs a finishing school where she teaches children of the country's new elite to pronounce "Givenchy" and "Versace." A Canadian socialite who surrounds herself with all things frilly and froofy says she has modeled her life after candy-factory heiress Truly Scrumptious from *Chitty Chitty Bang Bang*. We see Dubai's most lavish hotels, Moscow's oligarchical opulence. Everywhere, Greenfield succeeds in finding the most extreme absurdities and ironies that emerge from gross inequality, like the Russian models who wear designer "peasant chic" clothes. American hip hop producer will.i.am "regards his eight-bedroom home [in Los Feliz] as a place to create rather than a living space and typically sleeps in a small apartment down the block." At a Santa Monica charity auction, women drink Moët and bid on designer handbags to benefit disadvantaged children. Another fundraiser for poor kids is described as "the social event of the year."

EVEN AMIDST THIS VAST CARNIVAL of profligacy and waste, however, Florida couple Jackie and David Siegel stand out. The Siegels, who have made a fortune in the timeshare business, are in the middle of building the largest single-family home in America, a 90,000 square foot faux-château just outside Walt Disney World. They call it "Versailles," and when completed it will feature six pools, two movie theaters (one for adults, one for children), and an ice skating rink. The master bedroom alone is 10,000 square feet (which Mrs. Siegel acknowledges is "larger than most people's homes.")

The Siegels have taken conspicuous consumption to another level entirely. Jackie Siegel wears $10,000 ostrich-feather pants, and her shopping budget is up to $1 million a year. She has 13 children, because "when I found out I could have nannies, I just kept having kids." ("I think she's from South America," Jackie says of one nanny. Another nanny—who has not seen her own children in nearly 20 years—lives in an outbuilding originally designed as a playhouse for the kids, who rapidly grew bored of it.) The Siegels are upgrading to Versailles because they feel as if their current 26,000 square-foot house is too small, even though they have to travel round it on Segways and call people in other rooms via cell phone. Asked why he has decided to build a 90,000 square foot home, David Siegel replies: "Because I can." (Unsurprisingly, Siegel is a fan of Donald Trump, whose presidential victory he calls "the best thing that has happened to me since I discovered sex.")

Greenfield is not just interested in the spectacle of exorbitant wealth, however. She wants to know not only how those at the very top behave, but how the aspiration for needless material goods has come to affect individuals from *all* classes. She is interested in what she calls "the influence of affluence," the powerful hold that the fantasy of material prosperity has come to hold over the popular imagination. Greenfield implies that the "American Dream" has morphed from a desire to have a decent but modest life to a lust for as much as one can get, that instead of striving for relative comfort people now pursue gain for its own sake.

So we don't just see the kids in Santa Monica; Greenfield also photographs working-class teens in East L.A. and South L.A., to show how wealth shapes the value systems of even those who don't have it. A Hispanic high schooler spends two entire years saving the $600 necessary for a limousine and clothes for his prom. People will spend what little they have on status symbols like high-priced sneakers and brand-name T-shirts. Greenfield reiterates the classic critique of consumption: that people come to find meaning in the stuff they have, or the stuff they *think* they'll have someday, rather than in community, friendship, and family ties. Life becomes hollow and superficial, as jeans and jewels take the place of human beings in our hierarchy of values and priorities.

That superficiality goes beyond an obsession with couture clothes. Greenfield's photographs also document the pernicious effects of the beauty industry in packaging and selling impossible ideals of women's bodies, whether through Barbie dolls or child beauty pageants ("I'll be a superstar. Money money money. I would have money as big as this room," says six-year-old pageant contestant and reality TV star Eden Wood). Greenfield has some disturbing portraits of the world of plastic surgery, as women and girls (we see an L.A. teenager recovering from a nose job) modify themselves, sometimes to extremes, chasing an illusory perfection fed to them by mass media.

At the extreme end, women's bodies are simply commodified and sold outright, through strip clubs and pornography. While she does not give an opinion on whether and how sex work should be regulated—a virtue of the book is that the photographs' subjects are allowed to speak for themselves, with Greenfield's voice seldom intruding—it is clear that Greenfield is dubious about the contemporary progressive notion that sex work can be liberating or is indistinguishable from other work. Greenfield is clear that *stigmatizing* sex workers is wrong (we meet a college student who was kicked off the track team after it was discovered that she stripped to pay her tuition), and that these occupations can provide a certain *financial* freedom. Nevertheless, she wants us to be disturbed by an industry that turns women into lumps of flesh to be sold, an industry that only exists *because* women need money and men have it. Sex work, for Greenfield, is definitely degrading, though perhaps not much more so than any other kind of work that reduces the human being to a product.

IN THE BACKGROUND OF ALL OF THIS lurks Donald Trump, the man who has spent a lifetime selling people on a fantasy of the good life, and whose operation of the Miss Universe pageant and notorious abuse of women tie him closely to Greenfield's idea of a capitalism that is ruthlessly predatory and patriarchal. Trump's election makes for a fitting dénouement to Greenfield's thirty-year story, embodying all of her themes: greed, reality television, wealth without taste, the hollow lust for fame and power, sexism and objectification, and lies upon lies. As she says:

> *Our highest public servant is a real-estate developer and reality-TV star who lives in a penthouse on the sixty-sixth floor emblazoned with his name and decorated in a Louis XIV style, with ceilings painted with 24-karat gold, marble walls, and Corinthian columns.*

Trump's pitch to the American people was the same poisonous fiction that capitalism has been telling them for decades. As inequality worsens, Trump says: vote for me, and you can have it all. Unfortunately, you can't have it all. All you end up with, like the students who spent $30,000 on a "Trump University" education, is a cardboard cutout of Donald Trump. He still lives in Trump Tower, and you still live in your shitty apartment. You can max out your credit cards to buy a Louis Vuitton handbag, but the people who run the world will still run it, and the doors of the club are never going to actually be open to you. If you're lucky, the billionaires may generously allow you to pay them every cent you have for the privilege of *feeling* like you're in the club.

But lies can never be lived indefinitely, and Greenfield's book is also a chronicle of what happens when bubbles burst and people come face to face with reality. In the aftermath of the 2008 financial crisis, we meet the families who thought they had it made, only to suddenly find themselves with nothing. Greenfield surveys an America of broken dreams, empty swimming pools, and ghost estates. People squat in foreclosed houses, and half-built, uninhabited subdivisions are slowly reclaimed by nature.

The Siegel family never finishes building Versailles. People stop buying timeshares and David Siegel is forced to lay off large numbers of his employees and household staff, and to rent out his Rolls Royce. One of the Siegels' daughters, Victoria, who seemed to have a pretty skeptical and down-to-earth perspective on her family's outrageous lifestyle, dies of a prescription drug overdose at the age of 18.

There is a deep sadness that runs through *Generation Wealth*. Over and over, the oldest clichés about money and happiness are proven correct. People with money are lonely, cruel, and unfulfilled. Their lives are marked by divorce, drug abuse, and cultural degeneracy. Tolstoy's famous observation that "every unhappy family is unhappy in its own way" is shown to be nonsense. At least among the rich, unhappy families look the same wherever you go.

The lessons are confirmed through testimony from some recovering one-percenters. A former Wall Street trader can't believe he once thought a $3.6 million dollar bonus was disappointingly small, and has dropped out to found a charity. A German fraudster wanted by the FBI has now (possibly cynically) embraced asceticism and Christianity, and declares that the pursuit of wealth will lead to ruin, since "capital has no conscience, it just wants to multiply."

It's not just those who have left the rat race who realize how laughable and meaningless it all is. One of the striking things about *Generation Wealth* is just how many people are fully cognizant of the silliness of their material lusts. They joke at their own expense, they know they are spending money on foolish things and that they have no good justification for why they want the things they want. Yet just as with racial prejudice or sexual desire or any of the other mysterious forces governing human behavior, knowing you have it doesn't allow you to will yourself to be free of it.

Prestige and status are such strange things. You can be aware that they're irrational yet still intensely desire them. You can realize that the cool kids are all a bunch of assholes who will grow up to live largely miserable lives, yet still feel flattered when they like you and rotten if they ignore you. *Generation Wealth* shows just how fundamentally ridiculous people's value systems can be, yet how totally inscrutable the process is by which those value systems are implanted in the human subconscious. Why is it that everybody can know something leaves them unhappy yet continue to do it? If money doesn't buy true satisfaction, and nobody would deny that, why haven't people stopped spending their lives chasing dollars? Money must buy *something*. David Siegel says that it just allows you to be "unhappy in a good section of town." Still, even after learning that lesson, Siegel himself continued to work twelve-hour days trying to rip people off with time-shares so that he could build a palace. He never saw his daughter, and had no idea she was addicted to drugs until her body was found after the overdose. Now, he's seen the full tragic consequences of the worship of money. Yet as of 2016, Siegel was *still* trying to build the palace, *still* worshiping Trump. How can a force be so strong that even the death of a child can't prise a person free from it?

Greenfield has compiled a bleak document of contemporary life. To her, social mobility is "fictitious and provided by designer brands." We have witnessed the "erosion of family, religious, and community ties," and are now locked in a endless futile cycle of aspirational consumption, buying stuff we don't need to sustain a dream that will never come true. Everything is bought and sold, nothing is sacred, and the shopocalypse is nigh.

In this vision, America is Las Vegas, Los Angeles, and Wall Street. It is *Toddlers & Tiaras* and *My Super Sweet Sixteen*. It's McMansions. It's Lil Jon's diamond grill. It is Hugh Hefner's house and Kim Kardashian's ass. It is a country of strip clubs, casinos, and prosperity gospel megachurches. It is TrumpLand. The final photograph in *Generation Wealth* is of a naked stripper crawling to pick up dollar bills from a pile on the floor. It is clear what Greenfield thinks of us.

BUT THERE ARE MORE THINGS in heaven and earth than casinos and strippers. The TrumpLand vision of America and the 21st century is neither fully complete nor fully accurate. Like all attempts to formulate grand, all-encompassing theories, *Generation Wealth* sacrifices complexity and nuance for the sake of rhetorical effectiveness. As a result, we get a more depressing view of the world than we necessarily ought to hold.

Because she is a top-flight photojournalist, Greenfield has managed to track down some uncommonly vapid people. Yet it is not clear how typical they actually are. Greenfield's understanding of the world was forged during her youth in Los Angeles and her undergraduate years at Harvard. But these places are not the world, and the world is not these places. Southern California is *known* for its unusually high quantities of shallow and self-absorbed backstabbing ladder-climbers, who are drawn there because it is the hub of the entertainment industry. Thus if we want to understand what "people" are like, focusing disproportionately on L.A. will give us a funhouse-mirror perspective, one that exaggerates the prevalence of certain noxious traits.

As a piece of sociology, then, *Generation Wealth* is tainted by "selection bias": Greenfield wishes to demonstrate how greedy and materialistic our society is, and has done so by finding and photographing lots of greedy and materialistic people. But that doesn't actually address the question the book is supposedly answering, namely "How important is wealth in defining people's identities today?" That's because we're looking only at the people whose identities *are* defined by wealth, rather than looking at a random cross-section of the human population.

Now, we might think that Greenfield is right, that this tendency *is* shared widely, meaning there's nothing unrepresentative about her sample of airheaded Angelenos, billionaire Muscovites, chain-wearing hip-hop artists, Wall Street fraudsters, aging Playboy bunnies, bankrupted condo flippers, and Florida timeshare kingpins. But I suspect that's not the case. After all, *Generation Wealth* rarely dwells on the lives of those we see in the background: the nannies and dog groomers themselves. When we do hear from them, they *don't* actually seem to have bought into the value system that Greenfield ascribes to "us." In fact, they seem somewhat bemused by it all.

But Greenfield explicitly wants to make a statement about what "we" are like, rather than what a particularly revolting subsection of us are like. As she says, her book is about how "we, as Americans, have gone from a traditional ethos, underpinned by Judeo-Christian values, of modesty, thrift, humility, and discretion... of helping others less fortunate, to a culture of bling, celebrity, and narcissism." She asks: "How have we afflicted ourselves with a pathological state of material longing?" She even brings in lefty doom-preacher Chris Hedges, who says that nowadays "commodities and celebrity culture define what it means to belong, how we recognize our place in society, and how we conduct our lives."

It's the "we" that is such a problem. One is tempted to answer: "Well, *you*, maybe. But leave 'we' out of this." What does it even mean to say that "we" are "pathological" in our material longings, that "we" no longer have humility, and live in a culture of bling? Does it mean that everyone does? And if it's only some people, then which people, and how many? It's obviously true that the tendencies Greenfield describes are present in American life, and that large numbers of people embrace them. But saying that those tendencies *are* American life, that they define us, risks mistaking a cartoon for reality. It's certainly tempting, now that Donald Trump is the president, to think of Trumpism as a kind of national philosophy. But the vast majority of this people in this country *didn't* vote for Donald Trump. He was hugely unpopular. A suggestion that Trump is a representative ambassador for the American ethos is simply wrong.

The question of representation comes into sharp relief whenever Greenfield photographs African Americans. In a photography book over 500 pages long, ostensibly about the role of wealth in "our" lives, nearly every black man in the book is a rapper (though Al Sharpton also pops up), and many of the black women are strippers. But, and this should not need to be said, *most black men are not rappers*. Greenfield has singled out the most materially ambitious subset of black males she can find, the ones who most embrace the kind of lifestyle that she is attempting to document, and suggested we can extrapolate from them. But we can't. We should no more judge the black community by its most hedonistic rappers than we should judge white people by *Duck Dynasty* or NPR. You do not obtain a useful sociological understanding of a group by singling out its most ludicrously stereotypical members. It would be different if Greenfield had found the same tendencies among black teachers, truck drivers, insurance agents, postal workers, and clergy. But we should probably not allow the kids who want to throw fistfuls of dollar bills in the air to "make it rain" to speak on behalf of their race.

THE GOOD NEWS, THEN, is that the world probably isn't full of the kind of narcissistic people that Greenfield's photos so vividly depict. We are not, thank goodness, all living in one enormous Southern California. Dog plastic surgery and toddlers in thongs are the exception rather than the rule. The ruthless pursuit of lucre is only one of the myriad ways in which people fill life's deep existential void. But there are lots of others.

Still, it's not necessary to believe that "we" are in a "generation wealth," or to buy into the apocalyptic ravings of Chris Hedges, in order to accept that capitalism does incubate a kind of cultural sickness. Everything Greenfield documents *is* disturbing, and it's certainly also common. The Trumpian wealth fantasy may not be everyone's dream, but heaven knows it's plenty of people's. And rampant consumerism does seem to be grinding up all worldly resources to build luxury sedans and shopping plazas.

I do think the problem is properly defined as "consumerism" or "capitalism" rather than "materialism," though. A mild materialism is fine and harmless. Nice things are nice, and people should get to have comfortable chairs, big computer monitors, and soft fabrics in a variety of colors. An appreciation for quality objects is one of the joys of being alive. The problem seems to come when acquisition becomes the end rather than the means, when you cease to actually *enjoy* the things you buy, and begin to be compelled by the act of buying itself.

This is the dangerous tendency that capitalism engenders. Because it needs constantly to extract our money in the pursuit of profit, it does not tell us to have and enjoy lots of high-quality goods. It tells us to keep buying and buying, *no matter what*. The moment you get an iPhone—a truly incredible product, if we're being honest—your model will be outdated and you will be encouraged to upgrade. It's not the materialism that's the problem, but the anxiety that comes of being told you never have enough. The problem isn't that you and the Joneses both bought hot tubs, it's that you are counting the number of jets in each other's jacuzzis rather than sitting back and enjoying the bubbles.

The result of the status competition is that there are intolerable amounts of waste, and that that waste is *for nothing*, because it does not produce happiness. I am all for wasting resources on frivolity, if we all have a good time. But when we don't, when we destroy the earth and all we get in return is a spiritual vacuum (and a stupid T-shirt), then some terrible mistake is being made.

As I say, though, not all of us are dwelling in a dystopia of nihilism and shopaholism. It is not Black Friday all over the world. Capitalism does indeed create a pernicious ugliness and lack of values. It does cause people to buy some of the most utterly pointless rubbish at the most outrageous prices (although, oddly enough, it's often the consumption habits of women in particular, such as handbags and shoes, that are portrayed as the most absurd and unjustifiable, even such a feminist-friendly project as *Generation Wealth*). And it does cause people to be simultaneously incredibly busy, incredibly insecure, and incredibly sad. But it's not all there is, and one should remember that for every person maxing out their credit cards at the mall or throwing wads of dollar bills at a stripper, there is another hanging out with friends at a dive bar, getting ice cream with their parents, or falling in love by a fire.

As a "theory of everything" that tells us "who we are now," *Generation Wealth* is far too broad. As a document of the lives of certain people, and a particular hideous cultural consequence of capitalism, it is extraordinarily thorough and disturbing. Greenfield has made a serious contribution to a neglected area of sociology, and helped address the disparity between studies of the poor and studies of the affluent. She has probed, using incredibly vivid photographs and revealing interviews, the little-explored links between economics and culture. But it's important to remember that we are not, all of us, a generation wealth. We are, like human beings of every generation, motivated by a conflicting and complicated set of aspirations and motivations. Capitalism has the terrifying tendency to turn people into the sorts of insatiably avaricious people depicted in this book. But it has not yet come to define us all.

And God willing, it won't.

It's Basically Just Immoral To Be Rich

HERE IS A SIMPLE STATEMENT OF PRINCIPLE that doesn't get repeated enough: if you possess billions of dollars, in a world where many people struggle because they do not have much money, you are an immoral person. The same is true if you possess hundreds of millions of dollars, or even millions of dollars. Being extremely wealthy is impossible to justify in a world containing deprivation.

Even though there is a lot of public discussion about inequality, there seems to be far less talk about just how patently shameful it is to be rich. After all, there are plenty of people on this earth who die—or who watch their loved ones die—because they cannot afford to pay for medical care. There are elderly people who become homeless because they cannot afford rent. There are children living on streets and in cars, there are mothers who can't afford diapers for their babies. All of this is beyond dispute. And all of it could be ameliorated if people who had lots of money simply gave those other people their money. It's therefore deeply shameful to be rich. It's not a morally defensible thing to be.

To take a U.S. example: white families in America have 16 times as much wealth on average as black families.[1] This is indisputably because of slavery, which was very recent (there are people alive today who met people who were once slaves).[2] Larry Ellison of Oracle could put his $55 billion in a fund that could be used to just give houses to black families, not quite as direct "reparations" but simply as a means of addressing the fact that the average white family has a house while the average black family does not. But instead of doing this, Larry Ellison bought the island of Lanai.[3] (It's kind of extraordinary that a single human being can just own the sixth-largest Hawaiian island, but that's what concentrated wealth leads to.) Because every dollar you have is a dollar you're not giving to somebody else, the decision to retain wealth is a decision to deprive others.

Note that this is a slightly different point than the usual ones made about rich people. For example, it is sometimes claimed that CEOs get paid too much, or that the super-wealthy do not pay enough in taxes. My claim has nothing to do with either of these debates. You can hold my position and simultaneously believe that CEOs should get paid however much a company decides to pay them, and that taxes are a tyrannical form of legalized theft. What I am arguing about is not the question of how much people should be given, but the morality of their retaining it after it is given to them.

Many times, defenses of the accumulation of great wealth depend on justifications for the initial acquisition of that wealth. The libertarian-ish philosopher Robert Nozick gave a well-known hypothetical that is used to challenge claims that wealthy people did not deserve their wealth: suppose millions of people enjoy watching Wilt Chamberlain play basketball. And suppose, Nozick wrote, that each of these people would happily give Wilt Chamberlain 25 cents for the privilege of watching him play basketball. And suppose that through the process of people paying Wilt Chamberlain, he ended up with millions of dollars, while each of his audience members had (willingly) sacrificed a quarter. Even though Wilt Chamberlain is now far richer than anyone else in the society, would anyone say that his acquisition of wealth was unjust?

Libertarians use this example to rebut attempts to say that the rich do not deserve their wealth. After all, they say, the process by which those rich people attained their wealth is totally consensual. We'd have to be crazy Stalinists to believe that I shouldn't have the right to pay you a quarter to watch you play basketball. Why, look at Mark Zuckerberg.

Nobody has to use Facebook. He is rich because people like the product he came up with. Clearly, his wealth is the product of his own labor, and nobody should deprive him of it. People on the right often defend wealth along these lines. I earned it, therefore it's not unfair for me to have it.

But there is a separate question that this defense ignores: regardless of whether you have earned it, to what degree are you morally permitted to retain it? The question of getting and the question of keeping are distinct. As a parallel: if I come into possession of an EpiPen, and I encounter a child experiencing a severe allergic reaction, the question of whether I am obligated to inject the child is distinguishable from the question of whether I obtained the pen legitimately. It's important to be clear about these distinctions, because we might answer questions about systems differently than we answer questions about individual behavior. ("I don't hate capitalism, I just hate rich people" is a perfectly legitimate and consistent perspective.)

I therefore think there is a sort of deflection that goes on with defenses of wealth. If we find it appalling that there are so many rich people in a time of need, we are asked to consider questions of acquisition rather than questions of retention. The retention question, after all, is much harder for a wealthy person to answer. It's one thing to argue that you got rich legitimately. It's another to explain why you feel justified in spending your wealth upon houses and sculptures rather than helping some struggling people pay their rent or paying off a bunch of student loans or saving thousands of people from dying of malaria. There may be nothing unseemly about the process by which a basketball player earns his millions (we can debate this). But there's certainly something unseemly about *having* those millions.

One of the reasons wealthy people rarely have to defend their choices is that "shaming the rich" is not really compatible with any of the predominating political perspectives. People on the right obviously believe that having piles of wealth is fine. Centrist Democrats can't attack rich people for being rich because they're increasingly a party for rich people. And socialists (this is the interesting case) tend to believe that questions about the morality of having wealth are relatively unimportant, because they are far more interested in how the state divides up wealth than in what individuals choose to do with it. As G.A. Cohen points out in *If You're an Egalitarian, How Come You're So Rich?*, Marxists have been concerned with eliminating capitalism generally, which has kept them from thinking about questions of the justice of people's personal choices. After all, if the problem of inequality is systemic, and rich people do not really make choices but pursue their class interests, then asking whether it is moral for wealthy people to retain their wealth is both irrelevant (because individual decisions don't affect the systemic problem) and incoherent (because the idea of a moral or immoral capitalist makes no sense in the Marxist framework). In fact, there is a certain leftist argument that giving away wealth in the form of charity is actually bad, because it allows capitalism to look superficially generous without actually altering the balance of power in the society.[4] "The worst slave owners were those who were kind to their slaves, because they prevented the core of the system from being realized by those who suffered from it," as Oscar Wilde ludicrously put it. (In our book *Blueprints for a Sparkling Tomorrow*, Oren Nimni and I parody this perspective by portraying two leftist academics who insist on being rude to servers in restaurants, on the grounds that being polite to them obscures the true brutality of class relations.[5])

But I think it is a mistake to avoid inquiring into the moral justifications for wealth. This is because I think individual decisions do matter, because if I am an extremely wealthy man I could be helping a lot of people who I am choosing not to help. And for those people, at least, it makes a difference when a billionaire decides to retain their wealth rather than rid themselves of it.

Of course, when you start talking about whether it is moral to be rich, you end up heading down some difficult logical paths. If I am obligated to use my wealth to help people, am I not obligated to keep doing so until I am myself a pauper? Surely this obligation attaches to anyone who consumes luxuries they do not need, or who has some savings that they are not spending on malaria treatment for children. But the central point

I want to make here is that the moral duty becomes greater the more wealth you have. If you end up with a $50,000 a year or $100,000 a year salary, we can debate what amount you should spend on helping other people. But if you earn $250,000 or 1 million, it's quite clear that the bulk of your income should be given away. You can live very comfortably on $100,000 or so and have luxury and indulgence, so anything beyond is almost indisputably indefensible. And the super-rich, the infamous "millionaires and billionaires," are constantly squandering resources that could be used to create wonderful and humane things. If you're a billionaire, you could literally open a hospital and make it free. You could buy up a bunch of abandoned Baltimore rowhouses, do them up, and give them to families. You could help make sure no child ever had to go without lunch.

We can define something like a "maximum moral income" beyond which it's *obviously* inexcusable not to give away all of your money. It might be 50 thousand. Call it 100, though. Per person. With an additional 50 allowed per child. This means two parents with a child can still earn $250,000! That's *so much money*. And you can keep it. But everyone who earns anything beyond it is obligated to give the excess away in its entirety. The refusal to do so means intentionally allowing others to suffer, a statement which is true *regardless* of whether you "earned" or "deserved" the income you were originally given. (Personally, I think the maximum moral income is probably much lower, but let's just set it here so that everyone can agree on it. I do tend to think that moral requirements should be attainable in practice, and a $30k threshold would actually require people experience some deprivation whereas a $100k threshold *indisputably still leaves you with an incredibly comfortable lifestyle better than almost any other had by anyone in history.*)

Of course, wealthy people do give away money, but so often in piecemeal and self-interested and foolish ways. They'll donate to colleges with huge endowments to get needless buildings built and named after them. David Geffen will pay to open a school for the children of wealthy university faculty, and somehow be praised for it.[6] Mark Zuckerberg will squander millions of dollars trying to fix Newark's schools by hiring $1000-a-day-consultants.[7] Brad Pitt will try to build homes for Katrina victims in New Orleans, but will insist they have to be architecturally cutting-edge and funky-looking, instead of just trying to make as many simple houses as possible.[8] Just as the rich can't be trusted to spend their money well generally, they're colossally terrible at giving it away. This is because so much is about self-aggrandizement, and "philanthropy" is far more about the donor than the donee. Furthermore, if you're a multi-billionaire, giving away $1 billion is morally meaningless. If you've got $3 billion, and you give away 1, you're still incredibly wealthy, and thus still harming many people through your retention of wealth. You have to get rid of *all* of it, beyond the maximum moral income.

The central point, however, is this: it is not justifiable to retain vast wealth. This is because that wealth has the potential to help people who are suffering, and by not helping them you are letting them suffer. It does not make a difference whether you earned the vast wealth. The point is that you have it. And whether or not we should raise the tax rates, or cap CEO pay, or rearrange the economic system, we should all be able to acknowledge, before we discuss anything else, that it is immoral to be rich. That much is clear.

The Meaning of Exploitation

ACCORDING TO A YEAR-LONG INVESTIGATION from—of all places—
USA Today, truckers around the Port of Los Angeles are suffering through
extraordinary financial and physical hardships.[1] They work incredibly
long hours, rarely seeing their families, yet frequently take home less than
minimum wage. The situation is made possible by the unique structure of
the contracts between truckers and trucking companies: drivers pay for
their trucks on a "lease-to-own" model, meaning that most of their original gross income goes straight back to the company to pay for the vehicle.
Worse, when drivers lose their jobs, they lose the truck and everything
they have paid into it. As *USA Today* reports:

> *Trucking companies force drivers to work against their will—up
> to 20 hours a day—by threatening to take their trucks and keep
> the money they paid toward buying them. Bosses create a culture
> of fear by firing drivers, suspending them without pay or reassign-
> ing them the lowest-paying routes... Employers charge not just for
> truck leases but for a host of other expenses, including hundreds of
> dollars a month for insurance and diesel fuel. Some charge truckers
> a parking fee to use the company lot. One company, Fargo Truck-
> ing, charged $2 per week for the office toilet paper and other sup-
> plies... Many drivers thought they were paying into their truck like*

*a mortgage. Instead, when they lost their job, they discovered they
also lost their truck, along with everything they'd paid toward it.*

The newspaper profiled some of the truckers who struggled under the
rent-to-own system. The stories are devastating:

> *Reyes Castellanos, 58, has gallstones and no health insurance,
> because he's labeled an independent contractor instead of an
> employee. Near-constant pain causes him to wince repeatedly as he
> talks from the cab of his truck. He keeps a giant thermos of coffee on
> the passenger seat. By his feet, a bottle he uses to avoid bathroom
> stops. Money is tight and it's not getting any better. Castellanos'
> 2015 tax return shows that he grossed $94,000. But he took home
> just $21,000 after truck expenses, including the lease-to-own pay-
> ment he makes to his employer every week. His wife told him to
> quit K&R Transportation and leave the truck behind. But Cas-
> tellanos isn't sure what other work he could find. "The truck is the
> only thing putting food on the table," he told her. "So we lost the
> house," Castellanos said. "I lost the house."*

Some workers have taken home as little as 67 cents per week after
paying for the lease, insurance, gas, and maintenance on the trucks. The
contract model means that drivers have all of the responsibility that
comes with owning a truck, but none of the benefits of actually being
their own boss. They're trapped in a never-ending cycle of toil and debt,
as their health breaks down and their family life disappears.

To me, it seems that any halfway morally decent human being has to
call what is done to these truckers "exploitation." The companies are
squeezing out every last ounce of the drivers' energy, and giving as little
as possible in return. It's a cruel, cruel situation in which hard-working
people's lives are being consumed and destroyed to enrich the owners of
trucking companies.

There is, however, a problem. The truckers' situation is obviously horrifying. But under the basic principles of a free market, there's nothing

either wrong or illegal about it. Several things the trucking companies have done are obvious violations of the law (e.g. demanding that employees lie about their hours on timesheets in order to violate federal maximum-hours safety standards). But in order to stop many of the most harmful features of the arrangement, one would have to support significant government interference in people's "freedom of contract." After all, this is a purely "voluntary" transaction between the drivers and the companies: nobody made the drivers agree to a lease-to-own arrangement. *USA Today* says that drivers were "forced to work against their will" and "not allowed to leave" because they would lose their jobs and trucks if they did not agree to the terms. But accepting that this is true requires us to reject the libertarian conception of "force" and "allow." In fact, it requires us to admit that Karl Marx was right: that workers don't really have a "choice" when entering into contracts with companies, because the "choice" they have is between working and starving, which isn't a choice at all. (We heard that in the words of trucker Reyes Castellanos: he would leave, but the truck is the only thing putting food on the table.)

This notion, that under capitalism workers are forced to enter exploitative agreements with employers, is explicitly rejected by free market thinkers. Philosopher Robert Nozick, in *Anarchy, State, and Utopia*, addresses those who believe that the agreements made by "workers accepting a wage position" are "not really voluntarily because one party faces severely limited options." Nozick concludes that this is nonsense:

> *Whether a person's actions are voluntary depends on what is it that limits his alternatives. If facts of nature do so, the actions are voluntary… Other people's actions place limits on one's available opportunities. Whether this makes one's resulting action non-voluntary depends on whether these others had the right to act as they did.*

Thus, if someone puts a gun to my head and tells me to do something, my action is involuntary, because the person did not have the right to do so. But if they act within their rights, and the constraints upon me arise "naturally," then it does not make sense to call an action involuntary. Nozick asks us to consider a group of people who pair off into couples. Let's call them Man A, Man B, Man C going down to Man Z, and Woman 1, Woman 2, Woman 3, going down to Woman 26 (I am using heterosexual couples just to make the example clearer, but it works with any set.) The people are ranked from most to least desirable, with A and 1 being most desirable and Z/26 being least desirable. Now, the couples pair off. A and 1 partner off. B would like to partner with 1, but since 1 has partnered with A, B settles for 2. Likewise, 2 would like to partner with A, but settles for B. 3 wants to partner with A or B, but settles for C, and so on, until only Z and 26 are left. Both Z and 26 would like to partner with anyone other than each other. But since there's nobody left, Z partners with 26.

Nozick uses this needlessly convoluted example to prove the following point: even though Z and 26 had only one option, as a result of choices made by other people, their decision to partner was still not "involuntary." They could simply have chosen to remain alone. He compares this situation with the labor market:

> *Similar considerations apply to market exchanges between workers and owners of capital. Z is faced with working or starving; the choices and actions of all other persons do not add up to providing Z with some other option... Does Z choose to work voluntarily?... Z does choose voluntarily if the other individuals A through Y each acted voluntarily and within their rights... A person's choice among differing degrees of unpalatable alternatives is not rendered nonvoluntary by the fact that others voluntarily chose and acted within their rights in a way that did not provide him with a more palatable alternative.*

Under a free market, according to Nozick, the idea that you are "forced" just because you have "no more palatable" alternative is false. He would scoff to read *USA Today*'s description of truckers being "forced" to continue working. They were not forced. They could simply have left their jobs and lost their trucks.

Nozick's "partners" comparison fails for an obvious reason: it isn't the correct analogue. If we wanted to test the principle with a comparable scenario, what we should really envisage is a situation in which people partner off into couples, and if you choose not to partner into a couple, you will starve to death. Instead of imagining a world in which there's not much of a consequence for not partnering, let's imagine a world in which there is one: a small group of people controls access to the community's food supply, and if you do not choose to marry someone, you will be denied access to the food supply and starve. In that situation, Z and 26's choice to partner, even though they have no interest in one another, seems a heck of a lot less "voluntary" than Nozick wishes for it to be.

The free-market conception of voluntariness therefore leads to an absurdity: it leads us to believe that people who choose between death and compliance are making a meaningful choice, even though this is precisely the same set of options provided to the person with a gun to their head. It believes that voluntariness rests not in the set of choices available to someone, but in whether other people are within their rights in creating that situation. That applies even if the person creating the situation is doing so intentionally. So I can deliberately construct a situation in which you are forced to either partner with Z or die (say, by bribing everyone other than Z to refuse to partner with you), and your choice is still perfectly voluntary under the Nozickian free-market framework. (I have previously posed a hypothetical "puzzle for libertarians" in which an entire village conspires to starve a child to death and then eat him, but does so entirely using free-market mechanisms rather than outright coercion.[2])

I dwell on this because I want to emphasize a key leftist insight: that in an important way, economic coercion using the market can operate like physical coercion. Leftists have always argued that the choice to "work or starve" is not much of a choice at all, and that this makes a lot of "freedom of contract" arguments untenable. The responses to this, even from the most thoughtful right-wing philosophers like Nozick, have not been persuasive. They require a definition of "voluntariness" that borders on the meaningless, or at least makes absolutely no difference to the individual actually faced with the choice (if I must work or watch my children perish, what difference does it make to me whether the people who have created that choice for me have acted within their rights or not?)

The California trucking scandal is therefore a useful case study of why it's crucial to reject a fundamental tenet of free-market thinking, and accept a fundamental tenet of leftist thinking. If we believe that all contracts are purely voluntary, then truckers like Castellanos are deliberately "choosing" a situation in which they never see their family, suffer from horrible, painful gallstones, and spend the vast majority of their income on a massive loan they will never pay off. But it's quite clear that this choice did not come out of nowhere: it was engineered by the party that offered him the contract. The trucking company could have paid Castellanos a decent wage and made him an employee with health benefits. Instead, it chose to present him with a choice between permanent indenture or starvation. Only one party in this situation has done anything meaningfully "voluntary."

SEPARATE FROM THE QUESTION of voluntariness is the question of exploitation. What the trucking company did to Castellanos seems intuitively "exploitative": if it's not exploitation for a company to attempt to financially ruin its employees for the sake of its own profits, then is anything exploitation? But the word "exploitation" is fraught and contentious, because it's difficult to figure out a precise definition. Marx offered the most famous formulation, but he grounded it in his notion of "surplus value," which is highly controversial.[3] My own conception is rather rough: to me, exploiting someone means extracting whatever you can from them without regard to their well-being (except, of course, to the limited extent that maintaining their well-being is necessary for you to further extract things). The trucking company exploits its workers because it only cares about their health and financial security to the extent that those things are minimally necessary in order to allow the drivers to keep working. Its drivers only matter to the company insofar as they are useful to it.

Once you adopt that definition, much of the labor that occurs under capitalism begins to appear pretty exploitative. A lot of companies see their employees as little more than fungible parts who exist to perform a function. Actually, Marx had an important description of how this relationship between the owner and the worker begins to look:

> In its blind unrestrainable passion, its were-wolf hunger for surplus-labour, capital oversteps not only the moral, but even the merely physical maximum bounds of the working-day.[4] It usurps the time for growth, development, and healthy maintenance of the body. It steals the time required for the consumption of fresh air and sunlight. It higgles over a meal-time, incorporating it where possible with the process of production itself, so that food is given to the labourer as to a mere means of production, as coal is supplied to the boiler, grease and oil to the machinery. It reduces the sound sleep needed for the restoration, reparation, refreshment of the bodily powers to just so many hours of torpor as the revival of an organism, absolutely exhausted, renders essential. It is not the normal maintenance of the labour-power which is to determine the limits of the working-day; it is the greatest possible daily expenditure of labour-power, no matter how diseased, compulsory, and painful it may be, which is to determine the limits of the labourers' period of repose. Capital cares nothing for the length of life of labour-power. All that concerns it is simply and solely the maximum of labour-power, that can be rendered fluent in a working-day.

That description is awfully similar to what happened to the truckers. They slept for just as many hours as were necessary for them to keep driving. Their bodies were broken down, their energies ruthlessly extracted. Marx points out that a profit-seeking company will burn through laborers without regard to their long-term health, because they can simply be replaced. The situation created by "freedom of contract" will be one in which people's lack of available options lead to their being exploited, used as disposable parts in a machine rather than respected as human beings who deserve fulfilled and prosperous lives.

In the absence of a mathematically precise theory like the one Marx offered, it may be difficult to measure degrees of exploitation. But the concept is extremely important: it describes a situation in which moral obligations toward people disappear, and they are simply utilized as means toward ends, even if this hurts the person being used. Under such a definition, the port truckers are a paradigmatic case of exploitation.

Most people who read *USA Today*'s report on the trucking industry were probably appalled; the drivers were classic examples of "upstanding, hardworking people" who received almost nothing in return for their labors. But it's essential to see not just that the situation is morally outrageous, but *why* it's morally outrageous. And the case shows why it's important to reject the idea that "voluntary contracts" are effective safeguards of people's interests, and to accept the value of "exploitation" as a concept for understanding the viciousness of the contemporary economy.

Private Fire Services and The Economics of Burning To Death

PRIVATE FIRE SERVICES DISTURB THE HELL OUT OF ME. That's because, more than just about anything else, they seem to hint at what a neo-feudalist dystopia might look like. The wealthy can buy firefighters and have their homes saved, while those who can't afford protection will have to watch as all of their possessions are incinerated. There will be two types of people in this world: those who can pay their way to safety, and those who will burn. In the fully-privatized world, the amount of money you have determines literally everything, and the privatization of basic services like firefighting seems to draw us worryingly close to that world.

During the 2017 California wildfires, according to the *Wall Street Journal*, some people received a little more fire protection than others.[1] Insurers sent in private firefighting forces to protect valuable homes, "sending out fire crews to clear brush, put down fire retardant around residents homes, set up sprinklers and then document the process via photos that are then sent to the homeowner." Only those homes that had signed up for special policies would be coated in fire retardant.

The use of private firefighters for the wealthy has apparently grown in recent decades. A 2007 report documented AIG's use of a "Wildfire Protection Unit" to serve its Private Client Group, a plan "offered only to homeowners in California's most affluent ZIP Codes—including Malibu, Beverly Hills, Newport Beach and Menlo Park." Online, you can find an extraordinary photo of AIG-branded firefighters in an AIG-branded fire truck. A homeowner recalled what it was like to know he was privately protected:

> *Here you are in that raging wildfire. Smoke everywhere. Flames everywhere. Plumes of smoke coming up over the hills. Here's a couple guys showing up in what looks like a firetruck who are experts trained in fighting wildfire and they're there specifically to protect your home. ... It was really, really comforting.*

Less comforting, perhaps, to the neighbors who also see a team of firefighters coming over the hills before realizing that they are only authorized to put out AIG-insured homes. In fact, not even just AIG-insured homes: special *elite* AIG-insured homes, though in one case the company was willing to benevolently extend protection to AIG customers with ordinary plans: "AIG said it did apply fire retardant to some homes of standard policyholders if they happened to be nearby, because it made financial sense." If saving your home doesn't "make financial sense," though, you're screwed.

The economics of the whole arrangement make perfect sense. An insurance company really does not want to see a multi-million dollar house burn to the ground, so of course it will be eager to provide extra fire services if doing so will substantially affect the amount of the subsequent claim. And it's clear why a wealthy person would want this kind of coverage: as the homeowner above says, it's really comforting to know that a corporation is sending you personal firefighters who will look out for you and you alone. Private firefighting is just like private security, or the mercenary soldiers that rich people hired in post-Katrina New Orleans to protect their properties from looting.

But though these deals make perfect sense to the parties making them, they have alarming implications. There's something outrageous about a world in which firefighters protect some people rather than others, and choose to let houses burn to the ground that could be saved. I am still haunted by the 2010 story of a local fire department who refused to put out a house fire because the owner hadn't paid his $75 annual fire protection fee. Emergency services seem like one area in which there ought to be a consensus that money shouldn't play a role. Obviously, that's far from true, as anyone who has gotten stuck with a $1000 bill for an ambulance ride knows well. But the more emergency response becomes a transaction rather than an equal and universal guarantee, the more literally true it is that some people's lives are worth more than others.

I am terrified of the future, and it's partly because I don't really see a way to stop these trends from getting worse. Public services will be under-resourced and wealthy people will have a strong interest in contracting for private services instead. This is already the situation in medical care, it's already the situation with police and the military,[2] why shouldn't it be the same with fire services? In every other domain of life, how much money you have determines what you will get in return, this just extends market logic to yet one more realm.

If we are not careful, this is what the dystopia will look like. Poor people around the world will burn to death in slums while a tiny group of rich people are insulated from all social problems and buy their way out of any trouble. Even if there is widespread climate catastrophe, those with nine houses can just hop from one to another as each successively tumbles into the sea. In fact, the world we're in already resembles the dystopia, the only major difference being one of scale. If wealth continues to be concentrated in a smaller and smaller group, and the vast majority of people are more and more excluded from power and left to fend for themselves, the word "feudalism" will seem less and less extreme as a descriptor.

It's tragic that there even is such a thing as the "economics of burning to death." But there is. And the more private fire services there are, the more your chances of having a house tomorrow will depend on whether you've paid off the right corporate protection racket.

Everything You Love Will Be Eaten Alive

HERE ARE TWO DIFFERENT VISIONS FOR WHAT A CITY ought to be. Vision 1: the city ought to be a hub of growth and innovation—clean, well-run, high-tech, and business-friendly. It ought to attract the creative class, the more the better, and be a dynamic contributor to the global economy. It should be a home to major tech companies, world-class restaurants, and bold contemporary architecture. It should embrace change, and be "progressive." Vision 2: the city ought to be a mess. It ought to be a refuge for outcasts, an eclectic jumble of immigrants, bohemians, and eccentrics. It should be a place of mystery and confusion, a bewildering kaleidoscope of cultures and classes. It should be a home to cheap diners, fruit stands, grumpy cabbies, and crumbling brownstones. It should guard its traditions and be "timeless."

It should be immediately obvious not only that are these views in tension, but that the tension cannot ever be resolved without one philosophy triumphing over the other. That's because the very things Vision 2 thinks make a city worthwhile are the things Vision 1 sees as problems to be eliminated. If I believe the city should be run like a business, then my mission will be to clear up the mess: to streamline everything, to prune the weeds. If I'm a Vision 2 person, the weeds are what I live for. I love the city because it's idiosyncratic, precisely because things *don't* make sense, because they are inefficient and dysfunctional. To the proponent of the progressive city, a grumpy cabbie is a bad cabbie; we want friendly cabbies, because we want our city to attract new waves of innovators. To the lover of the City of Mystery, brash personalities are part of what adds color to life. In the battle of the entrepreneurs and the romantics, the entrepreneurs hate what the romantics love, and the romantics hate what the entrepreneurs love. In the absence of a Berlin-like split, there can be no peace accord. It must necessarily be a fight to the death. What's more, neither side is even capable of *understanding* the other: a romantic can't see why anyone would want to clean up the dirt that gives the city its poetry, whereas an entrepreneur can't see why anyone would prefer more dirt to less dirt.

Vanishing New York: How A Great City Lost Its Soul is a manifesto for the Romantic Vision of the city, with Michael Bloomberg cast as the chief exponent of the Entrepreneurial Vision. "Nostalgic" will probably be the word most commonly used to capture Jeremiah Moss's general attitude toward New York City, and Moss himself embraces the term and argues vigorously for the virtues of nostalgia. But I think in admitting to being "nostalgic," he has already ceded too much. It's like admitting to being a "preservationist": they accuse you of being stuck in the past, and you reply "Damn right, I'm stuck in the past. The past was better." But this isn't simply about whether to preserve a city's storied past or charge forward into its gleaming future. If that were the case, the preservationists would be making an impossible argument, since we're heading for the future whether they like it or not. It's also about different conceptions of what matters in life. The entrepreneurs want economic growth, the romantics want jazz and sex and poems and jokes. To frame things as a "past versus future" divide is to grant the entrepreneurs their belief that the future is theirs.

Moss's book is about a city losing its "soul" rather than its "past," and he spends a lot of time trying to figure out what a soul is and how a city can have one or lack one. He is convinced that New York City once had one, and increasingly does not. And while it is impossible to identify precisely what the difference is, since the quality is of the "you know it when you see it" variety, Moss does describe what the change he sees actually means. Essentially, New York City used to be a gruff, teeming haven for weirdos and ethnic minorities. Now, it is increasingly full of hedge fund managers, rich hipsters, and tourists. Tenements and run-down hotels have been replaced with glass skyscrapers full of luxury con-dos. Old bookshops are shuttered, high-end boutiques put in their place. Artisanal bullshit is everywhere, meals served on rectangular plates. You used to be able to get a pastrami and a cup of coffee for 50 cents! *What the hell happened to this place?*

It's very easy, as you can see, for this line of thought to rapidly slip from critiquing to kvetching, and Moss does frequently sound like a cranky old man. But that's half the point. He wants to show us that the cranky old men aren't crazy, that we should actually listen to them. It's not a problem with them for complaining that the neighborhoods of their childhood are being destroyed, it's a problem with us for not caring about that destruction. Moss is a psychiatrist, and he does not see "nos-talgia" as irrational, but as a healthy and important part of being a per-son. We are attached to places, to the memories we make in them, and if you bulldoze those places, if you tear away what people love, you're causing them a very real form of pain.

Moss loves a lot of places, and because New York City is transitioning from being a city for working-class people to a city for the rich, he is constantly being wounded by the disappearance of beloved institutions. CBGB, the dingy punk rock music club where the Ramones and Patti Smith got their start, is forced out after its rent is raised to $35,000 a month. Instead, we get a commemorative CBGB exhibit at the Met, with a gift shop selling Sid Vicious pencil sets and thousand-dollar handbags covered in safety pins. The club itself becomes a designer clothing store selling $300 briefs. The ornate building that once housed the socialist *Jewish Daily Forward* newspaper, the exterior of which fea-tured bas-relief sculptures of Marx and Engels, is converted to luxury condos. Its ethnic residents largely squeezed out, bits of Little Italy are carved off and rebranded as "Nolita" for the purpose of real estate bro-chures, since—as one developer confesses—the name "Little Italy" still connotes "cannoli." A five-story public library in Manhattan, home to the largest collection of foreign-language books in the New York library system, is flattened and replaced with a high-end hotel (a new library is opened in the hotel's basement, with hardly any books). Harlem's storied Lenox Lounge is demolished, its gorgeous art-deco facade gone forever. Rudy Giuliani demolishes the Coney Island roller coaster featured in *Annie Hall*. Café Edison, a Polish tea house, is evicted and replaced with a chain restaurant called "Friedman's Lunch," named after right-wing economist Milton Friedman. (I can't believe that's true, but it is.) Judaica stores, accordion repairmen, auto body shops: all see their rent suddenly hiked from $3,000 to $30,000, and are forced to leave. All the newsstands in the city are shuttered and replaced; they go from being owner-operated to being controlled by a Spanish advertising corporation called Cemusa. Times Square gets Disneyfied, scrubbed of its adult bookstores, strip joints, and peep shows. New York University buys Edgar Allen Poe's house and demolishes it. ("We do not accept the views of preservationists who say nothing can ever change," says the college's president.)

The aesthetic experience of gentrified places is horrifying to Moss. They are "glittering pleasure domes for the uber-wealthy," empty spaces scrubbed of their authenticity. The "corporate monoculture" takes hold: new buildings are all glass boxes, full of grinning, shiny, happy people who don't really know what it's like to live. Moss talks about his first experience walking along the infamous High Line park; he was immediately told off by an official for getting too close to the plants. Moss was "creeped out by [the] canned, fabricated unnaturalness" of this "undead limbo": "I felt like I was in the home of a fussy neatnik with expensive tastes." A park should be a place to run around and have fun, not a museum. But the sort of people who live in the luxury condos around the High Line do not really understand the concept of unbridled joy. They are people who shun all risk, who want corporations to take care of them and make them comfortable: Applebees, Olive Garden, Starbucks, and Target are soothingly familiar, and make it easier to come to New York City from elsewhere without ever having to feel as if you've left home. "7-11 makes me feel safe," says one person thrilled about the chain coming to New York.

It's easy to criticize places like these as lacking "authenticity" compared to their counterparts: a tiny Italian restaurant in which actual Italians make third-generation recipes is simply *more real* than an Olive Garden. But I think "authenticity" is often a dubious criterion of value: there's no reason a Serbian or Japanese family can't open an Italian restaurant, if they can make the food well. The more important problems are those of centralization, homogeneity, and inequality. Starbucks is bad not because of its coffee (though the coffee is bad), but because Starbucks is turning the world boring and uniform, and power over how Americans drink coffee is concentrated in the hands of a single man, chief executive Howard Schultz.

This complaint against the demise of the mom-n-pops and the takeover of chain retailers is now decades old. And it has its flaws: sometimes labor practices can be better at large corporations than at the celebrated "small business," because there is actually recourse for complaints against abusive managers. If the only person above you is the owner, and the owner is a tyrant, there's not much you can do. Still, the core critique is completely valid. Chain retail exists to make the world more efficient, but ends up turning the world uninteresting. I have actually noticed that I am less inclined to travel because of this. Why would I go to New York when I can see a Starbucks right here? Monoculture is such a bleak future; local variation is part of what makes the world so wonderful. You can measure whether a place is succeeding by whether it's possible to write a good song or poem about it. It's almost literally impossible to write a good non-ironic poem about an Applebee's. Compare that with nearly any greasy spoon or dive bar.

THE MOST DISTURBING CHANGE, HOWEVER, is the inequality. The Romantic city is a democratic city: everyone has their little piece of it, nobody can simply reshape the entire place in accordance with their preferences. But the emerging version of New York City is a place where a disproportionate amount of power is held by landlords and developers, who can essentially do as they please. If you run a little café, they can multiply your rent by ten and get rid of you. If you own a home, they can seize it via eminent domain and build a new headquarters for a pharmaceutical company. They alone decide whether or not any given paradise will be paved, and whether a parking lot or a Duane Reade should be put in its place.

Developers often insist that they don't deserve their negative reputation. They wonder why some people hate them when all they do is build useful things that improve cities. But anyone who doesn't hate developers clearly hasn't understood things from the perspective of those who see their neighborhoods razed and beloved businesses shuttered. We know for a fact that, if developers were put in charge of the world, nothing would last if demolishing it would be profitable. I live in the French Quarter of New Orleans. I am dead certain that if someone could make $100 million by putting a skyscraper in the middle of it, they would. It's only thanks to the influence of wealthy residents that the area is able to keep the things that give it its charm. Even then, the neighborhood has been gentrified beyond recognition: what was once a thriving multi-ethnic residential neighborhood has become a ghost town full of rich people's empty *pied-a-terre* condos.

The very existence of landlords is staggeringly unfair. A person can live in a place 30 years, pay thousands of dollars a month in rent, and still have their home razed without having any say in the decision. One thing Moss's book shows very clearly is that a world of renters is a world in which people have little power to control what happens to them; those decisions rest in the hands of the people who actually own the properties. Eviction is an incredibly cruel and destructive process, yet landlords engage in it casually. (Over two million people are evicted every year in the U.S.) Moss brings up a set of often-ignored victims of gentrification: the elderly people who have run their stores for decades, and are suddenly forced out. Many are bewildered and depressed by the sudden change, left without a sense of purpose.

The greed of landlords and developers is a prime reason that New York is steadily transforming into "Disneyland for billionaires." But government policy also bears direct responsibility. Throughout New York history, city officials like Robert Moses have either neglected or waged active war against the ethnic populations that stood in the way of development. ("Look on the bright side... the city got rid of a million and a half undesirables," a mayoral aide observed about the fires that destroyed countless tenements in the 1970s, allegedly partially due to the city's intentional neglect of fire services.) But Michael Bloomberg was explicit in his commitment to making New York a city for the rich. Bloomberg's city planning director, Standard Oil heir Amanda Burden, stated the administration's aspirations: "What I have tried to do, and think I have done, is create value for these developers, every single day of my term." Bloomberg himself was even more frank, calling New York City a "luxury product," and saying:

> "We want rich from around this country to move here. We love the rich people."
> "If we can find a bunch of billionaires around the world to move here, that would be a godsend... Wouldn't it be great if we could get all the Russian billionaires to move here?"
> "If we could get every billionaire around the world to move here it would be a godsend that would create a much bigger income gap."

It didn't even seem to cross Bloomberg's mind that a flow of wealthy people into the city might not be such a "godsend" for the small merchants who would see their rents shoot up. The consequences of Bloomberg's approach were exactly what you would expect: homelessness rates exploded and median rent is now more than $38,000 a year in a place where the median income is $50,000. Bloomberg's solution to the homelessness crisis was for the city to buy the homeless one-way bus tickets out of town. He was critical of the very notion of a "right to shelter," implying that shelters might be clogged with rich people taking advantage of the system: "You can arrive in your private jet at Kennedy Airport, take a private limousine and go straight to the shelter system and walk in the door and we've got to give you shelter."

The increasing inequality in New York City has led to some absurd results. Brand new skyscrapers are filled with residential condominiums without any actual residents in them; the properties are owned as investments by the international super-rich, while homeless people sleep out front. Developers only grudgingly put affordable units in buildings, and some new construction has even included class-segregated separate entrances for affordable units and luxury units (the infamous "poor door"). At the same time, developers have been lavished with tax breaks and incentives; it's estimated that Donald Trump, over his career in New York real estate, received $885 million in tax breaks, grants, and other subsidies. (Note: tax "breaks" and "relief" are propaganda terms meant to reinforce the perception that taxes are a burden rather than a necessity that makes economic activity possible in the first place.)

The effort to replace poor people with rich people is often couched in what Moss calls "propaganda and doublespeak." One real estate investment firm claims to "turn under-achieving real estate into exceptional high-yielding investments," without admitting that this "under-achieving real estate" often consists of people's family homes. (Likewise, people often say things like "Oh, nobody lives there" about places where many people do, in fact, live.) One real estate broker said they aspired to "a well-cultivated and curated group of tenants, and we really want to help change the neighborhood." "Well-cultivated" almost always means "not black," but the assumption that neighborhoods actually need to be "changed" is bad enough on its own.

In fact, one of the primary arguments used against preservationists is the excruciating two-word mantra: *cities change*. Since change is inevitable and desirable, those who oppose it are irrational. Why do you hate change? You don't believe that change is good? Because it's literally impossible to stop change, the preservationist is accused of being unrealistic. Note, however, just how flimsy this reasoning is: "Well, cities change" is as if a murderer were to defend himself by saying "Well, people die." The question is not: is change inevitable? Of course change is inevitable. The question is what kinds of changes are desirable, and which should be encouraged or inhibited by policy. What's being debated is not the concept of change, but some particular set of changes.

Even "gentrification" doesn't describe just one thing. It's a word I hate, because it captures a lot of different shifts, some of which are insidious and some of which seem fine. There are contentious debates over whether gentrification produces significant displacement of original residents, and what its economic benefits might be for those residents. *The New York Times* chided Moss, calling him "impeded by myopia," for failing to recognize that those people who owned property in soon-to-be-gentrified areas could soon be "making many millions of dollars." But that exactly shows the point: Moss is concerned with the way that the pursuit of many millions of dollars erodes the very things that make a city special, that give it life and make it worth spending time in. A pro-gentrification commentator, in a debate with Moss, said that he didn't really see any difference, because "people come [to New York City] for the same reason they always have: to make as much money as possible." That's exactly the conception that Moss is fighting. People came to New York, he says, because it was a place worth living in, not because they wanted to make piles of money.

MOSS HAS SUGGESTIONS FOR POLICY interventions that might help to reverse the troubling changes. They are: putting decisions over new developments and chain stores to a community vote, re-zoning the city to limit formula retail, instituting rent increase caps for small businesses, expanding landmarking to legacy businesses, vacancy taxes on *pieds-a-terre*, lowering fines for small businesses, and ending tax giveaways to developers. They're all worth thinking seriously about, though Moss doesn't go into much detail. But the more important thing is to at least get on the same page values-wise: New York City should not be a mega-mall, and should not look be indistinguishable from Dallas or Toledo. He also wants to convince us of one thing above all: "hyper-gentrification and its free market engine is neither natural nor inevitable." The belief that Development and Growth should be the goals of a city is a piece of propaganda. For one thing, these words are vacuous. Actually, "development" is a truly insidious word, because it automatically suggests that what developers do is progress. Who wants to "inhibit"? Everyone wants to develop. What that can mean in reality, though, is demolishing a beloved local library and putting up a high-end hotel in its place. Moss wants us to recognize that these are not the result of mystical forces, but of decisions made by human beings: landlords, developers, and city governments. When the Gap moved to the East Village, to much protest, a Gap employee observed that despite the protests, "like everywhere else, they will accept it." And they were right: the Gap stayed, people moved on. This seems to always happen: people complain, then things change, then they accept the new reality. Moss wants us to refuse to accept it, to recognize that we don't have to accept new things we don't like, that change should be organic and democratic rather than imposed by the will of the rich. *Vanishing New York* calls for people to take their cities back.

I HAVE TO CONFESS, I DIFFER A LOT FROM MOSS in my conception of what a good city should be like. I have always found New York City to be something of an armpit, and not because it's full of high-priced condos. Many of the people Moss adores, the bohemians and artists, I find fairly intolerable. Moss is a poet, and wants a city of poetry. I am not a poet, I generally detest poetry. Moss has a strange fondness for *mean* New York, the New York that told everybody else to fuck off. I thought that New York was kind of an asshole.

But that's okay: the philosophy of *Vanishing New York* is that cities shouldn't all be the same, that they should have different attitudes toward life and different cultures. If I am more New Orleans than Brooklyn, that means we have a diverse world in which New Orleans and Brooklyn are very different places. The one thing that we should all be scared of, wherever we live, is the collapse of those differences, the streamlining and homogenizing of everything.

And yet the logic of capitalism sort of demands that this occur. If efficiency is your goal, then you're going to have chain restaurants. They're just more efficient. If you must perpetually grow and grow, then you're going to have to demolish a lot of things that people dearly love. If everyone embraces the pursuit of financial gain, then landlords are never going to cut tenants a break merely because their business is a neighborhood institution. In a free market world, everything you love will be eaten alive, unless you're rich.

The great contribution of *Vanishing New York* is in showing what will continue to happen in a highly unequal world that places more value on innovation than romance. Unless and until social priorities change, the City of Mystery will be slowly destroyed, a gleaming, deathly boring City of Wealth rising in its place. We can have one of these, or the other, but we cannot have both. And I know which I'd rather live in.

Horrors

The Politics of Tragedies

BEFORE SCREAMING AT A MUSLIM WOMAN and stabbing two people to death on a bus in Portland, Jeremy Christian had paraded around the city draped in an American flag. He had held signs that said "Trump Makes America Great Again," attacked a black woman with a bottle of Gatorade, and shouted slurs about Christians, Muslims, and Jews.[1] Before shooting two NYPD officers in Brooklyn, Ismaaiyl Brinsley had posted "#RIPEricGarner" on Facebook and promised to put "wings on pigs."[2] He had also shot his ex-girlfriend in the abdomen after she dissuaded him from committing suicide. Before Omar Mateen took 49 lives at the Pulse gay nightclub in Orlando, he had been diagnosed bipolar, abused his first wife, and pledged allegiance to ISIS.[3] He was also rumored[4] to have had gay lovers[5] and been friends with drag queens at Pulse itself.[6] Before Craig Stephen Hicks killed three Muslim students in North Carolina, he had joined an online group called "Atheists for Equality" and posted quotes from Richard Dawkins on Facebook.[7] He had also obsessed over the Michael Douglas movie *Falling Down* and complained about his neighbors playing Risk too loudly. Before Seung-Hui Cho committed the Virginia Tech massacre, he had disturbed his classmates by writing a play called *Richard McBeef*, featuring copious amounts of violence, swearing, and references to child molestation.[8] And before Jared Loughner shot Gabrielle Giffords and

13 others at a town hall event in a Phoenix strip mall, he had publicly asked Giffords the inscrutable question "What is government if words have no meaning?"[9]

I've never liked the idea that you shouldn't "politicize a tragedy." Many tragedies are inherently political; they are the direct consequences of decisions made by people in particular positions of authority. The horrific 2017 London tower block fire, for example, was a story about inequality.[10] The residents of Grenfell Tower were some of the poorest residents of one of the richest boroughs in Britain. As *CityLab* documented, thanks to government austerity policies, local authorities tried to raise revenue by redeveloping properties to accommodate greater numbers of residents, possibly compromising fire safety features in the process.[11] Poor residents had been crammed into a death trap, and instead of installing a fire escape or a second staircase, the tower's owners had tried to make the building less of an eyesore to wealthy Kensington residents nearby through minor cosmetic improvements,[12] such as an exterior polyethylene cladding that may have been responsible for the near-instantaneous spread of the fire to all parts of the building.[13]

What happened at the Grenfell Tower can't be understood without understanding the operation of pressures toward privatization and gentrification. In recent years, the prevailing philosophy of British government (under both the Conservative *and* Labour parties) has been toward reductions in the role of the state, and toward letting wealth do as it pleases. Residents of social housing in othewise-rich districts like Kensington have therefore been willfully neglected by their local councils, who would much prefer to see such people pack up and leave. And people's safety and welfare have been placed in the hands of the private sector, who (shockingly enough) may not have their best interests at heart. In the case of Grenfell Tower, millions of pounds in taxpayer money had been paid to a management company that handsomely compensated its directors, while leaving the building in a state of utter neglect.[14] Even decisions as to whether to install fire sprinklers were left up to private companies[15]; the former Conservative housing minister had resisted implementing a mandatory sprinkler requirement, saying "We believe that it is the responsibility of the fire industry, rather than the Government, to market fire sprinkler systems effectively and to encourage their wider installation."[16] (Theresa May's government had ignored a report on the risk of fire in high-rise buildings like Grenfell Tower.[17])

Residents of the tower had known exactly what would result from this. Time after time they lodged complaints about fire safety with the management company and the local council. 90 percent of residents signed a petition calling for an investigation into the building's management.[18] One woman filed 19 complaints over fire safety, only to be rebuffed every single time. The residents' warnings are downright chilling to read. They insisted that the Tories on the local council were ignoring them because they were poor and marginalized,[19] and came to the depressing conclusion that they would only be listened to after the inevitable deadly inferno:

> [We] believe that only a catastrophic event will expose the ineptitude and incompetence of our landlord, the KCTMO, and bring an end to the dangerous living conditions [here]... Only an incident that results in serious loss of life of KCTMO residents will allow the external scrutiny to occur that will shine a light on the practices that characterise the malign governance of this non-functioning organisation. It is our conviction that a serious fire in a tower block or similar high density residential property is the most likely reason that those who wield power at the KCTMO will be found out and brought to justice!... We have blogged many times on the subject of fire safety at Grenfell Tower and we believe that these investigations will become part of damning evidence of the poor safety record of the KCTMO should a fire affect any other of their properties and cause the loss of life that we are predicting.[20]

It's somewhat stunning to read through the resident activists' blog about the tower, documenting their endless attempts to get somebody from the management company or local government to pay attention to fire safety. The residents had begged for their lives; they had essentially cried out: "They are going to burn us alive here, we are all going to die and nobody is going to care until it's too late." And they were right. It seems inexplicable that so many people in power could have been warned so frequently, and yet done nothing. (That is not strictly true: lawyers for the borough did send the bloggers a threatening notice demanding that they take down the allegations. This is not nothing.[21])

In fact, this only makes sense when we understand the tragedy in its political context. The Grenfell Tower fire was not the result of a criminal plot to burn the poor, nor was it a freak accident. It was the logical end result of a decision-making process driven by a particular philosophy of governance and a particular set of economic laws. If there is no money to be made in housing the destitute in safe buildings, and the prevailing ethos is that profit should be allowed to determine the social good, then destitute people will be housed in unsafe buildings. If wealthy Kensington residents have no financial interest in doing anything to improve the living conditions of poor Kensington residents (in fact, driving out the poor might improve property values for everybody else), and the local government responds to the interests of its most influential citizens, then poor Kensington residents will languish. These are not conspiracy theories; they do not depend on collusion or maliciousness on the part of some elite cabal. They are simply descriptions of how a society operating according to certain rules will produce certain results. Corporations are under a mandate to produce profit, not to safeguard human lives. Thus human lives will only be safeguarded to the extent that doing so directly coincides with the production of profit. For people with no wealth, it rarely will. Thus in the 1900s, the laissez-faire approach gave us the Triangle Shirtwaist Fire.[22] Today, it gives us Grenfell Tower and factory collapses in Bangladesh. It will be the same everywhere and always. The system of incentives put in place will create a set of predictable results. The Grenfell Tower resident bloggers knew it. But they also knew that the nature of the political system was such that nobody was going to listen to the powerless. That is, after all, what it means to be the powerless.

The degree of politics in any given tragedy varies, but most tragedies are political to some extent, just as nearly everything that human beings do is political to some extent. That's because politics is the process by which power and resources are distributed among people, and usually when something horrible happens, the question of who has power and resources will often affect the outcome in some way. Hurricane Katrina, for example, was a "natural" disaster, in that nature makes hurricanes. But it was also a man-made and politically-made disaster, because the question of who received help was a function of who had wealth, and who has wealth is determined by how wealth is distributed. (After the storm, Blackwater mercenaries were called in to guard the homes of wealthy Uptown residents.[23] Needless to say, most New Orleanians did not receive comparable protection.) How many people will die in car accidents is a function of the cost-benefit decisions taken by car companies over new safety measures. Whether a sacred burial ground is paved over and turned into condos depends on whether one lives in an economic system that incentivizes the production of condos, and whether one lives in a political system that cares about sacred burial grounds. Rich people have the power to destroy the lives of their enemies, while poor people have hardly any power at all, meaning that the question of what happens in the world is fundamentally dependent on how wealth is distributed.[24]

Yet there's a dangerous temptation one must be wary of. Because so many things are political in some respect or other, it's tempting to find politics everywhere, to believe that every event must offer some kind of obvious political lesson or message. Pretending that tragedies occur in a vacuum is irresponsible and exonerates those (like austerity politicians) whose decisions directly result in the loss of human life. But it's equally irresponsible to see every tragedy through the lens of one's pre-existing political commitments, and to use people's suffering and death to attack one's ideological opponents. There is a misleading and tawdry way of "politicizing" tragedies, which views every event as the confirmation of views one already holds.

In the United States, mass shootings have not just become regular lurid grist for television ratings, but also offer ongoing opportunities for commentators to discern larger political patterns from the actions of individual mentally ill people. Every time an angry nutcase opens fire in a public place (and because this is America, that happens frequently), people rapidly scramble to uncover the perpetrator's political inclinations through careful scrutiny of their social media accounts. Upon hearing the news, they keep their fingers crossed that the killer is from the other side. So, if you're a conservative, you want the shooter to be a radical Islamist or a Black Lives Matter supporter. If you're a liberal, you want them to be a Tea Party racist or Christian zealot.

I actually don't mean to sound excessively cynical or critical by saying that people "hope" a killer is from the other side. After all, we all know that when the killer is from our side, it's going to be used against us. I can't imagine the feeling of dread that must come over Muslims every time they hear the words "suicide bombing" on the news. After all, they know that any time some disturbed jihadist murders a bunch of children, bigots will use it as evidence against all Muslims and their families. For Muslim parents, a prominent jihadi attack means they have to live in greater fear that their children will suffer bullying and violence. In a climate where people are judged by the actions of those that share their demographic characteristics, it is natural to hope that the harm has been done by some group that doesn't easily reinforce dominant political narratives (e.g. Symbionese liberationists or Vermont separatists).

The shameful aspect, then, is less in the "hoping it's not your people" than in the extraordinary rapidity with which people conclude that a shooting is the direct consequence of something the other side did. After the atheist shot the Muslim students, there were instant calls for a "moment of reckoning" among atheists[25]; the Islamophobic rhetoric of Sam Harris and Richard Dawkins had allegedly created a kind of cocksureness among atheists that provided ready justification for murder. A *New Republic* article called the killings the "outgrowth of a system" that dangerously convinced people—young white men especially—of their superior rationality.

However, when we look at the full facts about mass killers, rather than the convenient ones, everything becomes much messier. When the two NYPD officers were shot in Brooklyn, conservative commentator Heather Mac Donald wrote that the attack was the "poisonous effect" of the "lies" of the "anti-cop left."[26] She treated the action as a direct consequence of an ideology. Yet she didn't mention that the killer had also shot his ex-girlfriend. That's because it didn't fit the narrative: if his violence was motivated by his support for the Black Lives Matter movement, why did he shoot the ex-girlfriend as well? In fact, the man was severely mentally ill and had a long criminal history.[27] But acknowledging the mental illness would undermine the idea that the killings were political, so Mac Donald simply didn't mention it.

It's the same every time. The Portland attack was taken as proof that Trump had unleashed an army of violent racists. After Gabrielle Giffords was shot, liberals instantly began pointing a finger at... Sarah Palin, of all people, who had once released an ad "targeting" Giffords' congressional district. In fact, Jared Loughner did not despise Giffords because she was a Democrat, but because she subscribed to the false belief that words had meaning, and had not taken seriously his attempt to prove that they do not.[28] In other words, the attack was not exactly "political" in the commonly understood sense. (Though, since everything is still political, untreated mental illness and the ubiquity of firearm access still raise serious policy questions.) But the desire to find a political narrative does not die easy; the *New York Times* recently resurrected the Palin/Loughner connection again, before being forced to issue a retraction.[29]

In June of 2017, a man named James Hodgkinson shot up a GOP congressional baseball game, wounding four people including Louisiana representative Steven Scalise. Before that, Hodgkinson had posted a bunch of anti-corporate memes and volunteered for Bernie Sanders' presidential campaign.[30] He was also alleged to have brutally abused his foster daughters, one of whom killed herself after only a few months of living with him by lighting herself on fire.[31]

Of course, with a congressman having been shot, it was not long before people began discerning a larger political message. Since Hodgkinson called Donald Trump a "traitor," some people blamed Democrats for pushing conspiracy theories about Trump and Russia.[32] Since Hodgkinson was anti-Clinton, others suggested he was "radicalized by Russian propaganda."[33] Meanwhile, conservatives blamed liberals (specifically "progressive terrorism"[34]) and liberals blamed Our Vitriolic National Political Discourse. (There were, of course, calls for A Renewed Commitment To Civility.)

The *New York Times* pondered whether Bernie Sanders himself might be at fault, in a piece by *Times* writer Yamiche Alcindor (who once asked Sanders whether it was "sexist" for him to run against Hillary Clinton[35] and who had posted, without comment, a video of an anti-Semitic rant about Sanders' "ties to Jewish real estate owners").[36] Entitled "Attack Tests Movement Sanders Founded," the article said that Hodgkinson's words were "not far from Mr. Sanders's own message," and quoted a Trump-supporting political consultant suggesting that Sanders was offering "a passive justification for the kind of violence we saw" and should "accept the consequences" of his words because by calling Donald Trump "dangerous," "you are empowering the people that follow you to take whatever sort of action that they deem necessary."[37] Alcindor said Sanders' supporters had "earned a belligerent reputation" and have "harassed reporters" in defending their "idol."

One can see how these incidents are used as excuses for dismissing opposing political viewpoints. The *Times*, which once hastily re-edited an article after publication so that it would not reflect too positively on Bernie Sanders, throws together the shooting, Sanders's critique of "corporate media," and allegations of harassment. In doing so, it provides those who already dislike Sanders with material to confirm their worldview. "This is the logical consequence of 'BernieBro' ideology," they can say. But we can do this for anything. Mass killers grab on to all kinds of semi-formed political ideologies, and if we always view such people as the logical consequence of whatever idea they choose to spout, we will end up indicting every single religion and political persuasion. Furthermore, we must be extremely selective: we ignore the case of the man who shot three people at a UPS warehouse on the same day, but the GOP baseball attack must have been the consequence of politics.[38]

All of this is made harder by the fact that sometimes such attacks prob-ably *are* fueled by ideologies. It would be foolish to deny that ideas have consequences, and if a charismatic leader demonizes and dehumanizes people, exhorting his followers to rid the earth of them, he certainly bears responsibility for whatever violence results. However, it's also incredibly difficult to actually draw concrete connections, and incredibly easy to make unwarranted assumptions. We might think it obvious that Omar Mateen was motivated by radical Islam. But the Newtown and Aurora shooters did the same thing without any belief that they were serving the will of Allah. The tendency seems to be that people become violent first and craft an ideological justification later. If 99.9999% of Bernie Sanders supporters do not shoot their congressmen or commit acts of hideous public violence, but a far higher percentage of serial domestic abusers do, and our suspect is both a Bernie Sanders supporter and a serial domestic abuser, which of his characteristics should be most rel-evant? For any belief system, there will be a psychopath who shares its tenets, and perhaps the best approach is statistical rather than anecdotal. Rather than asking "Did a person with Belief X commit Crime Y?" in order to assess the consequences of Belief X, we should ask "Is a per-son with Belief X statistically more likely to commit Crime Y?" Only then can we say something interesting about belief X, and probably not even then.[39]

It's tough, then: beliefs cause action, but not always, and it's not clear when and how much, and which kinds of evidence prove what kinds of connection. It would be strange to say that racists who beat up a home-less immigrant while yelling about Donald Trump are in no way influ-enced by Donald Trump.[40] Likewise, it would be strange to say that a Wahhabist who blows himself up at a teen pop concert was in no way influenced by Wahhabism. But when we look at the chaotic facts of peo-ple's lives, it usually becomes impossible to draw straight lines, and we're always going to see simple meanings and lessons when they aren't neces-sarily there. The human impulse is to tell stories, and as people reel after a devastating tragedy, it's more tempting than ever to find some obvious explanation to latch onto, anything that keeps us from having to face the difficult truth that sometimes the universe is absurd in its cruelty, and sometimes you get no answers.

The best thing we can do is to be cautious, consistent, and fair. Causal speculation is inevitable, but consistent standards have to be applied. If a mass shooting in the name of candidate A tells us something about Candidate A, then it must necessarily also do so in the case of Candidate Y. The unacceptable position is the one that says: "the tragedies that indict my political opponents are political, while the tragedies that indict my own politics are simply unfortunate accidents."

All tragedies are political; life is political, people are political and so are the things that happen to them. Demands to avoid "politicizing" a tragedy are frequently demands to forgo serious scrutiny of the social, economic, and ideological causes of human misery. Yet we can draw a distinction between two definitions of the term: if "politicizing" means intentionally injecting politics when it isn't there, and exploiting something horrible for ideological ends, then nobody should politicize. But if "politicize" means a serious and clear-headed search for political implications, then it is a necessity, for a true assessment of the political causes of tragedy is the only way to prevent their recurrence.

How To Defend Hiroshima

As Barack Obama prepared to become the first sitting President to visit the Hiroshima bombing site in Japan,[1] pundits were already offering a new wave of justifications for the attacks and criticisms of Obama's "apology tours."[2] Michael Auslin of *Forbes* put out an article claiming the attacks were inevitable and necessary, and that "no American president president need ever apologize" for it.[3] The "Patriot Post" mocked Obama for feeling sorry about "winning World War II."[4]

Vigorous defenses of America's conduct in the war, and its use of the atomic bombs, have been made since virtually the moment of their being dropped. The arguments made when Obama visited Hiroshima were be well-worn and familiar. Commentary surrounding the President's Japan visit followed predictable patterns that have now repeated themselves for over seventy years.

All kinds of hideous acts are justified every day for one reason or another, and, there is nothing truly remarkable about the fact that people continue to defend the annihilation of 125,000 human beings at Hiroshima and Nagasaki. But there is something curious about these inevitable outpourings of excuses for America's conduct. It's not the argument itself, but the intensity of the self-assurance with which the acts are justified. Seventy years on, not only do media experts rush to excuse the bombings, but they rush to excuse them with a certitude that one usually sees reserve for the most elementary scientific truths. To these writers, that Hiroshima and Nagasaki were justified is as obvious as the law of gravity. Argue with a defender of the bombings, attempt to inject the smallest portion of doubt into the consensus, and one will be accused of pacifism and the revisionist conception of history.

Commentary defending the attacks consistently exudes this hyper-confidence in their correctness. A 2013 *National Review* article on the subject was entitled "Remembering When We Were Strong: Hiroshima, Nagasaki, and the Moral Necessity of a Nuclear Strike."[5] The author, David French, took the "historically illiterate" and "Christian pacifist[s]" to task for failing to appreciate the costs of "weakness" and the virtues of "decisive force." In a *Forbes* article, Henry I. Miller wrote that slowly:

> *The "was it necessary?" Monday-morning quarterbacks emerged and began to question the military necessity and morality of the use of nuclear weapons on Japanese cities. Since then, there have been periodic eruptions of revisionism, uninformed speculation and political correctness on this subject...*[6]

Last year, with the 70th anniversary of the Hiroshima attacks, the same kind of confident defenses emerged again. *New Criterion* editor Roger Kimball described opposition to the bombings as the product of "the anti-American intelligentsia [and] other sentimentalists of limited worldly experience."[7] Toby Young, in the British *Spectator*, complained that because of the anniversary, he was hearing the "predictable wailing and gnashing of teeth about the horrors of nuclear weapons," even though the Japanese "brought their misfortune on themselves."[8]

That view is widely shared. Young and the others are all conservatives, but their opinion remains the majority one. A Pew poll taken last year found that 56% of Americans believe the bombings were justified, with only 34% believing they were unjustified.[9] That number does reflect a change; immediately after the war, 85% of Americans believed the bombings were justified. But a belief in the rightness of the attacks continues to persist.

The basic argument in support of this view is a familiar one. The bombings, defenders say, precipitated the Japanese surrender and ended the war. In doing so, they saved millions of lives, both American and Japanese, that would have been lost over the course of an impending American land invasion of Japan. Those who are horrified by the casualties of Hiroshima and Nagasaki are therefore putting unreasoned sentiment above practical necessity. The only moral choice was to drop the bombs, since they ultimately saved lives.

This argument was the one put forward in 1945, and the historical debate has not reached a clear resolution. Opponents of the bombings insist that the decision had little to do with the surrender; the Japanese were on the verge of surrendering anyway, and the bomb was intended to intimidate the Soviets rather than the Japanese.

If discussions of Hiroshima and Nagasaki occur on these terms, however, they are destined to be forever irresolvable and polarizing. First, running a historical counterfactual and determining what "would" have happened if the bombs had not been dropped is an impossibility. Second, people's underlying position on the question of whether nuclear weapons are acceptable is destined to influence their interpretation of the historical evidence. The more horrified one is by nuclear weapons, the more one is likely to want to believe that the Japanese were on the verge of surrender. The more one believes that American foreign policy is a force for good, the more one is likely to believe that the bombings were a well-intentioned effort to help people by a president concerned with minimizing casualties. Pre-existing political tendencies will inevitably color the interpretation of murky historical evidence.

But if the evidence is debatable, then the extreme confidence of the bombings' defenders is both unwarranted and disturbing. Even if we just have an *open question* as to whether the slaughter of over one hundred thousand civilians was a necessity or totally pointless, the stakes of the issue seem high enough that conservatives ought to be hesitant before issuing bluster in defense of mass death. With an impossible counterfactual to contend with, a hot dispute among scholars, and a brutal event under discussion, pejoratively writing off disagreement as "illiterate" and "wailing" somewhat undermines one's confidence in the writers' capacity for fair assessment.

Indeed, it is the sheer glibness of so much of the disdain that is worrying, that makes one question whether they are even concerned about the moral questions at all. Oliver Kamm, a liberal writer for *The Guardian* who prominently defends the bombings, felt so chuffed when Noam Chomsky once accused him of "tacit acquiescence to horrendous crimes" that he uses the phrase as a blurb for himself.[10]

Anyone who excuses the attacks will inevitably begin by conceding that they were horrible, but for some reason they tend to be remarkably casual. In Kimball's writing, this toss-off line is phrased in the jaunty phraseology of a Sarah Palinism: "Were those bombings terrible? You betcha."

Though everyone who supports the attacks' necessity insists that they *care very deeply* about the moral question, and that they simply believe the bombings were a tragic necessity, they always emphasize the "necessity" far more than the "tragedy." Kimball dismisses John Hersey's eye-opening work of journalism, 1946's *Hiroshima*, in one word: "manipulative."[11] Kamm just refers to the bombings as "terrible," before immediately launching into his explanation of how all opposition is confused and meritless.

Perhaps, then, it is worth injecting a small piece of Hersey's reportage, in order to convey some sense of what is written off or undiscussed in the arguments of atomic bomb defenders. Here, Hersey discusses Hiroshima in the immediate aftermath:

> *Mr Tanimoto... ran toward them by the shortest route, along Koi Highway. He was the only person making his way into the city; he met hundreds and hundreds who were fleeing, and every one of them seemed to be hurt in some way. The eyebrows of some were burned off and skin hung from their faces and hands... Some were vomiting as they walked. Many were naked or in shreds of clothing. On some undressed bodies, the burns had made patterns—of undershirt straps and suspenders and, on the skin of some women*

(since white repelled the heat from the bomb and dark clothes absorbed it and conducted it to the skin), the shapes of flowers they had had on their kimonos. Many, although injured themselves, supported relatives who were worse off. Almost all had their heads bowed, looked straight ahead, were silent and showed no expression whatever. After crossing Koi Bridge and Kannon Bridge, having run the whole way, Mr Tanimoto saw, as he approached the centre, that all the houses had been crushed and many were on fire. Here the trees were bare and their trunks were charred. He tried at several points to penetrate the ruins, but the flames always stopped him. Under many houses, people screamed for help, but no one helped; in general, survivors that day assisted only their relatives or immediate neighbours, for they could not comprehend or tolerate a wider circle of misery. The wounded limped past the screams, and Mr Tanimoto ran past them. As a Christian he was filled with compassion for those who were trapped, and as a Japanese man he was overwhelmed by the shame of being unhurt, and he prayed as he ran: "God help them and take them out of the fire."

The passage only gives the narrowest glimpse at the scale of the destruction. But it is hard to imagine how one could sensibly discuss the issue without attempting to envisage some of the suffering involved. Even someone who considers himself a steely-hearted utilitarian, who has no trouble causing 100,000 people to perish if it will save 100,001, must use his capacity for empathetic imagination in order to make an informed assessment of the costs. After all, some deaths involve truly hideous suffering, and without understanding what the situation looks like for its victims, is impossible to even know the stakes of what we are dealing with.

And yet defenders of the bombings never permit the survivors' stories to intrude upon their arguments. The neoconservative writer Max Boot says that "I don't think the atomic bombing of Japan was a uniquely reprehensible event."[12] He would insist that what he means is that the bloody bombing of cities had become commonplace on both sides by

1945, that the bombs were different in type and intensity but otherwise a continuation of existing policy. But in order to make this case persuasively, Boot would need to deal with the fact that survivors beg to differ. Akihiro Takahashi, who was 14 years old when Hiroshima was bombed, and lost his ears and became deformed, was asked directly how the bomb differed from conventional weapons:

A conventional bomb does not have a heat wave. But with the atomic bomb, at the moment of the explosion, a fireball is created with a temperature of millions of degrees Celsius, and the area on the ground below the bomb reached 3,000 to 4,000 degrees Celsius. Steel starts to melt at 1,530 degrees, so that was much hotter than molten steel. Then the wind from the atomic bomb affected an area with a radius of 16 kilometers. At the moment of the explosion, the shock wave spread and was followed by a wind that reached 440 meters per second. Even the most powerful typhoon to hit Japan had a speed of only 82 meters per second. I myself was blown 10 meters by the blast, and the wind caused skin to peel off, eyes to pop out, and intestines to be blown out of the stomach. I myself lost the skin on my arm, and it dangled down from my fingers.

Boot doesn't mention these unique horrors. In fact, absent from every single defense of the bombings is a vivid description of their consequences. Why is that? After all, *if* the argument is a practical one, that the bombings were necessary in order to avoid a worse outcome, it should not be necessary to downplay the suffering, or wave it aside in a sentence. But each of them knows that the moment they quote Akihiro Takahashi, the pro-bombing case will begin to sound absurd.

That really is the factor that should make every single Hiroshima defense suspicious. The writers' level of revulsion just isn't sufficient to indicate that they really know what they are talking about. *The New York Times* "human rights" journalist Nicholas Kristof, perhaps known best for his enthusiastic defense of sweatshops,[13] conceded in his own pro-bombing column that "[i]t feels unseemly to defend the vaporizing of two cities."[14] But anyone who finds this merely "unseemly" can have no appreciation for what the "vaporizing" of cities actually entails. To actually reckon with the reality, one would not have to feel a simple "unseemliness" in defending the bombings, but a deep and tormenting perversity. Again, that isn't to exclude the possibility of making the "better than the alternative" argument. It is merely to say that in order to justify the obliteration of 100,000 civilians, slight discomfort will not do. If the utilitarian case is ever to be made, it must be made through tears. Anything else means the discussion isn't being treated with the moral seriousness it requires.

Like Boot, Kristof knows that if he goes beyond the abstract, if he talks about the realities of two obliterated cities instead of the debates between Japan's military and its emperor, he case will be instantly sapped of its force. So matters are kept vague and hypothetical. Kristof considers the argument that the U.S. ought to have bombed a remote area instead of a highly-populated city, or waited before dropping a second bomb on Nagasaki. "Yes, perhaps" we should have, he says. But there are 100,000 lives at stake in that perhaps.

The other massive omission Kristof makes is one shared by nearly every published defense of the bombing, namely the mentioning of Dwight Eisenhower, Douglas MacArthur, and Herbert Hoover. All three believed the bombings to have been horrendous and a mistake. But bizarrely, even as the historical consensus has been somewhat unsettled, and the wisdom of the bombings has been questioned by a greater percentage of Americans, the words of these three figures are still seldom quoted.

Hoover did not mince his words: "The use of the atomic bomb, with its indiscriminate killing of women and children, revolts my soul."[15] General MacArthur said he saw "no military justification for the dropping of the bomb."[16] Eisenhower recounted in his memoirs that in the lead-up to the bombing, he was "conscious of a feeling of depression."[17] He says that he told the Secretary of State that dropping the bomb was "completely unnecessary," and "our country should avoid shocking world opinion by the use of a weapon whose employment was, I thought, no longer mandatory as a measure to save American lives." Eisenhower affirmed his stance in an interview with *Newsweek*, saying that "the Japanese were ready to surrender and it wasn't necessary to hit them with that awful thing."[18]

Nor were these three eminent figures the only high-ranking officials to regret the decision. Truman's Chief of Staff, Admiral William Leahy, said that in his opinion, "the use of this barbarous weapon at Hiroshima and Nagasaki was of no material assistance in our war against Japan."[19] The Commander in Chief of the Pacific Fleet, Chester Nimitz, said in 1945 that "the atomic bomb played no decisive part, from a purely military standpoint, in the defeat of Japan." Admiral William Halsey, Commander of the Third Fleet, said in 1946 that "The first atomic bomb was an unnecessary experiment... It was a mistake to ever drop it." Henry "Hap" Arnold, commanding general of the Air Force, said in 1949 that "it always appeared to us that, atomic bomb or no atomic bomb, the Japanese were already on the verge of collapse."

The quotes go on and on. One can cite dozens of senior military officers and cabinet officials, from the commander of the Strategic Air Force to the Undersecretary of the Navy, all of whom thought the bombing was unnecessary and abhorrent, and many of whom strongly believed it should have been dropped in an uninhabited area instead of in the middle of a hundred thousand civilians. When one reads all of the quotes together, one gets the very strong feeling that, even on the highly questionable assumption that there was a military necessity to the bombings, the decision was not taken with the casualty-minimizing humanitarian carefulness that supporters insist was at play.

Justifiers of the bombings are thus constantly evading the actual difficult questions and evidence. If they were serious, and meant what they said about the bombings being a tragic necessity, they would happily cite the words of Eisenhower, MacArthur, Nimitz, and Leahy to explain why they were all in error. They would tell us why the attacks could revolt the coarsened soul of Herbert Hoover, but do nothing to their own. Instead, they sweep all of these words away as if they were never spoken.

The final tactic used is the accusation of revisionism. Oliver Kamm says that revulsion at the bombings occurred long afterward, that it "is not how they were judged at the time." Michael Auslin says critics are "second guessing" at "decades remove." David French believes that the Left began to "control the narrative." Kristof cites the new "emerging consensus" driven by revisionism (of course, the poll results cited earlier prove him mistaken on the emergence of any actual "consensus.")

But it's false to say that this is mere hindsight, that all criticism is the work of the "Monday morning quarterbacks" in the contemporary left. Arnold and Eisenhower said they knew it was in error *at the time* of the decision. Nimitz spoke mere months after the bombing, and further criticism erupted within a year. Albert Einstein was quoted in 1946 "deploring" the use of the bomb, and many dissenting writers and thinkers saw the bomb as the harbinger of something deeply and truly terrible.[20] One haunting example comes from a *New Yorker* writer, Clifton Fadiman, who wrote the following in a 1946 introduction to a book of Ambrose Bierce stories:

> *On August 6, 1945, the planet, with the United States in the lead, passed half-consciously into an era of despair. With a noiseless flash over Hiroshima, homo sapiens issued the first dramatic announcement of his inability to make a biological success of himself. The next few years or decades seem almost certain to provide planetary wars that will rend and crack and shiver the earth's thin skin, years of wholesale suicide, years that will paralyze the moral and religious sense of mankind. Civilized man—unless he decides to use his reason—will fall forward into a new and almost unimaginable barbarism.*[21]

Fadiman's words, as well as those of Takahashi, Eisenhower, MacArthur, and Einstein, should trouble all of those who speak confidently and casually in defense of the atomic bombings of Hiroshima and Nagasaki. Something so wretched should never be justified with such glib self-assurance.

Meat and The H-word

I AM GOING TO BEG YOU. I am going to desperately plead with you. Let me say the word, and let me say why I'm saying the word, and then let's have a discussion about it. I know that for some people, even to suggest that the word might apply to this case is tantamount to denialism. Just to have the conversation is to dishonor the victims. I realize, too, that I don't strictly *need* this word, of all words, in order to discuss the subject. I have been advised that it is counterproductive: feelings about the word are so fraught that the offense caused will outweigh any good I could possibly do, and will cause me to be far less persuasive than I otherwise would be. And isn't this about persuasion, ultimately? But I can't help it: every time I examine the facts, I can't stop thinking the word. If I'm being honest with you, and I want to be, I need to be able to tell you the question that I'm stuck on, and the question contains the word.

The word is "holocaust" and the question is this: "Given the amount of suffering and death that it entails, why is it improper to describe the mass slaughter of animals for human consumption as a holocaust?"

I appreciate why people react badly to any description of the loss of non-human life as a holocaust. One of the most disturbing features of the capital-H Holocaust was the dehumanization process. David Livingstone Smith, in *Less Than Human,* describes how a common prerequisite to atrocities is reconfiguring perceptions of a group, to make them seem *not just metaphorically* but literally "subhuman."[1] We all know that the Nazis described the Jews as rats and the Hutus described the Tutsis as cockroaches. "Comparing people to animals" is such a common feature of organized brutality that any attempt to draw parallels between animal-victims and people-victims can be seen as partly replicating the very thought process that led to the actual Holocaust.

Here is something animal advocates are often quite bad at expressing, though: "comparing people to animals" can either be intended to diminish the people or to elevate the animals, and these two thoughts are so dissimilar that even to call them both "comparing people to animals" is misleading. The version that elevates animals is perhaps more properly thought of as "comparing animals to people": if you dehumanize a person by comparing them to a rat or dog, you are also implying that there is something disgusting and worthless about rats and dogs. If those creatures weren't considered "lesser," the animal-comparison wouldn't be an insult. Instead of encouraging us to "stop dehumanizing people by comparing them to animals," animal advocates are suggesting that we get rid of the whole idea that there are Men and there are Beasts. Besides, our animal pejoratives aren't even consistent. They're based on weird folk-stereotypes only partially grounded in the actual nature of various species: calling someone a *rat* suggests they're filthy, but calling them a *squirrel* means they're hyperactive, and there are no particular connotations associated with other rodents like gerbils and capybaras. (It really is strange how a culture can assign expected anthropomorphic traits to each species: the nervous ostrich, the grumpy walrus, the industrious beaver, the clever fox, the lazy ass.)

It's important to be able to clearly and carefully make the distinction between elevating animals and diminishing humans, but it's harder to do in practice than it sounds. Utilitarians like Peter Singer get into trouble all the time when they make some appalling remark comparing disabled children with chimpanzees. I happen to think people are right to find this insensitive, because nobody can just willfully ignore the connotations that certain words actually have in practice, or the *effect* that these comparisons might have in a world where dehumanization is so dangerous. But in their intention, the utilitarians often mean to say that chimpanzees are as important as humans rather than that some humans are as unimportant as chimpanzees. How callous you find this remark depends entirely on what your preexisting ideas about the value of a chimpanzee life are. We're so conditioned to think that monkeys and pigs are our lessers that it's hard not to hear these words as insults.

WE ALL KNOW, OR AT LEAST we can all figure out with a moment's honest reflection, that our dominant attitudes on animals are inconsistent. Someone can be incredibly disturbed by the notion of eating their puppy, but happily consume bacon every other morning, and the cognitive dissonance between the two positions never seems to cause any bother. If we're being serious, though, we know that many sows are smarter than chihuahuas, and that all of the traits that cause us to love our pets are just as present in the animals we regularly devour the murdered corpses of. (I am sorry, that was a somewhat extreme way of putting it.) This is a commonplace observation, but in a way that's what makes it so strange: it's obvious that we have no rational reason to think some animals are friends and others are food. The only differences are tradition and the strength of the relationships we happen to have developed with the friend-animals, but that's no more a justification of the distinction than it would be to say "I only eat people who aren't my friends." Yet ven though nobody can justify it, it continues. People solve the question "Why do you treat some animals as if they have personalities but other equally sophisticated animals as if they are inanimate lumps of flavor and calories?" by simply pretending the question hasn't been asked, or by making some remark like "Well, if pigs would quit making themselves taste so good, I could quit eating them."

The truth is disturbing, which is why it's so easily ignored. I'm sure I don't have to remind you of all the remarkable facts about pigs. First, the stereotypes are false: they are clean animals and don't sweat, and they don't "pig out" but prefer to eat slowly and methodically. They are, as Glenn Greenwald puts it, "among the planet's most intelligent, social, and emotionally complicated species, capable of great joy, play, love, connection, suffering and pain."[2] They can be housebroken, and can be trained to walk on a leash and do tricks. They dream, they play, they snuggle. They can roll out rugs, play videogames, and herd sheep. They love sunbathing and belly rubs. But don't take my word for it—listen to the testimony of this man who accidentally adopted a 500-pound pig:

> *She's unlike any animal I've met. Her intelligence is unbelievable. She's house trained and even opens the back door with her snout to let herself out to pee. Her food is mainly kibble, plus fruit and vegetables. Her favourite treat is a cupcake. She's bathed regularly and pigs don't sweat, so she doesn't smell. If you look a pig closely in the eyes, it's startling; there's something so inexplicably human. When you're lying next to her and talking, you know she understands. It was emotional realising she was a commercial pig. The more we discovered about what her life could have been, it seemed crazy to us that we ate animals, so we stopped.*[3]

I want to note something that often passes by too quickly, which is that the sentience of animals like pigs and cows is almost impossible to deny. Animals can clearly feel "distress" and "pleasure," and since they have nervous systems just like we do, these feelings are being felt by a "consciousness." If a human eyeball captures light and creates images that are seen from within, so does a pig's eyeball, because eyes are eyes. In other words, pigs have an internal life: there is something it is like to *be* a pig. We'll almost certainly never know what that's like, and it's impossible to even speculate on, but if we believe that other humans are conscious, it is unclear why other animals wouldn't be, albeit in a more rudimentary way. No, they don't understand differential calculus or Althusser's theory of interpellation. (Neither do I.) But they share with us the more morally crucial quality of being able to feel things. They can be happy and they can suffer.

Critics suggest that this is just irrational anthropomorphism: the idea of animal emotions is false, because emotions are concepts we have developed to understand our own experiences as humans, and we have no idea what the parallel experiences in animals are like and whether they are properly comparable. The temptation to attribute human traits to animals is certainly difficult to resist; I can't help but see sloths that look like they're smiling as *actually* smiling, but these sloths almost certainly have no idea that they are smiling. Likewise, whenever I see a basset hound I feel compelled to try to cheer it up, even though I know that sad-eyed dogs aren't really sad. Even if we do posit that animals feel emotions, nobody can know just how distant their consciousnesses are from our own. We have an intuitive sense that "being a bug" doesn't feel like much, but how similar is being a water vole to being an antelope versus being a dragonfly? All of it is speculation. David Foster Wallace, in considering the Lobster Question ("Is it all right to boil a sentient creature alive just for our gustatory pleasure?"), noted that the issues of "whether and how different kinds of animals feel pain, and of whether and why it might be justifiable to inflict pain on them in order to eat them, turn out to be extremely complex and difficult," and many can't actually be resolved satisfactorily.[4] How do you know what agony means to a lobster? Still, he said, "standing at the stove, it is hard to deny in any meaningful way that this is a living creature experiencing pain and wishing to avoid/escape the painful experience... To my lay mind, the lobster's behavior in the kettle appears to be the expression of a preference; and it may well be that an ability to form preferences is the decisive criterion for real suffering."

And lobsters are a trickier case than other more complex creatures, since they're freaky and difficult to empathize with. As we speak of higher-order creatures who have anatomy and behavioral traits more closely paralleling our own, there is at least good evidence to suggest that various nonhuman animals can experience terrible pain. (Again, hardly anyone would deny this with dogs, and we just need to be willing to carry our reasoning through.) Once we accept that these beings experience pain, it next becomes necessary to admit that humans inflict a lot of it on them. We massacre tens of billions of animals a year, and their brief lives are often filled with nothing but fear and agony. The "lucky" ones are those like the male chicks who are deemed "useless" and are "suffocated, gassed or minced alive at a day old." At least they will be spared the life of torture that awaits most of the creatures raised in factory farms. I don't know how many atrocity tales to tell here, because again, this is not something unknown, but something "known yet ignored." I can tell you about animals living next to the rotting corpses of their offspring, animals beaten, shocked, sliced, living in their own blood and feces. I could show you horrible pictures, but I won't. Here's Greenwald describing a practice used in pig farms:

> *Pigs are placed in a crate made of iron bars that is the exact length and width of their bodies, so they can do nothing for their entire lives but stand on a concrete floor, never turn around, never see any outdoors, never even see their tails, never move more than an inch. They are put in so-called farrowing crates when they give birth, and their piglets run underneath them to suckle and are often trampled to death. The sows are bred repeatedly this way until their fertility declines, at which point they are slaughtered and turned into meat. The pigs are so desperate to get out of their crates that they often spend weeks trying to bite through the iron bars until their gums gush blood, bash their heads against the walls, and suffer a disease in which their organs end up mangled in the wrong places, from the sheer physical trauma of trying to escape from a tiny space or from acute anxiety.*[5]

Separate from the issue of "conditions" is the issue of killing itself. Obviously, it is better if an animal lives in relative comfort before it is slaughtered, and better if their deaths are imposed "humanely." But personally, I find the idea of "humane slaughter" oxymoronic, because I'm disturbed by the taking of life as well as by suffering. This part is difficult to persuade people of, since it depends largely on a moral instinct about whether an animal's life is "inherently" valuable, and whether they should have some kind of autonomy or dignity. Plenty of people who could agree that animal torture is wrong can still believe that eating animals is unobjectionable in and of itself. My disagreement with this comes from my deep gut feeling that opposing torture but endorsing killing is like saying "Of course, the people we eat shouldn't be kept in tiny cages before we kill them, that's abominable." Once you grant that animals are conscious, and have "feelings" of one kind or another, and "wills" (i.e. that there are things they want and things they don't want, and they don't want to die), the whole process of mass killing seems irredeemably horrifying.

I WANT TO COME BACK TO THE H-WORD. I think about the Holocaust a lot, the capital-H one. I'd imagine I think about it more than most people I know. I'm almost the opposite of a Holocaust denier: I find it so real, and the implications of its reality so unsettling, that it is difficult for me to ever quite get it out of my head. I almost think that in order to get on with your life, you have to operate in some state of quasi-denial: affirming intellectually that the Holocaust happened, but avoiding feeling viscerally what that actually means. "Six million" remains an abstract, the victims are black and white photos rather than conscious beings with pulses and itches and toes like yourself. The idea of watching your children be dragged away from you and shuffled off toward a gas chamber, it's just... it's too much, and you almost have to deny it, or at least not dwell on it frequently, because it's just so unbelievably sad.

My morbid inability to let go of the Holocaust leaves me thinking a lot about those varying states of denial. Nearly everyone is in some degree of denial about how much pain there is in the world, because grasping its full dimensions is, first, impossible, and second, would be paralyzing and make life unbearable. Because we have to overlook enormous amounts of suffering if we're going to live, have to stop thinking about the old people crying alone in their hospital beds, and the sick children whose every second of life has been spent dying, it is going to be very easy to miss an atrocity in our midst. It has never been a mystery to me how ordinary Germans could ignore what was going on around them. They did it the same way we ignore all of the pain that millions of strangers are going through at any given moment. As long as other people's terror isn't in the room with you, as long as it's off behind barbed wire a few miles away, it's not just easy to ignore but almost impossible to notice.

Walk through any American city on a nice day and see how easy it is to forget that the country has two million people in its prisons. They're off in rural counties, and as long as you don't go looking for them—and as long as you're not among the populations from whose numbers the incarcerated are mostly drawn—none of it will even exist for you. (For three years, I used to do the same ten minute walk from my apartment to school and back every day. It was only in the third year, after noticing it on a map, that I realized I had been walking directly past a jail with hundreds of inmates in it. People were locked in rooms, living lives, and I passed by unawares.)

Because people slip so naturally into oblivious complicity, it's crucial to actively examine the world around you for evidence of things hidden. What am I missing? What have I accepted as ordinary that might in fact be atrocious? Am I in denial about something that will be clear in retrospect? Every time I apply this kind of thinking to meat-eating, I get chills. Here we have set up *mass industrial slaughter*, a world built on the suffering and death of billions of creatures. The scale of the carnage is unfathomable. (I know sharks aren't particularly sympathetic, but I'm still shocked by the statistic that while sharks kill 8 people per year, humans kill 11,000 sharks per hour.) Yet we hide all of it away, we don't talk about it. Laws are passed to prevent people from even taking photographs of it. That makes me feel the same way I do about the death penalty: if this weren't atrocious, it wouldn't need to be kept out of view. "Mass industrial slaughter." There's no denying that's what it is. Yet that sounds like something a decent society shouldn't have in it.

I've tried my best to figure out a way to avoid my conclusion, because I know only a small fraction of other people share it. But it's a simple and, to me, inescapable deduction: (1) nonhuman animals are conscious beings capable of suffering, (2) unnecessarily causing conscious beings to suffer and die is morally reprehensible, (3) humans cause billions of nonhuman animals to suffer and die every year, mostly for their own pleasure, (4) by killing and eating animals, humans are doing something deeply wrong. (Jeremy Bentham's formulation is still powerful and hard to escape: "The question is not, Can they reason? nor, Can they talk? but, *Can they suffer?*") The difficulty of avoiding this conclusion is what disturbed David Foster Wallace during his time at the Maine Lobster Festival. He realized that it seemed preachy and extreme, but as a thoughtful and philosophically rigorous individual, he couldn't escape the morally troubling implications of boiling lobsters alive. The lobsters just didn't seem to want to be killed, and however normalized the practice may be, however easily we may take it for granted that these creatures are of little moral worth, once you begin to scrutinize these assumptions, to see that they're built on very little, and that a creature does seem to be going through something resembling pain, it becomes tough to defend our actions.

I still know I'm taking a risk by using the word "holocaust." The dictionary definition may be "any mass slaughter or reckless destruction of life" (and the word even originally referred to the burning of sacrifices, i.e. animals), but there are plenty who are skeptical even of applying the term to *other genocides.* To speak of a "pig holocaust" can seem trivializing and insensitive. *And yet:* once again, ideas that seem true and reasonable by instinct become harder to defend once scrutinized. It's true that how bad you believe the industrial slaughter of animals is, compared to the industrial slaughter of humans, depends on whether you believe suffering is suffering no matter which conscious entity it happens to, and the degree to which its gravity depends on the intellectual sophistication of the sufferer. You might also think that certain atrocities perpetrated on 100 million pigs are not as bad as those same atrocities committed against five fully-functioning human beings. A lot depends on your subjective weighting of the value of very different lives, and none of that has any obvious "true" answer. Personally, though, I keep having that feeling of being unable to escape my discomfort: knowing what's out there, knowing the cages, the blood, the billion squeals of pain, I hear over and over those same questions: "Why is this different? How can it be justified? What are you choosing not to realize?" And yet again that same terrible word: holocaust.

Famous Leftists I Have Loved

The Anti-Nationalist Legacy of Rudolf Rocker

"On the banner of the International was not written 'Proletarians of all lands, kill each other!' but 'Proletarians of all lands, unite!'"
– Rudolf Rocker, "War: A Study in Fact"

When Rudolf Rocker's *Nationalism and Culture* was released in 1937, it was hailed by no less an assemblage of luminaries than Albert Einstein, Bertrand Russell, and Thomas Mann. The historian Will Durant called it "magnificent" and "profound," and even the *New Republic* gave it a positive notice. It was an unusual level of mainstream acclaim for a book of political philosophy by a German anarchist refugee, especially one published by a group called the "Rocker Publication Committee," a Los Angeles-based venture set up for the sole purpose of releasing *Nationalism and Culture*.

Yet in the years since, Rocker's work has settled into the obscurity for which it was perhaps always destined. Unlike *The Decline of the West* (1926), Oswald Spengler's meditation on the destiny of civilizations, to which it was compared at the time, *Nationalism and Culture* is rarely cited. Though it proposes and defends a comprehensive theory of nationalism, Benedict Anderson does not even acknowledge it in *Imagined Communities* (1982). Contemporary mentions of the book are largely confined to anarchist circles, and even there it is an awkward outsider, its humanistic cultural analysis and rich love of history out-of-step with the contemporary anarchist inclination to immolate all sacred things.

The eclipse of Rocker's magnum opus is hardly mysterious. It is a book that accords with few of our conceptions of how such books ought to be written, a book that deliberately scorns almost all prior wisdom, and a book whose very existence is difficult to square with common understandings about its time. Rocker is a German who mocks both Hegel and Hitler in equal measure, and who writes in the uncompromising and eclectic voice of the autodidact, shunning the toothless evenhandedness demanded of academics. And writing as an atheistic Berlin anarchist in 1933, Rocker offers living proof of his own contention that individuals must not be made prisoners of stereotypes about national spirit.

Nationalism and Culture is, primarily, a 600-page exploration of the origins and development of nationalism, and a scathing denunciation of the corrosive effect of national feeling on the human spirit. Yet it is one of those works, like Robert Burton's *Anatomy of Melancholy*, that springboard from their stated purpose to discourse on everything under the sun. Architecture is analyzed, socialism is defended, and Rembrandt's paintings are scrutinized at length. It is at once a treatise on the state's relationship with culture and a manifesto for an enlightened leftism. Most of all, it is a clear-eyed plea for sanity at a moment when nationalist and religious irrationalism threatened to swallow the globe. It could not be more relevant today.

THE HUMANISTIC STANDPOINT of *Nationalism and Culture* is reflected in the author's cosmopolitan life. Born in Mainz in 1873, Rocker was not Jewish but spent almost his entire life in Jewish communities as an agitator and educator. During his twenty years in the East End of London, he edited a Yiddish paper, gave lectures in Yiddish, and was given the honorary title of "rabbi" by his devoted students. Rocker even recounts being chased through the streets by children shouting anti-Semitic slurs at him.

Rocker found nothing remarkable about the ease of his assimilation and believed he could have operated among the working class of any origin. But he felt a special kinship among the working-class Jews of London, whose combination of revolutionary ardor and love for education were in tune with his temperament. Even Emma Goldman pronounced herself puzzled at his affinity.

Like most radicals of any era, Rocker spent time on the receiving end of harassment by the state. Imprisoned by the British government during World War I, Rocker gave his fellow inmates lectures with titles like "The General Conditions and the Various Intellectual Movements in Europe After 1848-1849." He also spent time composing his only novel, *The Six* (1938), in which the moral failings of six characters from world literature, from Hamlet to Don Quixote, reveal why unity among disparate peoples is the only path to the new society.

The premise of *The Six* exemplified Rocker's humanist bent, which involved drawing from the best practices of each culture to create a new, universal one. He remained influenced by the Yiddish novelists whose books he had taught to workers. The libertarian inclinations he witnessed on lecture tours through the United States led him to write *Pioneers of American Freedom* (1949), a book that attempted to claim Lincoln for the anarchists.

It was *Nationalism and Culture*, however, into which he poured each ounce of his conviction and wide learning. Rocker penned the book in Berlin, during the Nazis' rise to power, and its original German publication was scheduled for 1933. After the Reichstag was burned, Rocker fled the country, taking with him only one possession: the just-completed manuscript of *Nationalism and Culture*.

ROCKER'S THESIS IS STRAIGHTFORWARD: Nations are the products of states, rather than vice versa. They are manufactured to serve the goals of the powerful, to divide human beings and keep them from recognizing their common interests. Rocker argues this point with a litany of historical examples, from the Renaissance to "the stupid and stumbling provisions of the Versailles treaty."

But en route to this thesis, Rocker finds himself addressing the entire history of Western political philosophy; with a lawyerly precision, he takes a score of celebrated thinkers to pieces. Plato and Aristotle are witheringly castigated for defending slavery. He takes turns with Calvin ("a unique monstrosity"), Kant ("He knew nothing else but the stark, implacable 'Thou shalt!'"), and Hegel ("reactionary from top to bottom"). St. Augustine receives a brutal lashing for his efforts to extend the reach of the church, and Rousseau is singled out as the philosopher who most laid the groundwork for totalitarian perversities.

Rocker also elaborates his objections to Marxism and to materialist philosophies that overemphasize the role of economic motivations in determining the course of history. So much, says Rocker, depends on the will to power; even capitalism does not operate according to the pure pursuit of profit, which is only one manifestation of the desire for domination. The emergence of Amazon, a profit-less behemoth whose modus operandi is simply to devour all things, would not have surprised Rocker a whit.

Rocker spends a great deal of time attending to scientific racism arguments, an understandable focus considering the conditions under which he wrote. Albert Jay Nock, a favorite of libertarians from Ayn Rand to William F. Buckley, has his essentialist theories of Jewish Oriental origin demolished. Rocker elaborates the theories of various "race astrologers," and gives arguments against them that could have been reprinted almost word-for-word upon the release of *The Bell Curve* or Nicholas Wade's 2014 *A Troublesome Inheritance*. "The essential error of every race theory, the reason for their inevitably false conclusions," Rocker states, is that they simply cannot prove the genetic determinism they claim; nor will they ever, for it is ideas like the nation that determine so much of human life, and "external race-marks have nothing to do with the intellectual and moral qualities of" humans.

Rocker does get around, in *Nationalism and Culture*, to discussing both nationalism and culture. Nations, for him, are ever unnatural and imposed from above. They do not spontaneously emerge from the people, but are put in place in order to serve political or economic ends; counterintuitively, nations tend to arise among dissimilar peoples, not similar ones. Rocker examines their rhetoric to show how leaders from Robespierre to Mussolini gave the state a religious character, and tracks the arbitrary processes by which nations combine and dissolve. It is only by historical accident that Californians are not a nation and Chileans are. He also points out the cynicism with which nationalist sentiment is exploited by the owning class, despite the fact that "the love of his own nation has never yet prevented the entrepreneur from using foreign labor if it was cheaper and made more profit for him."

To buttress his theory, Rocker undertakes a sweeping analysis of art, intending to show that the more a work of art reflects the soul of the nation, the less it reflects the soul of the artist, and thus the more compromised it is. He offers a compare-and-contrast study of Michelangelo and Leonardo da Vinci, including a warm tribute to the Mona Lisa, where "in this profoundest emotion of the man and the artist there breathes no breath of national feeling." He loves the Italian Renaissance, but aims to reclaim it from those who would dare to see it as Italian. Art does not follow national trends, Rocker insists, and succeeds only when it opposes them. We can appreciate art because it awakens our human feeling. Thus great art could have no national limitations, for if it is truly great it can be appreciated universally.

Rocker's remedy for national divisions is international socialism. But he fears factionalism among the left, and critiques those who march under its banner without fighting for its values. Rocker's description of the capitulation of socialist parties reminds one of the modern Democratic Party or of New Labour, who "have everywhere shown themselves incapable of guarding the political legacy of the bourgeois democracy, for they have everywhere yielded up long-won rights and liberties without a struggle."

ITS DISPARATE LINES OF INQUIRY make *Nationalism and Culture* shaggy and occasionally exasperating. Rocker's mind meanders here and there, though its prose and ideas are always clear. Further, despite Rocker's mountain of evidence, his lack of nuance and too-easy conflation of God, king, and nation, weaken his case. (One might grant the occasional overstatement to a man who saw Brownshirts outside his window as he wrote.)

But for all that Rocker might blur or get wrong, it is also astonishing what he gets right. He condemns Hitler, the Soviet Union, religion, and capitalism with equal vigor; he distrusts all ideologies that ask us to place something above our shared humanity. If he is mistaken in his theory, he is perfect in his temperament. He imbues one with an outlook that can be turned toward all earthly affairs. One can anticipate precisely what this honorary "rabbi" would feel about the present-day Palestinian situation: a firm rejection of nationalistic sentiment on all sides, aghast at both militant Zionism and the theocratic authoritarianism of Hamas. It is a lesson that might well be absorbed by a left that occasionally lets support for the Palestinian political cause drift into a romantic nationalism.

Yet despite the achievement of this blueprint for a humanist left, Rocker is forgotten by all except anarchists. After the initial acclaim, *Nationalism and Culture* quickly slipped out of print. (Today, AK Press sells an edition.) Rocker has been the subject of a short biography, 1997's *An Anarchist "Rabbi"* by Mina Graur, and is occasionally referred to by Noam Chomsky. But he is largely absent both from discussions of nationalism and from the pantheon of leftist heroes.

The neglect is unfortunate, for Rocker's work is both a vital contribution to the literature on nationalism and an elegant historical document. After all, here is Rocker, as chaos envelops Berlin, crying out for faith in human beings and the rejection of the state. Here is Rocker, tracing the ghastly history of Europe up until his moment and yet daring to express optimism at a moment of terrible darkness.

In our own time of rising national sentiment, of the UK Independence Party, Golden Dawn, and Marine Le Pen, *Nationalism and Culture* has much to teach the left. It is simultaneously an exposition of anarchist philosophy, a history of the world, a theory of the nation-state, and an indictment of power-worshiping sophistry and all human tyrannies. It is a declaration and a demonstration of how to think clearly, how to love language and culture and humanity, and how to approach a troubled time without falling into the snare of fatalism. Rudolf Rocker's humanist philosophy is a gift bequeathed to all; the "rabbi" that so enchanted the poor tailors of East London should continue to delight us today.

Life Sings With Many Voices: The Vision of Eduardo Galeano

IN THE SPRING OF 2014, when the Uruguayan writer Eduardo Galeano made some rueful comments about his classic anti-globalization, anti-imperialist history *Open Veins of Latin America* (1971)[1], the *Economist* was delighted.[2] At last there could be agreement that "capitalism is the only route to development in Latin America," the magazine crowed. Galeano's recantation could hardly have been more significant: "it was almost as if Jesus's disciples had admitted that the New Testament was a big misunderstanding."

Indeed, in the forty years since its publication *Open Veins* had achieved semi-mythic status. Uncompromising and accusatory, the book told of a centuries-long capitalist plunder operation, in which fruit companies, oil drillers, slave traders, and conquistadors collaborated to despoil the Americas. That story, containing more than a little truth, resonated with populist movements. The book became an international bestseller and the scourge of right-wing governments. It may have reached the height of its notoriety when Hugo Chavez gave Barack Obama a copy at the Summit of the Americas in 2009.[3]

Hence the shockwaves when Galeano publicly recanted the work. *Open Veins*, he said, was badly dated. He found his leftist prose unreadable. The *New York Times* reported that Galeano's disavowal "set off a vigorous regional debate, with the right doing some 'we told you so' gloating, and the left clinging to a dogged defensiveness." *Monthly Review*'s Michael Yates dismissed Galeano as just another writer gone conservative in old age.

On April 13 of 2015, Galeano died at the age of seventy-four. His legacy quickly began crystallizing in obituaries that portrayed him as no more than a once-brash post-colonialist who lost his political fire[4] and recently produced some fine writing on soccer.[5] But this narrative is mistaken. It omits Galeano's most important literary-political achievements: the beautiful new form of writing he crafted and the revealing lens through which he came to view human affairs.

By the time Galeano published *Open Veins* in 1971, he had already gained some notoriety as a leftist journalist. But his signature style would come later. Beginning with 1978's *Days and Nights of Love and War*, he developed an inimitable collage technique that he would deploy for the rest of his life.

The Galeano method is difficult to precisely describe, but it is easy enough to read. The word most often applied is "fragmentary," though the fragments are carefully arranged into unified wholes. Such works consist, usually, of brief stories, never much more than a page, each a snapshot of some moment in the life of a person, a country, the world. The subjects range from famous writers to dictators to nameless members of the underclass, all depicted in Galeano's sparse, graceful prose. A sample from *Mirrors* (2009):

> *Reichstag, Berlin, May 1945.*
> *Two soldiers raise the flag of the Soviet Union over the pinnacle of German power.*
> *This photograph by Yevgeny Khaldei portrays the triumph of the nation that lost more sons in the war than any other.*
> *The news agency TASS distributes the picture. But before doing so, it makes a correction.*
> *The Russian soldier wearing two wristwatches now has only one.*
> *The warriors of the proletariat do not loot dead bodies.*

The piece has all the hallmarks of Galeano's late writing. He uses not a word more than necessary, yet the style feels poetic rather than skimpy. The sentences are terse, but emotional impact is never sacrificed for brevity. His former dogmatism has been displaced by a sense of the absurd that does not take predetermined sides. But his humanist sympathies are also clear. He views war as a colossal folly and expresses compassion for struggling people bound by circumstance.

Galeano collected thousands of these anecdotes, all poignant or ironic. He sifted the raw material of history, gathering not just the textbook turning points but also scores of ordinary human moments with something to convey. He lovingly escorts the reader through his vast gallery, a wise and captivating tour guide. The name of Scheherazade has understandably been invoked in describing Galeano; it is hard to think of anything in our time comparable to his magical trove of a thousand and one little tales.

Galeano's greatest achievement is *Memory of Fire* (1982–86), a trilogy encompassing the entire history of the Americas, from creation myths to the publication of *Memory of Fire* itself. He wrote it out of his growing dissatisfaction with *Open Veins*. That book, he worried in 1983, "may reduce history to a single economic dimension" when life "sings with multiple voices." Thus, over nearly a thousand pages, Galeano brings us not just the pillaging of mineral rights but a grand kaleidoscope of the Western Hemisphere.

He crosses the continents chronologically, drawing scenes from every sphere of life—high and low, transformative and quotidian. We visit Cuzco in 1523, Key West in 1895, Chile in 1973. With the Spanish colonist Gonzalo Fernández de Oviedo, we taste guavas, medlars, and pineapples. Among all the New World fruits, the pineapple is best: "Oviedo knows no words worthy of describing its virtues. It delights his eyes, his nose, his fingers, his tongue. *This outdoes them all, as the feathers of the peacock outshine those of any bird.*" In 1917 we stand on a hillside with Pancho Villa as he contemplates the retreat of General Pershing. Then it's off to New Orleans to witness the invention of jazz.

Galeano reproduces classified ads selling slaves; vendors crying in the streets of Mexico City, 1840 ("Candies! Coconut candies! Merr-i-i-ingues!"); excerpts from revolutionary oratories; President William McKinley's speech exhorting the United States to civilize the Philippines. The cast of characters is one of the grandest in all of literature, full of saints, devils, and rogues: José Martí, Augusto Pinochet, Simón Bolívar, Toussaint L'Ouverture, Pablo Neruda. Cantinflas and Leon Trotsky, Carmen Miranda and Eva Peron. Sergei Eisenstein shoots films in Mexico, and Enrique Santos Discépolo composes tangos in flea-ridden Argentine dressing rooms. We witness hurricanes, slave revolts, military coups, torture, bloodshed, romance, soccer. Occasionally, we find heroes. Bartolome de las Casas, champion of the Indians, tries to "halt the plunder that uses the cross as its excuse." Far more common, though, are close-ups of the wars and abuses whose memories are so often buried with their victims. The Viceroy of New Spain watches as heretics are hanged in 1574; 380 years later, the CIA installs a repressive dictatorship in Guatemala. Yet if Galeano focuses on memorializing suffering, he also depicts simple pleasures, as when Buster Keaton and Charlie Chaplin perform together for the first time in their careers, in *Limelight* (1952). There are love affairs and dances and endless ordinary people fighting to preserve their dignity. Alongside folly, mishap, and travesty are painful beauty, coincidence, and wonder. *Memory of Fire* documents what it feels like to be alive at one's moment in time.

In his subsequent books, Galeano continued to experiment with formats, concocting his singular brew of journalism, memoir, folktale, and history. *Upside Down* (1998) presents satirical lessons from a comically bizarre syllabus on the "inverted" world wrought by globalized capitalism. Quotes from Noam Chomsky join macabre woodcut drawings of skeletons, alligators, and aristocrats. In *Soccer in Sun and Shadow* (1995) he applies his method to sports, producing an eclectic (and acclaimed) history of the game.

For their inventiveness alone, Galeano's books would be a treasure. But to truly appreciate their significance one must understand their author's evolution. He was a propagandist who became an artist. Galeano realized that all-explaining stories, such as the Marxist story and the cap-italist story, fail to capture the chaotic mosaic of human existence. He decided that we should never see our realities through the filter of our politics, but our politics should emerge from our realities. Thus he came to detest those "dogmatic versions of Marxism that proclaim the Only Truth and that divorce man from nature and reason from emotion." The lack of overarching moral narratives, the abandonment of linear storytelling, the shattering of the text into hundreds of tiny shards—all reflected the growing sophistication and humility of Galeano's thought.

But as he changed, Galeano never renounced his leftist economic analysis. He was enriching his commitments rather than discarding them. His later works are still full of references to capitalist robbery and U.S. imperialism. But he layered new insights atop these. Economics was not life; life was also ideas, geographies, cultures. Sometimes corporate predation destroyed people, and sometimes bureaucracy destroyed them. Sometimes they destroyed themselves. The important thing was to always be with the victims against the victimizers, to show boundless compassion, and to bear witness.

Galeano sought to gather up the overlooked injustices of history, to ensure that, whatever their lessons, they would never be lost. He insisted he was not a historian but "a writer obsessed with remembering." In his words, forgetting is "the only death that really kills." His way of serving the people he loved was to keep as many of them alive in his work as he could.

This was not the project of *Open Veins*. As Galeano admitted, that book is marred by its Marxist materialism. The best parts of it—the sensitive storytelling, the sense of monumental historical sweep, the moral clarity—would be deepened in subsequent writing. The parts that didn't work—the communist orthodoxy, the mono-causal trajectories, the leaden economics—would be ditched.

Open Veins took off because it gave readers what they most wanted: a straightforward explanation of why things are and how they came to be. Later, as Galeano's sociological eye became more refined, he would realize that simple answers are cheap, that life takes forked paths, that the "thousand voices" of the earth are irreducible. Meaning, such as it can be found, cannot be imposed but must arise naturally from recurring patterns in the emergent composition. Galeano had once wanted to be a painter, and it was with a painter's sensibility that he realized human beings were too intricate to be depicted in broad strokes.

There was a wry irony in Chavez's gift to Obama. It could fit perfectly into one of Galeano's collections of scraps: the story of one ruler giving another ruler a book opposing all rulers, a book neither of them would read. Those leaders didn't understand Galeano, just as the *Economist* didn't understand him, just as the Marxists who thought he had turned right-wing didn't understand him. Subtlety is unintelligible to the fanatical.

Through his evolution as an artist and a thinker, Galeano showed how to free oneself from the dogmatists, how to remain radical in sympathy for the weak and hatred of tyranny while never sacrificing one's integrity or independence of thought. He demonstrated not just a dynamic new way of writing, but also a way to form our ideas, to see ourselves in history, and, above all, to remember.

Lessons From Chomsky

IT HAS BEEN 50 YEARS SINCE Noam Chomsky first became a major public figure in the United States, after publishing his essay "The Responsibility of Intellectuals," which argued that American academics had failed in their core duty to responsibly inquire into truth.[1] Over the past five decades, he has paradoxically been both one of the most well-known and influential thinkers in the world *and* almost completely absent from mainstream U.S. media.

Nobody has been more influential on my own intellectual development than Chomsky. But I recently realized that what I've learned from Chomsky's work has had almost nothing to do with the subjects he is most known for writing about: linguistics, U.S. foreign policy, and Israel. Instead, where I feel Chomsky's influence most strongly is in a particular kind of *approach* to thinking and writing about political, social, and moral questions. In other words, it's not so much his conclusions as his method (though I also share most of his conclusions). From Chomsky's writing and talks, I have drawn an underlying set of values and principles that I have found very useful. And I think it's easy to miss those underlying values, because his books often either consist of technical discussions of the human language faculty or long and fact-heavy indictments of United States government actions. So I'd like to go through and explain what I've found and why I think it's important. The lessons I've learned from Chomsky have encouraged me to be more rational, compassionate, consistent, skeptical, and curious. Nearly everything I write is at least in part a restatement or application of something I picked up from Noam Chomsky, and it feels only fair to acknowledge the source.

1. Libertarian Socialism

In the United States, "libertarianism" is associated with the right and "socialism" with the left. The libertarians value "freedom" (or what they call freedom) while the socialists value "equality." And many people accept this distinction as fair: after all, the right wants smaller government while the left wants a big redistributionist government. Even many leftists implicitly accept this "freedom versus equality" distinction as fair, suggesting that while freedom may be nice, fairness is more important.

Libertarian socialism, the political tradition in which Noam Chomsky operates, which is closely tied to anarchism, rejects this distinction as illusory.[2] If the word "libertarianism" is taken to mean "a belief in freedom" and the word "socialism" is taken to mean "a belief in fairness," then the two are not just "not opposites," but necessary complements. That's because if you have "freedom" from government intervention, but you don't have a fair economy, your freedom becomes meaningless, because you will still be faced with a choice between working and starving. Freedom is only meaningful to the extent that it actually creates a capacity for you to act. If you're poor, you don't have much of an actual capacity to do much, so you're not terribly free. Likewise, "socialism" without a conception of freedom is not actually fair and equal. Libertarian socialists have always been critical of Marxist states, because the libertarian socialist recognizes that "equality" enforced by a brutal and repressive state is not just "un-free," but is also *unequal*, because there is a huge imbalance of power between the people and the state. The Soviet Union was obviously not free, but it was also not socialist, because "the people" didn't actually control anything; the state did.

The libertarian socialist perspective is well-captured by a quote from the pioneering anarchist Mikhail Bakunin: "Liberty without socialism is privilege and injustice; socialism without liberty is slavery and brutality." During the 1860s and 70s, 50 years before Soviet Union, Bakunin warned that Marxist socialism's authoritarian currents would lead to hideous repression. In a Marxist regime, he said:

> *There will be a new class, a new hierarchy of real and pretended scientists and scholars, and the world will be divided into a minority ruling in the name of knowledge and an immense ignorant majority. And then, woe betide the mass of ignorant ones!... You can see quite well that behind all the democratic and socialistic phrases and promises of Marx's program, there is to be found in his State all that constitutes the true despotic and brutal nature of all States.*

This, as we know, is precisely what happened. Unfortunately, however, the bloody history of 20th century Marxism-Leninism has convinced many people that socialism *itself* is discredited. They miss the voices of people in the libertarian socialist tradition, like Bakunin, Peter Kropotkin, and Noam Chomsky, who have always stood for a kind of socialism that places a core value on freedom and deplores authoritarianism. It emphasizes true democracy; that is, people should get to participate in the decisions that affect their lives, whether those decisions are labeled "political" or "economic." It detests capitalism because capitalist institutions are totalitarian (you don't get to vote for who your boss is, and you get very little say in what your company does), but it also believes strongly in freedom of expression and civil liberties.

Libertarian socialism seems to me a beautiful philosophy. It rejects both "misery through economic exploitation" and "misery through Stalinist totalitarianism," arguing that the problem is misery itself, whatever the source. It's a very simple concept, but it's easy to miss because of the binary that pits "communism" against "capitalism." Thus, if you're a critic of capitalism, you must be an apologist for the most brutal socialist governments. But every time there has been such government, libertarian socialist critics have been the first to call it out for its hypocrisy. (Usually, such people are the first ones liquidated.) The libertarian tradition in socialism is precious. And Chomsky, skeptical of corporate and governmental power alike, is our foremost public exponent of it.[3]

2. Pragmatic Utopianism

The problem with utopians is that they're not practical, and the problem with pragmatists is that they often lack vision. If you dream of elaborate perfect societies, but you don't remain anchored in real-world realities and have a sense of how to get things done, all of your dreams are useless. You may even end up destroying the progress you have already made for the sake of an ideal you'll never reach. But if you don't have a strong sense of what the ultimate long-term goal is, you're not going to know whether you're moving closer to it or not.

Chomsky's approach to "political reality" seems to me a good balance of both radicalism and pragmatism. He is an anarchist in his strong skepticism of authority, and a utopian in his belief that the ideal world is a world without social class or unjust hierachies of any kind, a world without war or economic deprivation. But he is also deeply conscious of the realities of the world we live in and the need for a politics that actually cares about moving towards this utopia to be willing to take small step rather than just wait for a revolution.

Consider Chomsky's approach to voting. Chomsky believes simultaneously that (1) voting is not a very important part of politics, because it doesn't change much thanks to the combination of the typically awful candidates and the low impact of a single vote and (2) you should still vote, and if you live in swing state, you should vote for the Democratic candidate for president. He is radical in that he believes we need far broader political action than simply voting once every few years for the least-worst of two major party candidates, but practical in that he also believes that it's better if Democrats get into office than Republicans. Chomsky understands that you can simultaneously work to save ObamaCare *and* believe that it's a pitiful substitute for a genuine healthcare guarantee, and we need much more radical change.[4]

3. Rejecting Simple Binary Distinctions

Both of the above examples are part of a tendency in Chomsky's thought that I have consistently found helpful: trying not to fall into simple binary distinctions. So, if the question is: "Do you support the Democrats or do you believe in third parties?" the Chomsky answer is, roughly, "It depends on the circumstances. If a third party, whose principles are closer to mine than the Democrats, had a viable chance of winning, I'd vote third party. But if the only thing the third party is likely to do is split the progressive vote and put the Republicans in office, I'd hold my nose and vote for the Democrat." Or, if the question is: "Should we be reformists or revolutionaries?" the Chomsky answer is "Well, it depends what each of those would entail. Let's talk about what we mean by each of those terms and which one is likely to get us to our goal."

You can see this tendency at work in Noam Chomsky's attitude toward the Boycott, Divestment, and Sanctions (BDS) movement against Israel. Chomsky is known as a critic of Israel, but he has received criticism from BDS members for questioning the efficacy of their tactics.[5] This has led to suggestions that Chomsky "opposes BDS."[6] In the world of binaries, you have to either support something or oppose it. The idea of "supporting the goal of improving the welfare of Palestinians" *and* the tactic of boycotts, *but* opposing particular actions by the BDS movement does not fit within the existing binary.

Likewise, Chomsky has been accused of rejecting the comparison of Israeli treatment of the Palestinians with Apartheid South Africa, with a critic saying he "dismisses the apartheid designation."[7] In fact, what he has tried to do is draw a distinction: in Israel itself, the racial division is not on the level with South African Apartheid, but in the Occupied Territories, it's actually *worse* than Apartheid.[8] But to some supporters of BDS, hearing that the situation within Israel is not as brutal as Apartheid will mean Chomsky is "dismissing" the Apartheid comparison, even though he actually thinks the situation for many Palestinians is *worse* than Apartheid. The nuance can be difficult to appreciate unless we set aside our existing binary classifications.

George W. Bush is famously associated with the phrase "You're either with us or you're against us." But this feeling is shared across the adherents of many political ideologies, with nuance seen as betrayal. The Chomsky answer to whether "you're with us or against us" is "Well, I'm with you to the extent that you do good things, and I'm against you to the extent that you do bad things." But that response is usually met with "Oh, so you're against us, then."

4. THE CONSISTENT APPLICATION OF MORAL STANDARDS

One of Chomsky's simplest principles is among the most difficult to apply in practice: you should judge yourself by the same moral standards that you judge others by. This has formed the core of his critique of U.S. foreign policy, and yet it is often insufficiently appreciated even by those who embrace his conclusions. Many people think that Chomsky is uniquely "anti-American." In fact, his criticisms of the United States are so strong largely because when this elementary moral principle is applied to the facts, the conclusion is inevitably deeply damning. It simply turns out that if you judge the United States by the standard that it uses to judge other people, the United States does not look very good. If you take the facts of, say, the bombing of Laos[9] (where the United States secretly dropped 2.5 million tons of bombs in the 60s and 70s, massacring and maiming thousands of peaceable villagers, 20,000 of whom were killed or injured in the decades *after* the bombing when unexploded bombs went off),[10] and you imagine how it would appear to us if the roles had been reversed and Laos had been bombing the United States, you begin to see just how inconsistent we are in our evaluations of our own actions versus the actions of others. 500,000 people died in the Iraq War. If Iraq had invaded the United States and 500,000 people had died (actually, the proportional population equivalent would be closer to 5,000,000), would there be any way that anybody in the country could conceive of Iraq as a "force for good" in the world in the way that the U.S. believes people should think we are? It's laughable. If Vietnam had invaded the United States the way the United States had invaded Vietnam, could such an act ever be considered justified?

This idea of moral consistency, of trying to treat like behaviors alike, is the simplest possible notion in the world. It's so elementary that it sounds childish to even pose the questions. And yet the power of latent patriotic sentiment is so great that it makes a clear-eyed and fair assessment incredibly difficult. It's *hard* to see the world through other people's eyes, to see what our self-justifications look like to those who are on the receiving end of our actions. And when we do it, it's deeply discomforting. But this is the foundation of Chomsky's critique: it's not enough to have "values" (e.g. "terrorism is bad"), you must apply those values consistently (i.e. if something would constitute terrorism if done against us, it must constitute terrorism if it is done by us). Chomsky is seen as being "anti-American" for pointing out that if the Nuremberg principles were applied consistently, essentially every postwar U.S. president would have to be hanged. But this is just a result of the application of consistency: the crime of "aggressive war" that was so forcefully condemned at Nuremberg has been committed repeatedly by the U.S.

In both linguistics and politics, Chomsky often uses his famous "Martian coming to Earth" example: try to imagine what our planetary affairs would look like to someone who was not part of one of the particular human societies, but was separate from them and able to see their commonalities. They would perceive the similarities between human languages, rather than the differences, and they would see the bizarre ways in which each country perceives its *own* acts as right and everybody else's as wrong, even when the same acts are being committed.

The principle of treating all human beings consistently has an incredible power to illuminate, because it helps us clarify what our values actually are and make sure we are following them. But it also helps us become true "universalists," in the sense that we can begin to view things from a human perspective rather than a nationalistic perspective.

5. CLEAR AND ACCESSIBLE WRITING

Even though Noam Chomsky is not exactly known for the memorability or emotional force of his prose, he helped teach me to write. That's because he writes and speaks in a very particular way: in clear language, maximally designed for people to actually be able to understand it. Chomsky is one of the few writers on the left who entirely shuns highly abstract theoretical lingo in favor of straightforward, plain-language argumentation. In his political writings he follows the principle, which I share, that it is the writer's job to make himself understood, rather than the reader's job to try to figure out what the hell the writer is talking about.

This actually follows from Chomsky's "libertarian socialist" politics. The great libertarian socialists have generally been incredibly clear writers. (Compare the experience of reading Rudolf Rocker's *Nationalism and Culture* with the experience of reading Louis Althusser.[11]) This is partially because they have a strong belief in "democratic education": they believe that everyday people should have access to knowledge and understanding, and that intellectual endeavors shouldn't be the purview of a specialized caste of privileged people. They believe that ordinary workers should get to read the classics and to understand science and mathematics, because they do not believe in social class and hierarchy. The libertarian socialists have always been critical of the more "Leninist" mindset, which sees social change coming from a "vanguard" of intellectuals who know what's best for the people. For the anarchistic socialist, the power to change their lives should be in people's *own* hands. Thus writing, even on complicated subjects, should be in the clearest language possible, because it shouldn't just be available to academics and people who have had elite educations.

Chomsky follows this principle through in a number of respects. Throughout his life, he has preferred to give talks to small activist organizations, churches, and community groups rather than to students at Ivy League schools (partly because he believes the latter are less likely to listen to anything). His writings can be complex, and sometimes require a lot of patience and mental effort, but they are never intentionally "difficult," and their meanings are always clear. Unlike many academics, who bury their points in layers of specialty jargon, Chomsky believes the job of a writers is to communicate the point, and to do so successfully.

6. Skepticism of Status

This one is particularly important for me. Chomsky's principle is that you should examine the quality of ideas themselves rather than the credentials of those voicing them. This sounds easy enough, but it isn't: in life, we're constantly expected to defer to the superior wisdom of people who have superior status, but who we're pretty sure don't know what they're talking about. There's always a little part of us that goes "Well, I know it *sounds* like he doesn't know what he's talking about, but he's my professor/priest/superior so perhaps I'm just stupid." Chomsky talks a lot about the way social status and privilege are generated; rewards and accolades often flow to people not on the basis of their superior knowledge, but on the basis of their ability to convince people that they have superior knowledge, which is quite a different thing entirely. People at the top often try to convince those at the bottom that you get to the top by being *smart*. In fact, Chomsky says, success is probably driven by the possession of greed, ambition, ruthlessness, and obsequiousness. Education, he says, selects for passivity: you do well if you flatter your teachers by repeating what they think, you do less well if you refuse to go along with the assignments you're given because you think they're stupid.

The education system in the United States, Chomsky suggests, does not really educate. It subdues. A genuine education involves helping someone through a process of self-discovery and curiosity, not just learning to regurgitate facts. Thus, because the people who do best in our current education system are those who got the most As, as opposed to those who developed their minds the most, we shouldn't trust a person to be wise just because they're educated. This is something a lot of people realize intuitively, but there are still a lot of "educated fools" who are listened to and given credence.

But what I love about Chomsky is that this *isn't* an embrace of igno-rance or "anti-intellectualism."[12] It's anti-intellectual in that Chomsky opposes the idea of having a "secular priesthood" of intellectuals who "are a special class who are in the business of imposing thoughts." But it's not anti-intellectual if "intellectual" means *the use of the mind*; in fact, this is precisely what Chomsky is encouraging. And it doesn't mean that you shouldn't learn from experts. Rather it means that you should try to crit-ically evaluate what an expert says, and determine on your own whether to accept it, and that you should judge an expert by her ideas rather than her *curriculum vitae*.

7. Self-Critical Science

Noam Chomsky's view of the correct way to do "science" is instructive. Many people on the left are critical of "science," or what they call "sci-entism," because they believe that in imposes some kind of rigid "tech-nocratic" or "Enlightenment" framework on how humans should think, suggesting that Western forms of reasoning are superior and insisting on a kind of "certainty" about scientific belief that ignores differing points of view. In turn, many people in the sciences reinforce this conception by defending a dogmatic conception of science; people like Sam Harris and Richard Dawkins, who use mockery to defend what they call "reason," affirm the worst stereotypes about the "scientistic mindset" that cannot see its ignorance due to its certainty of its own superior rationality.

Chomsky's conception of science is much more helpful, and once again illustrates his ability to get beyond simple binaries (i.e. you either accept "scientific fact" or you dismiss the "scientistic mentality"). Chomsky (and to be fair, he is hardly alone in this) views science as *uncertainty* rather than certainty. The scientific approach to understanding the world is an effort to do the best you can given the limits of your reason, but far from being blind to those limits, they are themselves a central subject for scientific investigation.

In fact, even though he is definitely a defender of the "Enlightenment tradition" insofar as he believes in using reason and logic to solve problems, Chomsky has voiced some of the most serious doubts of anyone in the sciences of human beings' potential to fully understand the world. Chomsky encourages us to appreciate that, because we are biological creatures, our capacities are very limited. Despite our unique faculties, we are more like pigs than like angels, and for us to assume we can ever achieve full knowledge of the universe is not much different from a farm animal thinking it could understand organic chemistry. Much of Chomsky's work has been on how human beings' innate capacities structure their thinking, and if that's your starting point, you will be a skeptic about how much science can ever hope to truly accomplish given the finite abilities of our brains and bodies. (Chomsky divides scientific questions into "puzzles," which can potentially be solved, and "mysteries," which may be beyond the limits of human comprehension. Consciousness and free will, for example, may simply be mysteries that our biological limitations will always prevent us from investigating deeply.)[13]

I like this point of view because I think it charts a helpful course between the extreme of "scientific certitude" and what we might call "radical relativism." It suggests that we should investigate the universe using scientific tools. But the phrase "scientific tools" doesn't refer to certainty and confidence. Ir refers to doubt, curiosity, and a cognizance of our own limitations. Science is not about declaring that you know what the universe is, it's about trying to think about the best explanations. Testing hypotheses, discarding hypotheses, asking yourself why you're testing hypotheses to begin with, asking yourself what you even *mean* by the word hypothesis, etc.

It also helpfully collapses the distinction between science and philosophy. Inquiring into how you know what you know is part of the scientific process, not something separate from it. Chomsky is a lot more like the broad-mined "natural scientists" of the 18th century than the highly specialized academics of today. "Natural science" didn't see a dividing line between science and philosophy; instead, it saw one task: understanding as much as possible, with whatever tools we have available. Reason is a critical part of that, but reason must also be used to recognize the boundaries of its own capacities.

For libertarian socialists, science is also conceived of as mirroring the process of participatory democracy: knowledge is pursued as a collective enterprise, with each person giving their bit, never reaching perfection, but hopefully moving us towards a better and more knowledgeable state of affairs. Like democracy, it is messy, and moves in fits and starts, but it's the best means we know of of trying to come to understand the universe together, just as democracy is the best means we know of for trying to govern ourselves.

8. Commitment to Open Inquiry

Because the libertarian socialist tradition has always so strongly valued freedom and deliberative democracy, it has a strong commitment to freedom of expression. Unlike many forms of authoritarian socialism, which swiftly produce justifications for why certain forms of reactionary speech must be suppressed for the good of the multitude (or because "speech is power and power is hierarchy" or any other justification you like), libertarian socialists generally believe very strongly in permitting all points of view and generally look skeptically on efforts to respond to morally objectionable speech with censorship rather than with more rational and persuasive speech.

Noam Chomsky's commitment to radical free speech has landed him in trouble before, even with other members of the left. Most notoriously, he wrote in support of the free speech rights of Robert Faurisson, a French literature professor who had denied the existence of Nazi gas chambers and called Anne Frank's diary a forgery. Faurisson was dismissed from his position, repeatedly convicted in the French criminal courts, and even brutally beaten and sprayed with stinging gas.[14] Chomsky, who has called the Holocaust "the most fantastic outburst of collective insanity in human history," wrote an essay defending Faurisson's right to free speech and signed a petition drafted by Faurisson's (Holocaust-denying) supporters calling for him to be allowed to freely publish his "findings" and for the government to "do everything possible to ensure [Faurisson's] safety and the free exercise of his legal rights."[15]

French intellectuals pilloried Chomsky for his support of Faurisson, and he has repeatedly been accused of being an apologist for Holocaust denial.

It's strange that anyone would think Chomsky sympathetic to Holocaust denial. After all, socialists despise Hitler, who liquidated leftists by the score. But once again, binary thinking takes hold: if you "support" someone, it is impossible to support them for the narrow and limited purpose of believing we should get to hear and examine whatever argument and evidence they think they have produced about the Holocaust. You must either endorse their conclusions or not support them at all. But this way of thinking leads to the curtailment of rights for those who we find reprehensible, and when rights don't exist for those people, they don't exist at all: *"Goebbels was in favor of free speech for views he liked. So was Stalin. If you're really in favor of free speech, then you're in favor of freedom of speech for precisely the views you despise. Otherwise, you're not in favor of free speech."* [16]

9. Critiquing Power Without Conspiracy Theories

Noam Chomsky is sometimes accused of holding the "smoke-filled room" view of politics: everything is a grand conspiracy among the powerful to oppress the powerless. In fact, this is precisely the opposite of the Chomsky view of conspiracy. The real view is, again, a thing of nuance: the belief that oppression does *not* require a conspiracy, and that the "smoke-filled room" concept misunderstands how power works.

Chomsky is a consistent critic of conspiracy theories. Why? Because generally there doesn't need to be any kind of "conspiracy" to create the kinds of gross inequalities and cruelties we see in our society. Most of it is right out in the open. Furthermore, conspiracy theories overcomplicate things. For example, in order to believe the "Bush did 9/11" conspiracy, you have to believe in an incredibly capable and competent government, that was able to plan and execute an extraordinary destructive act, without anyone leaking or blowing the whistle at any of the many levels it would have required to do such a thing.[17] That requires a view of government competence that is hard to maintain. A far simpler, and more plausible theory, is simply that the Bush administration used the 9/11 attacks to its advantage, that it found them politically convenient for carrying out its preexisting plan to invade Iraq. That doesn't require any kind of conspiracy. Likewise with the CIA: we *know* about many of the agency's foul deeds; its murders, coups, and torture. The problem is not that the information is hidden in darkness, it's nobody actually holds the agency accountable.

The same goes for Chomsky's theory of the press, the so-called "manufacturing of consent." It's accused of being a conspiracy: people are stupefied by a corporate media that gathers to plot ways to control them. In fact, it's nothing of the kind. It's a theory based in economics and sociology more than anything else, a theory that says the media has no economic interest in providing serious informational content, that in a profit-driven media environment, the incentives are going to be toward providing entertainment rather than material that serves the public good and truly illuminates news consumers. That's not the result of a malevolent conspiracy drawn up by executives who want to turn the public into zombies; it's just what happens when people want to make a lot of money. Never attribute to conspiracy what can be explained by the operation of rational self-interest.

10. SIMPLE THINGS ARE THE MOST COMPLICATED THINGS

Chomsky speaks frequently about how curiosity and the path to knowledge begin by doubting the things that seem most certain. As he says, "willingness to be puzzled by what seem to be obvious truths is the first step towards gaining understanding of how the world works." His investigations into language, which ended up revolutionizing linguistics, were driven by the desire to answer simple questions, like: "Why is it that even young children are able to use language in so many different kinds of ways?" It often turns out that the simplest questions are the ones that are the most difficult to answer, or the ones that people have overlooked because they assume we already know the answers.

Chomsky's willingness to ask very basic questions and ask simple things has strongly affected my own thinking. It's easy to feel as if simple questions are stupid questions; there's a fear of seeming childish by saying or asking something obvious. Getting over that fear was tremendously useful for me, because it enabled me to approach the questions that I felt were important but that it seemed as if everyone must already know the answers to. For example, it has led me to ask things like "Why don't we talk about nuclear war more?",[18] "Why are public schools good?",[19] and "Are we talking about climate change in a useful way?"[20] I spend more time wondering about issues I implicitly took for granted, like how I know what my values are and why I think what I think. I wonder why people say certain things, or dress certain ways, or believe certain things. (In fact, *Current Affairs* itself began with a Chomsky-type "simple question": *Why is it that even though I'm a leftist, I don't enjoy reading any of the leftist periodicals?*) This willingness to look at the notions you take for granted with a new kind of skepticism or puzzlement is an incredibly valuable tool, and can make you both more curious and more humble.

11. Not Liking Politics

Noam Chomsky was once asked which he enjoyed producing more, his linguistic writing or his political writing. The question apparently took him by surprise; he didn't know why anyone would think he "enjoyed" doing his political writing. He did it because he felt morally compelled to do it, not because it was pleasurable.

I am skeptical of anyone who "likes" politics. Perhaps if we lived in a world without injustice, and we were just debating what color to paint the new village merry-go-round, it would be possible to find politics a source of enjoyment. But in a world where there are serious human stakes to politics, it is not a game. Chomsky came into political activism because he was horrified that hundreds of thousands of Vietnamese people were being doused with napalm by the United States military. The idea of "liking" politics seems perverse. Those who know Chomsky have said that he is motivated by a deep and sincere compassion for the victims of atrocities committed by his country; Fred Branfman recalled a visit with Chomsky to the site of U.S. bombing in Laos, where Chomsky wept after hearing stories from Laotian refugees, displaying the "most natural, human response" of the foreign visitors when compared with the stony journalists who simply took notes.[21]

I've always been reminded by this to remember what "politics" is about: it isn't pro wrestling, it isn't a horse race. It's the process that determines how power is going to be used. And so, while every life should have fun and pleasure and joy, ultimately there's nothing fun when we're talking about war and economic misery. (I think of that often now in the days when the follies of the Trump administration provide such an entertaining daily spectacle; meanwhile, the DHS continues to deport people's families.)

12.   PUBLIC FEARLESSNESS, PRIVATE GENEROSITY

Chomsky's public persona appears somewhat prickly; he is serious, he is often acidic in his tone, and he can seem self-confident to the point of arrogance. To those, like Sam Harris, who have been on the receiving end of Chomsky's somewhat merciless rhetoric, the idea of him as a "nice person" would seem strange.[22]

And yet, Noam Chomsky is a nice person. Or at least, a person who is very kind and generous with his time. It's well-known that Chomsky responds to nearly every email sent to him by a member of the public. And when he does so, he is never rude or patronizing. In fact, he is almost limitlessly patient. I know this from personal experience, having emailed him quite foolish questions several times, despite not knowing him at all personally. (He also gave me incredibly kind words of encouragement after I sent him a book I had written, which he read in full.) I've never seen anything quite like Chomsky's willingness to engage with strangers. I know plenty of far less significant people who will only respond to people they deem notable or influential enough to be worth corresponding with, yet in keeping with the libertarian socialist principle that everyone is equal and deserves equal access to knowledge, Chomsky replies to them all. It makes me feel ashamed of my own terrible emailing skills; I have tens of thousands of messages in my inbox that I've failed to reply to as they've piled up. Meanwhile, nearly every single person who sends Chomsky a note gets a response.

The perception of Chomsky as "arrogant" arises largely from the fact that he doesn't really care how he is perceived. In private, he is warm and generous, but in public he is a stern and uncompromising debater. There's a kind of "selflessness" to him that I've never really seen in another person. He deprecates his own achievements in linguistics, he doesn't care about awards or prestige, fame means nothing to him, and he takes no real pride in his political work. Instead, if you ask him, he says he feels like a failure for not having been able to do more good with his life. In Tom Wolfe's ludicrously ill-informed recent book on Chomsky, Wolfe portrays him as haughty and self-important.[23] But it's a very strange thing: he isn't this at all. He's a genuinely humble person who cares about other people.

The "character" aspect has been just as important as any intellectual lesson for me. I always try to remind myself that I should be generous to strangers, should cultivate humility, and should always focus on the work rather than on the rewards.

13. No Gods, No Masters, No Idols

And yet here is the most important thing of all I've learned from Noam Chomsky: Noam Chomsky doesn't really matter. I am confident that he would hate to see himself written about as some kind of personal role model or idol, because he believes that you're supposed to care about the person's ideas rather than the person. Chomsky has cited Marxism as an example of how the veneration of *people* can lead to absurdity: your system of social analysis shouldn't be "Marx"-ist, it should just be *true*. To the extent Marx was right, you can incorporate his ideas, and to the extent he was wrong, you should reject them. To subscribe to a dogmatic and personalized "ism," though, is foolish; physicists don't practice "Einsteinian" physics, they practice physics, and Einstein just happened to be a good physicist. It's therefore somewhat ironic that people even speak of "Chomskyan linguistics," since it's a concept Chomsky himself would reject. (There's also a scene in the film *Captain Fantastic* in which the central characters celebrate "Noam Chomsky Day" and sing worshipful songs about him; I am certain he would cringe to see it.)

I therefore don't follow any kind of "Chomskyan" system, or see him as a "role model." He is simply a person, a person from whom I happened to have learned a fair number of things. But I have learned many other things from many other people, and I will write about them too.

I also have a number of criticisms of Chomsky. I think he is often insufficiently skeptical of left-wing sources. I think he dismisses many arguments too quickly without being fair to them. I think his insistence that he doesn't use "rhetoric" is false. I think he has too hastily signed his name to a couple of questionable things. I think he has maintained some mistaken positions too long in the face of contrary evidence. And there are plenty more.

But one of the great anarchist slogans is: No Gods, No Masters. The whole point is not to replace one idol with a better one, it's to get rid of idols. I think Chomsky would be very concerned if I *didn't* have criticisms. It would mean I had missed the entire point, which is that the truth is what matters, not the person investigating it, and since nobody has infallible access to truth, nobody should be beyond criticism. None of us is perfect, we're all just doing the best we can.

If I were to summarize the main points I've taken from Chomsky's writings and talks, they would be this: you should have both compassion and consistency, care about freedom and fairness alike, and be rational, curious, and humble. Note again that this doesn't matter whether you are a linguist or a political scientist; it's not the subject that matters so much as the method.

I have a crude generalization to offer (feel free to ignore it): people I have met whose political awakenings came through reading Chomsky have consistently tended to hold more humane and less dogmatic political beliefs than those whose political awakenings came through reading Karl Marx. I have met compassionate and thoughtful Marxists, and I have met obnoxious and unthinking Chomsky fans. But I believe that the *way* Chomsky introduces a person to politics, by offering observations and facts rather than an elaborate ideological structure, lends itself to more modesty and reflection than some of the more systematized political tendencies.

Of course, different people can come to the same destination by different paths, and the above lessons are not really "Chomsky lessons." They are simple human principles, easily accessed by contemplation and reason. But for me, personally, it would have taken a lot longer to reach them if it weren't for the guidance of Noam Chomsky, who has often been the one voice there to let me know that I'm not crazy, that the questions I have are reasonable, and that the thoughts I have are worth thinking.

Potpourri

The Uses of Platitudes

Nobody likes a platitude. Or at least, cool people don't like platitudes. Writers grimace at a platitude. It gives them physical pain. I have seen it on their faces. I have felt it myself.

"Death to all clichés" is one of the first rules of writing well. You can find good writers who use long sentences, good writers who use short ones, but you will never find a good writer whose work is full of clichés. This is because it's almost definitionally impossible to have clichés in a quality piece of writing. Writing should be original and creative, clichés are unoriginal and dull. Worse, they are the enemies of thought itself: since they have been repeated so much, they lose all meaning and fail to conjure any real images. And since they are such common and accepted parts of the language, we fail to examine whether they are actually true or coherent.

A platitude is even worse than a cliché. It's a sanctimonious cliché, a statement that is not only old and overused but often moralistic and imperious. A cliché can simply be innocently boring ("mountain out of a molehill," "taste of his own medicine"). It can also be creatively reworked. Instead of saying "plain as the nose on your face," Raymond Chandler wrote one of my all-time favorite analogies: "He looked about as inconspicuous as a tarantula on a slice of angel food cake." But platitudes have an aphoristic quality, they seem like timeless moral lessons.

They therefore shape our view of the world, and can lull us into accepting things that are actually false and foolish.

Some platitudes:

What's done is done. Money can't buy happiness. Every cloud has a silver lining. What doesn't kill you makes you stronger. Tomorrow is another day. Go with the flow. Nice guys finish last. Forgive and forget. Such is life. Time will tell. You gotta do what you gotta do. This too shall pass. No good deed goes unpunished. Good things come to those who wait. It is what it is.

Some common traits can be observed. Many platitudes are tautological. They're not just empty of content because they're overused, but because they literally contain no content to begin with. It is what it is. Well, of course it is. Everything is what it is. Nothing is what it isn't. You gotta do what you gotta do. Yes, because if you didn't, it wouldn't be a thing you gotta do. There is, of course, some implied meaning. "It is what it is" is assumed to mean something like "X is the unchangeable nature of things, and because the unchangeable nature of things cannot be changed, we must accept X as it is." But if we drew out what the phrase is actually implying in its usage, it would seem more debatable and invite more skepticism. How do we know that X is actually one of the unchangeable things instead of one of the changeable things? Structuring the sentiment as a tautology allows it to appear inescapable. It is a counsel toward resignation that seems impossible to argue with.

That "countenancing resignation" aspect of platitudes is common. Platitudes are often the things we say to people in order to "quell their cognitive unease," to find ways of either rationalizing or finding reassurance amid some kind of crisis. They attempt to make things okay, by explaining the seemingly inexplicable as part of a set of necessary and understandable rules followed by the universe. In long lists of platitudes we can detect something of a folk philosophy, the basic principles of which are: acceptance of things as they are, the need for hard work and patience, and confidence that the future will be good and the past isn't worth dwelling on.[1] After all, *everything happens for a reason.* Many of them contain the same sentiments as the first half of Reinhold Niebuhr's Serenity Prayer: "God, grant me the serenity to accept the things I cannot change." Fewer of them seem to adopt the other half ("... the courage to change the things I can, and the wisdom to know the difference"), which is a shame, because that's the half that encourages you toward reflection and action.

It's easy to see why platitudes are sometimes lumped into a category called "thought-ending clichés": many of them seem designed to turn you stupid. The most difficult questions about life are treated as settled rather than open. When we start questioning the platitudes, life begins to seem complicated and scary. What if everything doesn't happen for a reason? What if, while clouds have silver linings, human miseries often don't? What if money does, in fact, buy happiness? Platitudes create the illusion of a fair and orderly world, thereby preventing us from considering the possibility that it is, in fact, a grossly absurd and unjust world. They can keep us from appreciating the depth and completeness of certain tragedies, because they are designed to help us deal with our circumstances without losing our minds. And even when they are telling us that life is unfair or that nice guys finish last, the platitudes command us to conclude that *it is what it is* and you've gotta *go with the flow*. Platitudes, hammered into us from the time we first come to understand the language, discourage us from the kind of open inquiry that might lead to frightening conclusions, or that might cause us deep distress and disquiet. If it turns out that "what doesn't kill you" can still turn you into, say, a blind quadriplegic, the world can seem too awful to bear.

It's understandable that some writers have come to associate platitudes with totalitarian thinking. Hannah Arendt said that Adolph Eichmann "was genuinely incapable of uttering a single sentence that was not a cliché." George Orwell, in "Politics and the English Language," saw a direct link between the decay of language and the decay of independent political thought. Clichés eliminate mental effort by giving us a ready supply of stock metaphors and concepts. It's not surprising, then, that authoritarians embrace them. Orwell said that with a more judicious use of language, we can be "freed from the worst follies of orthodoxy," and hopefully keep our brains from being "anesthetized" by manipulative politicians.

Orwell likely overstated the connection between language and politics. I can very easily imagine fascists who use novel phrases (see Ezra Pound), and there are plenty of people who do good and are thoughtful while still relying largely on an old and simple phrase bank, such as those who subscribe to the humble moral teachings of Jesus. Perhaps that's just proof that there's little connection between critical thinking and moral goodness rather than between hackneyed language and uncritical thinking (i.e. that Orwell is right that stale language is a sign that a person doesn't question things, but wrong that people who ask questions will necessarily have fewer totalitarian instincts). But as a writer and a lover of literature, he was naturally inclined to see platitudes as the enemy, and to see a unity between that which is wrong in writing and that which is wrong morally.

The instinctive hatred of platitudes can be just as perilous as the thoughtless embrace of them. I have often seen people dismiss political essays as "trite" or "stale." I've sometimes had mine described this way: this says nothing new, or this reads like it's from the 1990s. But when it comes to moral and political writing, "unoriginal" is a strange pejorative. After all, we should probably be more concerned with whether an idea is good than whether it is new. The evaluation of works by their novelty has had devastating effects on parts of the academy, where scholars are rewarded for saying the most original thing rather than the truest thing. If producing something "stale" is considered shameful, writers may desperately try to produce something that is different from anything that came before, leaving aside all other considerations or quality or accuracy. (My colleague Brianna Rennix argues that the same fear is partly responsible for postmodern literature's refusal to simply tell a good story. She and I have also made the case that the field of architecture suffers similarly: building anything that looks like something that came before is considered nostalgic and unimaginative.)

The trouble with *throwing the baby out with the bathwater* when it comes to platitudes is that many of them express helpful and accurate sentiments, and do so succinctly and memorably. The Golden Rule, for example, is simply a good rule. *Do unto others as you would have them do unto you.* It's brilliant, beautiful, and timeless. In just a few words, it manages to provide a workable moral principle to cover almost any scenario. Think about what you'd want other people to do to you in this situation, and then do that to them. If actually internalized and followed, it's a succinct recipe for empathy and equal treatment. And it becomes no less applicable the more it ages.

It's the "actually internalizing" that's difficult, though. Because platitudes are old, it takes conscious effort to remind ourselves of what they mean. I've long felt this way about Gandhi's famous "Be the change you wish to see in the world." It's a coffee-mug-and-welcome-mat sentiment now. But it's also profound, if you actually spend time working through its implications. You cannot simply try to change the world, you have to change yourself to reflect the values that you'd like to spread. Taken seriously, that isn't meaningless, it actually has consequences. It means that you can't be a hypocrite. You have to live your values, and to reflect on what living your values actually entails. It's a very tough thing to actually do. It's no wonder we'd prefer for it to remain an empty, hippie-ish aphorism.

Of course, many of the platitudes are still bullshit. I hate a lot of them. I'm troubled by what they imply: that things are okay, that they will work out, that there is a plan. I don't think you should explain away the world's absurdities and injustices. It's only by facing them head-on, and recognizing that many of them *don't* have silver linings, that you can see just how important it is to fight them. If we accept suffering, for example, as natural and inevitable, then it is easier to be comfortable with the existence of large amounts of it. If it simply *is what it is*, then getting enraged by it is futile and irrational. But to me, that's monstrous. We have to examine things critically rather than passively accepting tautological justifications for them. To do otherwise is to be both morally and intellectually lazy.

The compromise, then, is that we shouldn't recoil at platitudes because they're platitudes, but should scrutinize them, because even the wisest ones carry no meaning unless we think about them carefully. It's senseless to accept something merely because it's old and sounds good, but it would be equally senseless to discard something over its age and popularity alone. Yes, we should be suspicious of conventional wisdom, but a sentiment may also have been passed through the ages because it happens to be correct. Novelty isn't virtuous by itself, but neither is tradition. Everything, after all, just is what it is.

The "Where Are You Coming From" Survey

ONE PROBLEM I OFTEN HAVE in navigating this baffling world is that I don't know where people are coming from. By this I mean that I dont really know anything about their worldviews, desires, self-conceptions, politics, knowledge bases, or histories. I find it very difficult to communicate with people when I have access to only tiny fragments of who they are and what their minds look like from the inside. In order to fill this gap, I have begun preparing this, my "Where Are You Coming From" survey. It contains the questions I would like to know everybodys views on before we speak.

- ♦ Is it presumptuous to tell another person about one's life unprompted? Would you ever go up to a person in a coffee shop and start talking to them? Under what circumstances is this appropriate?
- ♦ Do you have an identity? What is it? What aspects of it make it your identity?
- ♦ Have you ever been in love? What did it feel like? Was it a delusion?
- ♦ When you read a poem, what are you getting out of it? To what degree do you care about whether you are gleaning the meaning from the poem that the author intended?

♦ Is the word dialectics meaningful to you? If so, what does it mean? Why is it useful?

♦ How often do you think about the fact that underneath your skin, you are a skeleton? When you see other people, do you think about the fact that they, too, are skeletons?

♦ Do you think it is important to know what is going on in the world? Why is this important? Do you think one should know the names of the heads of state of foreign countries? Do you think one should be able to put countries on a map? Can you name lots of heads of state and put lots of countries on maps? Can you name the population of Romania to within 100,000 people? If you can't, does this trouble you? If you can, why is this necessary? Should knowledge be useful?

♦ Is it difficult for you to believe that history actually happened? Is it difficult for you to believe that Socrates existed, and that he possessed an asshole? Is there a difference in the degree to which you believe the President has an asshole and the degree to which you are convinced that you have one?

♦ Why do you like the music you like rather than some other music? Do you think your tastes in music are other than arbitrary? Can some music be better than other music, and if so what is the source of that value?

♦ If you are religious, what exactly do you believe about people of other faiths or no faith? Do you believe they are wrong? Do you believe you should try to convince them of your views? Do you believe religious feeling is the type of feeling which one can acquire through persuasion? If you are not religious, how do you reconcile the fact that you do not believe in a transcendent moral code with the fact that you behave as if you do?

♦ Why do you think people who are opposed to your political beliefs are opposed to them?

♦ Would you classify yourself as basically dysfunctional or basically functional? Do you think the world is comprehensible? Do you think life is manageable?

- What do you understand as the central insight of existentialism? Do you buy it? Please explain.

- Do you shop for pleasure? Why? Why does buying things give you pleasure? Are you uncomfortable in malls? When you see, say, millions of products on sale in a Target, do you think about what made those products and where they will go in the future? Are you horrified by civilization?

- Why should anyone care about the Constitution? If our Constitution were different, should we care about that one just as much?

- What would you say to someone who defended slavery? What do you think race is? Why are there races?

- Please list everything you know, in detail.

- Do you feel there is a fundamental difference between you and everyone else? If so, what is that difference? Do you think it is real, or a delusion? Do you think you have any delusions generally?

- How do you keep yourself from ignoring or downplaying evidence that contradicts your preconceptions?

- What does Utopia look like? Is government a necessary evil or a positive good? Should we think about utopias? What are your fundamental political principles? Do you think you act consistently with them? In what way do you act consistently? Why is it necessary to be consistent? Should conclusions follow from premises?

- What, of the things you believe, are you most certain of? What are you least certain of? What is belief? When did you last change your mind about something, and what made you do it?

- Do you think free will is a meaningful concept? Do you think God is a meaningful concept? Is communication possible when people mean vastly different things by the same words?

- Do you think, given sophisticated enough statistical techniques, your behavior, even your speech, could be reliably predicted? If so, do you think this has implications for whether you are exercising free will? Do you find it somewhat strange that everyone else on earth is experiencing consciousness just like you are?

♦ Do you find the song "Before I Grow Too Old" by Fats Domino to be sad? (If you have not listened to "Before I Grow Too Old, do so before moving to the next question.)

♦ Why should people love their children more than they love other people's children?

♦ Please transcribe a short piece of your internal monologue, as accurately as possible. Do not select the particular piece because it makes you seem interesting. Where is this monologue coming from?

♦ How much difference do you think there is between the way you see yourself and the way others see you? What factors about yourself do you think give people the most mistaken impressions about you?

♦ What do you most hope will happen to you soon? Being as specific as possible, what would you do given absolute power?

♦ Why do you care what other people think? If you answer that you do not care what other people think, why do you think you are lying?

♦ Do you worry about the percentage of outcomes in your life that are determined by mere chance? Does it concern you that you may have failed to meet the love of your life by failing to step in a certain puddle on a certain day?

♦ Is nationalism ever a positive force? What is nationalism?

♦ Do you enjoy your life? Have you ever had suicidal thoughts? Why did you not give into them? Please describe the lowest point you have ever felt. What are you striving for, and why do you think it will make you happy?

♦ Do you think there is any disjunction between what *is* produced as the result of the operations of a free market and what *ought* to be produced? Is there any use whatsoever in markets? Do you think it is acceptable that in a market, a person with more resources has more power than a person with fewer resources?

How is this different from one person having more votes in an election than another? Do you think people deserve whatever they are paid? What does it mean to deserve something?

♦ Where do rights come from? Are they eternal?

♦ How should rape prosecutions occur?

♦ What is bullshit? Do you bullshit?

♦ Do you feel the pain of others? Whose pain do you feel, and why? Do you feel the pain of people in your time more than people in a different time? Why? How often do you think about the victims of the Holocaust? Are there certain truths you avoid thinking about?

♦ Does death concern you? How do you deal with the fact that each step you take in any direction is necessarily a step toward death? To what degree does the fact of your inevitable death affect your actions in life?

♦ Do you think "I've never really thought about that" is a satisfactory answer to any of these questions? If you gave this answer to any of the above questions, why have you not thought about this before? Do you think it is worth thinking about?

Having the answers to these questions beforehand would make my interactions with people much more straightforward, because at least I would know where they are coming from.

The Professional Anarchist

"Professional anarchists, thugs and paid protesters are proving the point of the millions of people who voted to MAKE AMERICA GREAT AGAIN!"
—@REALDONALDTRUMP, FEB. 3, 2017

Hiring Committee
Office of the Professional Anarchist
University of California, Berkeley

To whom it may concern,

I am writing to inquire about the position of Professional Anarchist for the University. As a dedicated and bloodthirsty revolutionary with multiple years of experience in insurrectionary struggle, I believe I am highly qualified for the position and would be honored to be considered. I believe I could serve the University in a variety of capacities, ranging from performing ordinary administrative tasks to coordinating the violent overthrow of the capitalist state. A résumé is attached.

My particular areas of interest are in terrorizing the bourgeoisie, taking the streets, and roughing up fascists. Wanton destruction and mayhem are a particular subspecialty. My core competencies include burning, looting, and frightening unsuspecting commuters. I am highly skilled at both fomenting and inciting. I know a number of menacing protest chants, which frequently include vulgar references to police officers. I am also proficient in Word and Excel.

I have always been interested in pursuing a career in anarchism. As a child, when I was told I must do this or that, I obeyed only reluctantly, and frequently muttered comments of disdain toward my elders. In high school, I once became very frank with my trigonometry teacher, which resulted in a written disciplinary notice. Most of my time in the classroom was spent idly doodling circle-As on a notepad (sometimes, even on the desk itself). I persisted at this even in the face of repeated admonishment from parents, instructors, and peers. My anarchism, you see, has always been steadfast.

I hold a bachelor's degree in Political Theory from Brandeis University, *magna cum laude*, where I was a member of the Fuck Fascism Collective and made the Dean's List all semesters. I majored in Literature, but I would like to think I minored in misdemeanor arson. I occasionally distributed zines explaining how the twin behemoths of capitalism and the state oppress the working class, and was Vice President of one of the more notable *a cappella* groups on campus. I was not afraid to shake things up during my undergraduate years. In my honors thesis, I included a quote from Bakunin as an epigraph. As an anarchist, I was not afraid what the faculty would think of this.

In recent years I have honed my skill for setting large fires in public settings. When people have attempted to extinguish them, I have blockaded these people's passage, or distracted them with a flash grenade or some light conversation. I have always been a strong believer in setting nearby objects aflame and believe I could do very well at it in a professional setting. (You will find find a list of major conflagrations under "Extracurriculars," beneath the section on academic honors and awards.)

My background in true violent insurrection has been limited. I have not yet been afforded the opportunity to blow up an armaments train or poison a constable. I did, however, once toss an extremely heavy brick at the window of a Panda Express in Cleveland during the Republican National Convention. The window did not shatter, but my comrades praised the destructive spirit of the act. As an anarchist, I am prepared to dismantle the window of any shopfront by force. My most significant professional experience was in Seattle during 1999, where I did excellent work as part of the "black bloc" and was considered "detail-oriented" by peers for my careful selection of street lights to shatter. (In addition to this work, I overturned a policeman's motorbike. He pursued me to no avail. I am one slippery anarchist.)

I have other, non-related professional experience. I would ask you to look kindly upon my several law firm internships, which admittedly were not especially anarchistic. However, at these jobs I did intentionally misplace numerous important documents, generating considerable confusion among the associates. Supervisors nevertheless praised my punctuality and diligence, although as an anarchist I do not care what supervisors think. Soon there will be no supervisors. Death to all bosses. (I can still provide references as needed.)

I am strongly dedicated to putting anarchist philosophy into practice in my day to day life. When policemen come near me, I make a point of rolling my eyes and saying "Ugh." I frequently tweet rude things about the President of the United States. I do not care if he sees them. It does not matter to me if he becomes upset. I am an anarchist.

I am against all hierarchies. When I see a hierarchy, I destroy it. Or, at the very least, I raise very serious questions about it. If someone tells me to do something, I will frequently respond: "I am sorry, but I am unable to comply, for I am an anarchist." I am also not afraid to confront the state. I have four traffic infractions for a failure to yield at a stop sign. I freely confess to having committed these crimes. I am an anarchist. I yield to no one.

In my spare time, I enjoy gardening and reiki. I live with two cats, Emma and Johann, both of whom are named for famous anarchists. (Note that I do not say I "own" the cats. The cats are free. An anarchist must practice what he preaches.)

I know my record of serious vandalism may be somewhat more sparse than that of other candidates for this opening. But I am a highly motivated individual and willing to learn quickly. I am goal-oriented, and within the next five years I aspire to turn a limousine on its side and scrawl something lewd on the wall of a Wells Fargo branch. I am a team player and have an unquenchable thirst for the blood of capitalist parasites.

Thank you for considering me for the position. I look forward to hearing from you.

Down with the state,

Nathan J. Robinson

Light &
Dark

In Defense of Liking Things

NOBODY CAN REASONABLY ACCUSE ME of liking too many things. I am a veteran practitioner of the "Actually, This Thing You Thought Was Good Is Not Very Good At All" school of writing. I am promiscuous in my hatreds, grievances, and peeves, and I know well the pleasures of announcing that whatever my least favorite recent cultural development happens to be spells ruin for the civilized order.

But it's possible to take one's disagreeableness to excess. There is always the risk of becoming that most unwelcome of characters, the curmudgeon. At its best, written criticism can usefully point out social problems in ways that help clarify people's thinking. At its worst, it can be stuffy and joyless, a philosophy of "miserablism." If you're not careful, you can turn into P.J. O'Rourke, Joe Queenan, or even, *shudder*, Andy Rooney. The infamous "Whig View Of History" is the idea that things follow an inevitable trajectory towards progress, enlightenment, and decency. The curmudgeon's view of history is that everything is just getting worse all the time, that all of the things people like suck, and that they suck harder than anything has ever sucked in the history of things sucking.

The "fidget spinner" is a little plastic toy that has become popular recently among large numbers of children and modest numbers of adults.[1] You twiddle it in your fingers and it goes round and round. You can do nifty tricks with it. It seems like fun. It's even alleged to be good for kids with ADHD, because it gives them something to do with their hands.

Critics from the *Atlantic* and the *New Yorker*, however, have declared that the fidget spinner captures everything that is wrong with our century. Far from being an innocuous and amusing cheap little rotating thingamajig, the fidget spinner is, according to the *New Yorker*'s Rebecca Mead, an embodiment of Trump-era values.[2] It is a sign of a narcissistic and distracted culture, one captivated by trifles, ignorant of its own decline, and oblivious to all that is sacred, intelligent, and morally serious. We are fidgeting while Rome burns.

Mead's indictment of the fidget spinner is worth quoting at some length, in order that we may appreciate it in its full fustiness:

> *Fidget spinners... are masquerading as a helpful contribution to the common weal, while actually they are leading to whole new levels of stupid. Will it be dismissed as an overreaction—as "pearl-clutching," as the kids on the Internet like to say—to discern, in the contemporary popularity of the fidget spinner, evidence of cultural decline? ... Perhaps, and yet the rise of the fidget spinner at this political moment cries out for interpretation. The fidget spinner, it could be argued, is the perfect toy for the age of Trump. Unlike the Tamagotchi, it does not encourage its owner to take anyone else's feelings or needs into account. Rather, it enables and even encourages the setting of one's own interests above everyone else's. It induces solipsism, selfishness, and outright rudeness. It does not, as the Rubik's Cube does, reward higher-level intellection. Rather, it encourages the abdication of thought, and promotes a proliferation of mindlessness, and it does so at a historical moment when the President has proved himself to be pathologically prone to distraction and incapable of formulating a coherent idea... Is it any surprise that, given the topsy-turvy world in which we now live, spinning one's wheels... has been recast as a diverting recreation, and embraced by a mass audience? Last week, as the House voted to overturn the Affordable Care Act, millions of parents of children*

with special needs... began to worry, once again, about their children becoming uninsured, or uninsurable, an outcome the President had promised on the campaign trail would not occur. This week, after summarily firing James Comey... [Donald Trump] issued a baffling series of contradictory explanations for what looks increasingly like the unapologetic gesture of a would-be despot. Each day, it becomes more apparent that Trump is toying with our democracy, shamelessly betting that the public will be too distracted and too stupefied to register that what he is spinning are lies.

There are at least eight things that I love about this passage. First, it adopts the full New Yorker hierarchy of values: from elevating that thing called the "common weal" as the highest good, to "outright rudeness" being the basest of transgressions. Second, the idea that the fidget spinner is somehow "masquerading" as contributing to the common weal, as if fidget spinners come in packaging that promises a morally edifying and intellectually nourishing experience. Third, the idea that the fidget spinner's rise "cries out for interpretation." (Does it really?) Fourth, I love rhetorical questions where the obvious answer is the opposite to the one the author wishes us to offer. ("Will it be dismissed as an overreaction...?" Yes.) Fifth, the idea that unlike the selfish fidget-spinner, the noble and pro-social Tamagotchi encourages us to care about the feelings of others. Sixth, the hilariously overstated and totally unsubstantiated claims (spinning a fidget spinner is an act of "solipsism" that causes us to "abdicate thought" and put our interests above everybody else's). Seventh, the tribute to the great and deep "intellection" of the Rubik's Cube. Eighth, the tortuous and contrived Trump parallel, in which the fidget spinner now tells us something about James Comey and the Affordable Care Act.

But Mead is not alone in denouncing the spinner's effect on human values. Ian Bogost of the *Atlantic* analyzes the economic dimensions of the toy, seeing it as the logical conclusion of a capitalistic logic that wishes to pacify us with doodads and trinkets to keep us blind to our own exploitation and ennui:

[Fidgets spinners] are a perfect material metaphor for everyday life in early 2017... [They are] a rich, dense fossil of the immediate present... In an uncertain global environment biting its nails over new threats of economic precarity, global autocracy, nuclear war, planetary death, and all the rest, the fidget spinner offers the relief of a non-serious, content-free topic... At a time when so many feel so threatened, aren't handheld, low-friction tops the very thing we fight for?... Then commerce validates the spinner's cultural status. For no cultural or social trend is valid without someone becoming wealthy, and someone else losing out. And soon enough, the fidget spinner will stand aside, its moment having been strip-mined for all its spoils at once. The only dream dreamed more often than the dream of individual knowledge and power is the dream of easy, immediate wealth, which now amounts to the same thing.[3]

Now, I haven't played with a fidget spinner. I've never even seen one. My understanding is that their prime audience is the 12-and-under set, and I am friends with very few middle schoolers these days. But I will admit that from my limited experience watching videos of the things on YouTube, I did not begin to suspect that the fidget spinners displayed "the dream of individual knowledge and power."[4] Nor did I notice the parallels between the twirling of the spinner and the chaos of Donald Trump's presidency. Perhaps this shows the limits of my analytical capacities, or perhaps I am blinded by the pervasiveness of the American ideology of individualism. I'll confess, though, my basic reaction so far is that the toys look nifty and the tricks you can do with them are pretty cool.[5]

And I'd like to think that it's okay to feel this way. Not everything that exists in the time of Donald Trump has to be a metaphor for Donald Trump, and not every silly trinket produced by capitalism is evidence of our decline in intellectual vigor. Sometimes a cigar is just a cigar.[6] (Although in Freud's case, the cigar was a penis.) Cultural critics often display an unfortunate tendency toward "Zeitgeistism," the borderline-paranoid belief that there are Zeitgeists everywhere, massive social and historical essences to be found in all kinds of everyday practices and objects.

One problem is that the kind of theorizing done by Bogost and Mead amounts to the telling of "just so stories," unfalsifiable narratives that merely confirm the theorist's already-existing worldview. That means that anyone can tell whatever story they like about the fidget spinner. You could call it evidence of solipsism, because it causes humans to interact with the spinners rather than one another. But then I could offer a different story: the fidget spinner is evidence of social dynamism and of an increasingly tactile, physical, and body-conscious world. Which one of us is right? Neither. It's all B.S.

Any critic who wishes to offer the fidget spinner as evidence of some wider destructive social tendency faces another problem: it's not really any more pointless or individualistic than the yo-yo, and we've gotten along with those for about 2500 years. If you want to see fidget spinners as uniquely representative of Trumpism and so-called "late capitalism," you have to find a way to argue that it is fundamentally different from a yo-yo in some philosophically significant way. And since it isn't, and since if the fidget spinner shows civilizational decline then every dumb toy in history would necessarily have to prove the same thing, every cultural critic who tries to posit a Fidget Spinner Theory of Everything ends up somewhat stuck.

You can see this amusing dead-end whenever Bogost and Mead attempt to explain why the spinner is nothing like the generations of faddish knicknacks that came before it. (I'd imagine there were similar pieces in 2009 about how Silly Bandz explained the Obama era, or 1990's thinkpieces on what Beanie Babies could tell us about the Clinton economy.) Mead is at pains to come up with reasons why Rubik's Cubes and Tamagotchis are serious and worthwhile, while fidget spinners are decadent and stupid. Bogost, meanwhile, makes a hilariously convoluted attempt to meaningfully distinguish the fidget spinner from an ordinary spinning top:

A top is a toy requiring collaboration with the material world. It requires a substrate on which to spin, be it the hard earth of ancient Iraq or the molded-plastic IKEA table in a modern flat. As a toy, the top grounds physics, like a lightning rod grounds electricity. And in this collaboration, the material world always wins. Eventually, the top falls, succumbing to gravity, laying prone on the dirt... Not so, the fidget spinner. It is a toy for the hand alone—for the individual. Ours is not an era characterized by collaboration between humans and earth—or Earth, for that matter. Whether through libertarian self-reliance or autarchic writ, human effort is first seen as individual effort—especially in the West. Bootstraps-thinking pervades the upper echelons of contemporary American life, from Silicon Valley to the White House. ... The fidget spinner quietly attests that the solitary, individual body who spins it is sufficient to hold a universe. That's not a counterpoint to the ideology of the smartphone, but an affirmation of that device's worldview. What is real, and good, and interesting is what can be contained and manipulated in the hand, directly.

Since they had spinning tops in the 35th century B.C., for Bogost to confirm his belief that fidget spinners must embody "bootstraps thinking" and "the ideology of the smartphone," he knows he has to find some important difference.[7] "Ah, well, you see, the top touches the ground but the fidget spinner goes in the hand, and individuals have hands, therefore the fidget spinner is individualistic and libertarian while the spinning top is humble, worldly, and environmentalist." (Of course, Bogost is still powerless to deal with the yo-yo question. These both go in the hand and don't touch the ground. What about the yo-yo, eh, Bogost?)

I'm particularly irritated by this kind of cultural criticism because it embodies one of the most unfortunate tendencies in left-ish political thinking: the need to spoil everybody's fun by finding some kind of problem with *everything*. There is enough serious human misery in the world for the left to point out; there's no need to problematize the fidget spinner as well. Whenever I see something like, say, *Jacobin's* critique of Pokemon Go as being the "bourgeois" embodiment of an obedience-worshiping "technology of biopolitics," I can't help but think: "Do we really have to be these people? Because this isn't the side I want to be on."[8] We're allowed to like things. Even stupid things. And you don't have to rain on every single parade that passes by. Rule #1 for creating a left that people will want to join: don't be a humorless joykill who tells people that their stress toy makes them Donald Trump.

I might feel more sympathetic if these criticisms were intellectually rigorous or substantially true. But they aren't. They don't hold up to the most minimal logical scrutiny, because they fail to carefully answer the question of why we should consider the fidget spinner unique next to every other dumb little thing in history. They make ridiculous overstatements, and then don't explain why we should accept their just-so stories rather than another, equally contrived but opposing, set of just-so stories.

The reason that the fidget spinner is popular is not that it embodies our society's most depraved and fatuous tendencies, or that it signifies the erosion of our attention spans in the era of Trump. It's popular because it's a legitimately impressive little novelty device. Like all novelties, it will wear off. And there will be as much political significance to its disappearance as there was to its appearance: hardly any.

Fun is important, and sometimes people have fun by playing tiddlywinks or spinning a top or finding one of the myriad of other trivial diversions that keep us from having to face the full horror of our mortal existence. And people on the left shouldn't spend their time coming up with implausible theories for why everyone is delusional and stupid for enjoying playing with spinny-things. They should be trying to understand the roots of human suffering, and proposing ways to alleviate it.

Anything else is just a distraction.

Compassion and Politics

FOR A BRIEF MOMENT in May of 2017, it seemed as if McDonald's had gone political. From nowhere, the company's Twitter account began attacking the President of the United States, calling Donald Trump a "disgusting excuse of [sic] a president" and taunting him over the size of his hands.[1] It was an abrupt shift in tone from a social media account better known for conducting meaningless polls about hamburgers and engaging in clumsy attempts to keep up with the hashtag generation (e.g. "When bae is a Big Mac #relationshipgoals").[2]

Of course, the account had been broken into; anyone who thought American corporations would be capable of showing some moral and political backbone against Trump must have forgotten how the country's liberal-leaning tech CEOs turned from staunch opposition to capitulation and groveling immediately after Trump's election.[3] But the momentary flicker of controversy over the McDonald's tweet did provide one small insight into a certain prevailing political tendency. For, immediately upon hearing of the incident, *Business Insider* editor (and Democrat) Josh Barro decided to remark as follows: "This is a real brand misstep for McDonald's. Fat slobs with bad taste are a core Trump demographic."[4]

It was a nasty and elitist remark. (It was also wrong. As *Guardian* journalist Chris Arnade has documented, far from being for "fat slobs,"

McDonald's are often vibrant gathering-spots in working-class communities.[5]) Josh Barro has always been a proud elitist, though.[6] He believed the election of Trump proved it was better to let elites control political decision-making than to let the "masses" pick and has quite seriously declared that "elites are usually elite for good reason, and tend to have better judgment than the average person."

A small amusing fact here is that Barro himself is "elite for good reason." That good reason is that his father, Robert J. Barro, is the Paul M. Warburg Professor of Economics at Harvard University, a Harvard alumnus well-connected in the world of think tanks and financial journalism.[7] Little surprise then, that Joshua Barro grew up to be... a Harvard alumnus who has worked almost exclusively in the world of think tanks and financial journalism.[8] Elites are indeed elite for good reason, but it has precious little to do with the consequences of individual striving or merit.

In itself, though, an attack on McDonald's-goers by one *Business Insider* editor would be of little interest. *Business Insider* is, after all, a rag, and Barro's opinions are of no material consequence to humankind. But the attack exemplified a notable recent trend in the discourse of prominent wealthy Democrats: the heaping of limitless contempt upon poor people. Instead of heeding suggestions that greater amounts of empathy for working-class Trump constituencies might make Democrats less likely to lose these people's votes, lately some liberals have doubled down. As Clio Chang pointed out in *Jacobin*, figures including Paul Krugman ("I try to be charitable, but when you read about Trump voters now worried about losing Obamacare it's kind of hard") and Markos Moulitsas ("Be happy for coal miners losing their health insurance; they're getting exactly what they voted for") have reacted to stories about hardships and deprivation in Trump-leaning communities with unqualified disdain.[9] Ex-*New York Times* theater critic Frank Rich recently declared he had "no sympathy for the hillbilly," and suggested that:

> *Liberals looking for a way to empathize with conservatives should endorse the core conservative belief in the importance of personal*

*responsibility. Let Trump's white working-class base take responsi-
bility for its own votes—or in some cases failure to vote—and live
with the election's consequences... Let them reap the consequences
for voting against their own interests.*[10]

This kind of thinking isn't limited to media commentators. It seems
to be a strand in liberal thinking more broadly. Matthew Stoller collected a series of *Huffington Post* comments on an article about poor
whites dying from ill-health and opiate addiction:

◆ *"Sorry, not sorry. These people are not worthy of any sympathy. They
have run around for decades bitching about poor minorities not
"working hard enough," or that their situation is "their own fault."
Well guess what? It's not so great when it's you now, is it? Bunch of
deplorables, and if they die quicker than the rest of us that just means
the country will be better off in the long run."*

◆ *"Karma is a bitch and if these people choose to continue to vote
Republican and try to deny other [sic] from attaining the American
dream, they deserve no better than what they are getting!"*

◆ *"I for one have little sympathy for these despairing whites. If they can't
compete against people of color when everything has been rigged in their
favor, then there's really no help for them. Trump and his G(r)OPers will
do little to elevate their lot. If anything, these poor whites will be hired to
dig grave pits and assemble their own coffins."*[11]

The odd thing about all of this is that, just as Rich says, this is the conservative way of thinking about people experiencing deprivation. Rich
is a wealthy man telling poor people that their problems are their own
fault and they should exercise some personal responsibility. This does
not sound like the rhetoric of liberals, who until recently were supposed to be the hippie bleeding-hearts and the boosters of failed but
well-meaning Great Society entitlement programs. Now they're telling
the working class that they should either hoist themselves up by their
bootstraps or, better yet, die and make the world a better place.

Something seems to have happened here. And to see what it is, we might do well to return to the example of *Business Insider*'s Josh Barro. For while Barro is currently a Democrat, he wasn't always. In fact, after many years in the Republican Party, he only made the switch last year.[12] Someone, then, whose publicly-stated view is that the country should be run by its enlightened oligarchs and the children of its Harvard economics professors, thinks the Democratic Party is a more congenial home for his politics than the Republican Party.

That clearly shouldn't be the case. The Democratic Party, if it is adequately representing its fundamental democratic principles, should be a party that someone like Josh Barro would never want to join. The fact that he does want to join it should be serious cause for concern among the Democratic leadership. If the Democratic Party is actually on the left, then nobody who holds the views that Barro does (that the "masses" are incapable of judging for themselves and must be ruled by "elites") would ever voluntarily join it. In fact, we can design a kind of useful metric—a Barrometer, if you will—for determining whether your political party is adequately representing working people's interests. It's quite simple: if Josh Barro is in your party, then your party is failing to represent working people's interests. Having Barro turn up in your political camp is like when Zuckerberg shows up to Burning Man: it means the party's over.[13]

Now, there are multiple possibilities here. It may be that the Democratic Party actually represents wealthy snobs who think McDonald's is for fat idiots and think miners with black lung deserve their fate for Voting Against Their Interests. Or it may be that the party simply doesn't threaten the political interests of those wealthy snobs. But either way, it's clear that the contemporary Democratic Party isn't going to be making much of an attempt to redistribute power or wealth downward.

An important dimension of this is captured by *National Review*'s Kevin Williamson. Williamson is an uncommonly skilful writer and morally hideous human being who attained some notoriety when he decided that poor white communities "deserved to die" for failing to contribute anything to the global economy. He offers a standard right-wing take on poverty and deprivation: if your life sucks, you've nobody to blame but yourself. Capitalism, for Williamson, is a bringer of endless bounties, and the idea that it has "victims" is preposterous. (It is strange that such enthusiastic promoters of unregulated markets love to talk about the wondrous economic processes by which pencils are made[14] but have less to say about workers getting brutally maimed in auto parts assembly plants.[15])

But Williamson notes something puzzling: lately, a number of Democrats seem to agree with his view that poverty is a function of poor decision-making: "Today's Democrats talk about the Republican-leaning parts of the United States as though they were particularly unsympathetic Third World countries, populated by people who not only lost life's lottery but deserved it."

Williamson says that the Democrats are now the party of the "respectable upper middle-class"; they're the party of life's winners, and Republicans are becoming the party of the losers: after all, most of our country's most visible billionaires supported Clinton (Gates, Buffett, Bloomberg, Cuban, Zuckerburg, etc.), whereas the collapsing epicenters of the country's opiate epidemic are the heart of Trump Country.

Williamson's economic winners-and-losers framework is wrong in some important ways. (For one thing, it only works if you look solely at white people.) But he's right to detect a distinctly snobbish and bourgeois sensibility in contemporary Democratic politics. Yesterday's Rockefeller Republican is today's Clinton Democrat, and Rockefeller Republicans were fundamentally aristocratic in their inclinations.

Perhaps this explains why, as Bernie Sanders has noted, it's hard to figure out what the Democratic Party actually stands for these days. After all, what common political interests are shared by both black communities in Detroit and Warren Buffett? (Though we do know that Buffett has a longstanding passion for offering black people exorbitant mobile home loans.[16]) What unites a Hispanic domestic worker in Los Angeles with her studio executive boss? Only the most toothless and ineffectual political program could capture the wealthiest and the poorest alike.

But to see how Democrats might begin to reformulate an actual set of values, let's go back to Frank Rich. Rich says that Democrats "need to stop trying to feel everyone's pain," because this would "cater to the white-identity politics of the hard-core, often self-sabotaging Trump voters who helped drive the country into a ditch on Election Day." And herein lies a core fallacy: that in empathizing with people, you necessarily excuse them, and that by acknowledging someone's suffering, you thereby endorse their political agenda. You don't have to sign on to "white identity politics" in order to think that nobody deserves to have their health insurance taken away, no matter how stupid they've been either personally or politically. Rich writes that Democrats should "hold the empathy and hold on to the anger" because "if *National Review*['s Kevin Williamson] says that their towns deserve to die, who are Democrats to stand in the way of Trump voters who used their ballots to commit assisted suicide?"

The answer is that Democrats are supposed to be the ones who aren't callous assholes like Kevin Williamson, that they're the ones who are supposed to believe people don't bring their pain on themselves and that you don't discard people merely because they've made foolish decisions. (After all, the entire left argument about criminals is that poor decisions are frequently a product of bad circumstances rather than their cause, yet certain Democrats seem incapable of extending to Trump voters the logic that they would apply to religious terrorists or death row inmates.) Democrats are supposed to recognize the degree to which responsibility rhetoric ignores how little meaningful choice individuals have under the current economic and political system, and how ludicrous it is to blame them for things that are the product of massive structural forces. Since our lives are the product of our environments and our biology, and since we have almost no control over either of those things, talk of responsibility usually massively overstates the role of raw human willpower in shaping human destinies.

There's a perfectly simple and consistent principle from which Democratic (or progressive, or left, or just humane) politics are supposed to start: basic compassion for those who are suffering. The moment you find yourself saying "they brought it on themselves" or "I have no sympathy," you have ceased to practice the (often difficult!) basic moral principle that should drive left-wing politics, which is a deep compassion for people's struggles and a desire to help them make their lives better.

Note that this gets around common objections to having "sympathy for the hillbilly." It's sometimes suggested that instead of empathizing with Trump voters, we should empathize with those who will be victimized by Trump's policies, e.g. Muslims and the undocumented. But the whole idea of universal compassion is that you don't have to choose: you care about people in proportion to the amount they are being hurt, so the people who will be hurt the most can receive the most attention without diminishing the struggles of those who are being hurt somewhat less. This also means that nobody needs to have much sympathy for rich Trump voters (who, as it is often pointed out, constitute a disproportionate fraction of the Trump constituency). If you voted for Trump because you're a well-off bigot who thinks your taxes are too high, no hearts shall bleed for you.

A good statement of compassion-ethic was formulated by Arthur Schopenhauer (the most sensible, and therefore least-read, 19th-century German philosopher), who felt that the foundation of morality was in our ability to empathize with each other and care about the sufferings of the world. As he wrote:

> *Boundless compassion for all living beings is the surest and most certain guarantee of pure moral conduct, and needs no casuistry. Whoever is filled with it will assuredly injure no one, do harm to no one, encroach on no man's rights; he will rather have regard for every one, forgive every one, help every one as far as he can, and all his actions will bear the stamp of justice and loving-kindness. ... In former times the English plays used to finish with a petition for the King. The old Indian dramas close with these words: 'May all living beings be delivered from pain.' Tastes differ; but in my opinion there is no more beautiful prayer than this.*[17]

All living beings. That means caring about what happens rather than caring about who it happens to. It means valuing both the crime victim and the prisoner, or the families of both the dead U.S. soldier[18] and the dead Yemeni child.[19] It doesn't discriminate by race or nation, but only by the degree of harm being experienced.

Having compassion as your starting point doesn't lead to a particular necessary set of policy prescriptions. It doesn't make you a strict pacifist, or mean you need to think single-payer healthcare is practicable. But it does mean you can't end up like Frank Rich or Kevin Williamson, using the word "victims" in quotes and trying to determine who deserves to have a parent poisoned by industrial waste because they supported Trump's EPA nominee. It doesn't mean you can't think people are stupid, or can't think they should be making different choices, but it does mean that no set of bad choices means you should be afflicted with black lung or be crushed to death by industrial machinery.[20] Nor does it (or should it) necessitate being patronizing, and treating the destitute like infants or curiosities. In fact, in a certain way you actually grant someone their humanity by being frustrated over their choices rather than seeing them as little more than the helpless product of circumstance. But none of that means that you end up like Markos Moulitsas, taking pleasure in watching people reap the harmful consequences of the decisions you warned them against.

There are plenty of ways in which to reconstruct a moral foundation for liberal politics. People's inclinations on this may be different. But Schopenhauer was right. "May all living beings be delivered from pain." That's not a bad place to start.

Pessimism is Suicide

I AM NEITHER AN OPTIMIST NOR A PESSIMIST, because both positions seem unreasonable and foolish to me. The pessimist thinks the glass is half-empty, the optimist thinks the glass is half-full, but any reasonable person understands that both terms are equally applicable, and that arguments over which is more correct are futile and useless. The only sensible answer to the question of whether the glass is half-full or half-empty is "both," or "it depends what those terms mean," and if we want a precise understanding of what is going on with the glass, unclouded by normative values, we should simply say that water is taking up half of the glass.

You might think I'm taking the glass cliché too pedantically and literally. But it usefully shows why both optimism and pessimism should be avoided. If you're either one of these, then instead of assessing what the facts actually are, with as little bias as possible, you project your own prejudice onto any given situation in front of you. "Rose-colored glasses" are showing you a world that doesn't exist, but the same is equally true for glasses that make the world look bleak and dreary. In each case, your personal filter is keeping you from perceiving nature's true colors.

Actually, that's not quite right, since it's impossible to have some kind of objectively "true" perception in which the world is seen exactly as it is. You will always be a human being with prejudices, and all images will be bent by those prejudices. But if we want to have the best possible understanding of the world around us, our job is to try to figure out what those prejudices are and correct for them as much as possible. Thus nobody should embrace either optimism or pessimism, since doing so entails renouncing the quest to see things as clearly as possible.

Fortunately, I don't meet many optimists these days. I do, however, meet an awful lot of pessimists. As young people become ensnared in a lifetime of low-wage work and indenture to their debt, and are politically powerless and disengaged against the civilization-destroying forces of climate change and nuclear war, they understandably feel somewhat hopeless. It seems rational to believe that everything is heading straight for a miserable fiery hell in a rapidly-accelerating handbasket.

This position isn't rational, however. Think about what it actually requires to believe in unavoidable doom: you have to think that you know every single possible path that humanity's destiny could take. By taking a position that it is impossible to avoid calamity and extinction, a person asserts that they singlehandedly comprehend all possible futures. This is, to put it mildly, somewhat hubristic.

Thus another reason that pessimism is folly is that it is far too confident in the human capacity for prediction. Predictions are tricky things to make about anything, let alone the destiny of the species. Pessimism requires an unwarranted confidence in the inevitability of misfortune. But in order to understand the inevitable, you have to understand the universe, and if there is one thing human beings definitely do not understand, it is the universe.

It is wise to take a modest approach to anything that requires opining on the limits of the possible. A humble intelligence admits that it doesn't know how things will go. It realizes that any statement about the world as having a "trajectory" that can be extrapolated into the future requires adopting a phenomenal amount of confidence in one's own predictive capacity, and that both optimists and pessimists presume a kind of understanding of the rules and tendencies of the world that is actually impossible to attain.

People are always too quick to declare certain things impossible. They hardly ever actually know what's possible and impossible, but they will happily explain the limits on human action to anyone who dares to dream of something mildly beyond that which already exists. Of course, things once branded "impossible" happen every day, from the flying of airplanes to the election of Donald Trump as President of the United States. But as soon as the "impossible" happens and becomes the ordinary, instead of stopping using the word "impossible," people simply go and apply it to other things that they assume can't happen.

That's the key problem with use of the term "possible": it assumes that "I can't conceive of X" and "X can't happen" mean the same thing. Actually, since human beings are tiny creatures made of flesh and bone, the limits of our imagination may be much stronger than the limits of reality itself. Perhaps people should stop assuming that simply because they can't think of a way something could happen, there is no way something could happen.

I am always being told that my political beliefs are impossible. This is because I am a utopian: I believe in a world where all people are happy, free, and prosperous, and in which there is no war, destitution, or suffering. The arguments that are raised against this position amount to pessimism: human nature makes such a world impossible, and the things I dream of simply will never happen. But my answer to these criticisms is always the same: how the hell can you possibly know?

I worry about the consequences of all kinds of certainty, because of the "self-fulfilling prophecy" problem. The only way to know for sure that you will fail is to resign yourself to failure, and once you think you're doomed, you're not going to be able to muster the energy necessary to struggle against that doom. After all, why bother? Pessimism is therefore a kind of suicide, because it justifies dropping out and giving up. Personally, I am in a near-constant panic over nuclear weapons and environmental catastrophe, but pessimism itself almost seems a greater threat, since nothing better guarantees our doom than an embrace of the idea that we are doomed.

Shouldn't we be optimists, then? If prophecies can be self-fulfilling, shouldn't we assume that good things are going to happen? Isn't the correct disposition something like *The Secret* or the prosperity gospel, where if you believe in something enough, it will transpire?

I don't think it is. Optimism may bring comfort, but it's no less irrational than pessimism. The real task is not to find the best self-fulfilling prophecy, but to stop relying on prophecies altogether, and simply try to bring about the outcome you desire. Instead of believing that this or that good or bad thing will happen, we should simply say what we would like to happen, and do everything we can to make that thing happen.

The sensible position, then, is neither optimistic nor pessimistic, but hopeful: "I do not know what the future will be like, but I hope it will be good and I will try to make it good." Instead of trying to figure out what "is going" to happen, doom or utopia, as if we have no say in the matter, people should announce what they intend to make happen. Of course, you need some predictions in order to take any action. But generally, apocalyptic prophecies should be discarded, because they can't do anyone any good. (Besides, even if there is no hope, struggle against our inevitable fate can generate meaning in itself, as Albert Camus so appealingly argued in *The Myth of Sisyphus*.) The best thing one can do is to find some kind of "pragmatic hopefulness" that lies at the medium point between optimism and pessimism.

Nobody knows what is possible or impossible, and anyone who says they do is failing to recognize just how limited the human capacity for understanding is. Perhaps humanity is doomed. Perhaps it isn't. But the one thing we know is that it's suicidal to resign ourselves.

Imagining The End

THERE'S A QUOTE FREQUENTLY USED by leftists to illustrate how deeply ingrained society's prevailing economic ideology is: "today, it's easier to imagine the end of the world than the end of capitalism." First offered by Fredric Jameson, and now almost starting to lose meaning from overuse, the quote points out something that is honestly quite astonishing: it does seem far easier to conceive of the possibility of being boiled alive or sinking into the sea than the possibility of living under a substantially different economic system.[1] World-ending disaster seems not just closer than utopia, but closer than even a modest set of changes to the way human resources are distributed.

Jameson's quote is often used to show how capitalism has limited the horizons of our imagination. We don't think of civilization as indestructible, but we do seem to think of the free market as indestructible. This, it is sometimes said, is the result of neoliberalism: as both traditionally left-wing and traditionally right-wing parties in Western countries developed a consensus that markets were the only way forward ("there is no alternative"[2]), more and more people came to hold narrower and narrower views of the possibilities for human society. Being on the right meant "believing in free markets and some kind of nationalism or social conservatism" while being liberal meant "believing in free markets but being progressive on issues of race, gender, and sexual orientation."

Questions like "how do we develop a feasible alternative to capitalism?" were off the table; the only reasonable question about political intervention in the economy became: "should we regulate markets a little bit, or not at all?"

There's definitely something to this critique. It's true that, where once people dreamed of replacing capitalism with something better, today human societies seem to face a choice between apocalypse, capitalism, and capitalism followed shortly by apocalypse. Every attempt to speak of a different kind of economy, however appealing it may be emotionally, seems vague and distant, and impossible to know how to actually bring about. Plenty of young people today are socialists, but socialism seems a lot more like a word than an actual thing that could happen.[3]

Some of this is the result of a very successful multi-decade campaign by the right to present free-market orthodoxy as some kind of objective truth rather than a heavily value-laden and political set of contestable ideas. And the Jameson quote also partly succeeds through a kind of misleading pseudo-profundity: it's always going to be easier to imagine visceral physical things like explosions than changes in economic structures, and so the relative ease of imagining the former versus the latter may not be the especially deep comment on 21st century ideological frameworks that the quotation assumes.

But if socialism seems more remote than ever, it's also surely partly the fault of socialists themselves. If we ask the question "Why is it difficult to imagine the end of capitalism?", some of the answer must be "Because socialists haven't offered a realistic alternative or any kind of plausible path toward such an alternative." It's very easy to blame "neoliberal" ideology for convincing people that free-market dogmas are cosmic truths. Yet while Margaret Thatcher may have propagandized and evangelized for the principle that less government is always better government, she didn't actually prevent people on the left from using their imaginations. If our creativity has been stunted, it may also be because we have failed to use our minds to their maximal capacity, falling back on abstractions and rhetoric rather than developing clear and feasible pictures for what a functional left-wing world might look like.

I blame Karl Marx for that, at least somewhat. Marx helped kill "utopian socialism" (personally, my favorite kind of socialism).[4] The utopian socialists used to actually dream of the kind of societies they would create, conjuring elaborate and delightfully vivid visions of how a better and more humane world might actually operate. Some of these veered into the absurd (Charles Fourier believed the seas would turn to lemonade[5]), but all of them encouraged people to actually think in serious detail about how human beings live now, and what it would be like if they lived differently. Marx, on the other hand, felt that this was a kind of foolishly romantic, anti-scientific waste of time. The task of the socialist was to discern the inexorable historical laws governing human social development, and then to hasten the advance of a revolution. According to Marx, it was pointless trying to spend time drawing up "recipes for the cook-shops of the future"; instead, left-wing thinkers should do as Marx believed he was doing, and confine themselves "to the mere critical analysis of actual facts."[6]

But analysis doesn't actually create proposals, and it was because Marx believed that that things could sort themselves out "dialectically" that he didn't think it was necessary to explain how communism might actually function day-to-day. Ironically, given Marx's dictum that philosophers should attempt to change the world rather than merely interpreting it, Marx and his followers spent an awful lot of time trying to figure out social theories that would properly interpret the world, and precious little time trying to figure out which changes might actually improve people's lives versus which changes might lead to disaster. (Call me crazy, but I believe this tendency to shun the actual development of policy might have been one reason why nearly every single government that has ever called itself Marxist has very quickly turned into a horror show.)

The left-wing tendency to avoid offering clear proposals for how left ideas might be successfully implemented (without gulags) is not confined to revolutionary communism. The same affliction plagued the Occupy Wall Street movement: a belief in democracy and a hatred of inequality, but a stalwart refusal to try to come up with a feasible route from A-B, where A is our present state of viciously unequal neofeudalism and B is something that might be slightly more bearable and fair. By refusing to issue demands, or consider what sorts of political, economic, and social adjustments would actually be necessary to actualize Occupy's set of values, the movement doomed itself. The direct precipitating cause of its fizzling was Occupy's eviction from Zuccotti Park by the NYPD. But it's hard to think how a movement that isn't actually proposing or fighting for anything clear and specific could ever actually get that thing. (Occupy's "no demands" proponents would have done well to listen to Frederick Douglass, who declared that "Power concedes nothing without a demand.")

There's a bit of the same lack of programmatic strategy in the popular leftist disdain for "wonks" and "technocrats." Nobody finds D.C. data nerds more irritating than I do, but these two terms have become casual pejoratives that can seemingly be applied to anyone who has an interest in policy details.[7] Certainly, it's important to heap scorn upon the set of "technocratic" Beltway-types who value policy for its own sake, and allow political process to become an end in itself, drained of any substantive moral values or concern with making people's lives better. But in our perfectly justified hatred for a certain species of wonk, it's important not to end up dismissing the value of caring about pragmatism and detail.

In fact, I almost feel as if the term "pragmatism" has been unfairly monopolized by centrists, with the unfortunate complicity of many people on the left. "Pragmatism" has come to mean "being a moderate." But that's not what the term should mean. Being pragmatic should simply mean "caring about the practical realities of how to implement things." People like Bill Clinton and Tony Blair helped redefine "liberal pragmatism" to mean "adopting conservative policies as a shortcut to winning power easily." But being pragmatic doesn't mean having to sacrifice your idealism. It doesn't mean tinkering at the margins rather than proposing grand changes. It just means having a plan for how to get things done.

Thus leftism should simultaneously become more pragmatic and more utopian. At its best, utopianism is pragmatic, because it is producing blueprints, and without blueprints, you'll have trouble building anything. Yes, these days it's hard to imagine a plausible socialist world. But that's only partly because so many people insist socialism is impossible. It's also because socialists aren't actually doing much imagining. William Morris and the 19th century utopians painted vivid portraits of what a world that embodied their values might look like.[8] Today's socialists tell us what they deplore (inequality and exploitation), but they're short on clear plans. But plans are what we need. Serious ones. Detailed ones. Not "technocratic," necessarily, but certainly technical. It's time to actually start imagining what something new might really look like.

Conclusion: Socialism as a Set of Principles

NEARLY HALF OF MILLENNIALS describe themselves as sympathetic to "socialism" and not terribly fond of "capitalism." Yet if you asked each of them to explain the mechanics of how a socialist economy would function, I doubt many would have especially detailed answers. *Jacobin* magazine's *ABCs of Socialism* consists of answers to skeptical questions about socialism (e.g. "Don't the rich deserve their money?" "Is socialism pacifist?" "Will socialism be boring?") but notably "How will socialism actually work?" is not among them. With twelve million Democratic primary voters having cast ballots for a self-described "socialist," isn't it concerning that nobody has explained in detail how socialism will "work"? Embracing a new economic system without having a blueprint seems like it could only ever lead to something like Venezuela's collapse.

I think this criticism seems very powerful, and comes from an understandable instinct. But it has a mistaken view of what socialism actually means to the people who use the label. In the 21st century, for many of its adherents socialism is not describing a particular set of economic rules and government policies, some clearly-defined "system" that must be implemented according to a plan. Instead, it describes a set of principles that we want the economic and political system to conform to. Bringing the world into harmony with these principles will require experimentation, but that lack of rigidity is an asset. Because 20th century "socialist" states attempted vast social engineering projects, there is a tendency to think of "a socialist economy" in engineering terms. Capitalism is an engine, with its parts all working together to produce an effect. Socialists come along and say that the engine should be designed entirely differently, with a totally different set of rules in order to produce better effects. If this is what we're talking about when we're talking about "capitalism versus socialism," then it's completely right to ask for an explanation of how the proposed alternative works. We'd be very suspicious of someone who said they had reinvented the combustion engine but refused to tell us how the alternative would work and insisted that before trying it we destroy all of our combustion engines.

But this is a poor way of thinking about what is being advocated by socialists. Books are a better analogy. We have, in our hands, a badly-written manuscript and are trying to edit it into a well-written manuscript. There's no blueprint for the well-written manuscript. We create it through a process. Delete a passage here, insert one there, move this around, move that around. And in doing this, we follow a set of principles: we want it to flow well, we want the reader not to get confused, we want all our sentences to be forceful and precise. Those principles aren't handed down from on high, and there are lots of different ways we could write the book that would produce something satisfactory. But asking at the beginning of the process "Well, what will the finished product look like?" makes no sense. If we could present a blueprint for the finished book, we wouldn't need a blueprint because we would already have finished the book.

Socialism can be conceived of similarly: socialists are trying to make society better, so that its operations meet a particular set of ideal criteria. Here, I want to quote Leszek Kołakowski, the Polish scholar of Marxism, who was a vicious opponent of communist governments but drew an important distinction between socialism as a system and an ideal:

> [It would be] a pity if the collapse of communist socialism resulted in the demise of the socialist tradition as a whole and the triumph

of Social Darwinism as the dominant ideology... Fraternity under compulsion is the most malignant idea devised in modern times... This is no reason, however, to scrap the idea of human fraternity. If it is not something that can be effectively achieved by means of social engineering, it is useful as a statement of goals. The socialist idea is dead as a project for an 'alternative society.' But as a statement of solidarity with the underdog and the oppressed, as a motivation to oppose Social Darwinism, as a light that keeps before our eyes something higher than competition and greed—for all these reasons, socialism—the ideal, not the system—still has its uses.[1]

By his last years, Kołakowski was bitterly disenchanted by the left to an extreme I find off-putting. But even he offered high praise for the great socialists of early 20th century Europe, and the ideals they embodied. They "wanted not only equal, universal and obligatory education, a social health service, progressive taxation and religious tolerance, but also secular education, the abolition of national and racial discrimination, the equality of women, freedom of the press and of assembly, the legal regulation of labour conditions, and a social security system. They fought against militarism and chauvinism [and] embodied what was best in European political life."

Here we begin to see what socialist principles actually involve. How can they best be summarized? Kołakowski suggests it's "fraternity," but that seems too limited and too squishy. It does start there, though: with a feeling of connectedness and compassion for other human beings. "We are here to help each other through this thing, whatever it is," as Kurt Vonnegut said. Many socialists begin with that feeling of "solidarity" with people whose lives are needlessly hard and painful, and a sense that we are all in this together.

Socialism also has a firm idea of the kinds of deprivation that this "fellow-feeling" leads us to care about. Everyone should be meaningfully free to have the most fulfilling life possible. "Meaningfully" free means that they need to be able to have that life in reality rather than just in theory: if every child who can afford it can take a trip to Disney World, but some children cannot afford it, then not everyone is free to go to Disney World and it would be cruel and false to tell a poor child that they were free to go if they wanted to. We can debate the ingredients of a fulfilling life, but for libertarian socialists like myself they include a high degree of personal autonomy and the ability to shape your own destiny.

This is what leads socialists toward the idea about "collective ownership of the means of production," which is often cited as the core tenet of socialism. The reason socialists talk about "ownership" so much is that "ownership" refers to decision-making power. If I own a book, it means I am the one who gets to decide what happens to it. I can write in it, sell it, or throw it away. The instinct that "people should be able to shape their own destinies" leads socialists to endorse what I think is the core meaning of "democracy," namely the idea that *people should have decision-making power over those things that affect them.* If we think people's choices should be valued, then they should be included in decisions that affect them.

Hence all this business about the "means of production." The workers in an auto plant are strongly affected by the decision as to whether or not it should close and move production elsewhere. Yet because they do not "own" it (i.e. have any decision-making power), the choice will be made without the participation of those it will impact most. This violates the core principle of democracy. The whole reason socialists are critical of the concentration of private property in few hands is that it constitutes a concentration of socially consequential decision-making power. Say I have been renting my apartment for 30 years. I have made it my home, I have loved it and improved it. Yet I don't have decision-making power over what happens to it, because I am not the owner. The building can be sold and I can be evicted, without having any right to participate in the decision. It's not that I am necessarily entitled to get my way. But democracy does entitle me to have a share in the decision-making proportional to my stake in the outcome. Free market capitalism ensures no such participation; the ones who decide what happens are the ones who own the most resources.

This is also why authoritarian "socialist" regimes don't deserve the name. The whole purpose here is to increase people's control over their circumstances. If you're simply vesting that control in a government, and people have no say in that government, then there's nothing socialistic about what is going on, unless the term is meaningless. Collective ownership means collective decision-making power. Without democratic decision-making, then there's no collective ownership. There's just government ownership, and governments themselves only conform to the principles of socialism to the extent they are democratic. In fact, "democratic socialism" should be a redundancy, because socialism should consist of the application of democracy to all aspects of life.

There are plenty of different ideas for how to make the world more democratic, to ensure that people's lives aren't being controlled by mysterious private or state forces that they have no control over. Socialists have a variety of proposals for economic democracy, such as the Universal Basic Income, worker cooperatives, and mandating profit-sharing. But the democratic principle isn't just about economics. It's also what turns socialists into feminists and anti-racists. Sexism and racism are outside forces that are acting on people against their will, making their lives more difficult on account of demographic characteristics that they cannot choose. The principle "everyone should have the most fulfilling possible life" means that women shouldn't be harassed at work, transgender teens shouldn't be bullied, and people of color shouldn't face unique structural disadvantages.

One may think that by identifying ideas like "giving everyone a maximally fulfilling life" as core principles, I am draining socialism of meaning. After all, *who doesn't want people to have fulfilling lives*? If socialism just means "things should be good," everyone is a socialist. But that's part of the point: socialism tries to apply values that are essentially universal. What differentiates the socialist and the non-socialist is the "apply" part. Everyone talks about democracy and freedom and fulfillment, but socialists are concerned to figure out what those things would *really* entail, and ensure that they are meaningful components of everybody's lives, rather than only existing for some. The United States is "democratic," and people are "free." But when the public's views don't affect the government's policies, and when people can't get vacation time to go and take advantage of their freedom, these concepts are not being fully realized. Socialist principles may sound like platitudes, but when taken seriously they have radical implications: they mean a whole planet without war, crime, prisons, or vast wealth inequality. A socialist world would be very different from our current one.

The principles themselves, though, don't contain any definitive prescription for how to get there. My comparison with the "edit and rewrite" process may imply that I am advocating "piecemeal reforms" or "baby steps." But that's not what I mean by experimentation. Experimentation doesn't mean that you shouldn't be bold. It just means constantly checking to make sure you're upholding the principles. Preferring principles to systems doesn't mean you can never be a revolutionary, it means making sure your revolution is actually advancing your principles rather than "breaking a lot of eggs but never getting an omelet." Nor does it mean that "socialist" today means "social democrat," i.e. capitalism with a welfare state. It could mean that, if that were the best we could hope for. But genuine socialism is idealistic: the perfect application of its principles would only occur in a utopia, which means the work will never fully be done.

The millennial embrace of socialism, then, does not mean that millennials are trying to implement some complicated new economic system that they do not understand. It means that they measure any economic system by the degree to which it is humane and democratic, and they are angered by the degree to which our current one fails people. It means that they reject selfishness and believe in solidarity. And it means that they are determined to help each other build something better, whatever that may be.

CITATIONS

"DEMOCRACY: PROBABLY A GOOD THING"
pp. 19-28

1   Benjamin Wittes and Jonathan Rauch, "More professionalism, less populism: How voting makes us stupid, and what to do about it," *The Brookings Institution* (May 31, 2017).

2   Nathan J. Robinson, "This Is Why You Don't Listen When They Tell You That You'll Fail," *Current Affairs* (June 9, 2017).

3   James Kirchick, "The British election is a reminder of the perils of too much democracy," *Los Angeles Times* (June 9, 2017).

4   Bret Stephens, "The Year of Voting Recklessly," *The New York Times* (June 9, 2017).

5   Jason Brennan, *Against Democracy* (Princeton University Press: 2017).

6   Noam Chomsky, "Notion of Elite Guardian Class Dates Back to Founding of US," *Truthout* (Feb. 11, 2016).

7   Frank Moraes, "Josh Barro Is Blinded," *Frankly Curious* (June 6, 2016).

8   @jbarro, post on *Twitter* (June 23, 2016).

9   James Traub, "It's Time for the Elites to Rise Up Against the Ignorant Masses," *Foreign Policy* (June 28, 2016).

10   Daniel A. Bell, *The China Model: Political Meritocracy and the Limits of Democracy* (Princeton University Press: 2015), p. 30.

11   "Why we need to teach geography.mov," *YouTube* (Aug. 14, 2011).

12   Luke Savage, "The Democratic Deficit," *Jacobin* (July 7, 2016).

13   Lee Drutman, "What if 'more public participation' can't save

American democracy?" *Vox* (June 9, 2017).

14   "Superdelegate," *Wikipedia*.

15   Tim Weiner, *Legacy of Ashes: The History of the CIA* (Anchor: 2008).

16   "Gul Rahman," *Wikipedia*.

17   Justin Fox, "Voters Are Making a Mess of Democracy," *Bloomberg View* (July 6, 2016).

18   John Stuart Mill, Consideration on Representative Government (Gutenberg.org).

19   Adrian Jawort, "The Declaration of Independence — Except for 'Indian Savages,'" *Indian Country Today* (Sept. 23, 2017).

20   Thomas Jefferson, "Query XIV – The administration of justice and description of the laws?" (xroads.virginia.edu).

21   Andrew Green, "Why Western democracy can never work in the Middle East," *The Telegraph* (Aug. 16, 2014).

"THE CLINTON COMEDY OF ERRORS"
pp. 29-43

1   "Hillary Clinton to campaign in Arizona ahead of November general election," *KTAR* (Oct. 31, 2016).

2   Pamela Engel, "Clinton never set foot in Wisconsin — then she lost it, and it helped cost her the presidency," *Business Insider* (Nov. 9, 2016).

3   Shane Goldmacher, "Hillary Clinton's 'Invisible Guiding Hand,'" *Politico* (Sept. 7, 2016).

4   John Wagner, "Clinton's data-driven campaign relied heavily on an algorithm named Ada. What didn't she see?" *The Washington Post* (Nov. 9, 2016).

5   "Michael drives into a lake," *Vimeo* (2010).

6   Patti Zarling, "Clinton, Obama postpone Green Bay event," *Green Bay Press-Gazette* (June 12, 2016).

7   @HillaryClinton, posts on *Twitter* (Mar. 6, 2016)

8   Amy Chozick, "Hillary Clinton to Show More Humor and Heart, Aides Say," *The New York Times* (Sept. 7, 2015).

9   Matthew Yglesias, "A letter to historians of the future — the 2016 election really was dominated by a controversy over emails," *Vox* (Dec. 25, 2016).

10   Lauren Carroll, "FBI findings tear holes in Hillary Clinton's email defense," *Politifact* (July 6, 2016).

11   Erik Wemple, "New York Times sheds new light on its own controversial Clinton coverage," *The Washington Post* (Apr. 24, 2016).

12   Ryan Struyk and Liz Kreutz, "Hillary Clinton Jokes About Wiping Email Server 'With a Cloth or Something,'" *ABC News* (Aug. 18, 2015).

13   Mark Niquette and Alan Levin, "Clinton Goldman Speech Transcripts Show Little to Match Fuss," *Bloomberg* (Oct. 15, 2016).

14   Note that she did this even after *Current Affairs* had carefully explained how the idea of a nationwide mania for Hamilton is a myth that exists only among political and cultural elites. See Alex Nichols, "You Should Be Terrified That People Who Like Hamilton Run This Country," *Current Affairs* (July-Aug. 2016). Collected in *The Current Affairs Mindset* (Robinson, ed.)

15   Amy Chozick and Jonathan Martin, "*Where Has Hillary Clinton Been? Ask the Ultrarich*," *The New York Times* (Sept. 3, 2016).

16   Mark Hensch, "Dems selling 'America is already great' hat," *The Hill* (Oct. 9, 2015).

17   Luke Savage, "How Liberals Fell in Love With *The West Wing*," *Current Affairs* (June 7, 2017).

18   "Clinton vs. Bush in 1992 debate," *YouTube* (Mar. 19, 2007).

19   Ezra Klein, "Hillary Clinton's 3 debate performances left the Trump campaign in ruins," *Vox* (Oct. 19, 2016).

20   Sam Kriss, "Our Gutless Eviscerators," *Slate* (Oct. 10, 2016).

21   Matt Bruenig, "On Chelsea Clinton," *Medium* (Mar. 16, 2017).

22   Alex Shephard, "This is the most damning anecdote from the Clinton campaign tell-all *Shattered*," *The New Republic* (2017).

23   "9-9-9 Plan," *Wikipedia*.

24   "Ninety-five Theses," *Wikipedia*.

25   Alexander Mooney, "Clinton touts support from 'white Americans,'" *CNN* (May 8, 2008).

26   Anna Merlan, "Clinton Campaign Issues Cautious, Meaningless Statement As Protesters Are Arrested Near Dakota Pipeline," *Jezebel* (Oct. 28, 2016).

27   Ezra Klein, "Understanding Hillary," *Vox* (July 11, 2016).

28   (Bill Clinton is actually much more unprincipled in this respect; see Robinson, *Superpredator: Bill Clinton's Use and Abuse of Black America*.)

29   Matthew Yglesias, "Democrats are in denial. Their party is actually in deep trouble," *Vox* (Oct. 19, 2015).

30   Robinson, *Trump: Anatomy of a Monstrosity*.

31   Rebecca Savransky, "Nate Silver: Clinton 'almost certainly' would've won before FBI letter," *The Hill* (Dec. 11, 2016).

32   Nathan J. Robinson, "It Matters, Yes, But How Much?" *Current Affairs* (Jan. 8, 2017).

33   Nathan J. Robinson, "Nominating a Presidential Candidate Under FBI Investigation Is an Incredibly Risky Gamble," *Current Affairs* (Mar. 5, 2016).

34   "Obama criticised for '$400,000 Wall Street speech,'" *BBC* (Apr. 25, 2017).

"THE RACISM VERSUS ECONOMICS DEBATE, AGAIN"
pp. 44-52

1   Mehdi Hasan, "Top Democrats Are Wrong: Trump Supporters Were More Motivated by Racism Than Economic Issues," *The Intercept* (Apr. 6, 2017).

2   Chauncey Devega, "It was the racism, stupid: White working-class 'economic anxiety' is a zombie idea that needs to die," *Salon* (Jan. 5, 2017).

3   Dylan Matthews, "Taking Trump voters' concerns seriously means listening to what they're actually saying," *Vox* (Oct. 15, 2016).

4   Derek Thompson, "Donald Trump and 'Economic Anxiety,'" *The Atlantic* (Aug. 18, 2016).

5   Bernie Sanders, "Bernie Sanders: Where the Democrats Go From Here," *The New York Times* (Nov. 11, 2016).

6   Robinson, "The Necessity of Credibility."

7   Adam Cancryn, "David Duke: Trump win a great victory for 'our people,'" *Politico* (Nov. 9, 2016).

8   Clare Foran, "Hillary Clinton's Intersectional Politics," *The Atlantic* (Mar. 9, 2016).

9   German Lopez, "Study: racism and sexism predict support for Trump much more than economic dissatisfaction," *Vox* (Jan. 4, 2017).

10   Casey Quinlan, "This is racism," *ThinkProgress* (Nov. 9, 2016).

11   "Top voting issues in 2016 election," *Pew Research Center* (July 7, 2016).

12   Jonathan T. Rothwell and Pablo Diego-Rosell, "Explaining Nationalist Political Views: The Case of Donald Trump," *SSRN* (Aug. 15, 2016).

13   Jonah Bennett, "Bernie Sanders: Most People Voting For Trump Aren't Racist Or Sexist," *The Daily Caller* (Nov. 5, 2016).

14   Robinson, *Trump: Anatomy of a Monstrosity*.

15   "Mehdi Hasan goes Head to Head with Michael T Flynn," *YouTube* (Aug. 4, 2015).

"WHY YOU DON'T LISTEN WHEN THEY TELL YOU THAT YOU'LL FAIL"
pp. 53-64

1   Eleanor Rose, "Jeremy Corbyn delivers Labour's biggest vote share since Tony Blair's 2001 landslide," *Evening Standard* (June 9, 2017).

2   Nathan J. Robinson, "Theresa May's Refusal To Debate Jeremy Corbyn Really Is Shameful," *Current Affairs* (June 2, 2017).

3   Ashley Cowburn, "Theresa May's Conservatives are 21 points ahead of Labour in new poll," *Independent* (April 15, 2017).

4   Adam Bienkov, "The 'dementia tax' could cost Theresa May a landslide general election victory," *Business Insider* (May 22, 2017).

5   George Eaton, "Theresa May's police cuts have returned to haunt her," *New Statesman* (June 5, 2017).

6   Tom Peck, "Theresa May lasts just 30 seconds when asked on Marr 'not to use soundbites,'" *Independent* (April 30, 2017).

7   Ian Johnston, "New poll puts Labour ahead of Tories for first time since Jeremy Corbyn became leader," *Independent* (March 18, 2016).

8   Owen Jones, "Never mind the SNP. The real danger is if the DUP are in government," *The Guardian* (April 24, 2015).

9   "What would Labour's manifesto cost? Your at-a-glance guide," *The Guardian* (May 16, 2017).

10   Steven Erlanger and Stephen Castle, "Theresa May Loses Overall Majority in U.K. Parliament," *The New York Times* (June 8, 2017).

11   Sebastian Payne, "Canterbury tale: why a true blue corner of Britain turned to Labour," *Financial Times* (July 5, 2017).

12   Claire Zillman, "In U.K. Election, More Women Than Ever Won Seats in Parliament," *Fortune* (June 9, 2017); Tom Batchelor, Election

results: record number of LGBTQ MPs elected to Parliament,"
Independent (June 9, 2017); "Voters elect most diverse parliament
ever," *The Voice* (Sept. 6, 2017).

13   @Bencjacobs, posts on *Twitter* (June 8, 2017).

14   Joe Murphy, "Joe Murphy: Jeremy Corbyn will hang on as leader but
the battle is far from over," *Evening Standard* (Sept. 21, 2016).

15   "Scruffy Jeremy Corbyn winds up Tories in 1984 - BBC Newsnight,"
Youtube (Aug. 18. 2015).

16   Charlie Atkin, "The 7 most ludicrous stories about Jeremy Corbyn,"
Independent (Sept. 30, 2015).

17   Peter Dominiczak, Ben Riley-Smith and Christopher Hope, "Jeremy
Corbyn branded 'disloyal' after refusing to sing national anthem on day
of shambles for new Labour leader," *The Telegraph* (Sept. 15, 2015).

18   Michael Deacon, "From beans to drains: inside the blissfully boring
world of Jeremy Corbyn," *The Telegraph* (May 30, 2017).

19   Tim Newark, "Jeremy Corbyn's mad plan would take Britain back to
the 1970s, writes Tim Newark," *Express* (May 12, 2017)

20   Bart Cammaerts, Brooks DeCillia, João Magalhães and César
Jimenez-Martínez, "Journalistic Representations of Jeremy Corbyn
in the British Press: From Watchdog to Attackdog," *London School of
Economics*.

21   "Media coverage of the 2017 General Election campaign (report 2),"
Loughborough University (May 19, 2017).

22   Jack Maidment, "BBC Question Time special: Jeremy Corbyn heckled
over Trident and IRA," *The Telegraph* (June 2, 2017).

23   Ross Douthat, "A Very British Radical," *The New York Times* (June 7,
2017).

24   Steven Erlanger, "For Britain's Labour Party, a Mild Defeat May Be
Worst of All," *The New York Times* (June 3, 2017).

25   Daniel Boffey and Harriet Sherwood, "Jeremy Corbyn accused of
incompetence by MPs over antisemitic abuse," *The Guardia*n (Oct. 16,
2016).

26   Jonathan Freedland, "With each misstep, Jeremy Corbyn is handing
Britain to the Tories, The Guardian (Nov. 27, 2015); "Copeland
shows Corbyn must go. But only Labour's left can remove him," *The
Guardian* (Feb. 25, 2017).

27   Polly Toynbee, "Corbyn is rushing to embrace Labour's annihilation,"
The Guardian (Apr. 19, 2017).

28   Sadiq Khan, "Sadiq Khan: We cannot win with Corbyn... so I will vote

for Owen Smith," *The Guardian* (Aug. 21, 2016).

29   Susannah Butter, "Owen Jones: 'I don't enjoy protesting - I do it because the stakes are so high,'" Evening Standard (Feb. 3, 2017).

30   Nick Cohen, "Don't tell me you weren't warned about Corbyn," *The Guardian* (Mar. 18, 2017).

31   The anti-Semitism controversy would return with a vengeance in 2018.

32   Fay Schopen, "Corbyn's devotion to his allotment is just what you want in a leader," *The Guardian* (June 2, 2017).

33   Suzanne Moore, "Where's the socialism that involves sharing life's joys?" *The Guardian* (Aug. 12, 2015).

34   Suzanne Moore, "The Sun and Mail tried to crush Corbyn. But their power over politics is broken," *The Guardian* (June 9, 2017).

35   Andrew Grice, "The Tory manifesto is a menu without any prices. They're betting on the fact that voters won't notice until it's too late," *Independent* (May 31, 2017).

36   Jack Shepherd, "BBC Debate beaten by Britain's Got Talent in the ratings," *Independent* (June 1, 2017).

37   Andrew Sparrow, "Jeremy Corbyn sweeps to victory increasing his mandate as Labour leader – as it happened," *The Guardian* (Sept. 24, 2016).

38   Heather Stewart and Rajeev Syal, "Labour MPs to reject roles in Corbyn shadow cabinet," *The Guardian* (Sept. 22, 2016); Channel 4 News, "These are the times senior Labour figures and MPs said Jeremy Corbyn was a bad leader and would lead the party into an election disaster, video posted on *Facebook* (June 9, 2017).

39   Clio Chang, "J.K. Rowling: Jeremy Corbyn is not Dumbledore," *New Republic*; Anushka Asthana, "JK Rowling gave 'blast of reality' on Jeremy Corbyn, says Labour MP," *The Guardian* (Sept. 1, 2016); @jk_rowling, posts on *Twitter*.

40   Harriet Agerholm, "Jeremy Corbyn was just 2,227 votes away from chance to be Prime Minister," *Independent* (June 9, 2017).

41   Tim Ross, "May Hires Jim Messina for U.K. Conservative Election Team," *Bloomberg* (Apr. 24, 2017).

42   @GovHowardDean, post on *Twitter* (June 26, 2016).

43   Tony Blair, "Tony Blair: Even if you hate me, please don't take Labour over the cliff edge," *The Guardian* (Aug. 13, 2015).

"THE DIFFERENCE BETWEEN LIBERALISM AND LEFTISM"
pp. 65-71

1   Nathan J. Robinson, "Can Jeremy Corbyn Change British Politics?" *Current Affairs* (Nov. 23, 2015).

2   Nathan J. Robinson, "The Climate Change Problem," *Current Affairs* (Nov. 11, 2016).

3   Nathan J. Robinson, "Pretending It Isn't There," *Current Affairs* (June 7, 2017).

4   Nathan J. Robinson, "Compassion and Politics," *Current Affairs* (Mar. 26, 2017).

5   "Pelosi: 'Democrats are capitalists,'" *CNN*.

6   "Bernie Sanders Is Not a Capitalist," *Meet the Press* (Oct. 11, 2017).

7   Timothy Snyder, *On Tyranny: Twenty Lessons From the Twentieth Century* (Penguin Random House: 2017).

8   Robinson, *Trump: Anatomy of a Monstrosity*.

9   Nathan J. Robinson, "I Don't Care How Good His Paintings Are, He Still Belongs in Prison," *Current Affairs* (Apr. 19, 2017).

10   Krystal Reddick, "Self-Care as Revolutionary Action," *Huffington Post* (Jan. 6, 2015).

11   Savage, "How Liberals Fell in Love with *The West Wing*."

12   "Obama DNC speech (We are the UNITED states of America)," *YouTube* (Nov. 13, 2008).

13   Jackie Wattles, "Carl's Jr. and Hardee's workers: Don't make our boss Trump's labor secretary," *CNN Money* (Jan. 11, 2017).

14   Ben Mathis-Lilley, "If Leaked List Is Accurate, Hillary's Cabinet Choices Would Have Enraged the Democratic Left," *Slate* (Jan. 10, 2017).

"HOW TO BE A SOCIALIST WITHOUT BEING AN APOLOGIST FOR ATROCITIES"
pp. 72-78

1   Bret Stephens, "Communism Through Rose-Colored Glasses," *The New York Times* (Oct. 27, 2017).

2   Nick Slater, "Taking Orwell's Name In Vain" *Current Affairs* (Oct. 11, 2017).

3   Alexander Berkman, *Life of an Anarchist* (Seven Stories Press, Nov. 2, 2004).

4   Emma Goldman, n.d., "There Is No Communism in Russia" *American Mercury* (April 1935).

5   Bertrand Russell, *Bolshevism: Practice and Theory* (1920).

6   "Lenin acknowledging the intentional implementation of State Capitalism in the USSR," libcom.org.

7   Alfonso Chardy, "Fidel Castro is dead: He leaves behind a dysfunctional legacy," *Miami Herald* (Nov. 26, 2016).

8   Mikhail Bakunin, "Statism and Anarchy," *Bakunin on Anarchy* (1873).

9   "Mikhail Bakunin," *Wikipedia*

10 Suzi Weissman, "The Legacy of Vladimir Lenin," *Jacobin* (May 25, 2017); Tariq Ali, "What Was Lenin Thinking?" *The New York Times* (Apr. 3, 2017).

11 Terry Eagleton, *Why Marx Was Right* (Yale University Press, 2011).

12 Krithika Varagur, "Declassified files outline US support for 1965 Indonesia massacre," *Financial Times* (Oct. 17, 2017).

"COULD DEATH BE A BAD THING?"
pp. 81-89

1   Hugo Cox, "Aubrey de Grey: scientist who says humans can live for 1,000 years," *Financial Times* (Feb. 8, 2017).

2   Roger Cohen, "When I'm Sixty-Four," *The New York Times* (Dec. 24, 2013).

3   Nathaniel Rich, "Can Jellyfish Unlock the Secret of Immortality?" *The New York Times* (Nov. 28, 2012).

4   Tad Friend, "Silicon Valley's Quest to Live Forever," *The New Yorker* (Apr. 3, 2017).

"THE CLIMATE CHANGE PROBLEM"
pp. 90-94

1   "William Happer," *Wikipedia*.

"WHY IS THE DECIMATION OF PUBLIC SCHOOLS A BAD THING?"
pp. 95-102

1   Simon Maloy, "Donald Trump's debate dictator play: Like an authoritarian strongman, he promises to send Hillary Clinton to prison," *Salon* (Oct. 10, 2016).

2   Alex Shephard, "Donald Trump just promised to abuse his power as president and prosecute Hillary Clinton if elected," *The New Republic* (2016).

3   Don Watkins, *Equal Is Unfair: America's Misguided Fight Against Income Inequality* (St. Martin's Press, 2016).

4   "Betsy DeVos," *Wikipedia*.

5   Matthew Rosza, "'I can't imagine a worse pick': Critics slam choice of Betsy DeVos to be secretary of education," *Salon* (Nov. 25, 2016).

6   Kristina Rizga, "Trump's Billionaire Education Secretary Has Been Trying to Gut Public Schools for Years," *Mother Jones* (Nov. 29, 2016).

7   Nikhil Goyal, "Public schools may not survive Trump's billionaire wrecking crew," *The Guardian* (Nov. 30, 2016).

8   Valerie Strauss, "Study on online charter schools: 'It is literally as if the kid did not go to school for an entire year,'" *The Washington Post* (Oct. 31, 2015).

9   Matthew Yglesias, "Different Places Have Different Safety Rules and That's OK," *Slate* (Apr. 24, 2013).

10   Alana Horowitz Satlin, "Group Funded By Trump's Education Secretary Pick: 'Bring Back Child Labor,'" *Huffington Post* (Nov. 24, 2016).

11   L.M. Orbison, "When Public Schools Disappear," *Current Affairs* (June 13, 2016).

"A PUBLIC OPTION FOR FOOD"
pp. 103-114

1   Scott Alexander, "Contra Robinson On Schooling," *Slate Star Codex* (Dec. 2, 2016).

2   Douglas Main, "Seven in 10 American Adults Are Overweight or Obese," *Newsweek* (June 22, 2015).

3   Karen Kaplan, "Half of Americans have diabetes or a high risk for it —

and many of them are unaware," *Los Angeles Times* (July 18, 2017).

4   Andrew Jacobs and Matt Richter, "How Big Business Got Brazil Hooked on Junk Food," *The New York Times Magazine* (Sept. 16, 2017).

5   Michael Moss, "The Extraordinary Science of Addictive Junk Food," *The New York Times Magazine* (Feb. 20, 2013).

6   Andrew Jacobs and Matt Richter, "How Big Business Got Brazil Hooked on Junk Food," *The New York Times Magazine* (Sept. 16, 2017).

7   Michael Moss, "The Extraordinary Science of Addictive Junk Food," *The New York Times Magazine* (Feb. 20, 2013).

8

9   Michael Moss, "The Extraordinary Science of Addictive Junk Food," *The New York Times Magazine* (Feb. 20, 2013).

10   Dave Zinczenko and Matt Goulding, "Raisin Bran among 5 worst cereals for your diet," *Today* (Sept. 10, 2010).

11   Julia Belluz, "The FDA just made the most significant changes to the nutrition label in years," *Vox* (May 20, 2016).

"THIS LITTLE ROCK AND ALL WHO SAIL ON IT"
pp. 115-124

1   Address to the 42d Session of the United Nations General Assembly in New York, New York, *www.reaganlibrary.gov* (Sept. 21, 1987)

2   Danny Lewis, "Reagan and Gorbachev Agreed to Pause the Cold War in Case of an Alien Invasion," *smithsonian.com* (November 25, 2015).

3   "Was an ALIEN responsible for Reagan's presidency? Screen legend Shirley MacLaine says the actor turned politician spotted a UFO in the 1950s... and the extra terrestrial being told him to switch careers," *Daily Mail* (Sept. 19, 2012)

4   Raymond Bonner, "Time for a US Apology to El Salvador," *The Nation* (Apr. 15, 2016).

5   "The Day the Earth Stood Still," *Wikipedia*.

6   Eric Yosomono, "5 Simple Things You Won't Believe Are Recent Inventions," *Cracked* (Oct. 6, 2010).

7   "Buckminster Fuller," *Wikiquote*.

8   "Albert Einstein," *Wikiquote*.

9   Albert Einstein, "Why Socialism?," *Monthly Review* (May 1949)

10 Nathan J. Robinson, "Getting Beyond 'New Atheism,'" *Current Affairs* (Oct. 28, 2017).

11 Mike Fleming Jr, "Quentin Tarantino's 'Star Trek' Will Be R-Rated: 'The Revenant's Mark L. Smith Frontrunner Scribe," *Deadline* (Dec. 7, 2017).

12 Ed Pilkington, "Hookworm, a disease of extreme poverty, is thriving in the US south. Why?," *The Guardian* (Sept. 5, 2017)

13 Samual Bowles and Arjun Jayadev, "One Nation Under Guard," *The New York Times* (Feb. 15, 2014).

"ALL OF YOUR ATTEMPTS TO REDEEM MARTIN SHKRELI WILL FAIL"

pp. 127-136

1   "CEO: 5,000-percent drug price hike 'not excessive at all,'" *CBS News* (Sept. 22, 2015).

2   James Surowiecki, "Taking on the Drug Profiteers," *The New Yorker* (Oct. 12, 2015).

3   James Hamblin, "Pharma Bro Is the Face of U.S. Health Care," *The Atlantic* (Sept. 23, 2015).

4   Lydia Ramsey, "Why hated pharma CEO Martin Shkreli is the villain we need," *Business Insider* (Dec. 9, 2015).

5   Ibid.

6   Rick Newman, "Martin Shkreli is actually a great guy," *Yahoo Finance* (Feb. 4, 2016).

7   Bethany McClean, "Everything You Know About Martin Shkreli Is Wrong—Or Is It?" *Vanity Fair* (Feb. 2016).

8   Allie Conti, "Wine, Wu-Tang, and Pharmaceuticals: Inside Martin Shkreli's World," *Vice* (Jan. 27, 2016).

9   "10k," *InDefenseOfGettingOff* (Sept. 22, 2015).

10 Drew Salisbury, "Price-gouging pharma-dick Martin Shkreli once threatened employee's family," *Death and Taxes* (Sept. 22, 2015).

11 Jacklyn Collier, "My Tinder date with 'Pharma bro' Martin Shkreli," *The Washington Post* (Jan. 5, 2016).

12 Eve Peyser, "Here's What Happened When I Matched on Tinder With the Most Hated Man in America," *Mic* (Oct. 5, 2015).

13   Emma Court, "Here's why Daraprim still costs $750 a pill," *Market-Watch* (Feb. 4, 2016).

14   Conti, "Inside Martin Shkreli's World."

15   "IamA Martin Shkreli - CEO of Turing Pharmaceuticals - AMA!" *Reddit* (2015).

"WHY IS CHARLES MURRAY ODIOUS?"
pp. 137-158

1   Jason DeParle, "Daring Research or 'Social Science Pornography'?: Charles Murray," *The New York Times* (Oct. 9, 1994)

2   "The Bell Curve Co-author Charles Murray discussed his book, The Bell Curve: Intelligence and Class Structure in American Life," *C-SPAN* (Nov. 8, 1994).

3   Charles Murray, "Charles Murray's SPLC page as edited by Charles Murray," *AEIdeas* (Mar. 24, 2017).

4   Bo Winegard and Ben Winegard, "A Tale of Two Bell Curves," *Quillette* (Mar. 27, 2017).

5   Charles Murray and Richard Herrnstein, *The Bell Curve: Intelligence and Class Structure in American Life* (Free Press, 1994).

6   Noam Chomsky, "Rollback" (Jan. 1995).

7   "How Heritability Misleads about Race," *The Boston Review* (Jan. 6, 1996).

8   Steven Fraser, *The Bell Curve Wars: Race, Intelligence, and the Future of America* (Basic Books, 1995)

9   Charles Murray, *Human Accomplishment: The Pursuit of Excellence in the Arts and Sciences, 800 B.C. to 1950* (HarperCollins, 2003).

10   "To Thomas Jefferson from Benjamin Banneker" (Aug. 19, 1791).

11   Warren Throckmorton, "Thomas Jefferson: American Enigma," *The Center for Vision & Values at Grove City College* (July 3, 2012).

12   Paul Finkelman, "The Monster of Monticello," *The New York Times* (Nov. 30. 2012).

13   Charles Murray, "Afterword - The Bell Curve: Intelligence and Class Structure in American Life," publicism.info (1996).

"THE POLITICAL SOCIOPATH: TED CRUZ IN HIS OWN WORDS"
pp. 159-169

1   Catherine Treyz, "Lindsey Graham jokes about how to get away with murdering Ted Cruz," *CNN* (Feb. 26, 2016).

2   Tom Boggioni, "Neurologist explains why it's hard to look at Ted Cruz's creepy 'unsettling' face," *Raw Story* (Feb. 6, 2016).

3   Patricia Murphy, "Ted Cruz at Princeton: Creepy, Sometimes Well-Liked, and Exactly the Same," *The Daily Beast* (Aug. 19, 2013).

4   Matt Taibbi, "How America Made Donald Trump Unstoppable," *Rolling Stone* (Feb. 24, 2016).

5   Ted Cruz, *A Time for Truth: Reigniting the Promise of America* (Broadside: 2015).

6   Michael A. Cohen, "Hillary Clinton's move left is no flip-flop," *The Boston Globe* (Oct. 9, 2015).

"WHO ARE THE REAL NAZIS?"
pp. 170-180

1   Evgenia Peretz, "Dinesh D'Souza's Life After Conviction," *Vanity Fair* (May 2015)

2   Matthew C. Nisbet, "According to Dinesh D'Souza, Bin Laden Doesn't Hate the U.S., He Hates the Cultural Left," *Big Think*.

3   Dinesh D'Souza, *The Roots of Obama's Rage* (Regnery, 2010), p. 198.

4   Andrew Ferguson, "The Roots of Lunacy," *The Weekly Standard* (Oct. 25, 2010).

5   Ariel Kaminer, "Star Commentator Is Out as Christian College President After Scandal," *The New York Times* (Oct. 18, 2012).

6   "Fliptree: Best Idea - Dinesh D'Souza," *Youtube*.

7   @DineshDSouza, post on *Twitter* (Jan. 19 2015).

"HUGH HEFNER: GOOD RIDDANCE TO AN ABUSIVE CREEP"
pp. 181-185

1   Olivia Bahou, "The 15 Worst Things Playmates Have Said About Life in the Playboy Mansion," *Cosmopolita*n (June 11, 2015).

2   Maria Yagoda and Diana Pearl, "Everything We Know About Life in the Playboy Mansion, from Holly Madison and Kendra Wilkinson's Memoirs," *Peopl*e (Sept. 30, 2017).

3   Rachel McRady, "Holly Madison: Hugh Hefner Offered Me Drugs, Tried to Buy Me in His Will," *US Magazine* (June 10, 2015).

4   Victor, "Hugh Hefner Admits to Not Wearing Condoms" *The Blemish* (Jan. 4, 2011).

5   Olivia Bahou, "The 15 Worst Things Playmates Have Said About Life in the Playboy Mansion," *Cosmopolitan* (June 11, 2015).

6   Jessica Boulton, "Inside Playboy Mansion: 'It's like a prison and Hugh Hefner prefers tennis to sex,'" *Mirror* (Jan 3, 2015).

7   "Obituary: Hugh Hefner," BBC (Sept. 28 2017).

8   Matt Schudel, "Hugh Hefner, visionary editor who founded Playboy magazine, dies at 91," *Washington Post* (Sept. 27, 2017).

9   Laura Mansnerus, "Hugh Hefner, Who Built the Playboy Empire and Embodied It, Dies at 91," *The New York Times* (Sept. 27, 2017).

10 John Ortved, "The Dress Code for Power Lunching at the Four Seasons," *The New York Times* (Jan. 5, 2016).

11 Nathan J. Robinson, "I Don't Care How Good His Paintings Are, He Still Belongs In Prison," *Current Affairs* (Apr. 19, 2017).

12 Jeannette Catsoulis, "Hugh Hefner: A Radical, And Not Just In The Bedroom," *NPR* (July 29, 2010).

13 Anna Codrea-Rado, "Hugh Hefner's Memorable Interview Moments," *The New York Times* (Sept. 28, 2017).

"THE COOL KID'S PHILOSOPHER"
pp. 210-231

1   Nathan J. Robinson. "Socialists Are Winning The Battle Of Ideas," *Current Affairs* (Nov. 22, 2017).

2   Sabrina Tavernise, "Ben Shapiro, a Provocative 'Gladiator,' Battles to

Win Young Conservatives," *The New York Times* (Nov. 23, 2017).

3   "The Complete Transcript: Ben Takes Berkeley," *The Daily Wire* (Sept. 15, 2017).

4   "The Rise Of Asian Americans," *Pew Research Center* (June 19, 2012).

5   Matt Bruenig, "The Success Sequence Is About Cultural Beefs Not Poverty," *mattbruenig.com* (July 31, 2017).

6   "The mystery of high unemployment rates for black Americans," *The Economist* (Aug. 3 2017).

7   Amy Traub, Laura Sullivan, Tatjana Meschede and Tom Shapir, "The Asset Value Of Whiteness: Understanding The Racial Wealth Gap," *Demos* (Feb. 6, 2017).

8   Christopher Ingraham, "Black men sentenced to more time for committing the exact same crime as a white person, study finds," *The Washington Post* (Nov. 16, 2017).

9   Gwen Sharp, PhD, "Race, Criminal Background, and Employment," *The Society Pages* (Apr. 3, 2015).

10   "Ben Shapiro on Black Income Inequality – 'Everything to do with culture,'" *Youtube* (Nov. 21, 2016).

11   Ta-Nehisi Coates, "The Case for Reparations," *The Atlantic* (June 2014).

12   Amy Traub, Laura Sullivan, Tatjana Meschede and Tom Shapir, "The Asset Value Of Whiteness: Understanding The Racial Wealth Gap," *Demos* (Feb. 6, 2017).

13   "Ben Shapiro on Black Income Inequality – 'Everything to do with culture,'" *Youtube* (Nov. 21, 2016).

14   See Google image search: "Ben Shapiro."

15   Ben Shapiro, *Bullies: How the Left's Culture of Fear and Intimidation Silences American*s (Threshold Editions, 2013).

16   @benshapiro, post on *Twitter* (Sept. 27, 2010).

17   Peter Beaumont, "'The worst it's been': children continue to swim as raw sewage floods Gaza beach," *The Guardian* (July 31, 2017).

18   Ben Shapiro, "Israeli Settlements: Light In The Darkness," *WND* (June 4, 2008)

19   Ben Shapiro, "The Radical Evil Of The Palestinian Arab Population," *Creators* (June 19, 2017).

20   Ben Shapiro, "God's road map," *Townh*all (May 21, 2003).

21   Ben Shapiro, "Transfer is not a dirty word," *Townhall* (Aug. 27, 2003).

22   Ben Shapiro, "Transfer is not a dirty word," *Townhall* (Aug. 27, 2003).

23   Adam Taylor, "The forgotten story of when the Germans were the refugees," *The Washington Post* (Sept. 3, 2015).

24   Tara Zahra, "A Brutal Peace: On the Postwar Expulsions of Germans," *The Nation* (Nov. 28, 2012).

25   Ian Schwartz, "Ben Shapiro: Teaching Minorities They Are Perpetual Victims is False, Backward, And Hurts Them," *Real Clear Politics* (Sept. 16, 2017).

26   Ben Shapiro, "What Can Israel Do?" *Townhall* (Mar. 13, 2013).

27   Ben Shapiro, "Media Pay Homage to Trayvon Martin on 21st Birthday. Here's the Real Story," *Breitbart* (Feb. 5, 2016)

28   Christal Hayes and Caitlin Doornbos, "Records: George Zimmerman punched after 'bragging' about Trayvon Martin case," *Orlando Sentinel* (Aug. 4, 2016).

29   Ben Mathis-Lilley, "Guess Who's Back? George Zimmerman, Getting Kicked Out of a Bar for Using the N-Word," *Slate* (Nov. 11, 2016).

30   Alexandra Lasker, "George Zimmerman just committed a blatant racist sex crime on Twitter," *AOL* (Dec 3, 2015).

31   Hilary Hanson, "George Zimmerman's Horrific Twitter Is Gone, And It Won't Be Missed," *Huffington Post* (Dec. 4, 2015).

32   Khaleda Rahman, "George Zimmerman's sick Twitter rant: Killer shares photos boasting about his freedom with vulgar racist rant at Obama just hours after posting image of Trayvon's dead body," *Daily Mail* (Sept. 28, 2015).

33   "12 Tweets Proving George Zimmerman's Twitter Account is Even Worse Than You'd Expect," *Watch The Yard*.

34   Lori Grisham, "'Muslim-free' gun store sells George Zimmerman Confederate flag prints," *USA Today* (Aug. 18, 2015).

35   @benshapiro, post on *Twitter* (Feb. 5, 2016).

36   Sophia Tesfaye, "Patton Oswalt gloriously smacks down Ben Shapiro's absurd cries of anti-semitism," *Salon* (Dec. 16, 2015).

37   Ben Shapiro, "The PETA Nazis," *Townhall* (Mar. 5, 2003).

38   Ben Shapiro, "Obama's Philosophically Fascist State of the Union Address," *Townhall* (Feb. 3, 2010).

39   Ben Shapiro, "Barack Obama Proves His Anti-Semitism," *Townhall* (May 6, 2009).

40   "Gaza flotilla raid," *Wikipedia*.

41 Ben Shapiro, "The Presidential Anti-Semite Strikes Again," *Townhall* (June 2, 2010).

42 Ben Shapiro, "Barack Obama Proves His Anti-Semitism," *CNSNews.com* (May 6, 2009)

43 Jeffrey Goldberg, "What Rahm Emanuel Really Said at AIPAC," *The Atlantic* (May 5, 2009).

44 Roger L Simon, "Middle East Negotiations: This isn't Hollywood, Rahm," *PJ Media* (May 4, 2009).

45 Jeffrey Goldberg, "Rahm Emanuel and Israel," *The Atlantic* (Nov. 6, 2008).

46 Ben Shapiro, "Jews in Name Only," *Townhall* (May 25, 2011).

47 Ben Shapiro, "Self-hating Jews and the Jewish state," *Townhall* (July 26, 2006).

48 Hank Berrien, "Ben Shapiro Debunks Transgenderism And Pro-Abortion Arguments," *The Daily Wire*, (Feb. 9, 2017).

49 "Dea Debunks 'Ben Shapiro Debunks Transgenderism'," *Red Goner* (Feb. 10, 2017).

50 Scott Alexander, The Categories Were Made for Man, Not Man for the Categories," *Slate Star Codex* (Nov. 21, 2014).

51 Ben Shapiro, "Liberals Take Over Your Brain," *The Patriot Post* (Feb. 17. 2010).

52 "Ben Shapiro - Caitlyn Jenner is a MAN, not a Woman! - Joe Rogan Podcast," *Youtube* (Aug 2, 2017).

53 Ann P. Haas, Ph.D., Philip L. Rodgers, Ph.D. and Jody L. Herman, Ph.D., "Suicide Attempts among Transgender and Gender Non-Conforming Adults," *Williams Institute, UCLA School of Law* (Jan. 2014).

54 Greta R. Bauer, Ayden I. Scheim, Jake Pyne, Robb Travers and Rebecca Hammond, "Intervenable factors associated with suicide risk in transgender persons: a respondent driven sampling study in Ontario, Canada," *BMC Public Health* (2015).

55 Ben Shapiro, "Myths, Lies And Stupidity About Health Care," *WND* (June 24, 2009).

56 David Weigel, "'Friends of Hamas': The Scary-Sounding Pro-Hagel Group That Doesn't Actually Exist," *Slate* (Feb. 14, 2013).

57 "'Friends Of Hamas': How A Joke Went Wrong," *NPR* (Feb. 21, 2013).

58 "Daily News Reporter Admits: Breitbart 'Friends of Hamas' Story 'Accurate'" *Breitbart* (Feb. 20, 2013).

59 Ben Shapiro, "Monitor The Mosques!" *WND* (June 7, 2006).

60   Ben Shapiro, "Fighting the Michael Jackson culture," *Townhall* (June 22, 2005).

61   Ben Shapiro, "This Is A War, Blockhead" WND (July 28, 2005).

62   Ben Shapiro, "Rap is Crap" Breitbart (Mar. 29, 2009).

63   "Ep. 108 - Here's My Problem With 'Hamilton' (Audio)," *Youtube* (Apr. 20, 2016).

64   Ben Shapiro, "The Worst Ruling Since Dred Scott," *Creators* (July 1, 2013).

65   Ben Shapiro, "There's No Such Thing as 'Crony Capitalism'," *Townhall* (Sept. 7, 2011).

66   Ben Shapiro, "Why Socialism Breeds Racism" *Townhall* (Oct. 27, 2010).

67   Ben Shapiro, "Rap is Crap" Breitbart (Mar. 29, 2009).

68   Ben Shapiro, "No, Barack Obama Isn't a Feminist -- He's a Self-Aggrandizing Tool," *Creators* (Aug. 10, 2016).

69   Ben Shapiro, "Why the 'Chickenhawk' argument is un-American: Part I" *Townhall* (Aug. 17, 2005).

70   Ben Shapiro, "The case for policing pornography" *Townhall* (Sept. 21, 2005).

71   Ben Shapiro, "Why Atheism Is Morally Bankrupt" *Townhall* (Dec. 18, 2008).

72   "Gay Rights Vs. American Morality" *Orlando Sentinel* (April 26, 2003).

73   Ben Shapiro, "Why war in Iraq is right for America" *Townhall* (Aug. 10, 2005).

74   Ben Shapiro, "Should we prosecute sedition?" *Townhall* (Feb. 15, 2006).

75   Ben Shapiro, "The Worst Ruling Since Dred Scott," *cnsnews.com* (July 5, 2012).

76   See his irrelevant discussion of the "eggshell skull" doctrine.

77   "The Complete Transcript: Ben Takes Berkeley," *The Daily Wire* (Sept. 15, 2017).

"THE NECESSITY OF CREDIBILITY"
pp. 211-224

1   @realDonaldTrump, post on *Twitter* (Nov. 27, 2016).

2   Arnie Seipel, "Trump Makes Unfounded Claim That 'Millions' Voted Illegally For Clinton," *NPR* (Nov. 27, 2016).

3   Brett Edkins, "Media Perpetuates Trump's False Claim That Millions Voted Illegally For Hillary Clinton," *Forbes* (Nov. 28, 2016).

4   Glenn Kessler, "Donald Trump's bogus claim that millions of people voted illegally for Hillary Clinton," *The Washington Post* (Nov. 27, 2016).

5   Dan Spencer, "Team Trump Offers Evidence For Millions Voting Illegally," *RedState* (Nov. 28, 2016).

6   Jesse Richman and David Earnest, "Could non-citizens decide the November election?" *The Washington Post* (Oct. 24, 2014).

7   Michelle Ye Hee Lee, "Trump camp's repeated use of dubious sources on voter fraud," *The Washington Post* (Nov. 29, 2016).

8   Craig Silverman, "This Analysis Shows How Viral Fake Election News Stories Outperformed Real News On Facebook," *BuzzFeed* (Nov. 16, 2016).

9   Andrew Smith, "The pedlars of fake news are corroding democracy," *The Guardian* (Nov. 25, 2016).

10   Nicholas Kristoff, "Lies in the Guise of News in the Trump Era," *The New York Times* (Nov. 12, 2016).

11   Craig Timberg, "Russian propaganda effort helped spread 'fake news' during election, experts say," *The Washington Post* (Nov. 24, 2016).

12   Ari Shapiro, "Experts Say Russian Propaganda Helped Spread Fake News During Election," *NPR* (Nov. 25, 2016).

13   Yves Smith, "We Demand That The Washington Post Retract Its Propaganda Story Defaming Naked Capitalism and Other Sites and Issue an Apology," *Naked Capitalism* (Dec. 5, 2016).

14   James Carden, "'The Washington Post' Promotes a McCarthyite Blacklist," *The Nation* (Nov. 28, 2016).

15   Adrian Chen, "The Propaganda About Russian Propaganda," *The New Yorker* (Dec. 1, 2016).

16   Ben Norton and Glenn Greenwald, "Washington Post Disgracefully Promotes a McCarthyite Blacklist From a New, Hidden, and Very Shady Group," *The Intercept* (Nov. 26, 2016).

17   Matt Taibbi, "The 'Washington Post' 'Blacklist' Story Is Shameful and Disgusting," *Rolling Stone* (Nov. 28, 2016).

18   T. Rees Shapiro, "Jury finds reporter, Rolling Stone responsible for defaming U-Va. dean with gang rape story," *The Washington Post* (Nov. 4, 2016).

19   Franklin Foer, "Was a Trump Server Communicating With Russia?" *Slate* (Oct. 31, 2016).

20   Sam Biddle, Lee Fang, Micah Lee, Morgan Marquis-Boire, "Here's the Problem With the Story Connecting Russia to Donald Trump's Email Server," *The Intercept* (Nov. 1, 2016).

21   David Corn, "A Veteran Spy Has Given the FBI Information Alleging a Russian Operation to Cultivate Donald Trump," *Mother Jones* (Oct. 31, 2016).

22   Robert King, "Paul Krugman: Comey, Putin 'installed' the 'crazy, vindictive' Trump," *Washington Examiner* (Nov. 27, 2016).

23   Bob Bryan, "KRUGMAN: It's looking more and more like the election was swung by the FBI in virtual 'alliance with Putin,'" *Business Insider* (Nov. 17, 2016).

24   Nathan J. Robinson, "Democrats are Redbaiting Like It's 1956," *Current Affairs* (Jul. 27, 2016).

25   Paul Musgrave, "If you're even asking if Russia hacked the election, Russia got what it wanted," *The Washington Post* (Nov. 28, 2016).

26   Franklin Foer, "Putin's Puppet," *Slate* (July 4, 2016).

27   Anne Applebaum, "The Secret to Trump: He's Really a Russian Oligarch," *The Washington Post* (Aug. 19, 2016).

28   Michael Crowley, "The Kremlin's Candidate," *Politico* (May/June 2016).

29   Nathan J. Robinson, "Explaining It All to You," *Current Affairs* (Nov. 6, 2016).

30   Nathan J. Robinson, "Why Politifact's 'True/False' Percentages Are Meaningless," *Current Affairs* (Aug. 8, 2016).

31   Nathan J. Robinson, "What the Clintons Did to Haiti," *Current Affairs* (Nov. 2, 2016).

32   Sean Davis, "PunditFact: A Case Study In Fact-Free Hackery," *The Federalist* (Apr. 29, 2015).

33   Michelle Ye Hee Lee, "Carly Fiorina's 'secretary to CEO' career trajectory (Fact Checker biography)," *The Washington Post* (Sept. 25, 2015).

34   @realDonaldTrump, post on *Twitter* (Aug. 24, 2012).

35   Jon Greenburg, "Trump inflates wind turbine eagle deaths," *Politifact*

(May 31, 2016).

36   "Windfarms kill 10-20 times more than previously thought," *Save the Eagles International*.

37   Emma Bryce, "Will Wind Turbines Ever Be Safe for Birds?" *Audobon* (Mar. 16, 2016).

38   Hank Berrien, "Listen: Trump Surrogate Says Facts Don't Exist," *The Daily Wire* (Dec. 2, 2016).

39   Christian Datoc, "Kellyanne Pistol Whips Robby Mook: 'Biggest Piece Of Fake News In This Election Was That Trump Couldn't Win,'" *The Daily Caller* (Dec. 2, 2016).

40   McKay Coppins, "36 Hours On The Fake Campaign Trail With Donald Trump," *BuzzFeed* (Feb. 13, 2014).

41   Charlie Warzel, "FiveThirtyHate: Meet The Trump Movement's Post-Truth, Post-Math Anti-Nate Silver," *BuzzFeed* (Oct. 18, 2016).

42   Franklin Foer, "The Source of the Trouble," *New York* (June 7, 2004).

43   Joy-Ann Reid, "Can President Hillary Survive the Media's Fake Scandals?" *The Daily Beast* (Aug. 26, 2016).

44   David Roberts, "Why I still believe Donald Trump will never be president," *Vox* (Jan. 30, 2016).

45   David Roberts, "Everything mattered: lessons from 2016's bizarre presidential election," *Vox* (Nov. 30, 2016).

46   Emily Robinson, "Why Journalists Love Twitter," *Current Affairs* (Dec. 30, 2016).

"CAN THE NEW YORK TIMES WEDDINGS SECTION BE JUSTIFIED?"

pp. 226-229

1   @nytvows, *Twitter*.

2   The Kasper Hauser Comedy Group, *Weddings of the Times: A Parody* (St. Martin's Griffin: 2009).

3   Mark Shrayber, "Is This The Most Painfully Hipsterrific Wedding Announcement You've Ever Read? The Answer Is Yes," *Uproxx* (June 22, 2016).

4   David Brooks, *Bobos In Paradise: The New Upper Class and How They*

Got There (Simon & Schuster: 2001).

5   Weddingcrunchers.com

6   Todd Schneider, "How love and marriage are changing, according to 63,000 New York Times wedding announcements," *Vox* (May 31, 2016).

7   Eric Randall, "The Odds of Getting into The New York Times Wedding Section," *The Wire* (Dec. 1, 2011).

8   "How to Submit a Wedding Announcement," *The New York Times*.

9   Randall, "The Odds."

10   Lois Smith Brady, "The Sound of Music Is in His Blood and Now His Heart," *The New York Times* (June 17, 2016).

11   Clark Hoyt, "Love and Marriage, New York Times Style," *The New York Times* (July 12, 2009).

12   Ibid.

13   Patrick McGeehan, "New York Lags Behind Other Cities in College Graduation Rate," *The New York Times* (Sept. 27, 2012).

14   Timothy Noah, "Abolish the New York Times Wedding Pages!" *Slate* (Aug. 19, 2002).

15   "Marjorie Williams Marries," *The New York Times* (Aug. 12, 1990).

"HOW THE ECONOMIST THINKS"

pp. 230-236

1   James Fallows, "'The Economics of the Colonial Cringe,' about The Economist magazine; Washington Post, 1991," *The Atlantic* (Oct. 16, 1991).

2   "Inside the opioid epidemic," *The Economist* (May 11, 2017).

3   Edward Baptist, "What the Economist Doesn't Get About Slavery—And My Book," *Politico* (Sept. 7, 2014).

4   Henry Farrell, "When The Economist blamed Irish peasants for starving to death," *The Washington Post* (Sept. 5, 2014).

"THE HIERARCHY OF VICTIMS"
pp. 237-242

1   Art Swift, "Americans' Trust in Mass Media Sinks to New Low," *Gallup* (Sept. 14, 2016).

2   Sandra Tzvetkova and Max Roser, "Not all deaths are equal: How many deaths make a natural disaster newsworthy?," *Our World in Data* (July 19, 2017).

3   Note: there are disputes about how to measure global hunger statistics in particular, which could have an effect on these numbers, but the same patterns would show if we expanded beyond "disasters" to look at "deaths"; when people die (1) through long-term and comparatively more invisible causes or (2) in Africa they are paid far less attention than if they die violently and/or in a major Western city.)

4   Francesca Mirabile, "Chicago Still Isn't the Murder Capital of America," *The Trace* (Jan. 18, 2017).

5   Aaron Nelsen, "Mexico border journalist says violence is worse than ever seen before," *My San Antonio* (May 15, 2017).

6   "High blood pressure causing more deaths despite drop in heart disease, stroke deaths," *American Heart Association* (Dec. 19, 2014).

7   Ashley Seager, "Dirty water kills 5,000 children a day," *The Guardian* (Nov. 10, 2006).

"CNN WILL NEVER BE GOOD FOR HUMANITY"
pp. 243-249

1   AskNature Team, "Intricate relationship allows the other to flourish," *AskNature* (Dec. 14, 2015).

2   Marisa Guthrie, "CNN Chief Jeff Zucker Unveils Plan to Dominate Digital: New Shows, a $25M YouTuber and Donald Trump (Of Course)," *The Hollywood Reporter* (Mar. 1, 2017).

3   Don Kaplan, "Trump, CNN's Jeff Zucker enjoy special relationship — which may be why the new President reacts harshly to the network's reports," *NY Daily News* (Jan. 19, 2017).

4   Alex Weprin, "CNN chief says Trump's attacks are boosting morale," *Politico* (Feb. 16, 2017).

5   Brett Edkins, "CNN Thriving Despite Trump's 'Fake News' Attacks, Says Network President," *Forbes* (Feb. 17, 2017).

6   Paul Farhi, "One billion dollars profit? Yes, the campaign has been a gusher for CNN," *The Washington Post* (Oct. 27, 2016).

7   See Google Image Search: "Zucker and Trump."

8   Michael M. Grynbaum, "In Trump-CNN Battle, 2 Presidents Who Love a Spectacle," *The New York Times* (Feb. 26, 2017).

9   Hadas Gold, "Jeff Zucker has no regrets," *Politico* (Oct. 14, 2016).

10   Christiane Amanpour, "Journalism faces an 'existential crisis' in Trump era," *CNN* (Nov. 23, 2016).

11   Jack M. Balkin, "Trump's threat to democracy isn't free speech, it's this," *CNN* (Nov. 30, 2016).

12   Eliza Collins, "Les Moonves: Trump's run is 'damn good for CBS,'" *Politico* (Feb. 29, 2016).

13   Alex Weprin, "CBS CEO Les Moonves clarifies Donald Trump 'good for CBS' comment," *Politico* (Oct. 19, 2016).

14   Joe Concha, "CNN's Zucker: Trump's attacks 'badge of honor' for employees," *The Hill* (Feb. 17, 2017).

15   Tim Hains, "Cenk Uygur: When I Was At MSNBC, The Obama Administration Tried To Manipulate What I Said," *Real Clear Politics* (Dec. 16, 2016).

16   Guthrie, 2017.

17   @CNN, post on *Twitter* (Mar. 1, 2017).

18   Aaron Blake, "Trump critic Van Jones: 'One of the most extraordinary moments you have ever seen in American politics, period,'" *The Washington Post* (Feb. 28, 2017).

19   @DKThomp, posts on *Twitter* (Mar. 1, 2017).

20   David W. Dunlap, "1973 | Meet Donald Trump," *The New York Times* (July 30, 2015).

21   Christopher Lehmann-Haupt, "Books of The Times," *The New York Times* (Dec. 7, 1987).

22   Casey Neistat, "$18,000 a night HOTEL ROOM," *YouTube* (May 19, 2016).

23   Bryan Menegus, "35-Year-Old Teen Casey Neistat Says a Few Stupid Things," *Gizmodo* (Mar. 1, 2017).

24   AJ Willingham, "Haha guys, this bird looks like Donald Trump," *CNN* (Nov. 18, 2016).

25   "Squirrels eat potato chips," *CNN*.

26   Brenna Williams, "Hillary Clinton suggests cat gifs to cope with 2016;

Here's the whole election in cat gifs," *CNN* (Oct. 14, 2016).

27   Nathan J. Robinson, "The Sanders/Cruz Debate Was the Best Political TV in Ages," *Current Affairs* (Feb. 8, 2017).

28   Nathan J. Robinson, "Keeping the Content Machine Whirring," *Current Affairs* (Feb. 24, 2016).

"WHAT IS THE POINT OF POLITICAL MEDIA?"
pp. 250-253

1   "The Current Affairs Interview: Jamelle Bouie & Ryan Cooper," *Current Affairs* (May 4, 2016).

2   Stefano Dellavigna And Ethan Kaplan, "The Fox News Effect: Media Bias And Voting," *The Quarterly Journal of Economics* (Aug. 2007).

3   Shankar Vedantam, "Do Negative Ads Make A Difference? Political Scientists Say Not So Much," *NPR* (April 3, 2012).

"MASS INCARCERATION AND THE LIMITS OF PROSE"
pp. 257-268

1   Jeff Smith, *Mr. Smith Goes to Prison: What My Year Behind Bars Taught Me About America's Prison Crisis* (St. Martin's Press, 2015).

2   Bryan Stevenson, *Just Mercy: A Story of Justice and Redemption* (Spiegel & Grau, 2015).

3   Alice Goffman, *On the Run: Fugitive Life in an American City* (Picador, 2015).

4   Michelle Alexander, *The New Jim Crow: Mass Incarceration in the Age of Colorblindness* (The New Press, 2012).

"CAN PRISON ABOLITION EVER BE PRAGMATIC?"
pp. 269-278

1   Eugene V. Debs, "Statement to the Court," Marxists.org (Sept. 18, 1918).

2   "Prison abolition movement," *Wikipedia*.

3   Peter Kropotkin, "Prisons and Their Moral Influence on Prisoners," dwardmac.pitzer.edu (1927).

4   Clarence Darrow, "Crime and Criminals: Address to the Prisoners in the Chicago Jail," *Bureau of Public Secrets*.

5   Angela Y. Davis, *Are Prisons Obsolete?* (Seven Stories Press: 2003).

6   Gene Demby, "Imagining A World Without Prisons For Communities Defined By Them," *NPR* (Sept. 20, 2016).

7   Emma Goldman, "Prisons: A Social Crime and Failure," *Anarchy Archives*.

8   Demby, "Imagining A World."

9   "ACLU Policy Priorities for Prison Reform," ACLU.org.

10   "About the Florida Department of Corrections," *Florida Department of Corrections* (Revised April 2017).

11   "Louisiana profile," *Prison Policy Initiative*.

12   Andrew Cohen, "At Louisiana's Most Notorious Prison, a Clash of Testament," *The Atlantic* (Oct. 11, 2013).

13   "Anders Breivik: Just how cushy are Norwegian prisons?" *BBC* (Mar. 16, 2016).

14   "100 Safest Cities in America 2017," *Safewise*.

15   John Gramlich, "Voters' perceptions of crime continue to conflict with reality," *Pew Research Center* (Nov. 16, 2016).

16   Thomas C. Frohlich, Samuel Stebbins and Michael B. Sauter, "America's most violent (and peaceful) states," *USA Today* (July 29, 2016).

17   "The Facts: State-by-State Data," *The Sentencing Project*.

18   Oscar Wilde, "The Ballad of Reading Gaol" (1898).

"EVEN WHEN IT DOESN'T SAVE MONEY"
pp. 279-284

1   Loretta Taylor, "Prison education is a smart investment, reduces crime," *The Seattle Times* (Oct. 9, 2015).

2   Death Penalty Information Center, deathpenaltyinfo.org 3

4   Robert Frank, *Falling Behind: How Rising Inequality Harms the Middle Class* (University of California Press, 2013).

5   Richard Wilkinson, "How economic inequality harms societies," *TED* (July 2011).

6   "Grant Program," *Washington Center for Equitable Growth*.

7   Ben Eidelson, "Liberals are making the wrong case against racial profiling, *Salon* (May 9, 2010).

8   Alex Wagner, "Chambers of Pain," *The Atlantic* (Nov. 14, 2016).

"THE AUTOBIOGRAPHY OF ROBERT PRUETT"
pp. 285-307

1   Eleanor Dearman, "Appeal from South Texas man on death row denied U.S. Supreme Court Review," *Caller Times* (Oct. 2, 2017).

2   Nathan J. Robinson, "There's Never A Way To Make It Right," *Current Affairs* (Oct. 4, 2017).

3   "Exclusive interview: Death row inmate gets 3 stays of execution in disputed murders," *Crime Watch Daily* (Jan. 11, 2016).

4   John Rudolf, "Post-9/11 'Arab Slayer' Mark Stroman's Last Words Offer Message Of Peace," *Huffington Post* (July 21, 2011).

5   Timothy Williams, "The Hated and the Hater, Both Touched by Crime," *The New York Times* (July 18, 2011).

"HONESTY ABOUT THE DEATH PENALTY"
pp. 308-312

1   Death Penalty Information Center, deathpenaltyinfo.org.

2   "Cameron Todd Willingham: Wrongfully Convicted and Executed in Texas," *Innocence Project* (Sept. 13, 2010); Ed Pilkington, "The wrong Carlos: how Texas sent an innocent man to his death," *The Guardian* (May 14, 2012).

3   Nathan J. Robinson, "There's Never A Way To Make It Right," *Current Affairs* (Oct. 4, 2017).

4   Albert Camus, *Reflections on the Guillotine* (Calmann-Levy, 1957).

5   Tony Long, "Sept. 10, 1977: Heads Roll For The Last Time In France," *Wired* (Sept. 10, 2007).

6   George Orwell, "Revenge is Sour," *Tribune* (Nov. 9, 1945).

7   "Lethal Injection," *Amnesty International*.

"THINKING STRATEGICALLY ABOUT FREE SPEECH AND VIOLENCE"
pp. 316-334

1   Yesha Callahan, "Interview: 20-Year-Old Deandre Harris Speaks Out About Being Assaulted by White Supremacists in Charlottesville, Va.," *The Root* (Aug. 13, 2017).

2   "World War II casualties," *Wikipedia.*

3   Sara Ganim and Chris Welch, "Unmasking the leftist Antifa movement," *CNN* (Aug. 22, 2017).

4   K-Sue Park, "The A.C.L.U. Needs to Rethink Free Speech," *The New York Times* (Aug. 17, 2017).

5   Natasha Lennard, "Not Rights but Justice: It's Time to Make Nazis Afraid Again," *The Nation* (Aug. 16, 2017).

6   Nathan J. Robinson, "Money Talks," *Jacobin* (Jan. 26, 2015).

7   Nathan J. Robinson, "What We'll Tolerate, and What We Won't," *Current Affairs* (Feb. 21, 2017).

8   Nathan J. Robinson, "Why Is Charles Murray Odious?" *Current Affairs* (July 17, 2017).

9   Robby Soave, "A Professor Who Attended Charles Murray's Middlebury Talk Is Now Wearing a Neck Brace. Protesters Attacked Her," *Reason* (Mar. 3, 2017).

10   @GabeCohenKomo, post on *Twitter* (Jan. 20, 2017).

11   Mike Carter and Steve Miletich, "Couple charged with assault in shooting, melee during UW speech by Milo Yiannopoulos," *The Seattle Times* (Apr. 24, 2017).

12   Paul P. Murphy, "White nationalist Richard Spencer punched during interview," *CNN* (Jan. 21, 2017).

13   Maya Oppenheim, "Alt-right leader Richard Spencer worries getting punched will become 'meme to end all memes,'" *Independent* (Jan. 23, 2017).

14   Laura Vozzella, "White nationalist Richard Spencer leads torch-bearing protesters defending Lee statue," *The Washington Post* (May 14, 2017).

15   Tim Squirrell, "Linguistic data analysis of 3 billion Reddit comments shows the alt-right is getting stronger," *Quartz* (Aug. 18, 2017).

16   Fredrik DeBoer, "Looking Where the Light Is," *Current Affairs* (Mar. 1, 2017).

17   Ben Quinn, "Petition urges Cardiff University to cancel Germaine Greer lecture," *The Guardian* (Oct. 23, 2015).

18   Steven Blum, "Doxxing White Supremacists Is Making Them Terrified," *Broadly* (Aug. 15, 2017).

19   Michael Tracey, "On Firing Nazis," *TYT Network* (Aug. 18, 2017).

20   Emma Grey Ellis, "Whatever Your Side, Doxing Is a Perilous Form of Justice," *Wired* (Aug. 17, 2017).

21   Lennard, "Not Rights but Justice."

22   Amber Athey, "Dartmouth Professor Defends Antifa Violence ," *The Daily Caller* (Aug. 20, 2017).

23   Nathan J. Robinson, "'Debate' Versus Persuasion," *Current Affairs* (Mar. 16, 2017).

24   Eli Saslow, "The white flight of Derek Black," *The Washington Post* (Oct. 15, 2016).

25   R. Derek Black, "What White Nationalism Gets Right About American History," *The New York Times* (Aug. 18, 2017).

26   "Pepper sprayed Trump supporter says she was hit with flag poles at protest," *ABC 7 News* (Feb. 3, 2017).

27   Black, "What White Nationalism Gets Right."

28   "Should The Far-Right Be Confronted With Force?" *MSNBC* (Aug. 16, 2017).

29   Garrett Haake et al, "Thousands March in Boston for Counter-Protest to 'Free Speech Rally,'" *NBC News* (Aug. 19, 2017).

30   "The Anti-LARPers Manifesto w/ Freddie deBoer," *Dead Pundits Society*.

31   Nathan J. Robinson, "Lessons From Chomsky," *Current Affairs* (July 30, 2017).

32   "6 reasons why Chomsky is wrong about antifa," *Libcom* (Aug. 18, 2017).

33   "Judenrat," *Wikipedia*.

34   Martin Luther King, Jr., "Pilgrimage to Nonviolence," *Stanford King Encyclopedia*.

35   Simone Sebastian, "Don't criticize Black Lives Matter for provoking violence. The civil rights movement did, too," *The Washington Post* (Oct. 1, 2015).

36   Ronda Racha Penrice, "Why Malcolm X rifle image still strikes a chord," *The Grio* (Feb. 14, 2014).

37   James Barrett, "NY Times Reporter Admits Antifa Protesters In Charlottesville Were 'Hate-Filled' And Violent Before Left Forces Her To Backtrack," *The Daily Wire* (Aug. 14, 2017).

38   Athey, "Dartmouth Professor Defends Antifa Violence."

39   Dan McCarthy, video posted on *Facebook* (Aug. 19, 2017).

40   @Lepiarz, post on *Twitter* (Aug. 19, 2017).

41   "Cornel West & Rev. Traci Blackmon: Clergy in Charlottesville Were Trapped by Torch-Wielding Nazis," *Democracy Now* (Aug. 14, 2017).

42   David Freeman, post on *Facebook* (Aug. 14, 2017).

43   Bernie Woodall, "32-year-old Charlottesville victim Heather Heyer was passionate about social justice, her boss said," *Business Insider* (Aug. 13, 2017).

44   Kirsten West Savali, "Princeton Professor Keeanga-Yamahtta Taylor Cancels Public Appearances Amid Fox News-Fueled Death Threats," *The Root* (June 1, 2017).

45   Sophie Mann, "Claremont's Social Justice Warriors Face the Music," *The Wall Street Journal* (July 30, 2017).

46   Bradord Richardson, "College moves on from LGBTQ director suspicious of 'white gays and well meaning white women,'" *Washington Times* (July 10, 2017).

"'DEBATE' VERSUS PERSUASION"
pp. 336-341

1   Paul P. Murphy, "White nationalist Richard Spencer punched during interview," *CNN* (Jan. 21, 2017).

2   Laura Krantz, "'Bell Curve' author attacked by protesters at Middlebury College," *Boston Globe* (Mar. 5, 2017).

3   Allison Stanger, "Understanding the Angry Mob at Middlebury That Gave Me a Concussion," *The New York Times* (Mar. 13, 2017).

4   Richard Seymour, "The case against 'exposing' fascists," *Leninology* (Feb. 19, 2017).

5   Aristotle, *Rhetoric*, Book I, Part II.

6   Nathan J. Robinson, "Unless the Democrats Run Sanders, a Trump Nomination Means a Trump Presidency," *Current Affairs* (Feb. 23, 2016).

7   Michael Kinnucan, "Forget Swing Voters," *Current Affairs* (Feb. 22, 2017).

8   Martin Luther King Jr., "Letter From a Birmingham Jail," *African Studies Center – University of Pennsylvania.*

9   "The International," Marxists.org.

"LET THE KOOKS SPEAK"
pp. 347-356

1   @NoahShachtman, post on *Twitter* (Sept. 3, 2016).

2   Rafael Shimunov, "Who is Christopher Bollyn?" *Medium* (Sept. 3, 2016).

3   "Brooklyn Commons hosting antisemitic truther Christopher Bollyn," *JewSchool.*

4   Owen Jones, "Antisemitism has no place on the left. It is time to confront it," *The Guardian* (Aug. 26, 2015).

5   The Baffler Magazine, post on *Facebook* (Sept. 6, 2016).

6   "FAQs," *The Brooklyn Institute for Social Research.*

7   @BrooklynCommons, post on *Twitter* (Sept. 6, 2016).

8   "Letter from Melissa regarding Christopher Bollyn talk," *The Brooklyn Commons* (Sept. 7, 2016).

9   Matt Muchowski, "Following Politicized Dismissal, Norm Finkelstein Gives Details of Tenure Battle," *In These Times* (Jan. 23, 2012).

10   "Norman Finkelstein: On J S Mill's 'On Liberty,'" *YouTube* (Sept. 1, 2016).

11   Charlie Warzel, "Twitter Permanently Suspends Conservative Writer Milo Yiannopoulos," *BuzzFeed* (July 20, 2016).

12   Amanda Hess, "Why Did Twitter Ban Chuck C. Johnson?" *Slate* (May 28, 2015).

13   @ZaidJilani, post on *Twitter* (Aug. 25, 2016).

14   Julia Carrie Wong, "Mark Zuckerberg accused of abusing power after Facebook deletes 'napalm girl' post," *The Guardian* (Sept. 9, 2016).

15   Franklyn Haiman, "The Remedy is More Speech," *The American Prospect* (Summer 1991).

16   Debra Nussbaum Cohen, "9/11 Truther's Controversial Speech at Hipster Brooklyn Bastion Draws Protesters, Police," *Haaretz* (Sept. 9, 2016).

17   Jacob Siegel, "Jew-Hater Christopher Bollyn Brings 9/11 False Flag Act to the Brooklyn Commons," *The Daily Beast* (Sept. 10, 2016).

18   Sanders Korenman and Christopher Winship, "A Reanalysis of The Bell Curve," *NBER* (Aug. 1995).

19   Noam Chomsky, "Comments on Herrnstein's response," *Cognition* (1972).

20   Lauren Gill, "The 'truth' hurts: Staff at 9-11 truther talk attack spitting protestor," *Brooklyn Paper* (Sept. 8, 2016).

"GENERATION WEALTH"
pp. 360-372

1   "Of slots and sloth," *The Economist* (Jan. 15, 2015).

2   Lauren Greenfield, *Lauren Greenfield: Generation Wealth* (Phaidon: 2017).

"IT'S BASICALLY IMMORAL TO BE RICH"
pp. 373-378

1   Laura Shin, "The Racial Wealth Gap: Why A Typical White Household Has 16 Times The Wealth Of A Black One," *Forbes* (Mar. 26, 2015).

2   Nathan J. Robinson, "Slavery Was Very Recent," *Current Affairs* (Oct. 20, 2016).

3   Jon Mooallem, "Larry Ellison Bought an Island in Hawaii. Now What?" *The New York Times Magazine* (Sept. 23, 2014).

4   Jonathan Glennie, "Slavoj Žižek's animated ideas about charity are simplistic and soulless," *The Guardian* (Apr. 22, 2011).

5   Nathan J. Robinson and Oren Nimni, *Blueprints for a Sparkling Tomorrow: Thoughts on Reclaiming the American Dream* (Demilune Press: 2015).

6   Larry Gordon, "David Geffen gives $100 million to build a school for the children of UCLA staff and others," *Los Angeles Times* (Nov. 11, 2015).

7   Dale Russakoff, "Assessing The $100 Million Upheaval Of Newark's Public Schools," *NPR* (Sept. 21, 2015).

8   Lydia DePillis, "If You Rebuild It, They Might Not Come," *The New Republic* (Mar. 13, 2013).

"THE MEANING OF EXPLOITATION"
pp. 379-386

1   Brett Murphy, "Rigged," *USA Today* (June 16, 2017).

2   Nathan J. Robinson, "A Puzzle for Libertarians," *The Navel Observatory* (Jan. 19, 2015).

3   Ernest Mandel, "7. Marx's Theory of Surplus Value," *Ernest Mandel Internet Archive*.

4   Karl Marx, "Capter Ten: The Working-Day," *Capital Volume One* (Marxists.org).

"PRIVATE FIRE SERVICES AND THE ECONOMICS OF BURNING TO DEATH"
pp. 387-389

1   Leslie Scism, "As Wildfires Raged, Insurers Sent in Private Firefighters to Protect Homes of the Wealthy," *The Wall Street Journal* (Nov. 5, 2017).

2   David Amsden, "Who Runs the Streets of New Orleans?," *The New York Times* (July 30, 2015); Sean McFate, "America's Addiction to Mercenaries," *The Atlantic* (Aug. 12, 2016).

"THE POLITICS OF TRAGEDIES"
pp. 403-412

1   Allan Brettman, "Portland suspect in 2 slayings on train is known for hate speech," *The Oregonian* (May 27, 2017).

2   Tina Moore et al, "Two NYPD cops 'assassinated' in Brooklyn 'revenge' killing," *NY Daily News* (Dec. 21, 2014).

3   Barney Henderson, Harriet Alexander and Ruth Sherlock, "Omar Mateen: Everything we know so far about Orlando gunman," *The Telegraph* (June 15, 2016).

4   Molly Hennessy-Fiske, Jenny Jarvie and Del Quentin Wilber, "Orlando gunman had used gay dating app and visited LGBT nightclub on other occasions, witnesses say," *Los Angeles Times* (June 13, 2016).

5   "Man who says he was Omar Mateen's gay lover speaks out," *CBS News* (June 21, 2016).

6   Katie Zavadski and Lynn Waddell, "Drag Queen: Anti-Gay Terrorist Omar Mateen Was My Friend," *The Daily Beast* (June 12, 2016).

7   Adam Withnall, "Chapel Hill shooting: Craig Stephen Hicks condemned all religions on Facebook prior to arrest for murder of three young Muslims," *Independent* (Feb. 11, 2015).

8   "Virginia Killer's Violent Writings," *The Smoking Gun* (April 17, 2007).

9   Peter Walker, "Gabrielle Giffords shooting: Gunman linked to grammar 'judge,'" *The Guardian* (Jan. 10, 2011).

10   "London fire: Prime minister orders full public inquiry," *BBC* (June 15, 2017).

11   Feargus O'Sullivan, "Did London's Housing Crisis Help Spark a Fatal Blaze?" *CityLab* (June 14, 2017).

12   Andrew Griffin, "Grenfell Tower cladding that may have led to fire was chosen to improve appearance of Kensington block of flats," *Independent* (June 14, 2017).

13   Kyle O'Sullivan, "Structural engineer who warned of cladding dangers BEFORE horrific Grenfell Tower blaze explains why building was death trap," *Mirror* (June 15, 2017).

14   Gareth Davies, "Four managers at company paid £11million to manage inferno tower block shared more than £650,000 pay last year," *Daily Mail* (June 14, 2017).

15   Martin Robinson, "'No sprinklers or fire alarm' and residents told to stay INSIDE: Tower block's 'Third World' safety failures," *Daily Mail* (June 14, 2017).

16   Samuel Osborne, "Grenfell Tower: Tory minister urged against including sprinklers in fire safety rules as it could discourage house building," *Independent* (June 15, 2017).

17   Thomas Colson, "Theresa May's new chief of staff 'sat on' a review of fire safety in tower blocks like Grenfell Tower," *Business Insider* (June 14, 2017).

18   Robert Booth and Calla Wahlquist, "Grenfell Tower residents say managers 'brushed away' fire safety concerns," *The Guardian* (June 14, 2017).

19   "Grenfell Tower residents pleas fall on deaf Tory ears," *Grenfell Action*

Group (Dec. 9, 2015).

20   "KCTMO – Playing with fire!" *Grenfell Action Group* (Nov. 20, 2016).

21   Rob Waugh, "Council 'threatened blogger with legal action' over Grenfell Tower warnings," *Metro* (June 14, 2017).

22   "Triangle Shirtwaist Factory fire," *Wikipedia*.

23   Jamie Wilson, "Mercenaries guard homes of the rich in New Orleans," *The Guardian* (Sept. 11, 2005).

24   Nathan J. Robinson, "A Second Puzzle for Libertarians: The Infinitely Rich Man," *The Navel Observatory* (Jan. 21, 2015).

25   Nathan J. Robinson, "No, atheism does not need a moment of reckoning," *The Washington Post* (Feb. 13, 2015).

26   Heather MacDonald, "The war on cops: The big lie of the anti-cop left turns lethal," *Fox News* (July 8, 2016).

27   Matt Pearce and Tina Susman, "NYPD shooter had history of arrests and mental health treatment," *Los Angeles Times* (Dec. 21, 2014).

28   Nick Baumann, "Exclusive: Loughner Friend Explains Alleged Gunman's Grudge Against Giffords," *Mother Jones* (Jan. 10, 2011).

29   Maxwell Tani, "New York Times corrects editorial that drew huge backlash for blaming Sarah Palin in Gabby Giffords' shooting," *Business Insider* (June 15, 2011).

30   Nicole Gaudiano, "Alleged gunman James Hodgkinson volunteered on Bernie Sanders' campaign," *USA Today* (June 14, 2017).

31   Brandy Zadrozny et al, "Congressional Shooter Loved Bernie, Hated 'Racist' Republicans, and Beat His Daughter," *The Daily Beast* (June 14, 2017).

32   Michael Tracey, "Democrats, Paranoia, And Political Violence," *TYT Network* (June 15, 2017).

33   @ggreenwald, post on *Twitter* (June 15, 2017).

34   Osita Nwanevu, "Today in Conservative Media: Unpacking an Act of 'Lone-Wolf Progressive Terrorism,'" *Slate* (June 14, 2017).

35   Anna Merlan, "Bernie Sanders Has Testy Exchange With Reporter Who Asked If It's 'Sexist' For Him to Keep Running," *Jezebel* (June 6, 2016).

36   @Yamiche, post on *Twitter* (Apr. 9, 2016).

37   Yamiche Alcindor, "Attack Tests Movement Sanders Founded," *The New York Times* (June 14, 2017).

38   Thomas Fuller and Christine Hauser, "Gunman Kills 3 and Then Himself at San Francisco UPS Building," *The New York Times* (June

14, 2017).

39   "Confounding," *Wikipedia*.

40   Astead W. Herndon, "South Boston brothers plead guilty to brazen beating," *The Boston Globe* (May 16, 2016).

"HOW TO DEFEND HIROSHIMA"

pp. 413-421

1   Kevin Liptak, "Obama to make historic visit to Hiroshima," *CNN* (May 10, 2016).

2   Callum Borchers, "Obama's trip to Hiroshima, and the looming 'apology tour' narrative," *The Washington Post* (May 10, 2016).

3   Michael Auslin, "Obama Should Go To Hiroshima -- But Not For The Reason He Gave," *Forbes* (May 10, 2016).

4   Louis DeBroux, "America Owes No Apologies to Japan," *The Patriot Post* (May 11, 2016).

5   David French, "Remembering When We Were Strong: Hiroshima, Nagasaki, and the Moral Necessity of a Nuclear Strike," *National Review* (Aug. 8, 2013).

6   Henry I. Miller, "The Nuking of Japan Was A Military and Moral Imperative," *Forbes* (Aug. 5, 2014).

7   Roger Kimball, "Thoughts on an awful anniversary," *PJ Media* (Aug. 6, 2015).

8   Toby Young, "If the bombing of Hiroshima was a moral obscenity, blame Emperor Hirohito," *The Spectator* (Aug. 15, 2015).

9   Bruce Stokes, "70 years after Hiroshima, opinions have shifted on use of atomic bomb," *Pew Research Center* (Aug. 4, 2015).

10   oliverkamm.typepad.com

11   John Hersey, "Hiroshima," *The New Yorker* (Aug. 31, 1946).

12   Max Boot, "Why feel guilty about Hiroshima?" *Los Angeles Times* (Aug. 3, 2005).

13   Nicholas D. Kristof and Sheryl Wudunn, "Two Cheers for Sweatshops," *The New York Times Magazine* (Sept. 24, 2000).

14   Kristoff, "Blood On Our Hands?"

15   "Hiroshima: Who Disagreed With the Atomic Bombing?" Doug-long.com

16   Ibid.

17   "A Guide To Gar Alperovitz's 'The Decision to Use the Atomic Bomb,'" Doug-long.com

18   Timothy P. Carney, "'It wasn't necessary to hit them with that awful thing' --- Why dropping the A-Bombs was wrong," *Washington Examiner* (Aug. 8, 2013).

19   "American Military Leaders Urge President Truman not to Drop the Atomic Bomb," colorado.edu.

20   "Albert Einstein and the Atomic Bomb," Doug-long.com

21   Clifton Fadiman in Ambrose Bierce, *The Collected Writings of Ambrose Bierce* (Citadel Press: 1957).

"MEAT AND THE H-WORD"

pp. 422-430

1   David Livingstone Smith, *Less Than Human: Why We Demean, Enslave, and Exterminate Others* (St. Martin's Press, 2011).

2   Glenn Greenwald, "The FBI's Hunt for Two Missing Piglets Reveals the Federal Cover-Up of Barbaric Factory Farms," *The Intercept* (Oct. 5, 2017).

3   Steve Jenkins, "Experience: I accidentally bought a giant pig," *The Guardian* (Feb. 10, 2017).

4   David Foster Wallace, "Consider the Lobster," *Gourmet magazine* (Aug. 2004).

5

"LIFE SINGS WITH MANY VOICES: THE VISION OF EDUARDO GALEANO"

pp. 439-444

1   Larry Rohter, "Author Changes His Mind on '70s Manifesto," *The New York Times* (May 23, 2014).

2   "The gods that failed," *The Economist* (June 13, 2014).

3   Andrew Clark, "Chávez creates overnight bestseller with book gift to

Obama," *The Guardian* (Apr. 19, 2009).

4   Simon Romero, "Eduardo Galeano, Uruguayan Voice of Anti-Capitalism, Is Dead at 74," *The New York Times* (Apr. 13, 2015).

5   Billy Haisley, "Eduardo Galeano Has Died; Here Are Excerpts From His Classic Soccer Book," *Deadspin* (Apr. 13, 2015).

"LESSONS FROM CHOMSKY"

pp. 445-463

1   Noam Chomsky, "The Responsibility of Intellectuals," *The New York Review of Books* (Feb. 23, 1967).

2   "Libertarian socialism," *Wikipedia*.

3   "Noam Chomsky on Libertarian Socialism," *YouTube* (Oct. 21, 2014).

4   "Chomsky on Supporting Sanders & Why He Would Vote for Clinton Against Trump in a Swing State," *Democracy Now* (May 16, 2016).

5   Noam Chomsky, "On Israel-Palestine and BDS: Chomsky Replies," *The Nation* (July 22, 2014).

6   "WATCH: Noam Chomsky opposes BDS," *New Jersey Jewish Standard Times of Israel* (Mar. 31, 2016).

7   Yousef Munayyer et al, "Responses to Noam Chomsky on Israel-Palestine and BDS," *The Nation* (July 10, 2014).

8   "Noam Chomsky: Israel's Actions in Palestine are "Much Worse Than Apartheid" in South Africa," *Democracy Now* (Aug. 8, 2014).

9   Fatima Bhojani, "Watch the US Drop 2.5 Million Tons of Bombs on Laos," *Mother Jones* (Mar. 26, 2014).

10   Sarah Kolinovsky, "The Bombing of Laos: By the Numbers," *ABC News* (Sept. 6, 2016).

11   Rudolf Rocker, *Nationalism and Culture* (The Anarchist Library: 1933).

12   Nathan J. Robinson, "What Noam Chomsky Thinks of 'Intellectuals,'" *Current Affairs* (Sept. 5, 2016).

13   "Noam Chomsky - Mysterianism, Language, and Human Understanding," *YouTube* (May 30, 2016).

14   "Revisionist Historian Suffers Savage Beating," *CODOH News* (Sept. 16, 1989).

15   Noam Chomsky, "Some Elementary Comments on The Rights of Freedom and Expression," Preface to Robert Faurisson, *Memoire en defense* (Oct. 11, 1980).

16   "Noam Chomsky - Freedom of Speech for Views You Don't Like," *YouTube* (Feb. 3, 2017).

17   "Noam Chomsky discusses 9/11 Conspiracy Theorists," *YouTube* (May 7, 2011).

18   Robinson, "Pretending It Isn't There."

19   Nathan J. Robinson, "Why Is 'The Decimation of Public Schools' a Bad Thing?" *Current Affairs* (Nov. 30, 2016).

20   Robinson, "The Climate Change Problem."

21   Fred Branfman, "When Chomsky wept," *Salon* (June 17, 2012).

22   "The Limits of Discourse As Demostrated by Sam Harris and Noam Chomsky," *Sam Harris*.

23   Norbert Hornstein and Nathan J. Robinson, "1000 Ways to Misrepresent Noam Chomsky," *Current Affairs* (Dec. 7, 2016).

"THE USES OF PLATITUDES"

pp. 467-472

1   "The Giant List of Platitudes," City-Data.com (Apr. 5, 2015).

"IN DEFENSE OF LIKING THINGS"

pp. 487-491

1   Matthew V. Libassi, "The $500,000,000 Trend Spinning the Toy Industry Upside Down," *Fox Business* (May 12, 2017).

2   Rebecca Mead, "The Fidget Spinner Is the Perfect Toy for the Trump Presidency," *The New Yorker* (May 12, 2017).

3   Ian Bogost, "The Fidget Spinner Explains the World," *The Atlantic* (May 12, 2017).

4   Agoverseasfan, "Fidget Spinner Tricks for Beginners," *YouTube* (May 6, 2017).

5 JM Everything, "A Few Tricks You Can Do With Your Fidget Spinner," *YouTube* (Mar. 25, 2017).

6 "Sometimes a cigar is just a cigar," *Everything2* (Jan. 27, 2002).

7 "History of Spinning Tops," *Art of Play* (Nov. 21, 2016).

8 Sam Kriss, "Resist Pokémon Go," *Jacobin* (Jul. 14, 2016).

"COMPASSION AND POLITICS"
pp. 492-499

1 Bill Chappell, "McDonald's Tweet Blasts President Trump, And Is Quickly Deleted," *NPR* (Mar. 16, 2017).

2 @McDonalds, post on *Twitter* (Feb. 27, 2017).

3 Michael J. Coren, "Trump's meeting with Silicon Valley's elite was a naked power play, and they lost," *Quartz* (Dec. 16, 2016).

4 Greg P., "'Ugly elitism': Josh Barro SLAMMED for calling McDonald's/Trump demographic 'fat slobs with bad taste,'" *Twitchy* (Mar. 16, 2017).

5 Chris Arnade, "McDonald's: you can sneer, but it's the glue that holds communities together," *The Guardian* (June 8, 2016).

6 Frank Moraes, "Josh Barro Is Blinded By His (Elite) Privilege," *Frankly Curious* (June 6, 2016).

7 "Robert J. Barro" faculty page, Harvard.edu.

8 Justin C. Worland, "Legacy Admit Rate at 30 Percent," *The Crimson* (May 11, 2011).

9 Clio Chang, "Ending the Empathy Gap," *Jacobin* (Mar. 21, 2017).

10 Frank Rich, "No Sympathy for the Hillbilly," *New York* (Mar. 19, 2017).

11 Matthew Stoller, "On Mocking Dying Working Class White People," *Medium* (Mar. 24, 2017).

12 Josh Barro, "Why I left the Republican Party to become a Democrat," *Business Insider* (Oct. 16, 2016).

13 Felix Gillette, "The Billionaires at Burning Man," *Bloomberg Businessweek* (Feb. 5, 2015).

14 Kevin C. Williamson, "iPencil," *National Review* (May 20, 2013).

15 Peter Waldman, "Inside Alabama's Auto Jobs Boom: Cheap Wages,

Little Training, Crushed Limbs," *Bloomberg Businessweek* (Mar. 23, 2017).

16   Nathan J. Robinson, "The Good Billionaires," *Current Affairs* (Aug. 3, 2016).

17   Arthur Schopenhauer, *The Basis of Morality* (Macmillan: 1915), pp. 213-14.

18   " U.S. Service Member Killed, 3 Wounded in Surprise Yemen Raid," *CBS* (Jan. 29, 2017).

19   Iona Craig, "Death in Al Ghayil," *The Intercept* (Mar. 7, 2017).

20   Waldman, "Inside Alabama's Auto Jobs Boom."

"IMAGINING THE END"

pp. 504-508

1   Fredric Jameson, "Future City," *New Left Review* (May-June 2003).

2   "There is no alternative," *Wikipedia*.

3   Joel Kotkin, "The Screwed Generation Turns Socialist," *The Daily Beast* (Feb. 19, 2017).

4   "Utopian socialism," *Wikipedia*.

5   "Lecture 21 – The Utopian Socialists: Charles Fourier," *The History Guide*.

6   Karl Marx, "1873 Afterword to the Second German Edition," *Capital Volume One* (Marxists.org).

7   Robinson, "Explaining It All."

8   William Morris, *News From Nowhere* (Marxists.org).

"SOCIALISM AS A SET OF PRINCIPLES"

pp. 509-514

1   Leszek Kołakowski, "What Is Left Of Socialism?" in *Is God Happy: Selected Essays* (Basic Books, 2013).

Acknowledgments

Primary thanks go to every human being who lived before me, without whom history would not have been the same and I would not be living in the social and political context necessary to produce this book. I would particularly like to thank the various industrial workers who have built the products on which I have depended to produce this book, and the agricultural laborers who have grown the food necessary for me to think and write. Additional thanks go to those who developed the personal computer and the internet, as well as each and every person who built the city of New Orleans over time. I am grateful to each person who has contributed to the production of any object or idea that I have ever been exposed to, and those who created the conditions necessary for those objects and ideas to emerge. From the people who made my shoes to the people who made those people's shoes, this work would not have been possible without the collective labors of many billions of people, and those people's evolutionary ancestors, over a period of millions of years.

I would also like to thank my parents.

A Ready-Made Negative Review of This Book

IN THIS BLOATED AND SHAPELESS TOME, Nathan J. Robinson attempts to diagnose the world's ills and prescribe his eccentric and ahistorical brand of ideological medicine. The book, which consists almost entirely of recycled work previously published, roams across an esoteric and arbitrary assortment of subjects, none of which is given more than the most superficial treatment. Robinson's shallowness is matched only by his confidence, and he displays an off-putting certitude in the wisdom of his undertheorized, brand of so-called "luxury" socialism, which marries the self-righteousness of the radical left with the gray insipidness of bourgeois liberalism. Instead of hanging together as a cohesive whole, the collected pieces offer us little more than a series of badly-taken snapshots of the interior of a thoroughly pedestrian and simplistic mind. Robinson has clearly never taken so much as an introductory course in economics or metaphysics, and when he is not mangling the contents of complex philosophical doctrines he offers "insights" that have been well-known to scholars in the field for decades. An embarrassing and unnecessary volume of sophomoric analysis mixed with childish attacks on academics and the wealthy.

ABOUT CURRENT AFFAIRS

CURRENT AFFAIRS IS A BIMONTHLY PRINT MAGAZINE OF political commentary, journalism, and satire. It's a fresh, fearless, and independent antidote to contemporary political media. We focus on challenging preconceptions and undermining orthodoxies. *Current Affairs* showcases some of the country's best contemporary writers, and is edited by a highly experienced team of professionals with backgrounds in law, literature, design, technology, and politics. We bring a sharp critical eye to the absurdities of modern American life, and provide a new and unique set of perspectives on major political issues.

CURRENTAFFAIRS.ORG

Made in the USA
Columbia, SC
18 February 2020

88090736R00336